The Urbana Free Library

To renew materials call
217-367-4057

D0073272

CUBA

A Global Studies Handbook

Other Titles in
ABC-CLIO's
**GLOBAL STUDIES: LATIN AMERICA
& THE CARIBBEAN**
Series

GLOBAL STUDIES: LATIN AMERICA
& THE CARIBBEAN

CUBA

A Global Studies Handbook

Ted A. Henken

A B C ⬥ C L I O

Santa Barbara, California • Denver, Colorado • Oxford, England

11-07

55.00

Library of Congress Cataloging-in-Publication Data

Henken, Ted.
Cuba : a global studies handbook / Ted A. Henken.
    p. cm. — (ABC-CLIO's global studies series)
    Includes bibliographical references and index.
    ISBN 978-1-85109-984-9 (hard copy : alk. paper) — ISBN
978-1-85109-985-6 (ebook) 1. Cuba—History—1959-1990. 2.
Cuba—History—1990- 3. Cuba—Handbooks, manuals, etc. I.
Title.
    F1788.H38 2008
    972.9106'4—dc22

                                                    2007018990

12 11 10 09 08 1 2 3 4 5 6 7 8 9 10

This book is also available on the World Wide Web as an ebook.
Visit http://www.abc-clio.com for details.

ABC-CLIO, Inc.
130 Cremona Drive, P.O. Box 1911
Santa Barbara, California 93116–1911

Production Editor	Alisha Martinez
Editorial Assistant	Sara Springer
Production Manager	Don Schmidt
Media Editor	Ellen Rasmussen
Media Resources Coordinator	Ellen Brenna Dougherty
Media Resources Manager	Caroline Price
File Management Coordinator	Paula Gerard

This book is printed on acid-free paper. ∞
Manufactured in the United States of America

Para Ivet, mi esposa,
Quien me ha enseñado cosas de Cuba,
Que no se pueden aprender de ningún libro.

Contents

Series Editor's Foreword

In a world in which borders are blurring and cultures are blending at a dizzying pace, becoming more globally aware and knowledgeable is imperative. This is especially true regarding one's immediate neighbors, where the links are most intense and most profound. For this pragmatic reason, knowing more about Latin America is especially relevant to people living in the United States.

Beyond such a practical consideration, Latin America is a fascinating region of the world on its own terms, and it is worth the time and energy to get to know the region better simply as a matter of intellectual curiosity. By providing a readable and engaging introduction to a representative selection of the region's countries, this series hopes to engage readers and nurture their curiosity in the region and its peoples.

One point that this series will make abundantly clear is that Latin America is not a homogeneous region. For example, its population is remarkably diverse. Indigenous peoples are spread throughout the region, constituting the majority of the population in countries where the largest of the region's magnificent pre-Colombian civilizations were centered. Descendants of the Iberian European colonizers continue to dominate the region's political and economic landscape, though recently arrived immigrant populations from Europe and Asia have made significant inroads into the economic, political, and cultural aspects of these countries. The Atlantic slave trade network brought hundreds of thousands of Africans to Latin America to labor in the plantation economy. The African cultural legacy is particularly relevant to modern Brazil and the Gulf-Caribbean countries. And the process of racial mixture, or miscegenation, that occurred freely and consistently over the past 500 years of the region's history has created a unique *mestizo* identity that many modern Latin Americans embrace as their own.

Obviously, therefore, one characteristic of the region that makes it so intriguing is that it is so vastly different from one country to the next and yet, at the same time, the countries of the region bear striking similarities. In addition to sharing a physical continent and space in the Western Hemisphere, the countries of Latin America also share a basic, common history that stretches from the colonial period through the present day. And the region is also bound together in many ways by language and culture.

In terms of its geography, Latin America is a vast region, encompassing more than one-half of the entire Western Hemisphere. Further, its natural environment is one of the more diverse in the world, from the deserts in northern Chile to the lush and ecologically diverse rainforests of the Amazon River basin. It is also a region rich in natural resources, providing the world with many of its foodstuffs, energy and mineral resources, and other commodities.

A few basic statistics can help to illuminate the importance of learning more about the region. Latin Americans constitute approximately 12 percent of the world's total population, and Latin American countries make up approximately 6.5 percent of the world's landmass. By some estimates, the Spanish language is the most spoken language in the Western world and is second only to Mandarin Chinese among all linguistic groups worldwide. The vast majority of Spanish speakers reside in Latin America. Portuguese, the native language of Brazil, is among the world's ten most spoken languages.

Among the developing world, Latin America ranks consistently at the top in terms of most economic and social indicators in aggregate terms, but the region still struggles with chronic poverty and suffers from highly skewed patterns of income distribution. A consequence of this income gap has been growing out-migration, with more and more Latin Americans each year making their way to better opportunities in wealthier and more economically developed countries. Recent efforts to promote greater economic integration through regional free trade agreements throughout the Western Hemisphere also illustrate the growing importance of a greater knowledge and awareness of Latin America.

In terms of politics and governments, Latin America finds itself squarely in the traditions of Western liberal democracy. Most Latin Americans embrace the values of individual freedom and liberty and expect their political systems to reflect these values. While this has not always been the reality for Latin American countries, as of late democracy has been the norm. In fact, all of the countries of Latin America today with the exception of Cuba have democratically elected governments, and all are actively engaged globally.

The specific volumes in this series introduce Mexico, Brazil, Chile, Costa Rica, Cuba, and Argentina. They represent all of the different subregions in Latin America and they range from the smallest countries to the largest in terms of population, landmass, and economic wealth. The countries included in the series vary in terms of their ethnic and class composition, with Cuba and Brazil containing large Afro–Latin American populations and with Mexico representing a society shaped by a rich and vibrant indigenous culture. The inclusion of Cuba, which remains the region's stalwart socialist experiment, offers ideological variation within the series. Argentina, Brazil, Chile, and Mexico represent the region's top four economic regional powerhouses, whose places in the global economy are well established. These four countries are also the region's most influential actors in the international arena, serving not only as leaders within the Latin American region itself but also exercising influence in the world's premier international bodies. On the other hand, Costa Rica and Cuba demonstrate the challenges and possibilities for the region's many less influential global actors and smaller economies.

Finally, it should be noted that Latin American culture is seeping much more into the mainstream of U.S. culture.

People in the United States enjoy the foods, music, and popular culture of Latin America because they are all more readily available in and appealing to the U.S. population. In fact, one might argue that the United States itself is becoming more Latin. Evidence indicates as much, as the numbers of those who identify themselves as Hispanic or Latino in the United States are growing rapidly and disproportionately to other ethnic or racial groups. According to the 2000 U.S. Census, the Hispanic population in the United States constitutes about 12.5 percent of the total U.S. population and is now the country's largest ethnic minority group. Even more striking is the incredible growth rate of the Hispanic population in the United States relative to the total population. In just twenty years, the Hispanic population more than doubled, and if this trend continues, Hispanics will constitute a majority of the U.S. population in about fifty years. The fact that Hispanics in the United States maintain strong ties to their countries of origin and maintain an affinity for the culture and lifestyles common to the region makes Latin America all the more relevant to understand.

The volumes in this series provide a basic introduction to some of the countries and peoples of Latin America. In addition to a survey of the countries' histories, politics, economies, and cultures, each volume includes an extensive reference section to help point readers to resources that will be useful in learning more about the countries and even in planning to visit them. But above all, the hope for this series is that readers will come to a better appreciation for Latin America as a region, will want to learn more about it, and will eventually experience the richness that is Latin America.

—*James D. Huck, Jr.*
Series Editor

Preface

I began my own personal and professional odyssey with the island and people of Cuba more than ten years ago, in July of 1995, when I took on a nine-month assignment as a social worker for Catholic Social Services Refugee Resettlement Program in Mobile, Alabama. I was hired for the specific task of receiving and resettling Cuban refugees from the U.S. naval base at Guantánamo Bay on the southeastern tip of Cuba, where upwards of 20,000 Cuban *balseros* (rafters) were being held in indefinite detention. One anecdote from my nine months of work with that wave of Cuban immigrants indicates the origins of my interest in the complex and often contradictory world of Cuba and its diaspora.

Hesitant to bring up political matters with my new Cuban clients for fear of stirring up heated emotions or painful memories, I developed the habit of assuaging my curiosity about their reasons for migrating by playing the songs of two famous but very different Cuban musicians for them in my car while taking them to their various appointments: Cuban protest singer Silvio Rodríguez and Cuban-American crossover salsa sensation Gloria Estefan. Rodríguez, Cuba's best-known *nueva trova* singer, continues to live in Cuba and is seen throughout Latin America as an unofficial spokesperson for the revolution. In fact, he has even served as a member of the Cuban Parliament. Estefan, on the other hand, is a Cuban exile icon who upholds Cuban and Cuban-American culture with a tenacity equaled only by the vehemence of her opposition to the government of Fidel Castro.

Despite Rodríguez's semiofficial persona, the great majority of my Cuban refugee clients reacted enthusiastically to his music, singing along with gusto and even asking me for copies of his tapes to play at home. There was at least one refugee family, however, who wondered aloud why I would dare to play "communist" music for them. On the other hand, few of them knew Estefan's songs or had even heard her name before, though most enjoyed hearing her Cuban-derived rhythms and often poetic, always nostalgic Spanish lyrics about her (and their) "lost island." A handful even commented approvingly on the concert that Estefan had performed for them while they waited anxiously in detention at Guantánamo.

Such starkly different reactions and opinions among such supposedly similar refugees highlight the great difficulty in uncovering any single "truth" about Cuba or in remaining dispassionately objective on the subject of the island and its complex history and current reality. Recent developments since 2003 on the island, including a renewed crackdown on corruption, private enterprise, and prodemocracy dissidents, along with the recent illness of Fidel Castro, and among the exile community—including the arrest in Miami of two Cuban-American state university employees on espionage charges, a subsequent Florida state ban on all academic travel to the island, an effort to remove an "objectionable" children's book about Cuba from all Miami-Dade public libraries, and the appearance of admitted bomber Luis Posada Carriles on the streets of Miami—make an already difficult research terrain even more polarized and combative.

Thus, beyond the challenge of writing a comprehensive but concise reference book on a country with such an intricate history and rich culture as Cuba, writing a balanced, accurate, and provocative—but nonpolemical—overview of this unique and fascinating island nation has been a daunting task. How does one describe the innumerable ways in which Cubans have embraced and, indeed, internalized much of U.S. culture during the island's century of independent existence, while at the same time recognizing the fact that the United States has often wielded its power and influence in a manner ultimately harmful to Cuban sovereignty? Likewise, how does one do justice to the enormous initial popularity and impressive social achievements of the Cuban revolution, without ignoring the suffering endured by the Cuban people both on the island and in exile as a result of external aggression and internal rigidity and paternalism? As Cubans like to say, *No es fácil* (It ain't easy)!

Although writing and teaching about Cuba can be a political minefield of sorts, even for the most enterprising and sensitive of scholars, the country of Cuba, with its unique culture, and the people of Cuba, with their contagious charisma, passionate convictions, and gracious generosity of spirit, make the never-ending task of understanding the country and its people inestimably rewarding and enriching. In many ways, this book is the fruit of more than a decade of learning and teaching about Cuba as a graduate student and then as a professor at Tulane University and Baruch College. As such, it benefits from both the many wise and dedicated professors who have taught me and the many more eager and inquisitive students I have been privileged to teach. The book also benefits immeasurably from what I have learned about Cuba and its people on more than a dozen trips to the island since 1997. It is for this complex set of personal, political, and professional reasons that I have written this book.

This volume provides an up-to-date overview of Cuban historical, political, economic, and sociocultural development from the pre-Columbian period to the present day, with an emphasis on the Cuban revolution, U.S.-Cuban relations, Cuba's impressive cultural achievements, and the country's current socioeconomic reality. The book contains four narrative chapters, on (1) geography and history, (2) economics and development, (3) government institutions, and (4) culture and society. While the first chapter focuses almost exclusively on prerevolutionary Cuba, the bulk of the other three chapters is dedicated to chronicling the economic, political, and cultural changes that have taken place in Cuban society under the revolution.

The second part of the book is a reference section that provides a timeline of Cuban history and specific information on important people, places, and historical events, language, etiquette (national habits, traditions, cuisine, and holidays), and important organizations and websites. I end with an annotated bibliography that lists some of the most helpful resources used in preparing the volume (including books, newspapers, periodicals, and films), a discography, or listeners guide, to some of my favorite Cuban music, as well as a chart that traces the development of Cuban popular music over the course of the twentieth century. Finally, interspersed throughout the text in the appropriate places, are a series of informative sidebars, and more than forty-five photographs I have taken in Cuba since 1997.

While the official title of this book is *Cuba: A Global Studies Handbook,* my own subtitle for it is "The Island that Dreamed It Was a Continent" (after the title of a painting by Cuban artist and personal friend Sandra Ramos). In choosing such a sardonic subtitle, my aim is to highlight the passionate exceptionalism of the island and its people, sometimes facetiously referred to as the Cuban "superiority complex." Every nation tends to celebrate its own unique characteristics and exceptional qualities. However, for Cuba and Cubans, exceptionalism has become a defining national trait, leading Cubans themselves—as well as a long succession of U.S. administrations—to behave *as if* the island were of continental importance. Based originally on the island's singular geography, heightened by its unique history, and intensified by revolutionary politics, Cuban exceptionalism has been perpetuated in exile by the many members of the extensive Cuban diaspora and reinforced by U.S. policies that have consistently afforded inordinate attention to the island and special treatment to its emigres.

Following from this Cuban "superiority complex," I structure my book around six interconnected paradigms that are key to understanding Cuban history and society.

(1) *Passionate exceptionalism:* Despite its relatively small size and lack of the natural or mineral resources that have

This painting by Cuban artist Sandra Ramos, entitled La isla que soña-
ba con ser un continente *(The island that dreamed it was a continent),
1995, depicts the island of Cuba in the artist's likeness dreaming of its
own greatness. Sitting along the* Malecón, *Havana's famed seaside
promenade, are a series of 30 key figures from Cuba's history, including Columbus, Hatuey, Bartolomé de Las Casas, Félix Varela, Carlos
Manuel de Céspedes, Antonio Maceo, José Martí, Máximo Gómez,
Fernando Ortiz, José Lezama Lima, Wilfredo Lam, Che Guevara, Fidel
Castro, Silvio Rodríguez, and* La jinetera mulata. *(Courtesy Sandra
Ramos)*

given leverage to other nations in the region, Cuba has consistently been able to convert its "dream" of continental, even
global, significance into an ongoing reality.

(2) *Transculturation:* Like the idea of the United States as
a "melting pot," this key term understands Cuban national
identity as a unique mixture (often referred to as *ajiaco,* or
Cuban stew) that includes African and European (and, to a
lesser extent, Taino and Chinese) cultural elements as cocontributors, without claiming any one of them as the mainstream.

(3) *Cuba-U.S. relations:* The book emphasizes the impact
of American culture and U.S. economic and political policies
on the island over the past 150 years (from 1850 to 2007),
chronicling Cuba's varying responses to that influence
(annexation, independence, nationalist renovation, and
socialist revolution).

(4) *Frustrated nationalism and diasporic nation:* One
consistent feature of all of Cuba's twentieth-century govern-

ments, both before and since 1959, has been their undemocratic, top-down command structure, derived from a pervasive sense of frustrated nationalism, producing a diasporic nation fractured by ideology and dispersed across geography.

(5) *Continuity and change:* The book identifies a number of recurring themes that are surprisingly consistent over time, despite major changes throughout Cuban history: economic dependency and underdevelopment; international migration; an intransigent, often corrupt winner-take-all political culture; lighthearted mockery; and, as indicated above, exceptionalism.

(6) *Prodigious cultural production:* A final paradigm highlighted in the text, and especially in Chapter Four, is the astounding sophistication, variety, proliferation, and influence of Cuban culture during the twentieth century, both on the island and abroad.

In summary, in the following pages I will tell a provocative, critical, but sympathetic tale of Cuba's history and development that aims to appeal especially to curious observers who want to add some weight and depth to what they already know about this "island that dreamed it was a continent." At the same time, I will use these six paradigms as analytical tools to help readers make sense of what has been a long and complex political and historical process, and critically understand and appreciate the uniqueness of the island's deep cultural roots and vital, embattled society.

Finally, I would be remiss if I did not acknowledge the fact that many of the ideas and themes presented here were developed over years of conversation with Cuban friends and colleagues, both in Cuba and in the United States. The art of conversation, highly developed among Cubans, has been imparted to me again and again, usually accompanied by a strong cup of Cuban coffee or, better yet, a well-aged glass of Cuban *añejo* rum. With sometimes wildly differing convictions, opinions, and points of view, all these deeply reflective and warmly hospitable Cuban friends and colleagues want the best possible present and future for their beloved *patria* (homeland), yet painfully realize at the same time that their nation's options remain frustratingly limited because of the long-standing political intransigence and opportunism that reigns both in Havana and in Miami—not to mention the often self-serving and counterproductive policies that consistently emanate from Washington.

Some of these friends and colleagues include Julio César González, Arturo López Levy, William Sabourin O'Reilly, Roberto González Gómez and Amparo Pujol, Carlos Alzugaray, Hernán Pérez Concepción and Fé Pérez Dovale, Raisa Clavijo de la Uz, Katia Ramos, Leandis Díaz Ramírez, Bismarck Valerino, Isabel Holgado, Neili Fernández Peláez, Miguel and Silvia Álvarez, Julio Carranza, Pedro Monreal, Rafael Hernández, Leonardo Padura, Wilfredo Cancio-Isla, J. Timmons Roberts, Eloise Linger, Holly Ackerman, Siro del Castillo, Carmelo Mesa-Lago, Jorge Pérez-López, Aurelio Alonso, Katrin Hansing, Ariana Hernández-Reguant, Elena Sacchetti, Silvia Pedraza, Arch Ritter, Esther Allen, Jorge Domínguez, Reuters Havana correspondents Marc Frank and Anthony Boadle, Ricardo Zúñiga, Dan Sainz, Usha Pitts, and Michael Parmly of the U.S. Interest Section in Havana, Mauricio Font of CUNY's Bildner Center, Wayne Finke, Ken Guest, James DeFilippis, Glenn Petersen, Héctor Cordero-Guzmán, Lourdes Gil, and Arthur Lewin of Baruch College, Sachie Hernández Machín, Ricardo Sánchez, Phil Peters, Joe Scarpaci, Lisandro Pérez, Damián Fernández and Uva de Aragon of Florida International University's Cuban Research Institute, Lisandro Pérez-Rey and Cynthia Barrera, Ned Sublette, an honorary Cuban if there ever was one, Tomás Montoya of Asociación Hermanos Saíz in Santiago, Dagoberto Valdés and the staff of the *Revista Vitral* in Pinar del Río, Michael Turner and Meg Crahan of Hunter College, Sandra Ramos, Alejandro Báez Mafes, Rolo García Milián, and my die-hard revolutionary Havana taxi driver, counselor, and confidant, Ernesto Merchant.

This book was supported from its inception by my wife,

Ivet. As I say in the dedication, through countless hours of enlightening, often heated, and always heartfelt conversation, she has taught me things about Cuba that I never could have learned from any book. Each page bears the stamp of her passionate heart and careful, critical eye. Others who read parts of the manuscript and offered valuable feedback have included Juan Antonio Blanco, Ivan Pérez Carrión, Samuel Farber, G. Derrick Hodge, Ariel Fernández, Peter Roman, Iraida López, Antonio López, Manuel Martínez, Roberto G. Fernández, Robin Moore, and Emilio Rodríguez. I am also grateful to various individuals and institutions who have generously supported my Cuban research, including Nick Robbins and Ana López, the former and current directors of Tulane University's Cuban-Caribbean Studies Institute, Ariana Hall of CubaNola Collective, Pedro Pedraza of the CUNY-Caribbean Exchange Program at Hunter College, Wayne Smith of the Cuban Exchange Program at the Johns Hopkins University, and Jorge Gracia, director of a National Endowment for the Humanities summer seminar on Cuban-American identity and culture at the University of Buffalo, in which I was a participant in 2006.

At ABC-CLIO, I am indebted to Alex Mikaberidze, whose close and critical reading of the entire manuscript at different stages helped make the final draft as accurate, concise, and effective as possible. Ellen Rasmussen's expert technical skills as the photo editor helped bring my images to life. She also efficiently tracked down useful maps and hard-to-find photos of important historical figures. Likewise, Stella Varvaris and Jason Belland of the Baruch Computing and Technology Center (BCTC) walked me through the finer points of Photoshop, helped me transform old prints into vivid digital images, and made space available for me to work. Also, the Latin American series editor Jimmy Huck, my former teacher, colleague, and racquetball adversary at Tulane University in our beloved New Orleans, deserves *un fuerte abrazo* for thinking enough of my scholarship, sensibility, and stamina to entrust me with the Cuba volume.

Finally, this study of Cuba would never have moved beyond its initial stages if not for the trust, honesty, and generosity of scores of private Cuban citizens and émigrés who opened their homes, lives, and mouths to this inquisitive and sometimes pesky outsider. It is my sincere hope that I have represented their hopes, fears, words, and ideas accurately and justly in the following pages. It is also my hope that this book can serve as a bridge of understanding for those who read it, helping to reestablish respectful communication between Cuba and the world outside.

—*Ted A. Henken*

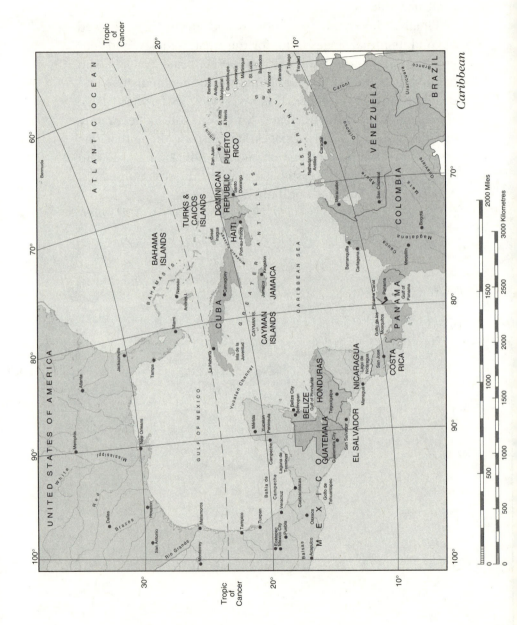

Caribbean

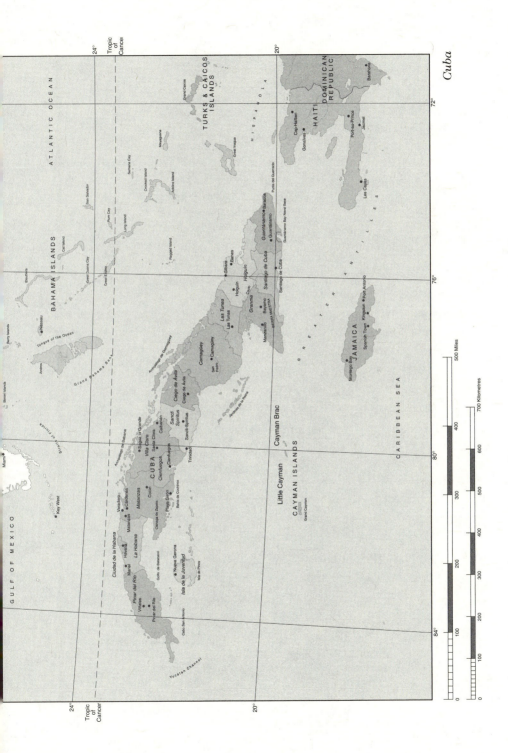

Cuba

PART ONE
NARRATIVE SECTION

CHAPTER ONE

Geography and History

GEOGRAPHY

Cuba is often referred to as being "just 90 miles" (145 kilometers) from Key West, Florida. However, just as important in the island's often turbulent history has been the fact that it is also just 130 miles (210 km.) east of Mexico's Yucatan Peninsula, 87 miles (140 km.) north of Jamaica, and 48 miles (77 km.) west of Haiti. Frequently and erroneously described as a "small island nation," Cuba is in fact a large island nation: far larger than any other single Caribbean island and roughly the same size (42,804 square miles; 110,869 square kilometers) as the rest of the Antilles combined. Cuba's large size and key geographic location at the confluence of the Gulf of Mexico, the Caribbean Sea, and the Atlantic Ocean have uniquely positioned it throughout its history to absorb, transform, and re-export new ideas, technologies, and fashions. Its strategic location at the crossroads of the three Americas (North, Central, and South) has also allowed it to play an important role in nearly every hemispheric and international craze and confrontation, from its founding as a Spanish colony at the dawn of "the age of empire," to its use as a springboard in the rise of the United States as an imperial power during the so-called Spanish-American War, to its role as the first "communist beachhead" in the Western Hemisphere during the Cold War, to the surprisingly pivotal if increasingly controversial position of the Guantánamo Bay Naval Base in today's "global war on terror."

Geographical Location: "Cuba Is the Key"

After taking a full week to parade slowly and symbolically across the island of Cuba from Santiago in the southeast to Havana in the northwest, Fidel Castro and his fellow revolutionaries swept into the capital on January 8, 1959, welcomed as liberators by jubilant crowds. Within two years the United States had broken off diplomatic relations with Cuba and would shortly attempt to overthrow its government. Soon thereafter Castro proudly declared, "I am a Marxist-Leninist and will be one until the last day of my life." Long before the dramatic triumph of Cuba's socialist revolution, however, the island of Cuba had already come to occupy a unique place of political and economic importance in the Western Hemisphere. This inordinate importance has little directly to do with either the much ballyhooed threat of communism or Castro's mythic charisma. Instead, it derives from Cuba's strategic location at the center of the Western Hemisphere, in the heart of the "American Mediterranean."

Throughout its long history, Cuba has played the role of a geographical hub, linking the peoples, cultures, and economies surrounding it. It has also long been coveted as a military defense post, given its proximity to strategic landmasses and vital sea lanes, including the peninsula and straits of Florida, the Yucatan peninsula and channel, the Windward Passage, the Gulf of Mexico, and the Isthmus of Central America. The island lies at the crossroads of every principal maritime passage in and out of the Caribbean. Both the Spanish and their many European rivals for predominance in the Caribbean knew this. Control of Cuba was key to supremacy in the New World.

The island was once home to perhaps four different groups of native inhabitants, each of which migrated there successively over a period of centuries from South America and the Florida Keys. Later, Cuba was the jumping-off point for Hernán Cortés in his three-year battle against the Aztecs in

Tenochtitlan (today's Mexico City), starting in 1519. After both Mexico's Aztecs and Peru's Incas were effectively conquered, Cuba was again used as a launching pad, this time for a number of expeditions to the North American continent, including the ill-fated campaigns of Alvar Núñez Cabeza de Vaca and Hernando de Soto. Later in 1565, the first permanent European settlement in North America was established by Pedro Menéndez de Avilés at St. Augustine, organized and equipped from Cuba (Martínez-Fernández 2004: 9). Also, because of its unparalleled natural port at Havana, Cuba eventually replaced Santo Domingo as Spain's central administrative city in the Caribbean. Later, the port of Havana became Spain's main roadhouse and weigh-station, the most important port city in the Caribbean. This importance derived from Havana's role as the officially mandated place of rendezvous for all Spanish treasure fleets (*la flota*), which would return to Spain together in a heavily guarded convoy bearing the booty from mainland conquests.

When the British finally succeeded in capturing the heavily fortified city of Havana in 1762, they threw open the port to two new, contradictory, and previously neglected ideas: free trade and slave labor. Although Cuba had experienced those things before, when the British departed a year later, they left an island irrevocably changed and eager to exploit these two new economic strategies. After independence in North America (1776), Haiti (1804), and most of the rest of Spanish America (the 1820s), Cuba's unique location contributed once again to its transformation. Trade exploded with the newly independent United States; French-Haitian slaves and slave holders arrived in great numbers to Cuba's Oriente (eastern Cuba) from the island of Hispaniola; and thousands of Spanish loyalists from the rest of the Americas descended upon the island. Those changes combined with and contributed to the startling growth of an economic system based on sugar monoculture and renewed African slave importation lasting until the 1860s.

At the same time, the growth of a powerful sugar-slave nexus in Cuba, together with its location 90 miles off the U.S. mainland, led to innumerable attempts on the part of various U.S. administrations (beginning with Jefferson in 1808, who called Cuba, the "key to the Gulf of Mexico") to buy or otherwise annex Cuba from Spain, adding it as a slave state. Ironically, a number of these annexation proposals were initiated by Cubans themselves, in order to link the island's destiny (and slave-based economy) to that of the United States. Even after American slavery ended in the 1860s, U.S. policy remained one of biding its time until the "ripe fruit" of Cuba, "incapable of self-support," would inevitably obey the "laws of political gravitation" and fall "towards the North American Union," which "cannot cast her off from its bosom"—as famously expressed in 1823 by secretary of state and future president John Quincy Adams (Pérez 1995).

At the end of the nineteenth century the bulk of the so-called Spanish-American War—which put an end to the last vestiges of a dying Spanish colonial empire and led to the birth of the United States as an imperial power—was fought in Cuba. Although the war grew out of the final episode in Cuba's ongoing war for independence from Spain (1868–1898), in the end Cuba was treated as another pawn (like Puerto Rico, the Philippines, and Guam) in the global chess match between the United States and Spain. Cuba's rebels were excluded from participating in the Treaty of Paris that officially concluded the war. Given the unique geography of Cuba, the framers of the Platt Amendment also saw fit to grant the United States the dual rights to "intervene for the preservation of Cuban independence" and to set up a naval station at a key location on the southeastern tip of the island, Guantánamo Bay, making it the oldest U.S. overseas military base. This imperial pattern of "protective invasion," first developed in Cuba, was re-employed again and again in other countries throughout the Caribbean Basin, America's infamous "backyard," between 1902 and 1934.

During World War II, to avoid the threat of torpedoes from German submarines the U.S. took advantage of Cuba's proximity by creating an "Emergency Land-Water Highway" in order to shuttle food and supplies from the U.S. mainland to Puerto Rico. Merchandise would first be shipped down to Havana from south Florida and then trucked overland to Santiago. Next, it would be shipped across the Windward Passage to Port-au-Prince, Haiti, and trucked across the island of Hispaniola. Finally, it would be shuttled by boat from San Pedro de Macorís, Dominican Republic, across the Mona Passage, and deposited at the U.S. port in Mayagüez, Puerto Rico (Martínez-Fernández 2004: 11).

Arguably the tensest moment of the entire Cold War, the Cuban Missile Crisis of October 1962, derived from a simple fact of Cuban geography: the unacceptable proximity of Soviet missiles on the island, just "90 miles" from the United States. U.S. government newsreels from the era pointedly emphasize the threat of "offensive" nuclear warheads on a once-friendly, adjacent island. A widely circulated Associated Press map from 1962, entitled, "World Revolves Around Cuba," depicted the island encircled by concentric rings with New York City, the Panama Canal, and Mexico City all shown to be an equidistant 1,250 miles from Havana at the epicenter (ibid.: 12). Furthermore, the ultimate decision to remove the missiles from Cuba, reached through a series of secret diplomatic cables between Kennedy and Khrushchev, illustrated once again Cuba's weak position as a pawn in the power struggles between other, greater powers.

Given the island's closeness to Miami and its burgeoning Cuban-American community, in 1980 the United States became the country of first refuge in a mass refugee migration for the first time. Over a period of less than six months, 125,000 Cubans came to the United States, ferried across the waters in small boats by their Cuban-American relatives. Never before had the United States received so many immigrants in one place, at one time. This was possible primarily because of the fact of geographic proximity. Miami Cubans could simply go and get their relatives. While not pleased with the open violation of its borders, the U.S. government was loath to arrest these "heroic" Cuban-Americans as "smugglers" or deny entry to Cubans as "illegal immigrants."

Even today, Cuba's unique geography has again given it a prominent place in international politics, landing it repeatedly in the headlines. For example, the Guantánamo Base was used as a "safe haven" for Cuban (and Haitian) rafters in 1994, when Castro once again called Washington's bluff by opening up his borders. More recently, the base was converted into a detention center for "enemy combatants" conveniently located within U.S. military control but outside the bounds of U.S. territory, and thus beyond the reach of the most basic of U.S. legal guarantees. Cuba's unique geography has even placed it at the center of heated accusations about its being used as a trans-shipment point by drug smugglers attempting to introduce narcotics into the United States from South America.

Each of these historical examples underlines the fact expressed most simply by the key that lies at the center of the Cuban national coat of arms: Cuba is the key that unlocks the "Indies," the Caribbean, and by extension the entire hemisphere. Whoever controls Cuba will have leverage and influence throughout the Americas. This may seem a lot to hang on the simple, seemingly arbitrary fact of Cuban geography. But if geography is not destiny, it is at the very least the first cause behind the riddle of Cuba's exceptionalism.

Geographical Features: Topography, Climate, Fora and Fauna, and Conservation

Topography. Cuba is the largest and westernmost island of the Greater Antilles. Its total area is 42,804 square miles (110,869 sq. km.), making it slightly smaller than Pennsylvania (46,058 sq. mi.; 119,288 sq. km.), or about half the size of the United Kingdom (94,527 sq. mi.; 244,820 sq. km). Cuba's area includes the mainland (40,520 sq. mi.; 104,945 sq. km.), the Isle of Youth (renamed Isla de la Juventud in 1976) to the southwest (850 sq. mi.; 2,200 sq. km.), and the more than 1,600 small islets, keys, and coral reefs (1,434 sq. mi.; 3,715 sq. km.) most of which are located on the northeastern coast or east of the Isle of Youth in the Gulf of Batabanó. Considered alone, the Isle of Youth is the sixth largest island in the Caribbean, after Cuba, Hispaniola, Jamaica, Puerto Rico, and Trinidad. Its large size and proximity to the Cuban mainland made it a perfect hideaway for pirates during the sixteenth and seventeenth centuries. For this reason, it is often said that the island, first christened *La Evangelista* by Columbus and later referred to colloquially as *Isla de Tesoros* by Cubans, was the inspiration for both Robert Louis Stevenson's *Treasure Island* and James Mathew Barrie's *Peter Pan* (ibid.: 2).

Cuba's coastline measures 3,570 miles (5,764 km.). By comparison, the coastline of Puerto Rico measures 310 miles (501 km.), and its total area is 5,324 square miles (9,104 sq. km.), making it about one-twelfth the size of Cuba. At its longest, measured from east to west, Cuba is 775 miles (1,250 km.) long and varies between 19.3 miles (31 km.) and 118 miles (191 km.) wide, with an average width of 50 miles (80 km.). If placed upon land, the distance between Cabo de San Antonio in the west to Punta de Quemado in the east would equal the distance from Miami to Nashville, or alternately from Paris to Budapest.

Cuba's topography is mostly flat savanna interspersed with rolling plains, called *llanos*. Roughly 60 percent of the land area is used for agriculture, but only about 12 percent of that land is highly productive deep and permeable soil. Twenty-one percent of the land is used for grazing or left fallow, while roughly a quarter of the total land area is still forested (though only a small portion of that is tropical rain forest). Only 6.3 percent of the land is occupied by human settlements. The island also boasts more than 200 natural harbors, many of which are deepwater ports well protected by bottleneck entrances. The majority of these are located on the northern coast, as are most of the island's more than 289 natural beaches.

The beaches on the northern coast tend to be longer and whiter, with breaking waves and a rolling surf. However, they are more affected by northern cold fronts, making bathing occasionally unpleasant in the winter. Cuba's southern beaches tend to be warmer in the winter months but are less attractive for bathers because of their rocky, swampy character and their abundance of sea urchins. Important exceptions are the attractive, popular destinations Playa Girón and Playa Ancón. The majority of the islands in Cuba's four archipelagos are also located off the northern coast, including Los Colorados north of the province of Pinar del Río and the Sabana and Camagüey Archipelagos located north of Villa Clara, Sancti Spíritus, Ciego de Ávila, and Camagüey provinces. Cuba's two other archipelagos are the Jardines de la Reina (Queen's Gardens), south of Ciego de Ávila province, and Los Canarreos, east of the Isle of Youth and south of the mainland.

Despite being the least mountainous of the Greater Antilles, with an average elevation of less than 328 feet (100 meters), Cuba is home to three mountain systems (or *sierras*), the Sierra Maestra in the Oriente region in the southeast; the Guamuhaya (containing the Escambray range) in the south-central provinces of Cienfuegos, Villa Clara, and Sancti Spíritus (peaking at 3,740 ft.; 1,140 m.); and the Guaniguanico system in the western province Pinar del Río, which contains both the Rosario and Órganos ranges (neither of which is higher than 2,293 feet; 699 meters). Pinar del Río is also home to the uniquely beautiful Viñales Valley, which features numerous underground limestone caves and high conical limestone hills, called *mogotes,* that rise abruptly from the valley floor. The Sierra Maestra contains Cuba's highest point, Pico Turquino, which rises to 6,474 feet (1,974 m.)

A stalactite formation in one of the many caves in the vicinity of Viñales in the province of Pinar del Río. (Ted Henken)

above sea level. Pico Turquino is the Caribbean's second highest peak after Pico Duarte of the Dominican Republic, which towers 10,407 feet (3,170 meters). Off the southern coast of Cuba, near the Sierra Maestra range, lies the Bartlett Trough and Cayman Trench, the lowest point in the Caribbean, which drops precipitously 23,720 feet (7,230 m.) below the sea between Cuba and Jamaica. This deep trench is the place where the North American and Caribbean tectonic plates meet, causing occasional earthquakes in the vicinity.

Cuba's rivers tend to be short, narrow, shallow, and non-navigable, making them of limited use as transportation channels in the history of the island's development. Major rivers include the Zaza (Sancti Spíritus, 65 mi.; 104 km.), Sagua La Grande (Villa Clara, 101 mi.; 163 km.), and Cauto, the island's longest at 230 miles (370 km.), which drains the northern slopes of the Sierra Maestra and flows westward out

Cuba's *mogotes* and caves

Part of the oldest geological formation in Cuba, the *mogotes* of Viñales Valley make the region one of the island's most picturesque natural wonders. Together with the region's extensive underground caves, such as the Gran Caverna de Santo Tomás, these enormous, roughly hewn, skyscraper-high slabs are what is left of a great limestone plateau that climbed out of the sea more than 150 million years ago. The underground caves hidden below the *mogotes* were first home to Cuba's Siboney Indians, giving their name to the fascinating if tourist-laden Cueva del Indio, an underground river within a massive limestone cave. Later, some of these same caves were inhabited by Cuba's famed runaway slaves, called *cimarrones* (the origin of the English names "maroon" and "Seminole," meaning "wild runaway"). Atop these *mogotes* are unique ecosystems, complete with endemic plants, mollusks, and Cuba's ancient cork palm, found only in the Viñales region. The valley economy is dominated by Cuba's rich tobacco, thanks to the ease with which the plant grows in the cool climate in the shadow of the *mogotes*.

of Santiago Province, emptying into the Gulf of Guanacayabo at Granma Province. Because of the lack of major navigable rivers to aid in transportation and the extractive nature of most economic activity in the colonial period, most early passenger and cargo transportation was by ship from port to port. For that reason nearly all of Cuba's early settlements were on the coast or on bays that had openings to the sea, not on rivers. An unwritten colonial rule stipulated that no sugar estate should be more than 50 miles (80 km.) from a port, since there were few serviceable roads in the interior. In fact, even though Cuba was the first Spanish-speaking country to develop a rail system, starting in 1837 (even before Spain), railroads were built to export sugar, not as a means of public transportation. The lesson, of course, is a key geographic one growing out of Cuba's economic history: major population centers grew naturally out of port towns, just as port towns grew from natural harbors (Pérez 1995).

The Cuban coastline's many keys and well-hidden and protected ports and bays allowed for the early development and dogged persistence of a ubiquitous contraband trade in sugar and slaves. Just as the wealth of natural harbors provided the opportunity for smuggling, Spain's attempt to monopolize trade necessitated it. Indeed, given the privileged position of the capital city of Havana, southeastern Cuba found itself both underpopulated and undeveloped (ibid.). Isolated from the rest of the island, parts of Oriente became important sanctuaries for communities of free blacks and *cimarrones* who formed their own communities (*palenques*), such as To' Tenemos ("We Have Everything"), Guarda Mujeres ("Women's Hideaway"), and Kalunga (a Congolese name for God) in what is today Guantánamo Province (Alvarado Ramos 1998).

Cuba's neglected Oriente was also home to many communities of small independent peasants, Cuba's *guajiros*. New immigrants often came to settle in the western provinces of Havana and Matanzas, but Oriente was always the most "Cuban" province on the island (Pérez 1995). Of course, "revolutionary Oriente," distant and scornful of authority, has also been the starting place for the great majority of the island's military conquests and revolutionary movements, including Diego Velásquez's scorched-earth campaign against the Indians starting in 1511, both of Cuba's wars for independence (1868 and 1895), and the Cuban Revolution itself, which began in the foothills of the Sierra Maestra in December 1956.

Prior to the 1850s, Cuba was administered exclusively through its capital city, with the captain-general ostensibly responsible to the Spanish Crown and acting as its official representative on the island colony. In practice, however, captain-generals often ruled with absolute power and saw their positions as a sure route to personal enrichment through payoffs for allowing contraband trade and the sale of *asientos* (exclusive rights to import slaves and other "goods"). Spanish restrictions on free trade were as extensive as they were notorious. Yet that only led to a greater disrespect for the law, since a high demand for goods was met with a chronically insufficient supply. Estimates are that as much as half of all Cuban commerce in the late seventeenth century arose from contraband trade.

In order better to administer the colony, in the 1850s the Crown reorganized its large and unwieldy western, central, and eastern departments, dividing the island instead into thirty-one districts, or *jurisdicciones*, split between new western and eastern departments, with Havana and Santiago as their capitals. In 1878, upon the close of the Ten Years' War and the rise of the Autonomist Party, the island's political and administrative divisions were overhauled again, out of which came 407 municipalities (townships) and the island's six traditional provinces: Pinar del Río, Havana, Matanzas, Las Villas, Camagüey (known as Puerto Príncipe before 1902), and Oriente.

Ironically, Cuban independence and prolonged U.S. influence did nothing to alter those administrative divisions, which remained in place for nearly 100 years. It was not until the first Congress of the Communist Party in 1976 that provincial divisions were again reorganized. To facilitate more effective administration, many of the 407 original municipalities were eliminated, leaving just 169. The original six provinces were divided into fourteen, with the Isle of Pines renamed the Isle of Youth and designated a "special municipality." From west to east, Cuba's fourteen provinces are Pinar del Río, Havana, City of Havana, Matanzas, Villa Clara, Cienfuegos, Sancti Spíritus, Ciego de Ávila, Camagüey, Las Tunas, Granma, Holguín, Santiago de Cuba, and Guantánamo.

Underlying these political and administrative divisions are Cuba's five major geographical subregions, each of which has

Oriente and the *orientales*

Despite the disappearance of Oriente as an official province, Cubans still speak of anyone hailing from the eastern end of the island as an *oriental* (an easterner, or Oriental). That is often done with haughtiness by overly proud *habaneros,* who commonly disparage their more provincial compatriots for their "strange" country ways, colloquial accents and expressions, and often darker complexions. It is common to hear Havana residents derisively describe arrivals to the capital from the east as being *de provincia* (from the provinces) or even *palestinos* (Palestinians)! Cuba's leading dance band since the early 1970s, Los Van Van, once even made a hit with a song that facetiously declared, *"La Habana no aguanta más"* ("Havana can't take any more"), indicating the extent to which overcrowding had become an issue in the capital city. Indeed, the government passed a migration law in 1997 that cut off housing and ration benefits to those unlawfully living in the capital, threatening them with deportation back to the provinces. Still, Cubans continue to migrate to the capital in search of housing and employment. Some even joke that Havana's two most famous *palestinos* are none other than Fidel and Raúl Castro, both of whom were born and raised in the town of Birán in Oriente, now part of Holguín province.

played an important historical role in the social, demographic, and economic organization of the island. These are the Occidental region, the Central or Las Villas region, the vast savanna of Camagüey, the Oriental region, and the Isle of Youth. The Occidental region, which includes the provinces Pinar del Río, Havana, and Matanzas, is the location of the most significant socioeconomic division in Cuba's history between its two signature cash crops, sugar and tobacco, both of which are grown abundantly in the region. This "counterpoint" between tobacco and sugar was famously described by Cuban writer Fernando Ortiz in his 1940 book *Cuban Counterpoint: Tobacco and Sugar.* Other regions either have specialized in one agricultural or industrial activity, as did

Camagüey in cattle ranching, or developed a diversified economic profile to match an equally diverse terrain, as did Oriente, which produces coffee, citrus, cacao, bananas, and sugar, as well as being home to its share of ranching and mining operations (Martínez-Fernández et al. 2002).

Climate. Cuba's subtropical climate is moderated by the prevailing trade winds coming in from the northeast, the surrounding water, and the cool air mass pushed down from the North American continent. Yearly mean temperature is 77 degrees Fahrenheit (25°C) and varies little during the year, from an average high of 81 degrees (27°C) in the summer months to an average low of 70 degrees (21°C) in the winter. The hottest part of the island is southern Oriente, where temperatures can reach beyond 106 degrees (41°C), especially in the lowlands of Guantánamo. Rainfall fluctuates during the year between a summer rainy season (May to October) that normally brings in between 8 and 10 inches (20–26 centimeters) of precipitation each month, and a winter dry season (November to April) that sees just 1 to 4 inches (3.2–10 cm.) per month, with an average of ninety-six rainy days each year. Almost two-thirds of the rainfall is concentrated in the wet season, in part because of the frequency of hurricanes during September and October. Central and western areas are occasionally known to endure a three- to five-month annual drought, known as *La Seca,* and recently the eastern provinces of Holguín and Las Tunas have had extensive droughts of their own.

Easily Cuba's most significant climatic phenomena are the Atlantic hurricanes that chronically threaten the island (the word originates from the Spanish *huracán,* based on the Taíno god of wind and rain, Uracán). A hurricane, more commonly called a *ciclón* ("cyclone") in Cuba, is produced when hot air rises from the surface of the Atlantic Ocean as cool air falls from the upper atmosphere and is sucked into a low-pressure area left behind by the rising heated air. The spinning of the earth causes the air being sucked in near the ocean's surface to spin counterclockwise around a central vortex, pulling water vapor in as it rises and acting much like a chimney; clouds and rain precipitate out the top of the spout. As long as the gathering storm remains over the warm, moist areas that act as its fuel, it will strengthen. Normally these storms wander northward into the eastern trade winds, which send the threatening mass on a direct collision course with the major islands of the Caribbean and the coastal areas in the Gulf of Mexico (Baker 2000).

The Atlantic hurricane season lasts from July through November, with Cuba's coast, especially its far west, subject to hurricanes from August to November. In general, the country averages one hurricane every other year. More than 150 recorded hurricanes have hit the island since 1498. Major storms include a 1768 storm that destroyed Havana, sinking sixty-nine ships in the harbor and leaving more than 1,000 dead. A 1791 storm, which also did extensive damage to Havana, left more than 11,700 head of cattle and 3,000 people dead. In the twentieth century, two storms are remembered for being especially destructive. A 1932 cyclone produced a tidal wave that destroyed the town of Santa Cruz del Sur and killed virtually its entire population of 3,000. In 1963, Hurricane Flora ripped through the island, leaving 4,200 dead and destroying more than 30,000 homes.

As a result of Cuba's finely honed civil defense system, just sixteen lives were lost between 1996 and 2002 despite six hurricanes, three of them major. This list includes hurricanes Lili ('96),' Georges ('98), Irene ('99), and perhaps the most devastating hurricane to strike Cuba in more than half a century, the category-four Hurricane Michelle ('01). The arrival of Michelle saw the evacuation of almost 800,000, with only five people dead, but it caused extensive damage to agriculture and livestock. The United States offered food aid, stipulating that "the Cuban people benefit and not the government." Castro refused, countering with a request to purchase American

---

Hurricanes and Cuban civil defense

As a result of the devastation caused by Hurricane Flora in 1963, together with the growing threat of foreign invasion, the revolutionary government developed a highly effective system of civil defense, with special training compulsory for all citizens starting in 1976. Cuba's highly centralized form of government helps make the civil defense plan work. Highly developed prestorm planning and the coordinated delegation of responsibilities have allowed the island to avoid high death tolls and become a recognized leader in disaster preparation. Also, because hurricanes are a normal part of life for Cubans, citizens are well versed in evacuation procedures, which are practiced each May. There are even measures in place to secure major appliances, pets, and other expensive belongings, so that no one stays behind for fear of looting. Finally, local and provincial officials double as civil defense officers, so that evacuees take orders from a familiar community leader, not an unknown federal official.

---

foodstuffs in hard currency. The offer was accepted, and for the first time since the early 1960s there was inaugurated a growing annual balance of cash-only food trade from the United States that continues despite political and bureaucratic obstacles.

Cuba's civil defense system was tested again in 2004 when Hurricane Ivan passed over the western end of the island. An amazing 2 million people were evacuated with no deaths or serious injuries. Most recently, after Hurricane Dennis struck the island in July 2005, leaving sixteen people dead, Castro refused the U.S. offer of $50,000 in aid, indicating that he would spurn even $1 billion as a protest against the ongoing embargo. The U.S. government seemed to strike back in September 2005, when it refused Cuba's offer of more than 1,500 doctors and over 25 tons of medical supplies after Hurricane Katrina destroyed large swaths of southeastern Louisiana and southern Mississippi (Martín 2005).

Flora and Fauna. Given its diversity of climatic zones, especially on its isolated keys, extensive coral reefs, and the
unmatched habitat of the Ciénaga de Zapata (Zapata Swamp),
Cuba enjoys a rich variety of plant and animal species. More
than 7,000 plant species are found on the island, many of
which are found elsewhere in the hemisphere because the
island was once attached to the continent. Still, over half of
these are endemic to Cuba. Prior to 1492 (and even as late as
the early nineteenth century before sugarcane planting
exploded), 90 percent of the island was covered with dense
tropical forests. However, by 1900 Cuban forests had been
reduced to just 54 percent of the island's total area, dropping
to just under 14 percent by 1959 (Moreno Fraginals 1976).
Today, 75 percent of the island is either savanna or plains, as
a result of the uncontrolled expansion of the population of
swine, the development of extensive cattle ranches, and the
heavy exploitation of sugarcane, especially during the nineteenth century. To combat the loss of forest, in 1987 the
revolutionary government instituted Plan Manatí, which succeeded in planting as many as 3 billion trees and increasing
the forested proportion of the island to almost 24 percent.
Unfortunately, most of those plantings were of either firs or
transplanted eucalyptus trees, not the original mahogany,
cedar, or ebony that originally flourished across the island.

Although greatly depleted during the sugar boom in the
nineteenth century, tree varieties still in existence include
the palm, cedar, ebony, mahogany, oak, pine, and extensive
coastal mangroves. Appropriately, Cuba's national tree is the
royal palm (*Reistonea regia*), which is featured on the
national coat of arms and can grow up to 130 feet (40 meters)
high. Unlike other, shorter palms, the towering royal palm
has a smooth, marblelike gray trunk topped by a curious
green bulb surrounded by a cascade of gracefully draped
palm leaves. Apart from its majestic beauty, the tree has been
very useful historically, with both the Taínos and Cuban Creoles exploiting different parts of the tree for a variety of uses.

For example, Cuba's famous thatched huts, called *bohíos* (still common in rural areas), were first engineered by the indigenous Taínos from the tree's palm fronds (called *pencas*). The sturdy bases of the fronds have been used as a naturally waterproof roofing and siding material. Also, palm honey and palm seeds have been used as animal feed, and the succulent heart of palm (*palmito*) is a highly sought after treat extracted from the center of the majestic trunk. Birds even feast on the tree's fruit, inadvertently helping to spread the seeds (*palmiches*) across the island and aiding in the tree's proliferation. Apart from other palm species, there are said to be as many as 20 million royal palms thriving across the expanse of the island today, almost double the island's human population.

Two other palm trees of note are the rare, prehistoric cork palm and the rounded, belly palm, *palma barrigona,* easily recognized by its distinctive shape. Other trees characteristic of Cuba include the transplanted royal poinciana, known in Cuba by its colloquial name, *flamboyán,* because of its flamboyant orange and red blooms that appear in December. There is also the wide-trunked *ceiba* or kapok (silk-cotton) tree, revered as sacred by Indian, African, and European cultures alike. Pine forests are most abundant in appropriately named Pinar del Río (Pine River) Province, as well as in eastern Holguín, central Guantánamo, and on the Isle of Youth (originally called Isle of Pines because of its extensive pine forests). A final tree variety that has proliferated in Cuba is the mangrove (*manglar*). Although not as majestic as the royal palm, mangroves are just as useful: they act as natural filters of water runoff, protect shorelines from erosion (and hurricane storm surges), and provide a nutrient-rich habitat for scores of small fish and birds. Though Cuba's mangroves are located in many of the island's coastal areas, they are most extensive in Cuba's massive Zapata Swamp on the southern coast of Matanzas Province, just west of the Bay of Pigs.

Cuba is also home to more than 300 species of wild orchid, with a number of sites dedicated to their cultivation, including an *orquidiario* built in the 1940s in the western town of Soroa with over 350 species, many of which are not found in the wild. Orchids are Cuba's largest and most diverse family of flowering plants, with flowers that range from less than a millimeter in size to hanging orchids with petals more than half a meter long. Another flower of note is the butterfly jasmine, Cuba's national flower, called the *mariposa blanca.* Because of its deep whiteness, the flower became associated with the Cuban nationalist ideals of rebellion, independence, and purity during the island's nineteenth-century independence wars, when Cuban women sympathetic to the rebel cause would wear the flower in their hair to transport secret messages. Perhaps the two most verdant locations on the island to find the richest diversity of Cuba's floral heritage are on the Isle of Youth and in the vast Zapata Swamp, the largest swampy wetland in the Caribbean. There are more than 750 botanical varieties in the swamp, 116 of them native to Cuba and 6 found only there.

The floral richness of the Zapata Swamp is matched only by its spectacular variety of fauna, including unique birds, amphibians and reptiles, marine turtles, fish and shellfish, offshore coral, mammals, bats, marine mammals, and insects and butterflies. Cuba boasts more than 300 species of bird, including the parakeet, owl, woodpecker, *sinsonte* (mockingbird), *ruiseñor* (nightingale), flamingo, and the famous *tocororo*, the national bird. Cuba's pink flamingos congregate in flocks of thousands in shallow swamps, keys, or lagoons. They feed on the high-salinity and larval- and algae-rich water, which also contains carotenoid pigments, a microscopic substance that gives the birds their distinctive pink color. Flamingos gradually gain their color as they grow to adulthood. Adults stand an average of 3.3 feet (1 m.) high and have a wingspan of 5 feet (1.5 m.). One look at the *tocororo* (also called *tocoloro*), a Cuban trogon of the Quetzal family, makes clear why it was chosen as Cuba's national bird. It has a blue head, white chest, and red belly. Like its Central American cousin, it is also distinctive for its short wings and long, flowing tail. Apart from the bird's tricolored plume, its nationalist significance stems from the legend that it is unable to live in captivity (*¡patria o muerte!*).

Even more fascinating and unique than its multicolored avian relative is the diminutive *zunzuncito* (bee hummingbird). This amazing Cuban creature is the world's smallest bird. Resembling more a bumblebee or large insect than a winged creature of the air, the male of the species weighs just 2 grams (less than a penny) and is slightly larger than a grasshopper. Cuba is also home to other of the world's smallest animals, including a tiny froglet (*Sminthillus limbatus,* the world's smallest frog), a dwarf bat, a pygmy owl called *sijucito* (or *sijú platanero*), and a Microtytus scorpion. On the other hand, large mammals include the *jutía*, a 2-foot-long Cuban tree rat found mostly on isolated keys among the mangroves (Baker 2000; Stanley 2000).

Given the nearness of the Cayman Islands, the Cayman Trench, and the fact that Cubans have even nicknamed their island *El caimán* (because of its elongated shape and its ability to endure), it is not surprising to find that the island is home to a number of important reptiles (80 percent of which are endemic), including both the caiman (alligator) and its longer and more feisty cousin, the crocodile (*lagarto criollo*). The diminutive caiman measures less than 6.5 feet (2 meters) long and is relatively common in Cuba's wet lowlands. The Cuban crocodile is found almost exclusively in the Zapata Swamp, where the government has worked over the past decade to save them from extinction. There are now around 6,000 Cuban crocs living in the wild. Unlike its American brother, the Cuban crocodile is an omnivore whose diet, though based on fish, also includes large mammals like wild boars, deer, and even the occasional unwitting birdwatcher.

The *zunzuncito*, Cuba's hummingbird

Like its larger cousin the hummingbird, the *zunzuncito* can perform amazing acrobatics because of the unbelievable rapidity of its wingbeat. Cuba has sixteen different species of hummingbird in all, each of whose wings beat faster than a naked eye can detect (up to 100 beats per second). Hummingbirds are unique in that they are the only species of bird that get lift from both their forward and backward wing strokes. This allows them to hover in place, turn upside down, and even fly sideways and backward. These abilities enable them to float as if by magic beside flowers as they extend their distinctive bills forward to extract nectar, simultaneously performing the symbiotic service of pollination for Cuba's flowers. Cuba's indigenous inhabitants revered these creatures as sacred, calling them *colibrís,* or "god birds." Even today, Cuban superstition has it that the best way to entrap prospective lovers is by having them drink a potion made from dried, ground-up hummingbirds.

The female croc actually helps to hatch her own eggs, taking her new offspring into a special pouch in her mouth and carrying them off to be fiercely guarded by both parents. Other common reptiles include iguanas, lizards, salamanders, marine turtles, and fifteen species of nonpoisonous snakes, of which the nocturnal *maja* python is the largest, reaching 13 feet (4 m.) long. There is also an 8-inch (20 cm.) long pygmy boa found only in the caves of Viñales.

Cuba has coastal waters filled with more than 900 species of fish and crustaceans. Crabs, turtles, thirty-five species of shark, and tuna are the most common. One sea animal that is in great abundance just off the perimeter of much of the island is the coral. The coral reef that stretches along Cuba's northern coast is the world's second longest, after the Great Barrier Reef of Australia. This animal, often not thought of as an animal at all, is better known for its "shell," the huge reefs that are the product of millions of tiny individual corals secreting an external calcium carbonate skeleton. More amazing still is the hidden secret to the growth of coral reefs, which is in the symbiotic relationship that these organisms have with the zooxanthellea, a single-celled alga that lives inside corals. Through a sunlight-induced process of photosynthesis, these algae produce oxygen and nutrients that enable the coral to live and grow. However, it is for this reason that coral reefs can grow only in shallow water that is exposed to sunlight, making the clear, shallow coasts of northern Cuba a perfect habitat (Baker 2000).

Apart from their beauty, intricate lifecycle, and complex structure, coral reefs function as a key growing ground for external algae and other plants that are the base of the marine food chain. Therefore, the loss of coral reefs is not simply an aesthetic matter. It also threatens the many fish and crustacean species that thrive in the coral habitat. Some of the marine life common in Cuba's coral-rich coastal waters, and often found on the tables of dollar-rich or well-connected Cubans, are shrimp, lobster, and the *caguama* (a protected but highly sought-after sea turtle). The diet of less affluent Cubans includes a variety of other abundant but less expensive fish, such as the *cherna* (grouper), swordfish, *pargo* ("red snapper"), *bonito* ("striped tuna"), and *aguja* ("gar" or "needlefish"). Still, the majority of these marine products are destined for international export or internal consumption by foreign tourists. Instead, Cuban nationals are more likely to consume small fish of lesser quality such as the *jurel* ("crevalle jack"), *macarela* ("mackerel"), or *merluza* ("hake"). A final nonedible crustacean, highly sought after (usually for sale to tourists) for its colorful striped shell, is the tiny *polimita* ("polymite") snail, found only in the Baracoa region.

Conservation and Environmental Challenges. The biggest threat facing Cuba's rich variety of flora and fauna is also the island's latest and most promising economic strategy: tourism. Like sugarcane before it, tourism promises a highly lucrative but also economically vulnerable, marginally sustainable, and environmentally threatening economic development strategy. In its zeal to attract greater numbers of tourists to the island, the Cuban government has begun to develop its northern keys into exclusive international resorts. Apart from the environmental impact of new hotels and their associated facilities, the government has built a series of massive stone causeways (*pedraplenes*) to facilitate access to those remote and once virgin keys. Such causeways do enormous damage to marine and coastal habitats, cutting wildlife off from food supplies and nesting sites, as has already happened at Cayo Coco and Cayo Guillermo.

Additionally, the construction and mineral extraction industries have led to the denuding of a number of natural areas, including the land surrounding the cement factory at Mariel and the nickel-mining operations at Moa in Holguín Province. Efforts have been made to clean up Havana's filthy harbor and reduce sulfur emissions from the many oil wells near Varadero, but there is still a long way to go. Cuba has few emission controls, but ironically the slow pace of development and chronic energy shortages have prevented extensive environmental destruction thus far. However, as Cuba recovers from the 1990s economic crisis, the government has few development options other than increased exploitation of its limited natural resources. The recent discovery of potentially large deposits of petroleum off Cuba's northwest coast is a case in point, both potentially lucrative and environmentally destructive.

On the flip side, Cuba's economic crisis has forced it to implement a number of sustainable-development strategies, including using *bagasse* (a sugarcane waste) and other biomass fuels to fire some industries (as was commonly done prior to the revolution), developing a respectable organic farming industry, and reaching into its popular traditions to promote "green" medicine. Also, much gas-powered transport has been converted to human or animal power, leading to the return of oxen and donkeys for farm labor and public transportation in many provincial cities and towns. Likewise, the once ubiquitous automobile has given way in many places to the bicycle. By 1993, Havana had more than 700,000 bicycles, up from just 100,000 in 1990. These mostly Chinese-made bicycles are used by private citizens, and after a difficult learning curve for a culture once as wedded to the automobile as is the United States, many roads and street signs recognize cyclers' rights and seek to protect them. The most common Chinese models—Phoenix, Forever, and Flying Pigeon—are available to Cubans on installment plans for between $60 and $120 pesos (the equivalent of between $2.30–$4.60 U.S. dollars), but still expensive when the average monthly salary remains around $260 pesos or $10 U.S. dollars. Inadvertently, that has worked to reduce air pollution and has given rise to a semilegal sector of private bicycle repair and parking services. At the same time, the increased time and energy needed to commute and the drop in industrial and agricultural output resulting from the use of such antiquated technologies have taken a heavy toll (Scarpaci and Hall 1995).

HISTORY

Pre-Columbian History and the Spanish Conquest

The island of Cuba was home to at least two major indigenous groups: the Siboney and the more advanced Taíno. A third group, known as the Caribs, who gave their name to the Caribbean (*el Caribe,* in Spanish), never actually set foot on the island of Cuba, though they were fierce challengers to the Taíno in many of the smaller islands of the eastern Caribbean. What is certain is that the Taíno were the dominant and most populous group on the island when Spanish conquest began in the early 1500s.

Set against a colorful, patriotic mural in Havana, this photo features a Forever brand of Chinese bicycle rented by the author on his first trip to Cuba in 1997. (Ted Henken)

Archeological evidence indicates that Cuba's earliest indigenous group, the Siboney, arrived on the island in 1000 BC. They were hunter-gatherer cave dwellers, living mainly on the western and southern coasts. Much of what we know of the

Siboney, including their name, was gleaned not directly from them but through contact with the larger and more advanced Taínos, who referred to them as *siba eyeri* ("cave-men" or "rock-men"). On the other hand, the indigenous name for the island, Cubanacán, as well as the modern nation that calls it home, Cuba, comes from the Siboney, not the Taíno.

Cuba's Taíno were part of the larger family of Arawak peoples who populated most of the rest of the Greater Antilles. Cuba's Taíno were in constant contact with their fellow Arawaks on the islands of Hayti (Santo Domingo) and Borinquén (Puerto Rico) to the east. In fact, the famed Arawakan cacique (chieftain) Hatuey was a kind of refugee who fled to the island of Cuba after witnessing the brutal repression and virtual enslavement of his brethren in the western part of the island christened Hispaniola by the Spanish (now divided between the modern nations Haiti and the Dominican Republic).

The Taíno arrived in Cuba from Hispaniola in two waves, the first in the ninth century and the second in the mid-fifteenth century, just before Columbus arrived in the Caribbean in 1492. The first group of Taíno (sometimes referred to as the Sub-Taíno) favored the north coast of eastern Cuba and left the largest number of settlement sites, most located in Cuba's Oriente. They pushed the Siboney out of the eastern portion of the island over the course of centuries, incorporating some of them into Taíno society as slaves, called *naboríes*.

Although some Taíno settlements were located near the coast, the Taíno preferred to live farther inland, near sources of freshwater. They built relatively large villages of 1,000 to 2,000 inhabitants, ruled over by a cacique, and lived in cone-shaped, thatched huts made of palm fronds, which they called *bohíos*. Larger, rectangular dwellings with porches, reserved for the cacique, were known as *caneyes*. Beside their homes, they built small storage structures that they called *barbacoas* (likely the origin of the English word *barbeque*). Each of these words, as well as the structures they describe, is still commonly used in modern Cuba, with *barbacoa* commonly used to refer to a split-level home, and *El Caney* doubling as the name of Cuba's oldest rum factory and as a suburb of Santiago where descendants of the Taíno lived for many years.

The Taíno would build a series of *bohíos* around a central area, called a *batey,* where important assemblies, festivals, and ball games took place. Again, the word (as well as the structure), *batey,* has been passed down to modern Cuba and is used today to refer to the living quarters and central plaza of a sugar plantation. A final Taíno word still occasionally used in modern Cuba is *areíto,* the name of the most important native celebration, in which the Taíno would sing and dance for hours on end as they recited the stories of their past to the young.

Like the Siboney, the Taíno subsisted on hunting and gathering, but they also cultivated small gardens in which they grew a variety of crops, including maize (corn), sweet potato (*boniato*), *yuca* (sometimes spelled yucca and called cassava or manioc in English), tomato, avocado, pineapple, and, for religious purposes, a plant that they called *cohiba*—tobacco. (*Cohiba* is also the brand name of contemporary Cuba's most sought-after cigar). Again, many of these crops, but especially *yuca*, from which the Taíno made a starchy kind of bread called *casabe*, and the sweet potato, continue to constitute the staples in the Cuban diet. Another innovation was their practice of keeping wild animals alive in captivity for the purpose of later consumption. The Taíno did this both with various mammals and reptiles they captured, including the *jutía* and iguana, and with mullet, which they managed to keep alive in specially constructed underwater pens. Finally, the Taíno were skilled craftsmen, weaving mats, nets, and hammocks, and carving ornaments and canoes—both the English words *hammock* (in Spanish, *jamaca*) and *canoe* (*canoa*) originate from the Taíno language.

Cuba's other band of Taíno inhabitants arrived sometime during the fifteenth century and settled in the far eastern coastal region in and around the town of Baracoa. This second group came to Cuba fleeing from the fierce and presumably cannibalistic Caribs, who were then in a process of expansion. Given their short time in residence on the island, there are few archaeological sites attributed to this group (Pérez 1995).

After first landing in Guanahani (renamed San Salvador by Columbus and today part of the Bahamas) on October 12, 1492 (a date subsequently celebrated in most of Latin America, but *not* in Cuba, as *El Día de la Raza* and in the United States as Columbus Day), Columbus continued on toward an island that the natives of Guanahani said was larger and offered more of what Columbus wanted: "gold, spices, and other merchandise." Guanahani natives were likely just trying to get rid of Columbus since Cuba never yielded much gold. However, Columbus arrived on the northeastern coast of Cuba (which he called alternately *Chipangu,* thinking it was perhaps Japan, and later *Colba,* mimicking a native name for the island) on Saturday evening, October 27, 1492. After this initial visit, the Spanish concentrated their efforts on colonizing the smaller island of Hayti to the east, which they renamed *La Española* (Hispaniola in English) after Isabella the Queen of Spain.

Rumors of abundant deposits of gold on the abandoned island turned attention back to Cuba when Columbus's son Diego was appointed governor of the Indies in 1508. Increasing disputes between Spanish conquistadors on Hispaniola over the dwindling tracts of available land and dwindling numbers of natives who could be forced to work also fueled the exodus. Hispaniola's governor Nicolas de Ovando (1502–1509) then sent Sebastian de Ocampo to Cuba in an attempt to circumnavigate and survey the island. Ocampo returned to confirm that Cuba was indeed an island. He also discovered numerous well-protected deep-water ports and brought news of gold deposits in the island's interior. Ovando reacted by entrusting a colonization campaign to his lieutenant, Diego Velásquez, who had already distinguished himself as a competent administrator, wealthy landowner, and stalwart soldier in early battles against Hispaniola's own band of Taíno.

The conquest, colonization, and settlement of Cuba proceeded in two waves. First, Velásquez landed at the eastern tip of Cuba near Maisí in 1511 with 300 men and moved westward along the coast to establish Cuba's first small Spanish settlement at Baracoa in 1512. Velásquez renamed Baracoa, calling it Nuestra Señora de la Asunción, and renamed the entire island Juana after the new queen of Spain. However, since Juana (*La Loca*) was then going crazy and had been placed in virtual captivity back in Spain, Velásquez renamed Cuba Fernandina, after King Fernando. Eventually, however, both Cuba and the town of Baracoa regained their indigenous names. Velásquez was accompanied in Cuba by his young and dashing personal secretary Hernán Cortés, who was soon named mayor of Baracoa and later of the island's second capital, Santiago. However, Cortés quickly grew tired of civic administration and trying to "tame" Cuba's land and native population. Just seven years later, in 1519, he would violate Velásquez's direct orders and set sail on his own voyage of discovery and conquest—in Mexico (Thomas 1993).

The second wave of the conquest of Cuba was led by Pánfilo de Narváez, who arrived at Cuba's southern coast near the Gulf of Guacanayabo with a smaller expedition from Jamaica. Given past experiences, Cuba's natives knew exactly what to expect from the arriving Spanish forces and resisted them tenaciously from the start. Resistance, however, was futile, given the Spaniards' far superior weapons and technology (horses, dogs, guns, and iron swords), as well as their most lethal secret weapon (secret even to themselves)—disease. In 1512, Velásquez and Narváez reconnoitered in Oriente, subdued the Taíno forces there, which included capturing and putting to death the Taíno cacique Hatuey. They then enacted a scorched earth campaign to subdue and colonize the rest of the island.

Velásquez and Narváez split up their forces into three regiments at Baracoa. Velásquez sailed along the southern coast, another group proceeded by ship along the northern coast, and Narváez's regiment headed over land, plundering and pillaging as it went. They rendezvoused more than a year later at Carenas Bay on the northern coast (later renamed San Cristóbal de La Habana in 1519), establishing Cuba's first seven European settlements along the way. Following Baracoa in 1512 were Bayamo (1513), Trinidad (1514), Sancti Spíritus (1514), Havana (1514, originally set up on the southern coast and moved to Carenas Bay, its present location, in 1519), Puerto Principe (1514), and Santiago (1515).

Unfortunately for the Spanish conquistadors, who came to Cuba hoping for more labor and better gold deposits than they had found on Hispaniola, neither the expected gold nor the desire of the natives to work as slaves ever panned out. Gold production peaked by 1519 and had all but ceased by the mid-1540s. Moreover, those natives not killed during the fierce and bloody battles of conquest rapidly succumbed to disease, committed suicide, or escaped into the mountains between 1516 and the mid-1540s, leaving the Spanish victors vanquished by their own brutality. These victorious conquistadors found themselves surrounded by vast tracts of fertile, virgin land, but left alone on an increasingly depopulated island. Although the bulk of natives on whom they had relied for labor were gone, the Spanish stubbornly refused to soil their hands by working the land like lowly farmers (Gott 2004).

The native population of Cuba upon Spanish arrival was roughly 112,000 (Pérez 1995). By the mid-1530s, it had been reduced to just 5,000–6,000, a catastrophic demographic loss of 95 percent. The causes of Taíno deaths were diverse and often cumulative. Cuban historian Juan Pérez de la Riva (2003) has estimated that war and massacres, as gruesome as they were, accounted for only about 12 percent of native deaths. Disease (25 percent) and suicide (35 percent) were much more significant causes of death. Finally, infant mortality (20 percent) and famines (8 percent) caused by the destruction of native plots rounded out this sad episode. However, the fact that Pérez de la Riva's numbers add up to a tidy

100 percent hints at his underlying assumption that Cuba's native population was completely wiped out. On the other hand, British historian Hugh Thomas indicates that even after the drastic demographic drop initially suffered by the Taíno, they probably still outnumbered Spaniards and African slaves as late as 1535. In that year, Cuba was home to approximately 300 Spaniards, 5,000 Indians, and 1,000 newly arrived African slaves (Thomas 1998).

What happened to those 5,000 remaining Indians? The answer lies in a final, as yet unmentioned factor. That is the supposition that those natives who did not succumb to the above depredations yielded instead to *mestizaje*—that is, they disappeared into Cuba's white Creole population over the next 350 years of colonial rule. Pérez de la Riva admits as much when he indicates that "[a]fter 1550, when the indigenous population had been reduced to some five or six thousand, *mestizaje* surely became the main cause of the extinction of the indigenous race" (Pérez de la Riva 2003: 24–25). However, one wonders whether "extinction" is the best word to describe the outcome of a process of *mestizaje*.

It is perhaps more accurate to say that Cuba's Indians were not eradicated so much as they were absorbed into its "white" Creole population very early on. Spaniards generally arrived without female companionship and so quickly began taking native women as their wives or concubines, making the majority of the first generation of native-born Cubans mestizo (the mixed offspring of native women and Spanish men). However, these children were not thought of as *indios* (Indians) or even as mestizos. Instead, they were raised and identified as "white" *criollos* (Creoles, meaning in this context, Spaniards born in Cuba), despite the fact that they were half Taíno (Thomas 1998).

The Spanish Crown and Catholic Church made various halfhearted attempts to protect the Taíno from abuse and extinction. However, given the overriding goal of military expansion and mineral extraction, along with the rigidity and paternalism of Spanish culture, it is unlikely that there was an alternate path to the one ultimately followed: brutal exploitation and epidemic disease, followed by centuries of syncretic compromise and transculturation. The solution eventually settled upon after self-serving and ultimately unsuccessful experiments with different systems of labor and land grants (*encomiendas* and *repartimientos*) was to place the remaining Indians in *reducciones* (reservations): towns set apart exclusively for them.

Imposed after the great majority of natives had already died, some of the original *reducciones* included El Cobre, near Santiago; Guanabacoa, now a suburb of Havana; Pueblo Viejo; Mayarí; Yateras; La Guira; El Caney; and Jiguaní. As late as the nineteenth century, remnants of these and other native communities still survived in towns like Yara, Dos Brazos, La Guira, El Caney, and Jiguaní. There are also towns scattered about Cuba today with names like Caridad de los Indios (Charity of the Indians) and La Escondida (The Hideaway), indicating their native origins.

Before this strategy was implemented, many Taíno had already chosen their own spontaneous form of resistance by simply escaping *al monte* or *a la manigua* (into "the wild," woods, swamps, or mountains). There were at least two types of communities of Taíno escapees or "runaways." The earlier group was known as the *indios cayos* (key Indians), a name based on their strategic use of Cuba's innumerable and isolated keys and islets, from which they would occasionally emerge to attack the Spaniards. A second, much longer lasting type of isolated native community hid itself in Cuba's vast, forested interior.

The Spanish initially referred to these escapees simply as *indios del monte* (mountain or wild Indians), but they were more commonly called *cimarrones* (a Spanish term meaning "wild" or "untamed" first applied to animals like horses or pigs that had broken free and gone to live in the wild).

Depending on the size, duration, and organization of these communities, they might be considered *palenques,* and the people who lived in them called *apalencados.* Given the rapidity with which the Taíno population collapsed and the Spanish colonists' subsequent turn to African slaves to replace them, many of these "rebel" Indian communities soon began welcoming runaway African slaves into their midst. In fact, the terms *cimarrón* and *palenque* are today more associated with African than native resistance. However, the first of these communities were founded by natives, became mixed during the second half of the sixteenth century, and were later dominated by escaped African slaves (Alvarado Ramos 1998).

Given the survival of many of the original *reducciones* and the extent of native resistance organized into *palenques,* it is not surprising that recent anthropological research indicates that the indigenous peoples of Cuba did not simply disappear in the 1500s. In fact, the very region first colonized by Velásquez in 1512, the Baracoa-Maisí region of Oriente, is still home to many Cubans who trace their heritage and traditions as Cuban *guajiros* (a Cuban term similar to *campesino,* meaning country farmer) back to the Taíno-Arawak people, whom the Spanish priest and defender of the Indians Bartolomé de Las Casas called *cubeños.* These family nuclei (*caseríos*), many with family names like Rojas and Ramírez, still plant *yuca* fields (which they continue to call *conucos*), bake and eat *yuca* bread (*casabe*), and get together to share Cuba's Taíno stew, *ajiaco* (Barreiro 2003). Perhaps most important, these Cubans continue to identify themselves as natives, using the fairly common Cuban word *guajiro* to capture that identity. For Cuba's urban majority, the word *guajiro* denotes a kind of exotic backwardness preserved by "one of them" (hick or country bumpkin). However, for *guajiros* themselves, the word means what it meant to the original Taíno, "one of us."

Depopulation and Abandonment, 1540–1760

In the decades following the conquest of Mexico by Cortés in 1521, Cuba quickly came to be seen as a vast, untamed backwater, compared with the unimaginable size and wealth of gold and Indian laborers in Mexico. Spanish conquistadors did not venture across the seas, risking their lives in battle to resume the lowly life of farmers. Upon leaving Cuba, Cortés himself declared, "I came here to get rich, not to till the soil like a peasant" (Gott 2004: 20). The conquistadors came to the Indies without the commitments of family and had little of the enduring patience of the religious refugees and yeoman farming families who would later settle in North America. Instead, they sought to become wealthy hidalgos (men of title), overseeing vast tracts of land and hundreds of workers. Realizing that such a future was rapidly becoming impossible for them in Cuba, many left for Mexico during the sixteenth century. This shift mirrored Spain's own goal of extracting mineral wealth from Mexico and later Peru. By the mid-sixteenth century, Cuba entered a long lethargy in which it served Spanish interests mainly as a port. And it is through Cuba's ports, especially at Havana, that the next 200 years of Cuban history would be written.

The Beginnings of the Slave Trade. Before abandoning the island, Spanish colonists sought to replace their dwindling Indian workforce with a new imported labor force. Unwilling to take on the harsh work of digging mines and cultivating fields themselves, they first attempted to substitute the Taíno with new Indians from Central America and the Yucatan. When that scheme failed, the colonists turned to what would later become the backbone of Cuba's labor force: African slaves. Intended to replace Indian labor, the first African slaves were brought to Cuba from the neighboring Spanish colony in Santo Domingo in 1522. One reason that they were chosen was the fact that they came originally from a place so distant that they would harbor no realistic hope of return. That was quite different from Cuba's Indians, who were made into virtual slaves on their own land and as such were always disappearing into the *manigua* (wilderness). Unfortunately for the Spaniards, the Africans were quick to learn this form of resistance from the Indians. However, African slaves had the advantage of being more resistant to the European diseases that had decimated the Taíno.

African slavery in the Spanish West Indies grew out of a labor system that had already existed in southern Spain since at least 1450, in which as many as 100,000 African slaves labored in agriculture, ports, and as personal servants by the early sixteenth century. Thus most slaves initially came to the Caribbean not to work in large-scale, export-oriented plantation agriculture, but as personal servants. When colonists began to realize that these initial slaves brought in from other parts of the Spanish empire were insufficient, they pleaded with the Crown for the right to bring in African slaves directly from Africa in order to avoid economic "ruin." That right was granted as early as 1527, but it never came to fruition since colonists lacked the funds to pay for them.

Since sugarcane had yet to take on an economic importance in Cuba, the island rarely received more than 100 African slaves each year during the sixteenth century, a trend that continued until the final decade of the eighteenth century. During this period life for Cuba's slaves was somewhat better than it became later, under the strict drive for profit that characterized the nineteenth-century Cuban sugar boom. For example, the practice of *coartación* (manumission, or the purchase of one's own freedom) was within reach of many urban slaves. There were even occasions when masters would free their slaves after they had performed a number of years of service. Unlike in the United States, the children of slaves were not automatically slaves. Also, the lack of Spanish women in Cuba led to the rapid growth of a second generation of mestizos and mulattoes, who made the population of free coloreds quite sizable.

The opportunity for slaves to become "free people of color" added an important and influential class of free blacks to Cuban society. Although often ignored in practice, Spanish law provided both slaves and free coloreds with certain legal protections against arbitrary abuse, allowing them to marry and providing space for the formation of African associations (called *cabildos de nación*). Thus, the peculiar combination of the protections of Spanish law, the paternalism of Spanish Catholicism, the island's underdeveloped economy, and the more lenient Spanish attitude toward sexual relationships with blacks led to a surprising level of racial integration in early colonial Cuban society.

Colonial Government and Institutions. Early Cuban colonial society can be characterized as a marginal part of the Spanish empire, focused much more on frontier survival than on leading the charge of empire. Spanish laws, often devised by faraway colonial bureaucrats, were rarely observed. As a result smuggling flourished, and distrust of government authority became a deeply ingrained Cuban characteristic. Attack from escaped natives and fugitive slaves living in the forests or mountains, or from foreign pirates lying in wait just beyond the horizon, were constant threats. This perpetual state of insecurity, combined with the potential for violent siege, led to the development of a brutal, authoritarian, and corrupt political culture (Suchlicki 1997).

Like most colonial societies, colonial Cuba was acutely stratified based on ethnic origin, race, and class. The dominant political class was made up of the Spanish and their descendants, but divided, with increasing tension, between the Cuban-born Creoles (*criollos* or *naturales*) and the Spanish-born *peninisulares,* who constituted the cadre of colonial representatives, military officers, and Catholic clergy. While there was significant Creole participation in government in the beginning, senior colonial officials were universally drawn from the ranks of the resident Spanish military officers, who were more concerned with the defense of Spanish territory and mercantilist monopoly than with the development of the local economy (Pérez 1995: 36).

In theory, the Spanish governor of Cuba during the sixteenth century was subordinate to both the *audiencia* in Santo Domingo and New Spain's viceroy (in Mexico), and ultimately to the Spanish monarch. However, given the isolation and communication difficulties, the governor often acted as a monarch himself. As Spanish organization and administration improved, however, the governor was increasingly torn between responding to the demands of the local Cuban colonists and serving the interests of his Spanish superiors. As the legal head of all civil and military operations on the island, the governor (later called the captain-general) normally delegated important financial dealings to a series of royal officials who were appointed from Spain. Often these royal-level officials and institutions would come into fierce conflict with the local government that grew up from the island's Spanish colonists (Suchlicki 1997).

In the first decades of the Cuban colony, the *cabildo* (town council) was the leading local institution and, apart from the governor, was composed of various *acaldes* (judges/mayors) and *regidores* (councilmen), who were responsible for organizing and funding public services including the police, buildings, roads, and the jail. Although they worked in conjunction with the governor, the *cabildos* often exercised a great deal of autonomy and even selected a *procurador* (solicitor) who would represent the colonists' interests to the Spanish Crown, often coming in direct conflict with the governor himself. In 1532 the office of the *procurador* was crushed by the governor, and by midcentury this centralizing tendency won out as the Crown initiated the practice of appointing these councilmen for life, and even selling local offices to outsiders. This change began a tradition whereby Spanish-appointed councilmen routinely used their offices as a means to personal enrichment, monopolizing trade, hoarding scarce laborers, and speculating with royal funds and property. Thus the seed of latent Creole hostility toward outsiders sent by Spain to manage and extract wealth from the colony was planted, only to sprout with full force in the second half of the nineteenth century (ibid.).

For the next 200 years most of Spain's attention was focused on the colonial mainland, from which it extracted ever greater amounts of agricultural and especially mineral wealth. Cuba was given attention only to the extent that it served the Spanish mercantilist policy as a gateway and strategic meeting point for the fleets of ships heading back to Spain. The only real Spanish investment in Cuba between 1550 and 1750 was the construction of a complex defense system to protect the uninterrupted flow of goods back to the mother country. Cuba was important as a pipeline through which passed products reaped from other lands—not because of the as yet untapped potential of its vast and fertile soils. Still, Spain came to realize that ignoring developments in Cuba, especially given the growing challenge from rival European powers, was not an option. Cuba may have been on the margins of empire, but its strategic position made its defense essential (Pérez 1995).

The Pirates of the Caribbean. Because the Spanish were the first to establish colonies in the Caribbean, it was against Spain that France, Britain, and Holland fought to wrest control of these islands. However, those incursions were rarely carried out by the naval forces of the respective nations. Instead, the constant attacks at sea and raids on landed settlements were led by the legendary pirates of the Caribbean, the proto-bounty hunters, hired guns, and contrabandists of the age (alternately known as corsairs, privateers, freebooters, or buccaneers). Often working in cahoots with local Spanish officials and almost always licensed and paid by the royal family of one or more of Spain's rival European powers, the infamous privateers were outlaws in a time of frontier justice. Laws were often as arbitrary and unjust as they were unenforceable. Although detested by the Spanish Crown for constantly threatening their settlements and violating prohibitions against contraband, privateers were more often welcomed by desperate colonists who were used to getting fleeced by the Spanish monopoly on trade (Suchlicki 1997).

Cuba saw four major pirate attacks between the mid-sixteenth century and the epoch-making British occupation of Havana in 1762. The first major attack was led against the young city of Havana (not yet Cuba's official capital) by the French privateer Jacques de Sores in 1555. De Sores managed to capture Havana and burn it and its priceless archives to the ground. This attack grew out of the almost continual state of war that existed between the Spanish-based Holy Roman Empire (led by Charles V) and France (led by Francis) between 1519 and 1559. Hoping to gain a foothold in the Spanish West Indies, Francis's Caribbean strategy was to fund French privateers who would attack Spanish settlements there. Indeed, French buccaneers carried out attacks on various Cuban ports, including Baracoa, Havana, and Santiago, throughout most of the early sixteenth century, culminating in De Sores's decisive campaign against Havana in 1555.

After his victory De Sores was forced to beat a quick retreat, since the French were not yet prepared to defend a major Spanish city like Havana. Unlike previous French attacks on Cuban ports, one footnote to De Sores's attack on Havana is that it provoked a local Creole resistance for the first time that, though unsuccessful, indicated the appearance of a protonationalism among its colonists. The chief result of De Sores's success was to provoke Charles V's son, Philip II, to improve Cuba's dismal defenses. Havana was converted into the best fortified port city in the Western Hemisphere. Philip II appointed Pedro Menéndez de Avilés to coordinate Cuba's land defenses as well as convert the vulnerable Spanish trade convoy into a powerfully armed sailing force defended in 1564 by battleships that would henceforth

The defensive walls that once encircled the full 4,892 meters of the city perimeter of Colonial Havana (Habana Vieja) were begun in 1674 and dismantled almost 200 years later, starting in 1863. It took a crew of African slaves twenty-three years to complete the 10-meter-high, 1.4-meter thick walls. The walls once held nine defensive citadels, 180 cannons, and served as a barracks for as many as 3,400 soldiers. (Ted Henken)

accompany the treasure fleets back to Spain on each return voyage.

Cuba was converted into a roadhouse, weigh station, and stronghold of Spain's mainland booty, based on its advantageous location in the center of the Atlantic trade winds. Spanish ships would proceed south from the Iberian Peninsula to the African coast, where they would catch the westerly winds that brought them to the port of Santiago at Cuba's southeastern coast. After collecting treasure from South America and Mexico at Cartagena and Vera Cruz, all treasure ships would rendezvous back at Havana and ride the easterly trade winds to the northeast through the Bahamas into the North Atlantic and back to Spain. Thus "Havana became the fulcrum around which Spanish commerce with the Americas was to revolve over the next three centuries" (Gott 2004: 29).

The fact that Havana became the Western Hemisphere's crossroads for American raw materials heading east, and

European manufactured goods going west, turned the port city into a bustling marketplace of carpenters, shopkeepers, shipbuilders, bankers, businessmen, gamblers, peddlers, and prostitutes, all of whom served the diverse needs of the itinerant merchants, sailors, soldiers, revolutionaries, and contrabandists. At the same time, the city became a veritable cosmopolitan emporium of new ideas, the latest fashions, and the most innovative musical styles, making Havana different from the rest of the country. For example, though the musical genre called son originated in Oriente, it was Havana's shipyard that gave birth to the hard wooden pegs (produced by the thousands for shipbuilding) that were quickly transformed by an anonymous stevedore into the clave, the sine qua non of son, and the "rhythmic key" to all Cuban dance music. Musicologist Ned Sublette reminds us, "For two and a half centuries, Cuba was not a country so much as it was a port" (2004: 84).

Before Philip II could complete his defense plan, a new threat against Havana emerged from Spain's newest rival, Britain. England's Queen Elizabeth offered a regular privateering commission to Sir Francis Drake. Already feared throughout the Spanish Caribbean as *El Draqui,* Drake set sail in 1585 for the Caribbean from England at the head of an imposing English fleet. Drake first sacked Santo Domingo in January 1586 and then turned his sights on the pearl in the Spanish Caribbean Crown, Havana—or so thought the terrified and still largely unprotected *habaneros.* Instead, Drake decided to take the city of Cartagena de Indias on the South American coast. Although he did eventually land on the far southwestern point of Cuba at Cabo San Antonio, he never made an attempt on Havana.

Realizing that Cuba had dodged a bullet, Spanish King Philip II proceeded to build, in Havana and Santiago (and later in San Juan, Santo Domingo, and Cartagena), a series of defensive fortresses at the mouth of each settlement's main port. Havana soon became home to a small fort on the west side of the entrance to its harbor, San Salvador de la Punta, and to the larger and more distinctive fortress, El Castillo del Morro, to the east. These fortifications, designed by the Roman military engineer Gian Battista Antonelli and begun in 1586, the very year of Drake's false alarm, were not finished until more than forty years later, in 1630.

After losing most of its sea power in the defeat of the Spanish Armada by the English in 1588, the Spanish fleet was embarrassed once again by the staunchly Protestant Dutch. This time, however, the Spanish were routed just off the coast of the Cuban port of Matanzas, losing the entire Spanish silver fleet in 1628. Dutch Admiral Piet Heyn led this legendary attack sailing for the Dutch West India Company.

The final chapter in Cuba's pirate wars was written by the famous Welsh buccaneer Captain Henry Morgan. Morgan was sent to southern Cuba from Port Royal in British Jamaica in 1688 to discover whether the Spanish intended to retake Jamaica. Morgan pushed ashore at Puerto Principe with ten ships and 500 men and marched 50 miles north to the central city of Camagüey, where he managed to pilfer much of the city's wealth before returning victorious and wealthy to Jamaica. Morgan was not strictly a pirate, since his group of buccaneers was under license as "privateers" for the British. However, he was later arrested by the British and deported to England because of his excessive cruelty. In the end his luck changed, and he was released, knighted Sir Henry Morgan, and allowed to return to Jamaica as its lieutenant governor.

As a result of the mutual insecurity caused by these continuing incursions, the Spanish and British agreed to call a truce at the Peace of Madrid in 1670. Spain accepted British control over Jamaica and the Cayman Islands and allowed the British free movement in the Caribbean, while the British agreed to desist from trading in recognized Spanish territories. Spain also sat down at the bargaining table with France in 1697 at Ryswick. Spain recognized French authority over the western third of Hispaniola (today's Haiti), provided that

Originally built between 1589 and 1630, the Castillo de los Tres Santos
Reyes Magos del Morro, *universally known to Cubans simply as "El
Morro," did not receive its signature look until more than 200 years
later when Cuba's first lighthouse (pictured here) was added in 1845.
El Morro guards the eastern shore of the entrance to Havana's harbor.
(Ted Henken)*

the French agreed to call off their constant and costly bucca-neer attacks on Cuba and the rest of the Spanish Caribbean.

Cuban Agriculture. During these years, Cuba began to lay the foundation for what would become its two signature export crops, tobacco and sugar. Sugarcane cultivation, transplanted originally from the Pacific but arriving in Cuba directly from southern Spain through Santo Domingo, first took hold in and around the city of Matanzas. Cane process-ing, however, remained technologically rudimentary, as it depended upon the use of animal traction and wooden imple-ments to produce a low-grade brown sugar. In fact, Cuban cattle ranchers were the first to install sugar mills on the island and begin to produce small amounts of sugar, most of which was consumed locally. These ranchers lacked access to the three elements necessary to turn sugar cultivation into an export industry: capital, labor, and official sanction (Suchlicki 1997).

Tobacco, an indigenous crop, was originally kept at arm's length by Creole planters. In fact, it was first adopted by slaves and free coloreds who began to grow and successfully market it to Cuba's many visiting sailors. Only later did Cre-oles begin to see the economic potential in systematically cul-tivating tobacco, which they did mainly in the fertile lands south and west of Havana. Ironically, Creoles proceeded to pass laws that prohibited blacks from profiting from what had initially been considered *cosa del negro* (a black thing). Tobacco cultivation remained in Creole hands for most of the sixteenth and seventeenth centuries.

The Crown later turned the tables on the Creole planters in Pinar del Río. As the trade and profitability of tobacco cultiva-tion grew, Spain placed increasingly complex regulations and taxes on the sale of the product (Pérez 1995). Then, in 1717, the government enacted the hated *factoría* system, which made the cultivation of tobacco an official monopoly for the next 100 years. Cuba's fiercely independent *vegueros* (tobacco growers) were forced to accept a new system whereby the Spanish Crown would advance them money with the requirement that they sell their harvest to the government at a fixed price (Suchlicki 1997: 27). Ironically, such an arrangement could just as easily describe the current communist government's relationship with Cuba's private farmers.

This new arrangement immediately provoked a violent *vegueros* revolt and an increase in contraband trade. Despite the fact that the intention of the *factoría* system was to put an end to the contraband tobacco trade, it is likely that in the years after 1717 as much as 75 percent of all Cuban tobacco production was purchased illicitly by smugglers from British Jamaica, French Saint-Domingue (Haiti), or the North American colonies. Tobacco was a perfect contraband commodity, given its light weight, lack of bulk, and the high prices it commanded in Europe. Furthermore, it required little capital, little land, and few workers—especially when compared with the arduous, expansive, and expensive cultivation of sugarcane (Pérez 1995; Suchlicki 1997).

By the end of the eighteenth century, Cuba's *vegueros* found themselves pressured to sell their land as its value shot up because of the growth of the much more profitable, but unstable and labor-intensive crop, sugarcane. The Spanish Crown encouraged this shift, since the more lucrative sugar trade could provide greater revenue. Throughout the colonial period (and even after independence), there was little consideration of developing a local manufacturing economy or of diversifying Cuba's monocultural agricultural industry. In fact, over time Cuba became less, not more, agriculturally diversified. The Crown discouraged local entrepreneurship, preferring that the island depend upon it for the basics, allowing Cuba to continue to specialize as a producer of raw materials for Spain—the very definition of mercantilism.

Aiming to eliminate contraband trade and increase profits, the new Bourbon rulers of Spain moved decisively to check the growing political and economic power of Cuba's Creoles.

Starting in 1740, the Crown began to implement a rigid and ambitious system aimed at exercising absolute control over Cuban trade, the Real Compañía de Comercio de La Habana (Royal Company of Commerce of Havana). This incongruous name highlights Spain's attempt to find an effective balance between notoriously corrupt and inept "royal" enterprises and the much more productive and efficient private "companies." The hope was that this new "Royal Company" could perform the royal task of funneling all production surpluses back to Spain (putting an end to smuggling, piracy, and contraband trade), while at the same time making the process of production, marketing, and sale more efficient and profitable. However, the Real Compañía met with only limited success before it was eventually abandoned after the British occupation of Havana in 1763.

The unpopularity and ultimate failure of the Real Compañía among Cuban residents owed in part to the fact that they were now paid a pittance by the company for products that they had previously sold (legally or through contraband) for much more. Even worse, the company now had an exclusive right to provide the island with all its imported manufactured goods, which were notoriously expensive given the company's monopoly on sales. On top of all that was a never-ending series of new taxes designed to transfer to Spain a greater portion of the colony's wealth, including an import tax (the *almojarifazgo*), a sales tax (the *alcabala*), and a fleet tax (*avería*), in addition to the church (*diezmo*) and mining taxes (*quinta*) already in place (Pérez 1995).

In the end, a system put into place to make production more efficient and profitable for Spain and prevent contraband only provoked ever more contraband and smuggling. Also, the Real Compañía was put into place at a time when Cuban protonationalism was beginning to awake from its 200-year slumber, first signaled by the abortive *vegueros'* revolt of 1717. Other indications of the growing sense of Cuban identity included the establishment of the first printing press

(1723), the founding of the University of Havana (1728), the recognition of Havana as an independent bishopric (1748), the building of the first Cuban post office (1754), and the incorporation of an association to promote national economic development, the Sociedad Económica de Amigos del País (1792).

La Prosperidad Británica: The British Occupation of Havana, 1762–1763

The British invasion of Havana in 1762 is in many ways the beginning of the history of modern Cuba. That is so because it helped put an end to the island's relative isolation from the political and economic forces that had already remade the rest of the Americas and ushered in its incorporation into the modern world economy as something more than a roadhouse between Europe and the Americas. The arrival of a British invasion force at the small fishing village of Cojímar (15 miles east of Havana) on June 6, 1762, signaled the beginning of the end of Spain's 250-year uninterrupted dominion over the island of Cuba. More important, the ten-month British occupation of Havana marked a major reversal of fortune for an island that had until then served Spanish royal interests principally as a stopover point for Spain's returning treasure fleets. Unlike most other European colonies in the Caribbean, Cuba was not (yet) a sugar factory.

The brevity of the British occupation belied the significance of its long-term commercial impact on Cuba. The British threw open the island to trade with new British and North American markets and products, shocking the island's Creole merchant class out of a Spanish-imposed monopolistic lethargy. When the Bourbons regained sovereignty over the island (under King Carlos III) in June 1763, it was with an enlightened awareness that Cuba's Creole class had tasted the benefits of free trade and would not willingly return to the status quo ante. Cuba and its economy would never be the same.

The impact of the British occupation was heightened by the extremely repressed nature of Cuban commerce under Bourbon mercantilist practices prior to 1762. There was palpable discontent among Cuban Creoles who had been straightjacketed under the constraints of the Royal Company. This discontent was exacerbated by a growing resentment against Spanish officials who exercised inflexible and centralized institutional control over local affairs in the interests of remote Spanish authority. To make matters worse, the colonial administration was deeply corrupt, with royal agents viewing their positions as a means to amass personal wealth and sell favors to the highest bidder.

In this context, the Creole leadership was delighted at the British occupation and proceeded to collaborate actively and openly with the new administration after the *peninsulares* had been disgraced. During the successful ten-month collaboration between the British and the Creoles (often referred to as simply *la prosperidad británica*), Cuban Creoles quickly learned that there was money to be made in Cuba (Thomas 1998). English capital and low-priced slaves entered the island's economy, and an emerging Creole elite was made increasingly aware of the benefits of trade with Europe and North America. Cubans began to acquire a taste for non-Spanish goods and markets, forcing Spain to re-examine its mercantilist policies. The British also introduced novel enlightenment political ideas, customs, and forms of organization to the island, making the stifling consequences of the Spanish colonial system all the more apparent and unacceptable to the local Creole class.

An estimated 10,000 slaves were brought to the island during the occupation, a number equal to what would have normally arrived in ten years (Pérez 1995). This expansion of slave labor was accompanied by new markets for Cuban products, the most important of which were sugar and tobacco. In fact, this mutually reinforcing sugar-slave nexus, expanded under the British, would come to define Cuban society and link it in a dependent position to the world economy in the nineteenth and twentieth centuries. At the time, however, few Creoles, recently relieved from the excessive restrictions of Spanish mercantilism, were concerned about overdependence on sugar and slave labor, or about the contradiction between free trade and a captive labor force. They were more interested in finally being able to tap Cuba's formidable economic potential, which had so long been stymied by Spanish mercantilism (Syrett 1970).

When Spain regained control over Havana on February 10, 1763, enlightened Bourbon rulers returned to a much-changed city and proceeded to enact a series of previously unimaginable commercial liberalization measures during the final decades of the eighteenth century. In 1765, Madrid ended the trade monopoly of Seville and Cádiz, allowing seven other Spanish ports to do business with Cuba. Trade was also initiated with other Spanish Caribbean islands, and all previous taxes and duties were replaced by a flat 7 percent ad valorem tax. Between 1778 and 1803 eight other Cuban port cities were authorized to trade directly with Spain and other Spanish colonies. Owing to a labor shortage in the rapidly expanding sugar sector, between 1789 and 1791, Cuban Creoles successfully petitioned Carlos III to allow unlimited free trade in slaves to merchants of any nationality. Finally, in 1817, Spain repealed the hated *factoría* system, allowing the unrestricted cultivation and sale of tobacco once again (Pérez 1995: 59).

As a result of these administrative changes, Cuba was transformed into a major player in the sugar industry and slave trade in the thirty years following occupation. Whereas just 60,000 slaves had been introduced into Cuba in the 250 years after 1512, between 1764 and 1790, 50,000 new slaves were imported at a rate of 2,000 per year. This stable supply of slave labor allowed for the expansion of land under cane cultivation. Whereas in 1762 the size of the average sugar plantation was 320 acres, worked by six to eight slaves, thirty years later the average plantation had grown to 700 acres and was home to nearly 100 slaves. During those same years the total acreage under sugar cultivation increased from 10,000 to 160,000 (Thomas 1998). In sum, the British occupation of 1762 and the subsequent relaxation of Spanish trade restrictions between the 1760s and the 1790s were harbingers of a more complete transformation of Cuba into the world's richest colony and largest sugar producer by the 1820s (Kuethe 1986).

Sugar and Slavery: Cuban Economy and Society, 1763–1886

Of the many liberalization measures enacted in Cuba by Carlos III as a result of the British occupation, the most important was the decision to allow unlimited trade in African slaves. Whereas over the previous two centuries Cuban planters had relied on either foreign companies or unlicensed smugglers to provide them with a labor force, now the new liberalization of slave trading made the supply stable. At the same time, new markets for Cuban products were opening up, especially in newly independent North America, which could make an expansion of sugar production extremely profitable. Thus the combination of new markets and new access to labor signaled the beginning of sugar's ascendancy in Cuba and led to a black majority (slave and free colored) in Cuba by the middle of the nineteenth century.

Small-scale sugar production gave way to plantation dominance and the rise of a wealthy, influential Creole planter class led by the likes of Cristóbal Madan, Miguel Aldama, and most of all Francisco de Arango y Parreño. Arango's tireless efforts as Havana's representative to the Spanish court in 1789 resulted in the open introduction of slaves into Cuba directly from the African coast. Like many of his contemporaries, Arango combined a belief in modern liberal economic ideas with an insistence on the need for an expansion of

Table 1.1 – Estimated Cuban Slave Imports, 1512–1865

Years	Total Numbers	Average Annual Numbers
1512–1763 (251 years)	60,000	239
1763–1789 (26 years)	30,875	1,188
1790–1799 (10 years)	50,516	5,052
1800–1809 (10 years)	52,958	5,296
1810–1819 (10 years)	115,931	11,593
1820–1829 (10 years)	58,109	5,811
1830–1839 (10 years)	92,085	9,209
1840–1849 (10 years)	31,754	3,175
1850–1859 (10 years)	63,600	6,360
1860–1865 (6 years)	8,000	1,333
Totals (353 years)	**563,828**	**1,597**

(Source: Thomas 1998)

slavery on the island. These men constituted a new type of plantation owner, possessing shrewd business sense, large amounts of capital, efficient exploitation of labor, enlightened use of modern technology, political savvy, proto-nationalist sentiment, and intellectual curiosity. Unfortunately for Cuba, the potential of sugar and promise of slave labor would turn out to be a prison of global dependency and national inequality, not a palace of modernity and development. This was due in no small part to the inherent contradiction between free trade and forced labor (Thomas 1998).

The powerful combination of demand from new markets and access to new slaves, however, would never have come together to produce a new type of sugar aristocracy if not for one final key element that allowed for the true explosion in Cuba of an economy based on sugarcane, slave labor, and relatively free trade. That element was a slave revolt in the neighboring French colony of Saint-Domingue that transformed itself into a full-fledged revolution. The impact of what became known as the Haitian Revolution on the subsequent development of Cuban commerce and culture can scarcely be overestimated. Cuba's biggest rival in sugar production was effectively destroyed. This sudden contraction in sugar production led to great profits for Cuba as the price of sugar on the European market doubled between 1788 and 1795. In addition to bringing new cane cultivation techniques and slaves to the island, the arriving French exiles injected the Cuban planter class with a heavy dose of fear of slave rebellion that would influence political developments in Cuba and relations with the emerging United States at least until the abolition of slavery on the island in 1886.

The great irony of Cuban slavery is that it experienced its greatest, most concentrated spurt of growth only after the slave trade had been officially outlawed by a treaty between Spain and Britain in 1820. In the entire 302 years between 1518 and 1820, Cuba received a total of 385,000 slaves, whereas 468,000 came in illegally during the 52 years between 1821 and the last clandestine arrival in 1873. The explosive growth of slave labor contributed to the development of the island's economy and the wealth of sugar planters and especially slave merchants, who often acted as Cuba's only bankers providing essential credit to planters. However, the rapid growth of Cuba's slave population caused increasing alarm among Cuba's Creoles, who feared a repeat of the lopsided population distribution that brought ruin to Saint-Domingue's (Haiti's) planter class and freedom to its slaves. Indeed, in 1841, Cuba's 436,000 slaves together with its 153,000 free people of color made up almost 60 percent of the island's population of 1 million. While this population distribution shifted back toward a white majority in the second half of the nineteenth century, there was relatively little white Spanish immigration during the early decades of the century.

If the size of the African presence were not cause enough for worry, white Creoles pointed in panic to the proliferating and sometimes secret African organizations on the island. These organizations were based on the different "nations" from which slaves had originated and thus were given the name *cabildos de nación*. The most influential of these groups came in the nineteenth century from what is today

Nigeria: the Lucumís (who spoke the Yoruba language and came from Benin) and the Carabalís (who were mainly composed of members of the Ibo and Efik tribes, who hailed from Biafra, and whose name derives from the larger geographical region from whence they came, the Calabar). A third, smaller, but more deeply established group came in the late sixteenth century. Referred to in Cuba as Congos, most of these slaves came originally from modern-day Angola, near the region where the Congo River flows into the sea. Smaller groups were the Mandingas and the Gangás, who came from Sierra Leone, and the Minas, who were brought from an area of the Gold Coast that is today Ghana (Sublette 2004).

Toward Independence and Emancipation. Not surprisingly, it was out of these groups and their sometimes secret societies that emerged Cuba's first attempts at emancipation and independence. The first three embryonic movements for independence were led by a small community of educated and well-connected free coloreds sometimes in collaboration with progressive whites. The third and most significant of these early nineteenth-century conspiracies was led by José Antonio Aponte (Cluster and Hernández 2006). The Aponte conspiracy was anathema to both Spanish authority and the conservative Creole elite, because its stated purpose was none other than "to abolish slavery and the slave trade, and to overthrow colonial tyranny, and to substitute the corrupt and feudal regime with another, Cuban in nature, and without odious discriminations" (quoted in Gott 2004: 50).

Like its forerunners, Aponte's plan was betrayed just as it came to climax in 1812, with its leaders, including Aponte, sentenced to hang and their heads later displayed at the city's entrance as a warning to others. In each of these conspiracies, as well as in the subsequent and equally unsuccessful conspiracy of the 1820s, Soles y Rayos de Bolívar, led by José Francisco Lemus, black conspirators were almost always brutally executed, while their white counterparts were more often imprisoned or exiled. One reason that these initial independence movements were unsuccessful and so harshly repressed is that they could always be portrayed by Spanish officials as aiming at the creation of a black republic, following Haiti's example. Officials would unapologetically play the race card against white Cuban Creoles by reminding them that only Spain and its soldiers could protect them against the "African hordes" on the one hand, and ensure the profitability of their slavery-dependent sugar fortunes on the other (ibid.: 52).

The increase in Spanish repression, sustained attacks on Cuban slavery by British abolitionists, and a burgeoning slave population that had come to surpass Cuba's white population by 1841, led to rising expectations among Cuba's slaves followed by brutal, reactionary repression ordered by Captain-General Leopoldo O'Donnell (1843–1848). Known as the Escalera conspiracy, the series of slave rebellions and the harsh repression that followed between 1843 and 1844 was the early nineteenth century's most significant challenge to colonial rule. Captain-General O'Donnell saw the rebellion as a golden opportunity to crack down on a number of leading white abolitionist intellectuals, including Domingo del Monte and José de la Luz y Caballero, teach Cuba's growing slave population some needed discipline, and finally have a pretext to deport a portion of Cuba's "subversive" free black immigrant population.

After the uprising was brutally put down, O'Donnell ordered a macabre, months-long series of Inquisition-like interrogation sessions in which scores of blacks were literally tortured to death as the authorities sought more information about the phantom conspiracy. It was these interrogations, conducted with prisoners strapped to wooden ladders (*escaleras*), that gave the episode its name. More than a thousand people were imprisoned, and an almost equal number of free coloreds (many of them immigrant workers from nearby islands) were forced into permanent exile. O'Donnell even banned the immigration to Cuba of any emancipated slave or free person of color (Gott 2004).

Cuban society under sugar and slavery. As a result of the often contradictory forces that structured the lives of Cuba's slaves, a significant free black and mulatto population developed on the island during the nineteenth century. The ability to purchase one's freedom, the frequency of mixed unions, and the fact that children were not normally kept as slaves, allowed the free blacks and mulattos to constitute as much as 15 percent of the Cuban population of 1 million by 1841. Moreover, a detailed code regulating the treatment of slaves slightly mitigated the harshness and inhumanity of Cuban slavery as it spread across the island in the nineteenth century. Slaves were considered to have souls and given a place (albeit at the bottom) in the social and religious system. They were considered to be both moral and legal personalities in the sense that they could marry, hold property, and theoretically even use the courts if wronged (Thomas 1998). Despite these legal protections, however, Cuban slaves imitated their native predecessors in devising numerous ways to resist and rebel. Suicide, escape, and rebellion were the three most common types of resistance, apart from the tactic of preserving their religious traditions by "hiding them in plain sight" in syncretic combination with Catholic saints and ritual (Sublette 2004).

The world of the Cuban *ingenio* (sugar plantation) can be captured with reference to five characteristic individuals: an aloof owner, an intelligent if scheming *maestro* (master sugar engineer), a hated *mayoral* (overseer), a small group of slaves who worked indoors and in the more technical aspects of sugar production, and a mass of field slaves who labored for unimaginably long hours in the fields cutting and hauling cane and clearing and preparing the fields during the sustained five- to six-month harvest. The slave and plantation owner was usually an individual of Spanish birth. He lived at least part of each year on his plantation, though he was not usually directly involved in the production process or in disciplining slaves. These tasks were left to the *maestro* and *mayoral*, respectively. Many times future slave owners began their careers as Spanish merchants, eventually acquiring a plantation through foreclosure (Thomas 1998).

While the *maestro* was fairly educated and responsible for the technical side of sugar production, the *mayoral* was a universally hated and feared figure who trusted no one and was always found carrying a whip and sword. Since he was used by the owner to discipline the slaves, the *mayoral* was sometimes a black or mulatto offered his brutal position as the price for his relative freedom. Because of fear of alliances in the wake of the Haitian Revolution, however, after 1800, Cuban overseers were almost always white.

Although it seems impossible to believe, Cuban slaves on sugar plantations in the nineteenth century were allowed only four hours of sleep during the five- to six-month harvest season. During the off-season, slaves typically rose between 2:00 and 3:00 A.M., when they would start the day cleaning the grounds and workhouses of the plantation. Responding to the ringing of a bell, the slaves would then head out to the cane fields and start harvesting at between 4:30 and 5:00 A.M., working until noon, when they would have an hour lunchbreak. They returned to the fields at 1:00 P.M.. and worked until 8:00, at which time they were allowed to retire to their *barracones* ("barracks"). During the harvest season slaves would often work until well past 10:00 P.M., with those working in the mill itself up even later in order to process all the cane cut as rapidly as possible so as not to lose any sugar to rot or spoilage (ibid.).

The average annual mortality of Cuba's slave population during the nineteenth century has been estimated at between 8 and 10 percent, with the majority of deaths occurring during the harvest. Death came from overwork, accidents, epidemics, punishments, and outright murder. Accidental death or dismemberment was especially gruesome, as it normally involved a slave being crushed to death in the mill's machinery, boiled alive in a vat of sugar-juice, or losing a hand to one of the cane rollers. Reports of masters severely punishing or even killing a slave for minor or even invented offenses were legion. Finally, the advent of more modern plantations with steam-driven mills toward the end of the nineteenth century led to slaves being treated worse, inasmuch as they were more likely to be "regarded and treated as economic rather than human units" (ibid.: 176). As a result, slave uprisings became more common.

The constant fear of a slave rebellion injected a nearly ubiquitous tension into the lives of Cuba's sugar planters. Since slaves and equipment were often bought on credit, mill owners found themselves in a state of continual and absolute dependency on merchants and slave traders. Also, since Spain had officially outlawed the slave trade in 1820, Cuban planters were always anxious that they would have to give up their slaves because they were illegally obtained. Finally, planters feared that their slaves would rebel as they had done in Haiti. This difficult position forced most planters to continue to support both the slave system and the colonial domination that protected it.

Annexation and Rising U.S. Interest in Cuba. U.S. policy toward colonial Cuba during the nineteenth century set the parameters that would influence relations between the United States and an independent Cuba in the twentieth century. Perhaps the most telling summation of U.S. policy toward the island came from Secretary of State John Quincy Adams in 1823:

> There are laws of political as well as physical gravitation, and if an apple, severed by a tempest from its native tree, cannot chose but fall to the ground, Cuba, forcibly disjoined from its own unnatural connection with Spain, and incapable of self-support, can gravitate only toward the North American Union,

which, by the same law of nature cannot cast her off from her bosom. (Quoted in Pérez 1995: 108)

This vivid declaration indicates that as early as the 1820s the United States already had designs on Cuba. Furthermore, Americans assumed that Cuba's connection with Spain was unnatural and that the island was incapable of existing as an independent, self-sustaining unit. Both of these assumptions would survive until the end of the nineteenth century and drive U.S. policy during the so-called Spanish-American War. The second assumption influenced the U.S. approach to a nominally independent Cuba and still drives American policy toward the island today.

Although former president Thomas Jefferson shared Monroe's inclination of making Cuba part of the American union, going so far as to offer to purchase the island from Spain in 1808, he understood that the United States could gain the island only through violent conquest, which he wanted to avoid at all costs. "I have no hesitation in abandoning my first wish [of annexation] to future chances," Jefferson wrote in an 1823 letter to then President James Monroe, "and accepting its independence . . . rather than its association, at the expense of war and her enmity" (quoted in Gott 2004: 58). Unfortunately, this wish to avoid the enmity of Cuban patriots and respect the island's sovereignty has not been shared by many subsequent U.S. lawmakers.

In fact, during the nineteenth century various factions both in the United States and Cuba actively lobbied for Cuba's annexation to the United States. Whether Cuba could be added to the union as a new slave state was the driving reason for U.S. interest in the island during the 1840s and 1850s. Likewise, many increasingly disenfranchised Cuban Creoles felt that they would fare better under U.S. tutelage than as second-class citizens under Spanish rule. As a result of this annexationist fervor, the United States offered to buy the island outright from Spain on three different occasions in midcentury. Finally, the Ostend Manifesto of 1854, issued by U.S. ministers at an international meeting in Ostend, Belgium, defended U.S. designs on the island, warning Spain and other world powers: "We shall be justified in wresting it from Spain if we possess the power" (Pérez 1995: 110). In fact, that warning became a reality forty-four years later, when the United States invaded the island, snatching victory and sovereignty—if not formal independence—out of the hands of Cuban revolutionaries and transforming a Cuban war of liberation into a war of U.S. conquest.

The End of Cuban Slavery, 1880–1886

While the outcome of the American Civil War put to rest the idea of Cuba's annexation as a way to preserve American slavery, it also led many Cuban planters to grudgingly accept the fact that the days of Cuban slavery were numbered. By this time, Cuba's clandestine slave trade had ended, with the last known slave arrival in 1873. Cuban planters began searching for new sources of labor to replace Cuban slaves. Also, some planters had begun to realize that the skyrocketing price of slaves made the institution of slavery economically obsolete. It was becoming preferable to consider using contract laborers from Galicia, the Canary Islands, Ireland, the Yucatan, and, most prominently, China, since they could be inexpensively employed for a period of eight years without long-term obligations or fears of rebellion. In fact, as many as 130,000 Chinese coolies arrived in Cuba between 1847 and 1873 (Dana 2003; Guanche Pérez 1999; Thomas 1998).

Given the harsh treatment endured by Cuba's new contract laborers, it is clear that the end of slavery in Cuba had little to do with a change of heart on the part of Cuban planters. It is likely that living and labor conditions for both emancipated slaves and those freed through the *patronato* (a system of gradual emancipation between 1880 and 1886), as well as for contract laborers, were actually worse than those

This impressive gateway marks the entrance to the Chinese Cemetery, reserved for the descendants of the Chinese indentured workers who began coming to Cuba in 1847. The small cemetery is adjacent to the Colon Cemetery, the massive, ornate, and architecturally priceless city of the dead in the Vedado section of Havana. (Ted Henken)

of slaves, since planters had no obligation or financial incentive to feed, clothe, or house these workers properly. In fact, many planters freed their slaves and turned to Asian contract workers since they had no status and therefore no legal protections, nor did they provoke the same condemnation as did the institution of slavery.

The increase in technical innovation on Cuba's sugar plantations in the late nineteenth century further undermined the economic logic of slavery. The introduction of new technology tended to push out smaller planters because of the prohibitive costs of new equipment. Also, as a result of the illegality of the slave trade after 1820 and Britain's stepped-up enforcement thereafter, the price of newly arrived slaves continued to rise, placing them out of reach of most small planters. Only those planters with sufficient capital benefited from innovation,

Table 1.2 – Chinese Imports to Cuba, 1847–1873

Year	Number of Vessels	Chinese Shipped	Chinese Died at Sea	Chinese Landed	Mortality Rate
1847	2	612	41	571	6.70
1853	15	5,150	843	4,307	16.37
1854	4	1,750	39	1,711	2.23
1855	6	3,130	145	2,985	4.63
1856	15	6,152	1,182	2,970	19.21
1857	28	10,101	1,554	8,547	15.38
1858	33	16,411	3,027	13,384	18.44
1859	16	8,539	1,332	7,207	15.60
1860	17	7,227	1,008	6,219	13.95
1861	16	7,212	290	6,922	4.02
1862	1	400	56	344	14.00
1863	3	1,045	94	951	9.00
1864	7	2,664	532	2,132	19.97
1865	20	6,810	407	6,403	5.98
1866	43	14,169	1,126	13,043	7.95
1867	42	15,661	1,247	14,414	7.96
1868	21	8,400	732	7,668	8.71
1869	19	7,340	1,475	5,864	20.10
1870	3	1,312	63	1,249	4.80
1871	5	1,827	178	1,649	9.74
1872	20	8,914	766	8,148	8.60
1873	6	3,330	209	3,121	6.28
Totals	**342**	**138,156**	**16,346**	**121,810**	**11.83**

(Source: Thomas 1998)

simultaneously reducing the number of *ingenios* and increasing the size of those that remained. Finally, technical innovations mechanized the harvesting and refinement process and allowed production to skyrocket, while reducing the need for slave labor on many plantations.

The age-old Cuban *ingenio* was transformed in the 1880s and 1890s into the massive *central,* an enormous factory in the field that was completely mechanized and used only free labor. Cuban *centrales* typically subcontracted the growing and harvesting of sugarcane to dependent *colonos* (tenant sugar farmers), who worked on the fields surrounding the centrally located and capital-intensive sugar mills (thus, the name *central*). While *central* owners paid *colonos* for producing and harvesting the cane, they normally owned both the land itself and the extensive network of railroads that were used to transport it to the mill and later to Cuba's ports. The increase in mechanization and the end of slave labor actually increased stratification and placed more power in the hands of fewer owners, who were increasingly likely to be foreigners.

Independence and Its Aftermath, 1868–1901

Cuba's first full-fledged war aimed at independence from Spain, the Ten Years' War, began in 1868 with the Grito de Yara. Led by the prosperous plantation and slave owner, Carlos Manuel de Céspedes, the war was largely contained within Oriente province in eastern Cuba. Trouble on the Spanish throne sparked Céspedes to free his slaves, declare Cuban independence, and commence the war on October 10. Although there was disagreement within the revolutionary coalition over the issue of slavery, Céspedes moved to abolish slavery in Cuba in 1870. Although celebrated today (together with José Martí) as the "father of the Cuban nation," Céspedes was in fact impeached by the more conservative members of his government-in-arms on October 27, 1873, accused of being dictatorial. Many also took issue with his unwavering commitment to total independence, staunch opposition to any negotiation with Spain, and distrust of Cuban annexationists.

Ostensibly aimed at Cuban independence, the war was more than a simple struggle between Cuban revolutionaries and Spanish troops. Internal conflict among the Cuban-born Creole elite, many of whom sought independence as a means of economic self-determination, weakened the rebel cause. Furthermore, while some powerful Cuban landowners favored independence via annexation by the United States so as to preserve their economic position, others sought absolute

Known to Cubans as El Titán de Bronce *(The Bronze Titan), mulatto rebel leader Antonio Maceo was one of the most effective mambises, or independence fighters, leading troops into battle against the Spanish in both the Ten Years' War and the second War for Independence that began in 1895. (Ridpath, John Clark,* Ridpath's History of the World, *1901)*

independence leading to an immediate end to slavery and the establishment of a representative democracy on the island. These issues divided the rebel forces and poisoned the eventual peace treaty that closed the war.

Ending less in defeat of the rebels than in mutual exhaustion, the war concluded in 1878 with the Zanjón Pact. However, Antonio Maceo, the distinguished mulatto soldier from

Santiago de Cuba who would later become a general in the second War of Independence, refused to accept the terms of the peace treaty and staged what has since become known as the Protest of Baraguá. Maceo met personally with Spanish general Martínez Campos in order to reject the peace treaty, since it failed to recognize Cuban independence and freed only those slaves who had fought as *mambises* (insurgents in the Liberation Army).

The period between the end of the Ten Years' War in 1878 and the start of the second Cuban War of Independence that began in 1895 was marked by three major developments: the Guerra Chiquita (1879–1880), the rise and decline of Cuba's Autonomist Party, and the founding and growth of José Martí's Cuban Revolutionary Party (PRC) in exile. The Guerra Chiquita occurred largely because of the bad peace made in the Zanjón Pact of 1878. Many of the rebel leaders, including the Dominican-born General Máximo Gómez, General Calixto García, and Maceo, rejected the peace treaty and opted to continue fighting or retreat into exile until a new revolt could be organized.

The formation of the Autonomist Party was a liberal response to the Zanjón armistice. While not seeking immediate, absolute independence, the party advocated self-rule for Cuba while remaining a colony of Spain. This gradualist approach gained significant support from an embattled public because of its rejection of violent revolt after a decade of bloody warfare, the end of slavery between 1880 and 1886, and nominal Spanish reforms. Lasting for twenty years (1878–1898), the Autonomist movement eventually lost momentum as a result of its inability to reduce inequalities between Creoles and *peninsulares* or gain any significant and lasting reforms from Spain. Although autonomy was formally declared by Spain in the early days of 1898, Cuban rebels saw it as a treasonous ploy aimed at preventing their eminent victory, refusing even to consider it as an option.

Stepping into this void and picking up the mantle of the Ten Years' War was José Martí and his intrepid Cuban Revolutionary Party. Though largely unknown inside the island because of a life lived in exile, Martí quickly gained predominance in the independence movement on account of his eloquence, untiring commitment to absolute independence, and unifying democratic vision that sought to establish justice and equality for all races and classes of Cubans. A lifelong adherent to social democratic ideals and a fierce opponent of hatred and oppression in all its forms, Martí's motto was: "Only love creates" (Aguilar 1993: 28).

Martí had hoped to fight a quick war, fearing that a drawn-out confrontation with Spain would lead to great loss of life and massive destruction of Cuba's infrastructure and productive capacity. He was also deeply troubled that a protracted war against Spain would marginalize his movement's civilian leadership and gradually give over unchecked power to the rebel military leaders. Perhaps Martí's greatest fear, however, despite his admiration for U.S. democracy and economic progress, was that a protracted battle would give the United States an excuse for intervention and eventual annexation of the island. In fact, that was exactly his state of mind when he sat down to write what would turn out to be his final letter, addressed to his Mexican friend and politician, Manuel Mercado.

> Every day now I am in danger of giving my life for my country and my duty—since I understand it and have the spirit to carry it out—in order to prevent, by the timely independence of Cuba, the United States from extending its hold across the Antilles and falling with all the greater force on the lands of our America. All I have done up to now and all I will do is for that. (Martí 2002: 347)

Later in the letter, Martí makes the famous declaration, "I lived in the monster," referring to his almost fifteen years in New York City, "and I know its entrails—and my sling is the

Poet, politician, orator, journalist, and revolutionary, José Martí was the intellectual author and moral inspiration of the second, ultimately successful War for Cuban Independence that began in 1895. Tragically killed in battle early that same year, Martí did not live to see his dream of a Cuba libre fulfilled. (Library of Congress)

sling of David" (ibid.). Coming from any other Cuban political or military leader, this declaration might sound demagogic. However, coming from the unblemished and single-minded

---

José Martí's letter to Máximo Gómez

Although less well-known than the letter he wrote the day before his death in 1895, Martí also penned an equally prophetic, impassioned letter to his comrade in arms General Máximo Gómez expressing the fear that Cuba's independence could just as easily be undermined by the very soldiers who fought so bravely to achieve it. As the civilian head of the Cuban Revolutionary Party (PRC), Martí was constantly in conflict with Gómez over civil-military relations. In fact, in 1884, Martí reluctantly withdrew from the independence movement out of fear that Gómez harbored dictatorial designs. In this little known letter to Gómez, Martí asked, "Are we the heroic, modest servants of an idea, or are we bold and fortune-favored *caudillos* who prepare to bring war to a nation in order to take possession of it for ourselves?" Then he famously reminded Gómez, "A nation is not founded, General, as a military camp is commanded" (ibid.: 258–259).

Martí and given the subsequent history of U.S. deep penetration of Cuba's social, economic, and political life, such a statement sounds more like a sadly accurate prophecy than a politician's scheming bombast.

Martí's hopes for a quick and decisive war were dealt a critical blow when, on the eve of the attack, the U.S. government seized the majority of the rebels' ships and supplies in Fernandina, Florida, early in 1895. Going ahead with the attack, Martí and Gómez rendezvoused in the Dominican Republic, where they jointly signed the Montecristi Manifesto as the respective civil and military heads of the independence movement. Just prior to this declaration of principles, rebels on the island issued their own *Grito de Baire* on February 24, 1895, signaling the start of the war. Initially, the Rebel Army did rather well and managed to spread their revolt west across the island and into all six provinces by 1897.

However, both Martí and Maceo were killed before the war was over, leaving Gómez as the commander in chief of the

Cuban rebel forces, while civilian control fell to a weak and unknown school teacher, Tomás Estrada Palma, back in New York. It had perhaps been suicidal for Martí, a middle-aged writer in failing health with no military training, to join the rebels in Cuba. However, he was likely trying to prove his mettle to the military leadership, counterbalance their ambition with his own selfless example, and deflect the criticism that he always ended up "giving the Cuban emigrants lessons in patriotism under the shadow of the American flag" while others were dying for the cause of Cuban liberation on Cuban battlefields (ibid.: 335).

Developing their own style of guerilla warfare designed to defeat the Spanish by destroying the country's productive capacity, the rebels took control of most of the island, leaving only the major cities in the hands of the disease-stricken and demoralized Spanish troops. In response, Spain turned to the brutally effective General Valeriano Weyler, who arrived in Cuba in early 1896 and rapidly put into place his infamous strategy of *reconcentración*. Weyler aimed to isolate the rebels by ordering all noncombatants into a handful of fortified towns. However, these "reconcentration camps" were not equipped to handle the hundreds of thousands of civilians who began to die en masse of starvation and disease. Weyler was ordered to return to Spain in late 1897 to quell rising protests, even though his ruthless tactics were the only thing that seemed to work against the determined Cuban rebels.

In the early months of 1898, three developments unalterably changed the nature and direction of the war, leading to the intervention of the United States. In response to Spanish commander Weyler's ruthless reconcentration policy, U.S. newspapers such as William Randolph Hearst's *New York Journal* and Joseph Pulitzer's *New York World* began to print sensational stories trumpeting Spanish atrocities and fanning war fever among the U.S. public. This circulation battle between New York's leading newspapers, forever since referred to as "yellow journalism," gave rise to Hearst's legendary (and perhaps apocryphal) directive, "You give me the pictures, I'll give you the war," when war correspondent Richard Harding Davis and artist Frederick Remington complained that they could find no battles to report (Cluster and Hernández 2006: 101; DePalma 2006).

Then, in the second week of February, two events combined to draw the United States irrevocably into the war against Spain. First, a U.S. paper published a letter from Dupuy de Lùme, the Spanish diplomatic chargé d'affairs in Washington, deriding President McKinley. Members of the Cuban Junta (exiled supporters of the rebel cause) intercepted the letter and leaked it to the press, trying to end U.S. neutrality, if not provoke direct intervention. Added to that insult was the mysterious explosion on February 15, 1898, of the warship *USS Maine,* which had been sent into the Havana harbor ostensibly to protect "American lives and property" during previous riots in the city. Although investigations were inconclusive at the time, this catastrophe took the lives of 266 servicemen and was used by U.S. expansionists to justify intervention, with the implication that Spain was responsible for the explosion.

Given the broad support in the United States for *Cuba libre* ("a free Cuba"), it seems ironic that the joint resolution passed in the spring of 1898 giving President McKinley authorization to intervene in Cuba did not grant recognition to the Cuban rebel forces. In fact, despite the widespread belief that the United States went to Cuba to win the island's independence, the resolution was not officially a declaration of war against Spain but merely an authorization of the use of force to end the Cuban conflict. President McKinley argued against recognition of the Cuban Rebel Army, as it would restrict U.S. movement on the island and subordinate U.S. troops to Cuban generals. At the same time, support for a free and independent Cuba was strong enough in Congress to have the Teller Amendment added to the joint resolution, stipulating that the United States "disclaims any intention to exercise sovereignty or control" over Cuba and would "leave the government and control of the island to its people."

Still standing today in a prominent place along Havana's *malecón* seaside boulevard is the slightly altered monument erected to the U.S. soldiers who perished aboard the USS *Maine*. Without the bronze eagle that once topped it and with the original English lettering replaced by Spanish, the monument quotes the final words of the long-forgotten Teller Amendment: "The people of the Island of Cuba are, and of right ought to be, free and independent." Ultimately, however, the Teller Amendment served not as a guarantor of Cuban self-rule but as a political ploy used to convince Cuban rebels of the beneficence of U.S. intervention and later as proof of the democratic intent behind the invasion (Cluster and Hernández 2006; Pérez 1998).

U.S. troops saw less than two months of action in Cuba before the Spanish were defeated. After U.S. forces under General William Shafter routed the Spanish fleet at the Battle of Santiago Bay, Cuban general Calixto García and his rebel army were barred from entering Santiago. The Cubans were also forced out of the formal handover of the city to the Americans on July 17, 1898, ostensibly to protect Spanish officials from Cuban reprisals. In July, an insulted García penned an outraged letter to General Shafter expressing his incredulity that the Americans had left the unelected Spanish authorities in control of Santiago, refusing to allow his men into the city. The ultimate insult to Cuban independence was added months later at the signing of the Treaty of Paris on December 10, 1898. While the United States and Spanish forces were represented, the Cuban rebels were not even invited.

In a supremely ironic and symbolic coincidence, General García died suddenly the next day in Washington, D.C., while awaiting news of the terms of the transfer of Cuban sovereignty to the Americans. At the same time, General Máximo Gómez refused to attend the ceremony for the raising of the

The statue on the left depicts José Martí holding a young boy. The inscription on the plaque at the base of the statue is from his final letter to Manuel Mercado (see above). On the right is the base of the USS Maine *monument, which quotes the Teller Amendment of 1898, in which the U.S. Congress recognized Cuban independence. The original English words were removed and replaced by Spanish lettering. (Ted Henken)*

U.S. (not Cuban) flag at Morro Castle in Havana. "Ours," he wrote, "is the Cuban flag, the one for which so many tears and blood have been shed. We must keep united in order to bring to an end this unjustified military occupation" (Sierra 2006). Despite such strident sentiment, a four-year U.S. military occupation of Cuba followed (1898–1902). The Spanish captain-general was replaced by a U.S. military governor, and more U.S. troops arrived in Cuba to enforce the occupation than had come to fight the war (Cluster and Hernández 2006: 104). The frustrated Cuban Rebel Army was disbanded, and Martí's PRC dissolved. True to the letter, if not the spirit, of the Teller Amendment, the U.S. military government left control of the island to the Cubans after Cuban representatives passed a new constitution in 1902.

However, U.S. insistence on the addition of the Platt Amendment to the constitution caused deep resentment among Cubans and undermined any real possibility for self-rule. Essentially, Cuban representatives were forced to choose between a "protected republic or no republic at all." The Platt Amendment fatally undermined Cuba's hard-won independence, granting the United States the right to intervene in the future to "preserve Cuban independence." Over the next three decades, the new Cuban republic lived out the dire consequences of U.S. occupation and "protection." In the postwar period, U.S. penetration of the island went far beyond its previous economic engagement, to include political, military, and cultural aspects that had largely been absent prior to the war. Also, the existence of the Platt Amendment, especially the article granting the United States the right (and obligation) to intervene whenever Cuban sovereignty was threatened, acted as a major obstacle for Cuban politicians to control their own political affairs or to learn by trial and error the imperfect art of democratic governance.

A Dubious Independence, 1902–1928

Throughout Cuba's republican period leading up to the revolution of 1959, political life on the island had little to do with ideology or party loyalty. Instead, Cuban politicians skillfully used the currency of corruption to garner and sustain support, transforming politics into a deeply balkanized exercise in personal power. Politicians owed their popularity not to their ideas or accomplishments, but to the patronage that they could dole out to their supporters. Likewise, the populace came to identify with and support different leaders not because of any unifying nationalist vision but simply because this or that politician had developed a personal reputation of providing his supporters with jobs, kickbacks, and public works projects, all looted from the public till.

In the first three decades of republican rule under the Constitution of 1902, Cuba was presided over by five different presidents, interrupted early on by a second U.S. occupation (1906–1909). When Cuba's first elected president, Tomás Estrada Palma (1902–1906), made a bid for re-election at the end of his first term, he provoked the newly formed Liberal opposition party to call for U.S. intervention to protect what it saw as an illegal attempt at a second term and a threat to Cuban sovereignty. Estrada Palma's supporters had already effectively purged all Liberal Party members from government posts, enshrining a winner-take-all political culture that rejected all negotiation and compromise. Estrada Palma then refused to step down after being re-elected in a clearly one-sided and fraudulent contest.

After the U.S. mediator (and future U.S. president) William Howard Taft worked out a political compromise acceptable to the Liberals, Estrada Palma rejected it as a betrayal and quickly resigned with the expressed intention of provoking a second U.S. intervention. While neither side could agree on how to govern, they did agree that another round of U.S. military government was preferable to their political enemies gaining power. Thus, the U.S. military returned to Cuba between 1906 and 1909, establishing a pattern, as well as a new "Plattist mentality," among Cuban politicians whereby difficult political decisions were deferred to Washington. Such a pattern would prove quite resilient and repeat itself with saddening predictability over the next thirty years.

During the second U.S. occupation the weak and contingent character of the Cuban government was established. The Platt Amendment encouraged disgruntled political elites to contest elections through armed rebellion, since they could always call on the United States to live up to its promise to preserve Cuban democracy and independence. This imperial relationship led to a pluralization of Cuban politics, as standing Cuban governments could never be sure of U.S. recognition. Whereas pluralistic political systems are usually understood as inherently positive and stable because of their broader and more democratic levels and forms of participation, all new republics must first establish order and legitimacy through a strong centralized state (Domínguez 1978). Chronically unable do this, Cuban governments remained vulnerable to criticism, attempting to establish legitimacy through corruption, and remained hopelessly disconnected from the socioeconomic forces driving the country. Although periodic elections and a formal constitution provided the government with a measure of legitimacy, that legitimacy was always suspect in the eyes of the Cuban people because of political corruption, electoral fraud, and the continuing humiliation of the Plattist constitution of 1902.

The end of the second U.S. occupation came in 1909 when José Miguel Gómez, nominally of the Liberal Party, was elected president. However, this return to electoral democracy failed to address the young nation's social and economic problems largely because politics had begun to function as a means for personal enrichment and patronage. Confronted with low levels of party loyalty, Cuban presidents owed their real loyalty to the United States and so cared little about the country's growing socioeconomic contradictions (ibid.). Gómez (1909–1913) distinguished himself as especially adept at making politics profitable (in part by reintroducing cock fighting and the lottery). Nicknamed *El Tiburón* (The Shark) for his high-profile political corruption and for harnessing the lottery as an efficient machine of political patronage, Gómez stepped down a rich man with the election of Conservative Mario Menocal in 1913 (Aguilar 1993: 43).

However, in the run-up to the 1912 election, the United States briefly invaded Cuba once again, this time reacting to a rebellion by members of Cuba's all-black Independent Party of Color (PIC). Using the threat of U.S. invasion as a pretext, outgoing president Gómez brutally crushed the uprising, killing its leader, the former slave and Independence War veteran Evaristo Estenoz. This event indicated that Cuba's fear of a race war had not died with the end of slavery and Spanish colonialism. Indeed, the twin issues of Cuban race relations and U.S. intervention would continue to hover in the air, influencing political discourse over the next fifty years. The brutal repression of the 1912 revolt also served to dampen black political participation in the years to come (Gott 2004).

As a former military man, a graduate of Cornell in engineering, and the former administrator of Cuba's largest sugar mill, Menocal was the first Cuban president to serve two consecutive terms (1913–1921). However, after successfully reigning in political corruption and passing nationalist economic legislation in his first term, Menocal provoked the same reaction as Estrada Palma when he announced his own bid for re-election in 1917. After the election Liberal Party leaders revolted, claiming electoral fraud. In fact, Menocal had placed military supervisors at many polls, resulting in 800,000 ballots cast by just 500,000 eligible voters. This time, however, the United States refused to intervene, having learned its lesson from being forced to intervene in 1906 and 1912.

Led by former president Gómez and Liberal candidate Zayas, the Liberal Party sought to use the military to force Menocal out. However, their cause was dealt a serious blow when a diplomatic cable from the U.S. State Department to its Havana envoy William González declared support for "legally established governments only." Instead of being provoked by Liberal claims of electoral fraud, the United States decided to throw its full diplomatic weight behind Menocal, quickly selling him arms that allowed him to defeat the Liberal uprising. In the future, Cubans would often refer to *las notas de Mr. González* as evidence of the constant threat of U.S. intervention and the inability of any Cuban president to rule without the blessing of the United States (Aguilar 1993: 45–46).

The Dance of the Millions. Corruption, already prevalent during the first three presidencies, was transformed into an art form during the four-year Zayas regime (1921–1925). That was combined with the increased volatility of the economy. Referred to historically as the "dance of the millions," starting in 1920, Cuba began to experience extreme fluctuations in the world price of sugar. That cycle of economic boom and bust for Cuba's main export commodity would continue into the future (especially during the 1920s and 1930s), provoking political instability and increasing levels of military and police repression.

The economic instability provoked by the 1920 collapse of the price of sugar led to the growth of *latifundismo* (large sugar estates) and forced many planters, especially Cuba's rural middle class, to sell their land to foreigners in order to survive. Mill owners brought in foreign contract workers from Jamaica and Haiti to keep wages low and ensure profits. However, as Zayas took office in the midst of this economic crisis in 1921, the economic shock awakened Cuba's sleeping nationalism and led to calls for national reform and renovation. Economic legislation that would put Cuban interests and workers first, a demand for public honesty, a departure from sugar monoculture, and resistance to doing the bidding of the U.S. government all became national issues (Aguilar 1993).

A weak presidency, largely unconnected to the social and economic problems experienced by the Cuban population, resulted in increasingly violent political upheaval, leading ultimately to renewed intervention by the United States in 1933–1934 (Domínguez 1978). The period between 1902 and 1928 can be characterized as dependent development and mitigated sovereignty, combined with a heavy dose of political corruption and rising levels of political violence (ibid.). By the late 1920s, many new interest groups appeared vying for control over the new nation's identity. Although largely ignored and relatively powerless at first, these groups (new political and nationalist organizations, cultural movements, anarchists, labor unions, students, and Afro-Cubans) were key players in the ultimate downfall of President Gerardo

Machado and the transition to a new political system (Pérez-Stable 1999).

The Fall of Machado and the Rise of Batista, 1928–1940

Having experienced at first hand the many wrenching contradictions of a monocultural, export-oriented, dependent sugar economy during the "dance of the millions," Cubans of all classes and political persuasions were beginning to reassess their supposedly protective relationship with the United States during the 1920s. While Cuba had grudgingly accepted the fact of extensive U.S. power and influence in nearly every aspect of national life, Cubans expected that such a privileged position came with an incumbent responsibility that the Americans seemed to be either ignorant of or unwilling to accept. Thus, as Cubans became aware that the effects of U.S. "protection" were not unambiguously positive, they began to call for a fundamental change in politics as usual (Thomas 1998).

The crucial decade of the 1920s in Cuba saw the emergence of nationalistic and increasingly anti-imperialist political, cultural, and intellectual movements. Most prominent among these were the National Association of Veterans and Patriots (1923); the more radical Anti-Imperialist League (formed by Julio Antonio Mella); the Cuban Communist Party, which was founded in 1925; and a group of young intellectuals calling themselves *los trece* (the thirteen), who published a devastating political tract that not only attacked the corruption of the Zayas regime but also condemned the entire Cuban political system (Aguilar 1993: 49–50).

On the cultural front, Cuba saw the rise of the journal *Cuba contemporánea* (1913–1927), which led the charge to revisit the life, work, and patriotic vision of José Martí. Also influential during those years was the *Grupo Minorista*, which included intellectual, artistic, and political luminaries such as Alejo Carpentier, Rubén Martínez Villena, Juan

Marinello, Emilio Roig de Leuchsenring, and Jorge Mañach, and which was responsible for publishing the important journal *Revista de Avance*. Members of this group were also involved in the artistic renaissance known as *Afrocubanismo,* which sought ways of challenging the complacency of Cuba's Creole bourgeoisie and to fix on and celebrate the unique elements of home-grown culture and art that could constitute a national culture.

Perhaps most prominent among these groups was the Junta Cubana de Renovación Nacional, founded in 1923 by the widely respected Cuban anthropologist Fernando Ortiz. Typical of this movement's goals and criticisms was Ortiz's complaint, expressed later in his famous book *Cuban Counterpoint,* that "Cuba will never really be independent until it can free itself from the coils of the serpent of colonial economy that fattens on its soil but strangles its inhabitants and winds itself about the palm tree of our republican coat of arms, converting it into the sign of the Yankee dollar" (Ortiz 1995: 65). This movement reflected a growing disgust with U.S. influence and a rise in Cuban nationalism. Their program called for the protection of national industry through a renegotiation of the U.S. reciprocal trade agreement; demanded labor, educational, and health reforms; and advocated for an end to the graft and corruption endemic to Cuban politics (Pérez 1995: 229–247).

The Machadato. The multiplying contradictions and nationalist frustrations of the early Cuban republic came to a climax during the Gerardo Machado incumbency (1925–1933). Former general Machado began his first term by instituting a series of nationalist reforms, including an increase in government oversight of the economy, limits on U.S. access to the economy, the expansion of public education, a recognition of trade unions, and a restructuring of Cuba's ineffective and arbitrary party system (Domínguez 1978). Although widely popular at first, these reforms could not endure in the face of

the near collapse of Cuba's economy during the Great
Depression. As a result of increasing instability, in 1928,
Machado forced the Cuban Congress to accept his own
unconstitutional re-election and turned increasingly to violent repression to deal with the social unrest brought about by
economic collapse and his own illegitimacy.

Despite Machado's mild attempts to increase state control
over the economy, by the late-1920s, it was obvious to Cuban
progressives and nationalists that all major industry was held
by foreigners and that those foreign owners naturally had foreign interests. Furthermore, no credible political system had
been established during the long years of U.S. "tutorial" in
self-government. Thus, Machado could not be trusted to carry
out nationalist reforms without first altering Cuba's close ties
with the United States. There was a rising, palpable outrage
among Cuban intellectuals, students, and progressives that
the ideals of Martí had been forgotten, as had the fact that
Cuba was a Latin American nation and not an Anglo-Saxon
colony (Thomas 1998: 599–602).

Ironically, many of these same nationalist voices calling for
a change in the U.S.-Cuban relationship found themselves
demanding U.S. intervention as Machado altered the constitution and began to protect his illegitimate rule with brutality
and corruption. As early as 1927, leading nationalist intellectual Fernando Ortiz petitioned the State Department to intervene, reminding the United States that the Platt Amendment
gave it the moral obligation to ensure "good government" in
Cuba (Pérez 1995: 259). By 1931, when Carlos Mendieta
appealed for U.S. intervention, such calls had become as commonplace as they were fruitless. Inadvertently, the United
States exhibited its approval of the Cuban president when
President Calvin Coolidge accepted Machado's invitation to
the opening of the sixth Pan-American Conference in Havana
in 1927. Machado responded to his opponents demands for
outside intervention by passing a law against any Cuban
found seeking outside interference in Cuban development.

Built under the presidency of Gerardo Machado in the 1920s and modeled on the U.S. Capitol building, this massive structure in Havana was the original home to the Cuban Congress. After 1959 it was turned into a museum and houses the Cuban Academy of Science. (Ted Henken)

As Cuba began to suffer from the economic aftershocks of the Great Depression, the fundamental dilemma of a history of Plattist intervention became clear. The election of Franklin D. Roosevelt in 1932 and the institution of his Good Neighbor Policy made intervention in Latin America off-limits, even as Cuban nationalists saw such heralded nonintervention as tacit support of the murder and political assassination associated with the Machado regime. One infamous example of Machado's brutal policies was the so-called *ley de fuga,* whereby Cuban police would murder suspected subversives in custody, washing their hands of the crime by explaining that the suspects had "died while trying to escape."

U.S. diplomat Sumner Welles, who came to Havana to mediate between Machado and the opposition in the summer of 1933, seems to have clearly understood the implications of this no-win situation for U.S. policy:

> To President Roosevelt two facts were clear. First, that while the existing treaty with Cuba gave this country the right to intervene, any such intervention would be contrary to the general line of inter-American policy which he had set for himself. Second, that a state of affairs where governmental murder and clandestine assassination had become matters of daily occurrence must be ended. (Quoted in Aguilar 1972: 129)

Disembarking in Havana on May 7, 1933, Welles was stepping into a situation in which the United States would be accused of irresponsibility by respecting the Good Neighbor Policy and *not* sending in the marines. "Each declaration of the Roosevelt administration reaffirming the Good Neighbor Policy and the desire of nonintervention in Latin America," Aguilar notes of the months leading up to Welles's arrival, "was hailed as a triumph for Machado and a setback for his 'anti-Cuban' enemies" (ibid.: 128). British historian Hugh Thomas agrees, writing:

> The threat of, or fear of, or desire for, a US intervention was the dominating theme of Cuban politics for thirty years after 1902. Few Cubans seriously wished for political absorption by the US, but they were anxious to use the US's apparently legal power (under the Platt Amendment) to intervene as a means of ruining their political opponents. (1998: 602)

For her part, Ruby Hart Phillips, a *New York Times* correspondent in Havana, agrees that while Cubans hoped that the election of Roosevelt would mean a "New Deal" for them too, they expected this to include some form of intervention against Machado. "Of course, we all know who have lived here," she writes, reflecting on the events of 1933, "that when Cubans get themselves into a situation where it is impossible to get out they shout for help from the United

States and are much aggrieved when it does not come. If it comes, a month later they are shouting 'Kick the Yankees out of Cuba'" (1935: 15).

This "Yankee-go-home; Yankee-come-back-please" attitude, elsewhere called the "Plattist mentality" by Cuban historians, characterized the history of the first Cuban republic from its inception in 1902 to its apogee in 1933, to its final replacement in 1940 by a new constitution. This same mentality also characterized the complex and rapidly unfolding developments during the second half of 1933, a period known in Cuba as the Revolution of 1933.

The Revolution of 1933. When U.S. envoy Sumner Welles arrived in Havana in the early summer of 1933, his purpose was to restore order and "democracy," prevent revolution, and protect U.S. financial interests. He sought to legitimize the moderate opposition made up of old political elites and simultaneously decertify the more radical groups. Indeed, many of these groups (the Student Directorate, the radical ABC, the Radical Left Wing, as well as the communists) would not have participated in the talks even if invited by Welles, since they were opposed to any negotiation with Machado, especially if mediated by the United States. Still, Welles's overriding goal was to orchestrate a constitutional solution to what he saw as a presidential crisis, while avoiding social revolution.

Ironically, while Machado shared the U.S. goals of ending the general strike of early August and bringing an end to a potentially revolutionary situation, he gradually came to resent Welles and began to publicly denounce U.S. intervention. As Machado began to sense that the real intent of U.S. mediation was to remove him from office, he became more intransigent in his original desire to remain in office until his term ended in 1935. His stubborn refusal to step aside finally melted when he lost the all-important support of the military. After his resignation on August 12, it seemed as if Welles had scored a complete victory, achieving all his goals: Machado was gone, revolution had been averted, the change in power had followed constitutional guidelines, and Carlos Manuel de Céspedes, the new president of Cuba, was a good friend of the United States, having been born and partially raised there (Aguilar 1972: 137–151).

However, Machado's ouster took an unexpected, and for Welles, undesirable turn on September 4, 1933, when a group of disgruntled enlisted soldiers took control of the country's main military base, Camp Columbia. Quickly realizing their untenable position, these soldiers were soon joined by members of the Revolutionary Directorate (DEU), a radical university student group, which arrived to give legitimacy and a revolutionary direction to the revolt. While the soldiers sought only better pay, housing, and benefits (Pérez 1995), the radical students hoped to push these limited military reforms in the direction of broad-based revolution that included the removal of Céspedes. Thus, when the leaders of the DEU arrived on the scene, a marriage of convenience was improvised that would serve both groups' needs. The mutinous soldiers would take over the military, and the revolutionary students would gain political power.

The chaotic series of events following the sergeant's revolt began with the formation of a *pentarquía* (five-member civilian junta), headed by a university professor selected by the revolutionary students, Ramón Grau San Martín, and given legitimacy by the support of the DEU and his radical minister of government, Antonio Guiteras. Within a week the *pentarquía* dissolved. Grau and Gutieras retained effective executive and legislative power, while the inexperienced Batista was promoted to chief of the Cuban Army. When recognition of their government did not immediately come, however, student leaders began to denounce both the United States and other Latin American governments.

A major reason that Washington refused to recognize Grau's "100-day government" was that it was made up of the very factions that Welles had previously tried to marginalize (Thomas 1998). Having rejected them earlier as those least likely to accommodate U.S. interests, it was unlikely that Welles would now embrace them as legitimate. Moreover, the series of radical nationalist reforms that Grau and Guiteras began to implement were aimed at doing away with old-guard politics as usual and redefining relations with the United States. The Platt Amendment was unilaterally abrogated, and all political parties that had participated in Machado's government were dissolved. Utility rates were lowered, women received the vote, and new labor rights were instituted, including minimum wage guarantees for cane cutters, an eight-hour work day, and a decree that required at least 50 percent of all workers in industry, commerce, and agriculture to be Cuban citizens (Pérez 1993: 70).

These ambitious reforms made the military half of the student-soldier coalition increasingly unsure of the wisdom of their gamble to accept these radical students as their partners in government. Welles noted this growing divide and worked quickly to exploit it. Meeting with Grau, Welles explained that the U.S. refusal to recognize his government arose from the fact that it was not supported by the "exceedingly important elements." He also warned that the United States could not support a government that had come to power through an unconstitutional army coup. Finally, Welles expressed doubt that the government could guarantee the protection of American lives and property without U.S. warships in Cuba's harbors (Aguilar 1972).

For his part, Grau argued that popular support even from the "important elements" would be forthcoming if only the United States would grant recognition. Welles responded, "US recognition could not be employed as a means of obtaining popular support" (Thomas 1998: 654). However, Welles knew that nonrecognition could destabilize a government just as effectively as recognition could stabilize one. Welles then met with Batista, informing him that he (not Grau) had the confidence of Cuba's most prominent commercial and financial leaders. He made it clear to Batista that he was a man who could be relied upon to protect U.S. interests in Cuba. Welles also indicated that the only major obstacle to a happy resolution of the military revolt was the "unpatriotic obstinacy" of the student coalition that was irresponsibly "playing politics" (Pérez 1993: 72).

By December 1933, Welles began to meet repeatedly with Batista in order to convince him that his days were numbered if he continued to insist on his marriage of convenience with the unacceptable and "unpopular" revolutionary Grau government. Welles also made it clear that the United States saw him as a trustworthy ally and potential bulwark of stability. By this time, Batista was especially concerned that the inability of the current government to ensure stability and gain recognition might provoke a U.S. military invasion (ibid.). Such an eventuality, he knew, would doom not only radical civilian leaders like Grau and Guiteras but also the members of the military leadership like himself who had linked their fate with them.

The End to the Grau Government and the Rise of Fulgencio Batista, 1934–1940

After getting assurances from the business and military sectors of the country, on January 15, 1934, Batista withdrew military support from Grau. Without a way to defend his rule Grau's resistance was short-lived, and he fled into exile on January 17, leaving Batista behind as kingmaker. After a rapid succession of provisional presidents, Batista anointed the anti-Machado politician Carlos Mendieta as president. Just five days later, Welles's replacement, U.S. ambassador Jefferson Caffery, extended to Mendieta Washington's official diplomatic recognition and proceeded bilaterally to abrogate the now clearly counterproductive and obsolete Platt Amendment.

Over the next six years Batista successfully managed to unify the army and the government into a single force with the window dressing of a series of ineffectual puppet presidents controlled by him. As in the past, these governments were the country's major source of public employment and political patronage, except that now these goods were administered and redistributed though Batista's army. After solidifying his relationship with the United States and coming to an accommodation with the Communist Party–controlled labor union at home, Batista felt confident enough to seek to fully legitimize his de facto rule of Cuba by allowing Congress to call a constituent assembly aimed at writing a new constitution and to make arrangements for a new election, for which Batista himself declared his candidacy.

Years of Hope and Betrayal, 1940–1952

Although the student revolutionaries were ultimately unsuccessful in 1933, their 100-day revolutionary experiment led to a fundamental shift both in Cuba's domestic politics and in its relationship with the United States. "The revolutionary episode of 1933," writes Aguilar, "was for Cuba a step forward, but only one step, and a step fraught with frustration and disillusionment" (1972: 239). Soon afterward, new political parties emerged, a massive labor organization (the CTC) was founded, and economic nationalism expanded with the number of Cuban-owned sugar mills and banks increasing significantly. Between the years 1940 and 1952, there would be progress toward the establishment of democracy on the island. Two major positive developments associated with this period (and directly related to the student hopes of 1933) were the passage of the progressive 1940 Constitution and the peaceful transition in 1944 from Batista to his democratically elected successor, Grau.

While Batista easily won election to the presidency after more than six years of running the country out of the military

Table 1.3 – Cuban Presidents and
U.S. Military Governors, 1899–2007

1899 (Jan.)	American General John R. Brooke
1899 (Dec.)	American General Leonard Wood
1902	Tomás Estrada Palma
1906 (Sept.)	Provisional U.S. Governor William Howard Taft
1906 (Oct.)	Provisional U.S. Governor Charles E. Magoon
1909	General José Miguel Gómez
1913	General Mario García Menocal (U.S. intervenes to protect 1916 reelection)
1921	Alfredo Zayas (governs with the oversight of U.S. envoy Enoch Crowder)
1925	General Gerardo Machado (ousted in August 1933)
1933 (Aug.)	Carlos Manuel de Céspedes
1933 (Sept. 3)	Five-man junta (*pentarquía*) (led by Ramón Grau San Martín)
1933 (Sept. 10)	Ramón Grau San Martín (ousted by Fulgencio Batista)
1934 (Jan. 16)	Carlos Hevia (appointed and controlled by Fulgencio Batista)
1934 (Jan. 17)	Manuel Márquez Sterling (" ")
1934 (Jan. 18)	Colonel Carlos Mendieta (" ")
1935 (Dec. 11)	José Antonio Barnet (" ")
1936 (May 20)	Miguel Mariano Gómez (" ")
1936 (Dec. 24)	Federico Laredo Bru (" ")
1940	Fulgencio Batista
1944	Ramón Grau San Martín
1948	Carlos Prío Socarrás
1952	Fulgencio Batista (assumes presidency after a military coup)
1959 (Jan.)	Manuel Urrutia (appointed by Fidel Castro)
1959 (July)	Osvaldo Dorticós (appointed by Fidel Castro)
1975	Fidel Castro
2006 (July 31)	Raúl Castro (assumes provisional presidency during Fidel Castro's illness)

(Source: Pérez 1995; Thomas 1998; Sierra 2006; Staten 2003)

barracks, he greatly miscalculated his overall electoral strength. As a result, the majority of the delegates elected to the constituent assembly in 1939 did not do his bidding, nor were they under his control. In fact, forty-one of the total seventy-six delegates came from opposition parties, while Batista together with the communists, his allies of the moment, took just thirty-five. As a result, the provisions of the new constitution were conceived in a spirit of national unity and reflected a desire for Cuba to become a progressive social democracy. At the close of the assembly, the leading communist delegate, Blas Roca, even declared that the final document had succeeded in "closing the revolutionary cycle that began in 1933" (Thomas 1998: 716).

The new constitution granted universal suffrage and freedom of political organization, recognized the legal and civil rights of all Cubans, abolished the death penalty, and provided social protections for women, children, and workers. Racial and sexual discrimination in the workplace was outlawed, and public education was made free and mandatory. Finally, on the important front of economic nationalism, private property was declared legitimate, but *latifundio* (vast lands held by a single owner) was outlawed. Limits were also placed on the rights of foreigners to own land. Thus free market principles were to be subject to significant state regulation.

One major problem with the constitution was that many of its articles were more goals to be achieved than mandates for immediate implementation. Still, the 1940 Constitution would act as an important symbol in the years to come, simultaneously serving as the embodiment of many of the radical goals of the thwarted revolution of 1933 and as a manifestation of the highest ideals of a clean, socially conscious, democratic Cuba. Sadly, this democratic vision was systematically betrayed under the subsequent incumbencies of the 1940s and 1950s. For that reason, the restoration of the 1940 Constitution would feature prominently in Fidel Castro's initial political "platform" as announced in his legendary defense speech at his 1953 trial, "History Will Absolve Me."

During Batista's administration (1940–1944), he demonstrated an unwavering support for the United States as it entered World War II. He also allowed the United States to construct airfields on the island, use Cuban ports for reconnaissance, and protect the Cuban coast as a way to keep German submarines out of the Western Hemisphere. Respected for having brought the country back to electoral democracy,

Batista was supported during his term in office by capitalists and communists alike. Political unity was facilitated by Cuba's strong alliance with the United States in the war against European fascism. Also, past expressions of anti-imperialism aimed at the United States were muted in the context of Germany's own imperialist actions, unifying most of the hemisphere on the side of the United States against fascist imperialism. As a result, these years marked the apex of "good neighborly" relations between the United States and Latin America during the twentieth century.

In the lead-up to the 1944 election, Batista's preferred candidate, Carlos Saladrigas, found himself in a tough battle against Ramón Grau San Martín, who had retuned from exile. Grau ran promising to achieve the nationalist goals set out in the heady days of 1933. Piquing the hopes of the populace, he won in a landslide. The smooth transition from Batista's government to the opposition was a positive sign. Moreover, it now seemed that the progressive, nationalist promise of the 1940 constitution would be fulfilled. Indeed, while in exile Grau had sought to rekindle Cuba's frustrated nationalism by naming his new party after the one founded (also in exile) by Cuban patriot José Martí a half a century earlier in 1892—the Cuban Revolutionary Party (PRC). However, given the betrayal of Martí's democratic vision by a long series of Cuban politicians claiming to govern in his name, Grau wanted to symbolically rescue the authenticity of Martí's hopes for Cuba by adding the nickname, *Los Auténticos* (or the Authentic Cuban Revolutionary Party, PRC-A).

Sadly, over the next eight years Grau, his party, and his successor, Carlos Prío Socarrás, went on to violate nearly every principle of good government in a fashion that would bring shame perhaps even to the utterly venal and corrupt politicians of Cuba's first republic. Instead of using their opportunity to make good on the frustrated hopes denied an entire generation, the Auténticos used their incumbency as a way to make good on their long-denied birthright as Cuban politicians: to quickly and lavishly enrich themselves. The great hope embodied in the Authentic Revolutionary movement turned out to be a disillusioning disappointment that was neither authentic nor revolutionary (Pérez 1993: 79). Even more disturbing was the fact that after setting hopes so high upon gaining power, the Auténticos' fall from grace was that much more detrimental to the legitimacy of Cuban electoral politics. This debasement of electoral politics and the later usurping of the entire democratic system by Batista would be the two main reasons that future revolutionaries would turn to armed struggle as their only option. In fact, in his four years in office Grau did more than perhaps any other single man to kill the hope of democracy in Cuba (Thomas 1998).

However, the fact that these were boom years in the Cuban economy mitigated the public reaction to the administration's increasing corruption, allowing Grau to pass power to his Auténtico successor, Carlos Prío Socarrás. In fact, Prío's anticlimactic election in 1948 was Cuba's last direct presidential election in its history as an independent nation. With the United States buying the 1945, 1946, and 1947 sugar harvest en masse in order to feed a Europe recovering from war, the cash flow allowed those controlling the purse strings of the Cuban economy to become masters of corruption. Civil servants were underpaid so that administrators could use the extra money for bribes. The national lottery created a nebulous fund that could be tapped to pay off critics or unfairly implicate government opponents. Many governmental departments had hundreds of phantom workers whose salaries were collected by political cronies, and the numerous public work projects allowed for unrestrained graft.

Another dangerous development during these years was the transformation of political debate into violent *gangsterismo*. Since political competition led to opportunities for personal enrichment, the battle over political positions and access to government sinecures often turned into violent gang wars worthy of Hollywood played out on the streets of Havana. Growing out of the University of Havana, many student groups operated as covers for what were in fact political action groups. However, political ideologies and nationalist ideals took a back seat to Byzantine rivalries and the settling of scores (Farber 2003; 2006).

Despite the economic flush of the late 1940s, the degeneration of serious politics into violent street battles and the growing malfeasance of the Auténticos provoked the consistent, eloquent criticism of one of its own. When former Auténtico stalwart Eduardo Chibás became aware of the depth and breadth of Auténtico corruption, he made it his personal mission to investigate, expose, and publicize every last detail of it over the airwaves in his famous Sunday afternoon news broadcasts. In May 1947, Chibás also founded a new splinter party to give an organizational home to his campaign of criticism. Called the Orthodox Party (Partido del Pueblo Cubano—Ortodoxo), Chibás's party sought to make a "clean sweep" of Auténtico corruption with its broom logo and resounding slogan, *Vergüenza contra Dinero* ("Shame against Money"). However, his excessive criticisms, elaborate sense of personal honor, and principled search for the truth seem to have contributed to his own tragic and untimely death.

On August 5, 1951, just a year shy of a national presidential election in which he was the leading candidate, Chibás vociferously denounced the corruption of Auténtico education minister Aurelio Sánchez Arango on his radio show. However, unable to produce definitive proof of his accusation, Chibás seemed trapped by his own unwavering honesty. Perhaps concluding that he had committed an unpardonable error, Chibás shouted what would be his last words as his radio address came to a close: "Comrades of Orthodoxy, let us move forward! For economic independence, political freedom, and social justice! Sweep the thieves from the government! People of Cuba, rise up, and move forward! People of Cuba, wake up! This is my last call!" (Chibás 2003: 299). As he uttered these words, Chibás shot himself in the stomach, hoping that the sound of the shot would resound over the airwaves in a powerful, symbolic suicide attempt. Whether this was a political stunt intended to rouse the nation to reform or an actual suicide attempt, Chibás's death days later and subsequent massive funeral acted as a symbolic burial of Cuban democracy itself.

Staggering toward the planned 1952 election without Cuba's most popular and charismatic public figure and after almost a decade of endemic graft and corruption, Cuban political life never arrived at that date with destiny. Instead, running a distant third in the coming election, Batista staged a bloodless coup, regaining power once again. His coup was as effective as it was rapid, and its ease was facilitated by the fact that he was but delivering "the coup de grâce to a moribund regime" (Pérez 1993: 83). The Auténticos had inadvertently done Batista the favor of so degrading Cuban electoral politics that his coup was seen by many as preferable to the debased political culture that had plagued Cuba during the previous eight years.

By 1952, Batista had amassed many friends and favors in Washington because of his stalwart support for the Americans in World War II. He also knew that he could easily exploit the Americans' fears of communist subversion in Cuba, thus gaining their solid support for his unconstitutional return to power. In Cuba itself, there was little organized resistance to the coup. Still, Cubans woke up on March 10 with a sickening awareness that they were now living under a military dictatorship, not in the civilized, modern democracy they had conjured up from the apparent wealth of the island's capital, Havana. Eight years of corruption made the Auténticos indefensible, and the death of Chibás had left the Ortodoxos defenseless. Mexican intellectual José Vasconcelos pronounced what is perhaps the best epitaph for the fall of Prío's presidency: "Prío fell like a rotten fruit, almost of its own weight" (Thomas 1998: 775). Such an epitaph could serve just as well for the entire Cuban democratic experiment from 1940 to 1952.

The fact that the planned 1952 election never took place frustrated a great many Cubans. One of them whose first run for a local elected office was upended by Batista's coup was a young, brilliant, ambitious, and exceedingly eloquent member of Chibás's Ortodoxo Party, who took the lesson of the coup to heart. He would never again run in an open, direct election, nor would he ever need to. A little more than a year later, living under Batista's unconstitutional dictatorship, he would take up arms instead. His name was Fidel Castro Ruz.

The Cuban Insurgency, 1953–1958: The Rise of Fidel Castro

Between Fidel Castro's abortive raid on the Moncada army barracks on July 26, 1953, and the dramatic conclusion to the Cuban Missile Crisis almost ten years later in October 1962, a complete transformation would take place in U.S.-Cuban relations. During that decade, Cuba went from being the closest and most prosperous client state under U.S. hegemony in Latin America to a fiercely independent, communist state under the increasingly authoritarian control of Fidel Castro. After coming to power, Castro further defied the United States by moving to consolidate the revolution's links with the Soviets and by openly challenging U.S. hemispheric hegemony by implementing a social revolution at home and supporting armed struggle abroad. How did this happen?

The answer to this riddle and the roots to the ultimately triumphant revolution that began with Fidel Castro's attack on Moncada lie neither in the conference rooms of the State Department nor in the hidden corridors of the Kremlin, but in Cuba's own tortured past. Whatever the path taken after Castro strode into Havana on January 8, 1959, and whatever the outcome of the increasingly hostile confrontations between his new government and that of the United States, the revolution that took power in 1959 was essentially nationalist in character and fought against the foreign and domestic enemies of the long-frustrated hope for political independence, clean and effective government, civilian control of the military, social justice, and national sovereignty.

Previous attempts to throw off colonial domination between 1868 and 1898 had ended with the disheartening U.S. occupation and the bitter pill of imperial domination that was the Platt Amendment. The growing corruption and dictatorship of the 1920s under Machado unified the country in a nationalist struggle leading to the abortive revolution of 1933. However, the progressive Constitution of 1940 was left unfulfilled by Batista and baldly betrayed by successive Auténtico administrations. The expectant candidacy of Eduardo Chibás, in many ways the last hope for a democratic Cuba, ended in his tragic suicide. Finally, the growing sense of national frustration produced by this long series of events was only exacerbated by Batista's coup of 1952, especially when he had the temerity to invoke the name and social democratic vision of Martí in his first public speech upon return to power.

From Moncada to Granma, 1953–1955. Fidel Castro's dramatic entree onto Cuba's political stage came just a year after Batista's 1952 coup. As fate would have it, this was also the centenary of Martí's birth in 1853. Castro's plan was to stage an audacious assault on the country's second most important army headquarters, the Moncada barracks in the far eastern city of Santiago de Cuba. Castro chose the city of Santiago and the date of July 26, 1953, for both strategic and symbolic reasons. Since July 26 marked the culmination of the week-long carnival celebration in Cuba's second city, it was likely that the barracks would be left unguarded. Furthermore, Castro knew that a revolt would have a much better chance of success if it began in the insular and historically neglected eastern province of Oriente. Nearly every successful rebellion in the island's history had begun in the east, gradually moving across the island into the more populated and better defended west. Having come of age in Oriente and studied as a boy in Santiago, Castro also knew that his small band of guerrillas could beat a quick retreat into the fastness of the nearby Sierra Maestra mountains if necessary.

The 150 members of the attack force recruited by Castro were drawn, like their charismatic leader, from the youth wing of the Ortodoxo Party. Only two members of his force were or had ever been Communist Party members: Castro's younger brother Raúl and one other. The rest were likely motivated by their rejection of Batista's illegitimate rule and by the progressive nationalist ideals of the Ortodoxo Party: social justice and anticorruption, but also anticommunism. Indeed, this is part of the reason that Cuba's Communist Party described the attack as a "putsch"—irresponsible and ill-timed adventurism—with no attention to coalition-building and no chance of success. Despite his later consolidation of the revolution under communist organization and ideology, "[t]he Castro strategy ran totally counter to Marxist-Leninist theories," argues Szulc, "which is why the Communists refused to support him for such a long time" (1986: 243). Castro knew that his handful of men could not win a war against the Cuban Army. However, he suspected that such an audacious attack, if successful, could inspire a nationwide uprising against the dictator and lead to the regime's eventual downfall (ibid.: 241).

Castro's plan was to take Moncada and then broadcast Chibás's "Last Call" over the city's radio stations. Castro hoped that his listeners, after hearing his group's revolutionary program, would spontaneously identify with the invocation of Cuba's frustrated nationalist aspirations. However, it was not his victory at Moncada that electrified the Cuban people, leading to mass rebellion and eventual revolution, but his defeat. This was no ordinary defeat. Batista's brutality in putting down the uprising and murdering most captured rebels afterward, combined with Castro's "spectacularly defiant stance afterward" (ibid.: 242), ignited the indignation of the Cuban people and led to an outpouring of support for the rebel cause and its charismatic leader.

As Castro was to do again and again throughout his long tenure as Cuba's "maximum leader," he was able to turn what was in all respects a lopsided military defeat into a resounding public relations victory. After the attack, Batista declared that his brave soldiers had successfully repelled the rebels, most of whom were supposedly killed in battle. However, in the four days after the attack, sixty-one men were captured and then assassinated, most of them being first horribly tortured. Only eight rebels had actually died in combat. Castro reacted by turning this brutality and duplicity into a powerful weapon with which he could expose Batista as a tyrant before the Cuban public. When Cuba's newspapers began to publish graphic pictures of bloody, dismembered, and mutilated bodies of scores of young Cuban men, the public discovered that Batista had not only ordered his army to brutalize and execute these brave young men but had then lied about it, trying to paint his own soldiers as brave defenders of the homeland.

A licensed lawyer and charismatic speaker, Castro refused the aid of Santiago's public defender and took on the task of his own defense. Batista moved to muffle the coverage of Castro's trial by holding the proceedings in the tiny examination room of a civilian hospital. However, the young journalist Marta Rojas, who sympathized with the rebels, took it upon herself to scribble down as much of Castro's mesmerizing speech as possible. Knowing that his guilt was predetermined and that the trial was aimed only at giving an impression of judicial impartiality, Castro decided not to defend his innocence. Instead, he used the trial as a public forum in which to meticulously and devastatingly indict the Batista regime itself.

Castro began his "defense" by invoking the right of rebellion against an illegitimate government. Then, as if on cue, prosecutors sought to learn the "intellectual author" behind the

This photo of the façade of the Moncada Army Barracks in Santiago de Cuba shows bullet holes left by the gunfire of rebel attackers. This detail was re-added after 1959 when the complex was turned into a museum and elementary school. (Ted Henken)

attack. Such a question was central to the case, since Cuban law placed equal responsibility on the "intellectual author" of a crime as on the actual perpetrator. Castro calmly responded that the attack's *autor intelectual* was none other than Cuban patriot José Martí. For the next two hours, Castro spoke directly to the panel of military judges before him. However, he knew that his real audience was the Cuban people. Invoking Martí in almost religious language, Castro intoned:

> It looked as if the Apostle Martí was going to die in the year of the centennial of his birth. It looked as if his memory would be extinguished forever, so great was the affront. But he lives. He has not died. His people are rebellious, his people are worthy, his people are faithful to his memory. Cubans have fallen defending his doctrines. Young men, in a magnificent gesture of reparation, have come to give their blood and to die at the side of his tomb so that he might continue to live in the hearts of his countrymen. Oh, Cuba, what would have become of you if you had let the memory of your Apostle die! (Quoted in ibid.: 297)

Subsequently, Castro's defense speech became the expansive if conveniently vague political platform for his new movement, announcing his goals to the nation and exposing Batista's tyranny and hypocrisy. However, few Cubans heard Castro's message, given the new controls over the press. Because of that, over the next few months an embellished and elaborated version of his speech was clandestinely distributed across the island. When Cubans read the words of this daring, charismatic figure, what they found was not only a litany of indictments against Batista's illegitimate regime but also a serious political program for national regeneration.

Castro indicated that had his attack been successful, he would have immediately decreed "five revolutionary laws": the restoration of the 1940 Constitution; agrarian reform; 30 percent profit sharing for workers in large enterprises; entitlement to a share of 55 percent of the profits of Cuba's powerful sugar mills for Cuba's *colonos;* and the confiscation of all property obtained through corruption. Additionally, Castro reassured the Cuban public that he intended to maintain a policy "of close solidarity with the democratic peoples of this continent." Finally, he hinted at what would become a defining characteristic of the revolution: solving the intractable socioeconomic problems common to underdeveloped countries like Cuba: "The problem of the land, the problem of industrialization, the problem of housing, the problem of unemployment, the problem of education, and the problem of people's health" (Castro 2003: 314).

Throughout his speech, Castro was also at pains to pledge that these new revolutionary laws and many ambitious goals would be accomplished together "with the restoration of civil liberties and political democracy." Finally, he concluded with the rousing declaration: "Condemn me. It does not matter. History will absolve me." Given the resonance of his nationalist, progressive message among the populace and his formidable talents as a public speaker, Castro's speech became a legend, catapulting him into national prominence.

Upon the close of the trial, Castro and his followers were sentenced to fifteen years in prison on the Isle of Pines. However, they served less than two years, benefiting once again from Batista's desire to enhance his tarnished reputation. In 1954, after winning an uncontested election, Batista announced an end to martial law, the return of constitutional guarantees, freedom of the press, and amnesty for all political prisoners, including Castro. In the meantime, Castro had converted his prison cell into a university of rebellion where he and many of his followers devoured the classics of the French Revolution (becoming especially enamored of Napoleon), the writings of Europe's leading social thinkers including Marx, as well as Cuban and Latin American history (Bardach and Conte Agüero 2007).

Castro was released along with his entire rebel force at noon on Sunday, May 15, 1955. Upon release, Castro quickly organized his group of followers into the *Movimiento 26 de Julio* (26th of July Movement). Realizing that Batista had effectively co-opted the legal opposition, Castro decided that clandestine armed struggle was his only option. On July 7, Castro left for exile in Mexico, knowing that he was a marked man in Cuba. Upon his departure, the magazine *Bohemia,* his ally in public relations in the wake of the Moncada debacle two years earlier, published his defiant parting message to the Cuban people:

> I am leaving Cuba because all doors of peaceful struggle have been closed to me. . . . As a follower of Martí, I believe the hour has come to take rights and not to beg for them, to fight instead of pleading for them. I will reside somewhere in the Caribbean. From trips such as this, one does not return or else one returns with the tyranny beheaded at one's feet. (Quoted in Szulc 1986)

In Mexico, Castro immediately became consumed with planning for the coming insurrection. Soon after arriving in Mexico City, at a party celebrating the second anniversary of the Moncada attack, Castro met an Argentine doctor named Ernesto Guevara de la Serna with whom he shared an immediate sympathy. Guevara exposed Castro to a more radical political ideology than he had perhaps up to then contemplated, and Castro gave Guevara exactly the revolutionary cause for which he had been traveling across half a continent to find. Returning home in the morning after a marathon ten-hour conversation with Castro, Guevara told his then wife, Hilda, that he had met "a great political leader, . . . a master of great tenacity and firmness. . . . If anything has happened in Cuba since Martí, it is Fidel Castro: He will make the revolution. We agreed profoundly . . . . Only a person like him would I be disposed to help in everything" (quoted in ibid.: 336). Guevara joined Castro's movement as its doctor. He later opted for the role of a soldier and quickly became known to his fellows as "El Che," based on his habit of addressing everyone he met in Argentine slang, "¡Che!"

After just fifteen months of fund-raising, training, and coordination with the movement's growing clandestine wing back on the island, Castro and eighty-one of his fellow would-be revolutionaries set sail for Cuba. The group departed from the small port town of Tuxpan, near Vera Cruz, in late November 1956 aboard the *Granma,* a yacht purchased from an American expatriate and named, presumably, after his grandmother. The small yacht was far too small to comfortably hold the eighty-two rebels, more than three times its capacity of twenty-five passengers. Overcrowded as the yacht was, things could have been much worse, since as many as fifty other rebels had to remain behind in Mexico.

The group's planned arrival at Playa Las Coloradas on the southwestern tip of Oriente was delayed for two days on account of bad weather. During the unanticipated seven days at sea, most of the men became seasick, one fell overboard, and most supplies ran out. Castro had originally planned his arrival to coincide with a simultaneous uprising in Santiago.

The attack went ahead as planned, dooming the rebel's chances of arriving undetected. Just before dawn on December 2, 1956, the *Granma* suddenly became lodged in a mud bank more than a mile from the beach at Las Coloradas. Guevara later wrote that the *Granma*'s heroic landing just off Cuba's mangrove-lined southeastern coast was really more of a shipwreck.

The crew was forced to leave the ship and most of their supplies behind and wade ashore. As they made their way through the maze of submerged tree roots, razor sharp sticks and vines, and swarms of ravenous mosquitoes, Castro was consumed by the fear that they had actually landed on one of Cuba's innumerable offshore keys. The group did not know where they were until one man managed to climb a tree and glimpse the majestic Sierra Maestra in the distance. Then, just as the group collapsed on solid ground, they were detected, and a merciless military bombardment began. The attack force of eighty-two was quickly dispersed and eventually reduced to less than twenty fighters. After wandering in the forest and hiding from military ambushes, eighteen of the original crewmembers managed to regroup in the Sierra Maestra (though revolutionary tradition dictates that there were just an apostolic twelve). Despite such an inauspicious beginning, Castro had been true to his pledge of returning to Cuba to resume the insurrection before the end of 1956.

The Long Road from the Sierra Maestra to Havana, 1956–1958. After regrouping with his handful of men now relatively safely hidden in the fastness of the mountains, Castro realized that they needed only to survive, since their very existence within Cuba constituted a challenge to the regime. Despite losing more than 80 percent of his fighting force early on, nearly all of Castro's leadership structure remained intact, including most of those who later became *comandantes* during the war: Che Guevara, Raúl Castro,

Juan Almeida, Ramiro Valdés, and Camilo Cienfuegos. For his part, Batista aimed to finish off the survivors of Castro's party, ordering his soldiers to remove peasants forcibly from the foothills of the Sierra Maestra, much as Spanish general Weyler had done sixty years before. However, as with Weyler, this policy backfired, because it only enlarged the rebels' "liberated" territory and made it easier for them to strike and then disappear into the forest.

Batista also exacerbated the hatred that many locals already felt for the rural guard by sending in a group of modern-day "volunteers" to terrorize suspected sympathizers. That group, who proudly called themselves *Los Tigres,* was led by the infamous and sadistic Rolando Masferrer and was more akin to the paramilitary death squads that would become so infamous later in Central America. *New York Times* journalist Herbert Matthews reported the results of this policy to the world in late February in a series of provocative front-page articles written after visiting Castro's camp: "One man told me how he had seen his brother's store wrecked and burned by government troops and his brother dragged out and executed. 'I'd rather be here fighting for Fidel, than anywhere in the world now,' he said" (Matthews 2003: 329).

In order to maximize the impact of his tiny rebel force, Castro and his followers developed two strategies that would help them defeat Batista's 40,000-member military: guerrilla warfare and propaganda. Used successfully sixty years earlier by Cuba's revered independence fighters, the *mambises,* guerrilla warfare was a strategic attempt to transform the liabilities of small numbers and weak firepower into assets by mastering the environment and effectively utilizing a hit-and-run strategy. In his many writings on irregular military tactics, Che Guevara coined the term *foco* (focus) to describe this method of warfare. Guevara also emphasized what he touted as the greatest asset of the irregular rebel army in the Sierra Maestra, which was that poor peasants, especially in isolated rural areas, could constitute a "tremendous potential revolutionary force" if presented with the right tactics and leadership. Guevara noted:

> [A]rmies are set up and equipped for conventional warfare. . . . When they are confronted with the irregular warfare of peasants based on their own home grounds, they become absolutely powerless; they lose ten men for every revolutionary fighter who falls. Demoralization among them mounts rapidly when they are beset by an invisible and invincible army which provides them no chance to display their military-academy tactics and their fanfare of war. . . . What is it that . . . makes those units invincible, regardless of the number, strength and resources of their enemies? It is the people's support. (Guevara 1969: 89–103)

From the time of their arrival in December 1956 and continuing on for the next twenty-four months through December 1958, Castro's guerrilla army was supported and often literally kept alive by the guidance, generosity, sacrifice, and eventual combat participation of the Sierra's peasants. Eventually whole networks of peasants came to their aid, despite having every reason to distrust them and look cynically on Castro's common introduction: "Have no fear, I am Fidel Castro, and we came to liberate the Cuban people." However, only rarely did any peasants betray the guerrillas. "It was not a peasant revolution that gave Fidel power," writes Tad Szulc, "but there would have been no revolution without the peasants" (1986: 380).

By early 1957, the arrival of Castro's forces had become common knowledge in Cuba and was on the verge of becoming international news. However, Batista had ordered a news blackout within Cuba censoring any news about the survival of the rebel forces. In fact, Batista faltered in trying to project an image of absolute confidence in his military, making the mistake of insisting to an expectant press that he had defeated the rebels and that Fidel Castro was among the dead. Seizing this golden propaganda opportunity, the urban leadership of the 26th of July Movement in Havana approached the bureau chief of the *New York Times*, Ruby Hart Phillips, to request that a reporter be sent to the Sierra Maestra to interview Castro. Reluctant to go herself, Phillips contacted Herbert Matthews, a veteran war correspondent and respected member of the editorial board of the *Times*. Thus was born Castro's second major public relations coup following his Moncada turnabout four years earlier. This time his audience would be global, and he was ready (DePalma 2006; Phillips 1959).

Matthews traveled to the Sierra from Havana in mid-February, feigning a holiday with his wife. Because of his own political sympathies and criticisms of press censorship, Matthews was eager to prove Batista a liar. However, prior to his historic meeting with Castro, Matthews had published editorials in the *Times* expressing great cynicism about the chances of success of the invading "terrorists." "Could anything be madder?" he asked rhetorically (DePalma 2006: 9–24). After a legendary interview with Castro in the foothills of the Sierra in the early dawn of February 17, 1957, Matthews published the first of three articles a week later on Sunday, February 24. Speaking to Matthews, Castro realized that he was addressing a worldwide audience. Projecting an image of military strength and popular support, Castro led Matthews to believe that he had a large number of men under arms. Casually mentioning the existence of two other guerrilla camps, Castro had a fellow soldier interrupt him with the news that a liaison from "column number two" had just arrived (Szulc 1986: 409). In fact, at the time of the interview there were eighteen men in Castro's force.

Clearly captivated, Matthews went on at length in his first article about the sharp political mind and "overwhelming personality" of a man he glowingly described as "a powerful six-footer, olive-skinned, full-faced, with a straggly beard." Matthews added, "It is easy to see that his men adored him and also to see why he has caught the imagination of the youth of Cuba all over the island. Here was an educated, dedicated fanatic, a man of ideals, of courage, and of remarkable qualities of leadership" (Matthews 2003: 329). Matthews also noted Castro's criticism of the sale of U.S. military equipment to Batista, which he was illegally using against the guerrillas. Finally, Castro indicated that his revolt was motivated only by democratic, pro-American goals, hoping to positively influence public opinion and quell any rising doubts about his commitment to democracy or desire for friendly relations with the United States. Echoing this sentiment, yet trying to capture the complexity of the movement's goals, Matthews reported:

> It is a revolutionary movement that calls itself socialistic. It is also nationalistic, which generally in Latin America means anti-Yankee. The program is vague and couched in generalities, but it amounts to a new deal for Cuba, radical, democratic and therefore anti-Communist. (ibid. 330)

After this laudatory report from within the Sierra Maestra, a place supposedly under tight military control, Batista exacerbated his problems by having his defense minister publicly assert that the article was a fabrication. However, the lies, brutality, and incompetence of his administration were exposed once again when the *Times* published a follow-up article featuring a grainy photo of Matthews standing beside a very alive Fidel Castro, each man sporting a heavy coat, cap, and signature Cuban cigar (De Palma 2006).

Over the next year, the Sierra rebel force gained momentum as Castro gradually distinguished himself as the most important opposition leader. On March 13, 1957, the student-led Revolutionary Directorate (DR) carried out an audacious attack on the presidential palace in Havana, with 100 men attempting to break past the guards and blast their way up into the third-floor presidential apartments where Batista was hiding. Despite successfully breaking into the palace and making it to the interior presidential offices, the assassination force could not penetrate to the third floor, since it was accessible only by a single elevator. Thirty-five rebels were killed in the attack, with only three

Fidel Castro, the leader of a small group of rebels known as the 26th of July Movement, sits in a guerrilla stronghold in the Sierra Maestra mountains of southeast Cuba. His younger brother, Raúl, stands on the left. This photo was taken on March 14, 1957, only weeks after New York Times' correspondent Herbert Matthews had made Castro's struggle a cause célèbre around the world. (AP/Wide World Photos)

managing to escape. Worse still, in the bloodbath that followed, most of the DR's leadership including its figurehead, José Antonio Echeverría, was killed.

While the attack made Echeverría into a martyr, it left the DR significantly weakened while greatly strengthening both Batista's base and Castro's position as head of the opposition. In the days following the attack, Batista received visits from a parade of powerful well-wishers who assured him of their continued support. Repression against student activists increased thereafter under the guise of investigating the attack. "Had the attack succeeded," reasons Szulc, "it would have left Fidel Castro in his mountains as a suddenly irrelevant factor in the revolutionary equation" (ibid.: 417). However, the first significant rebel victory against the army in the hamlet of El Uvero in the Sierra took place soon after the failed DR attack. As a result, "Castro's rivals had all been severely weakened or destroyed by the middle of 1957, and his tiny guerrilla army in the Sierra—still with only a hundred men in May—was now the only viable insurgent force on the island" (Gott 2004: 160).

Castro's forces grew and split up in order to bring the revolution across the entire expanse of eastern Cuba. By March 1958, Raúl Castro's sixty-five-man Second Front had established a foothold in the northeastern Sierra Cristal, while Juan Almeida managed to open another front north of Santiago. Likewise, Camilo Cienfuegos and Che Guevara departed the Sierra in mid-1958 to penetrate the west. As victory followed victory, Batista's government was forced to concede ever greater areas of "liberated territory" to the rebels. Batista was also faced with a series of new uprisings within the military, the most important of which was the successful takeover of the naval base at Cienfuegos. The liberation lasted only a day, after which B-26 bombers provided by the United States attacked the base. U.S.-supplied tanks and armored regiments then arrived from Havana, crushing the opposition. Despite Batista's victory, his illegal use of U.S. weaponry provoked an arms embargo by the United States, giving the opposition another symbolic victory and dealing another blow to Batista's legitimacy.

Frustrated in his attempts to convert his illegitimate rule into a legal, democratic presidency through transparent

Cuban President Fulgencio Batista addresses an estimated 150,000
people from the balcony of the presidential palace in Havana on
April 4, 1957, a month after surviving an assassination attempt in this
very spot. The address took place during loyalty demonstrations that
followed the failed attack on the palace. (Bettman/Corbis)

electoral fraud, Batista increasingly answered the opposition's
sabotage and subversion with violent repression, further dele-
gitimizing himself in the eyes of the Cuban people (Thomas
1998). Seeking to deliver a coup de grâce to Batista's faltering
legitimacy, the urban leadership of the 26th of July Movement

organized a general strike similar to the massive work stoppage that had ended Machado's reign of terror in 1933. Planned for April 9, 1958, the strike would rely on urban coordination, making it a test of the effectiveness of the movement's urban underground, which was often at odds with Castro's strategy and leadership in the Sierra. Castro grudgingly approved of the strike, which turned out to be a miserable failure, dealing a serious blow to the movement's urban leadership. At the same time, the failure justified Castro's increased symbolic and strategic importance as the leader of the opposition.

Batista reacted to the strike's failure by launching a final offensive against the rebels in the summer of 1958. Often near defeat, the rebels managed to fend off repeated attacks against their mountain positions, successfully outlasting the much larger and better equipped Cuban Army. The offensive ended on August 6, 1958. Just 321 men had held out against thousands of Cuban soldiers, who suffered as many as 1,000 casualties and lost scores of soldiers to rebel capture. The guerrillas' success was the last major turning point in the guerrilla phase of the revolution. In July and August, Castro began to implement an invasion of western Cuba. Guevara set out for Las Villas province, where he would score an important victory in Santa Clara. Camilo Cienfuegos was sent to Pinar del Río by way of the Escambray Mountains to assert control over a group of independent guerrillas there.

Two things were now clear. Batista's days were numbered, and the 26th of July Movement under Castro had achieved clear hegemony over all other revolutionary factions. Also, the PSP had finally decided to support Castro's movement, perhaps out of fear that they might be left powerless and irrelevant if he were to achieve victory. However, this was not a case of the 26th of July Movement turning communist. Instead of converting to communism, Castro successfully turned the communists into *Fidelistas*. Batista tried to hold on in the waning months of 1958 with a last-ditch election that fooled no one. Seeing the handwriting on the wall, the United States sent a secret emissary to plead with Batista to hand power over to a moderate junta, so as to prevent the looming Castro victory. Batista stubbornly refused, and Guevara's decisive victory in Santa Clara in December of 1959 sealed his fate. He reluctantly boarded a plane on December 31, leaving the country in the hands of Castro's bearded rebels as a new year, and a new era, dawned over the island.

The Revolution Begins Now, 1959–1962

Observers unacquainted with the complexities of the first three years of the Cuban Revolution often assume that Castro marched into Havana on January 8, 1959, a confirmed communist and a committed enemy of the United States. However, Castro's political ideology and foreign policy remained quite ambiguous, if increasingly radical, during his first years in power. In fact, socialist and anti-American rhetoric was much more important in consolidating a revolution under attack after January 1959 than it had been during the movement to overthrow Batista (Domínguez 1978). In January, Castro took up residence in Havana and declared his desire to remain the head of the military only. He moved quickly to create a new, rather moderate cabinet of ministers made up of leading liberal professionals who had opposed Batista but who were neither bearded guerrillas nor members of the Communist Party. Indeed, Castro's choice for president was Manuel Urrutia Lleó, a liberal, middle-class, anticommunist jurist.

On the other hand, it was immediately clear that Castro's ambitions were not limited to simply removing Batista from power. He rejected the possibility of a military junta or a new round of U.S. intervention as had occurred in 1898 and again in 1933. To prevent either eventuality, he called for a general strike that would paralyze the country and allow his guerrilla forces the time to rally the population and converge on

Havana. This time, the strike was absolute. "The history of 1898 will not be repeated," declared Castro over the radio on January 1, referring to how the U.S. occupying force had not allowed Cuban rebels to enter Santiago following Spain's defeat. Upon arriving in Cuba's second city on January 2, Castro marched into the Moncada barracks with wild crowds celebrating as he symbolically took possession of the fortress where he had begun the armed struggle five years earlier.

That evening, Castro spoke to a delirious throng of supporters, indicating that the real revolution had yet to begin. "The revolution begins now," he announced. "This time, luckily for Cuba, the Revolution will truly come into power. It will not be like in 1898, when the North Americans came and made themselves the masters of our country" (Szulc 1986: 459). Surprisingly, the United States responded by recognizing the new Cuban government almost immediately. This cordiality would be short-lived.

The first conflict between the United States and the new Cuban government erupted over the handling of trials for war criminals, which the U.S. news media began criticizing as "kangaroo courts." Castro angrily responded that no such complaints were aired when Batista was busy filling Cuba's streets and jails with the bloodied bodies of Cuba's youth. Invoking the right of the government to subject war criminals to what he called "revolutionary justice," Castro rejected what he saw as American hypocrisy, knowing that he enjoyed near total support of a populace well aware of the brutal crimes committed by Batista's secret police. Despite this confrontation, Castro paid an unofficial visit to the United States in April 1959, surprising officials by refusing to request any economic aid for his new government.

By the summer of 1959, indications began to surface that all was not well with many of the revolution's erstwhile moderate supporters. In fact, Castro's first cabinet broke apart in June over the issue of communist influence in the government, and President Urrutia was forced out in July. Finally, the respected Major Huber Matos publicly resigned in October to protest rising communist influence in the revolution. Despite this wave of defections, for an entire generation of Cubans 1959 was the best year of their lives. The vast majority saw themselves as active participants in an epoch-making event: the long-awaited fruition of a broad-based movement for national regeneration that both fed on and evoked an outpouring of human solidarity, humanistic altruism, and revolutionary effervescence.

If 1959 was the revolution's honeymoon, then 1960 started with increasing marital trouble and ended with an emphatic divorce as the United States cut diplomatic relations in January 1961. In fact, 1960 was the crucial year that defined the radical direction of the revolution, as well as the year in which the United States gave up on diplomacy and began preparing a military solution to its "Cuba problem." In February, the Soviet foreign minister, Anastas Mikoyan, paid a courtesy visit to Cuba accompanying a trade exhibition that had previously appeared in Mexico. The visit, quite ominous for the United States, resulted in the re-establishment of diplomatic relations between the two countries. Next, counter-revolutionary sabotage was suspected when the French freighter *La Coubre* exploded in March while delivering military equipment in Havana's harbor. Castro responded by pointing an accusing finger at the United States. Also in March, President Dwight D. Eisenhower secretly authorized the CIA to begin planning Castro's overthrow, what would become John F. Kennedy's most infamous fiasco—the Bay of Pigs.

Economic warfare between the two countries began in the summer, when two U.S.-owned petroleum refineries followed State Department instructions, refusing to refine the Soviet crude purchased by the Cuban government. Cuba quickly responded by nationalizing the two refineries. It is likely, however, that this whole episode was set in motion by Che Guevara, who accurately anticipated that the U.S. refineries would refuse to accept the Soviet crude even before he arranged to have it sent from the Soviet Union. Guevara knew that Washington would never tolerate the imposition of a radical socioeconomic experiment in its erstwhile economic colony. Much less would it sit idly by and watch its Cold War rival openly support such an experiment. Guevara also knew that a hostile U.S. reaction would facilitate the subsequent consolidation of the revolution under the socialism that he advocated.

When the United States eliminated Cuba's long-standing sugar quota in July, the USSR offered to purchase the balance of the quota and pledged to make a similar purchase the following year. In the waning months of 1960, economic warfare heated up again with the Cuban nationalization of all remaining U.S. properties and businesses, including utilities, sugar mills, banks, railroads, and factories. The United States responded by imposing the first elements of its now infamous trade embargo and recalling its ambassador, Philip Bonsal. Now clearly under threat from the United States, the revolution began to establish a series of mass organizations that would provide for national defense, promote mass mobilization, and effectively control all future political participation. These organizations included the People's Militia, the Committees for the Defense of the Revolution, the Federation of Cuban Women, the Union Communist Youth, and the National Association of Small Farmers.

The Bay of Pigs, April 1961. By the time Washington had severed its diplomatic relations with Cuba in January 1961, hundreds of thousands of Cubans had already fled to the United States. The Cuban exile invasion force that would attempt to oust Castro at the Bay of Pigs later that spring, Brigade 2506, drew its membership from that first group of exiles. Also among the exiles were the members of the Cuban Revolutionary Council, including its president, José Miró

Cardona, revolutionary Cuba's first prime minister. The council was set up in late March 1961, by Richard Bissell, deputy director of the Central Intelligence Agency (CIA). Organized just three weeks prior to the planned invasion, the council was expected to form the provisional government of Cuba once the Castro regime had been ousted.

The Cuban invasion was expected to proceed with the same ease that CIA-backed Guatemalan exiles had overthrown Guatemalan President Jacobo Arbenz and his reform government seven years earlier in Central America. However, CIA planners drastically underestimated the nationalist resolve and revolutionary commitment of the Cuban people. Unlike the counterintelligence and subterfuge successfully used against the Guatemalans in 1954, the CIA based its strategy in Cuba largely on wishful thinking and bad intelligence from biased sources within Cuba. They also misjudged Castro, who unlike the indecisive and fatalistic Arbenz, acted with resourcefulness and tenacity. Finally, Castro's deputy, Che Guevara, had witnessed the fall of Guatemala in 1954, steeling Cuban resolve to call Washington's bluff this time around (Schlesinger and Kinzer 1999).

On April 15, two days prior to the invasion, U.S. planes camouflaged as Cuban fighters and flown by exile pilots strafed various Cuban airports and military installations. Attempting to cripple the Cuban Air Force, the strikes only succeeded in killing several civilians, alerting the Cuban government to the imminent invasion, and provoking the ire of the Cuban people. During the massive state funeral for the dead that followed, Castro made a rousing speech in which he paraphrased Abraham Lincoln, calling his a revolution "of the humble, by the humble, and for the humble" (Cluster and Hernández 2006). Castro then wisely siezed this opportune moment of national unity and publicly declared the revolution a socialist one for the first time. "What the imperialists cannot forgive us for . . . is that we have made a socialist revolution under the nose of the United States," he roared. This audacious statement implicitly connected socialism to the defense of the Cuban nation, transforming the previously taboo socialist ideology into the revolution's guiding light and primary means of consolidation. Under attack from the American-supported exiles, the majority of the Cuban people seemed to rally to Castro's call. At the same time, Castro ordered the roundup and imprisonment of as many as 100,000 suspected sympathizers and collaborators in the counter-revolutionary movement.

On April 17, the exile invasion began at Girón Beach near the Bay of Pigs on Cuba's south coast. However, Brigade 2506 could make little headway beyond the shallow coral reef that protected the beach. Once ashore, their advance was stymied by the large and inaccessible Zapata Swamp. Like the *Granma* guerrillas only five years before, the *brigadistas* had to jump into the water and wade ashore, where they were quickly defeated. Survivors were taken prisoner and later ransomed to the United States in exchange for $53 million in food and medical supplies.

Designed to achieve the feat of overthrowing the revolution, while at the same time ensuring "plausible deniability" to President Kennedy, the Cuban invasion was a complete failure. One reason for the failure was that Kennedy had inherited a plan originally hatched by Eisenhower and so was never fully committed to supporting it. Despite his tough anti-communist rhetoric in his presidential debates against Richard Nixon the year before, Kennedy refused to allow any direct U.S. military involvement in the invasion. However, CIA planners deluded themselves into believing that Kennedy would change his tune once the invasion was afoot. Such wishful thinking and miscalculation doomed the invasion from the start. In the end, the failed invasion facilitated exactly the outcome that it was designed to prevent. The revolution was both radicalized and consolidated, allowing

This plaque, embedded in the side of a building on the corner of 23rd and 12th streets in Havana, commemorates Castro's declaration of the socialist nature of the Cuban Revolution. "This is a socialist, demo-cratic Revolution of the humble, by the humble, and for the humble," Castro proclaimed to a massive crowd on the eve of the Bay of Pigs invasion, which began on April 17, 1961. (Ted Henken)

Castro to disqualify all remaining moderates and purge the country with impunity. Also, this early attempt to overthrow the revolution justified Cuba's fear of subsequent invasion attempts, leading directly to the Cuban Missile Crisis.

The Cuban Missile Crisis, October 1962. "If the making of a radical revolution in Cuba required a break with the United States," writes Jorge Domínguez, "the defense of a radical revolution in the face of U.S. attack demanded support from the Soviet Union" (1993: 102). A full eighteen months after the failed attack at the Bay of Pigs, Cuba's newfound importance in world politics brought it once again to the forefront of international attention. With the threat of invasion now clear, Cubans sought greater Soviet protection through a public military pact with the Soviets that would demonstrate to the Americans that a second invasion would lead to war with the USSR. In fact, the Soviets had already planned to persuade Castro to allow them to place nuclear missiles on the island, using its strategic location as a counterbalance to the U.S. missiles that virtually encircled the USSR.

When the Cubans approached Khrushchev with the pact idea, he upped the ante with an offer to provide the missiles. However, Castro was concerned that accepting the missiles might compromise Cuban independence, since the missiles would be under exclusive Soviet control. He also preferred a public military pact, correctly fearing what might happen if the Soviet bases were discovered before they were fully operational. In the end, Castro accepted the missiles as a guarantor of the revolution. However, Khrushchev continued to hedge on making any public commitments to Cuba's military defense until the missiles were installed (Gott 2004).

Castro's fears were confirmed when a U2 spy plane discovered the missile sites nearing completion in mid-October 1962. Kennedy interpreted the move as a deliberate attempt to throw off the global balance of power by violating what had until then been considered America's sphere of influence. Kicking off a famous "thirteen days" of calculated threats and intense negotiations, Kennedy announced to the world on October 22 that the United States had discovered the missiles, that the Soviets must remove them, and that the U.S. Navy would "quarantine" the island of Cuba. While projecting a tough image, Kennedy also wanted to give Khrushchev the ability to respond to his demands without losing face. For that reason he labeled what was an illegal U.S. "blockade" of an independent country, a preventative "quarantine," refusing his generals' requests to authorize a military strike or second invasion of the island.

As the world held its breath, Kennedy projected a surprising toughness and poise in tense, sometimes cryptic negotiations with the Soviets, contrasting sharply with his previous missteps at the Bay of Pigs. For many exiles, however, Kennedy's earlier "betrayal" of Brigade 2506 was exacerbated when he helped to defuse this new crisis by secretly promising not to invade Cuba. Khrushchev showed his own negotiating skill by successfully using backdoor communications to defuse the crisis over the objections to Soviet hard-liners. However, when he removed the missiles without consulting Cuba, Castro was furious. While the Kennedy-Khrushchev agreement included a U.S. pledge not to invade Cuba, it also indicated that the fate of Cuba would again be decided by outsiders. The episode taught Castro that he could not fully trust his new Soviet sponsors. In fact, he would spend the remainder of the decade experimenting with insurgent subversion abroad and radical economic experimentation at home in defiance of Soviet advice. He would not reach out to them again until these radical experiments proved ruinous with Guevara's death in Bolivia in 1967 and Cuba's failed 10-million-ton sugar harvest of 1970.

Conclusion: The Ignorance and Arrogance of U.S. Policy

The history of U.S.-Cuban relations and the origins of the Cuban Revolution developed out of a close, yet inherently problematic, relationship going as far back as the colonial period, and culminating in 1902 in the semisovereign Republic of Cuba. This protected republic, despite massive amounts of initial aid from the United States and a growing, even thriving economy that developed in the 1940s and 1950s, was based on a series of fundamental contradictions (Farber 2006: 5). First, Cuba was a constitutional republic bedeviled by political underdevelopment and recurrent dictatorship. Second, the island's economic development was overly dependent on one crop (sugar) and one market (the United States), as well as compromised by the skewed distribution of wealth and by high levels of political corruption. Third, Cuba's intimate links with the United States, while seen by a small elite group as beneficial, were viewed with growing resentment and aversion by many others whose dreams of sovereignty had been thwarted by repeated U.S. interventions.

It was this sense of a growing yet frustrated nationalism that Castro symbolized for many Cubans in his first unsuccessful raid on Moncada, and again later in his triumphant two-year battle against Batista. For Cubans, the victory over Batista was much more than the ouster of a corrupt dictator. It was also an opportunity for Cuba to finally gain the independence it had been long denied. Many Cubans linked this denial to U.S. interests. Furthermore, American ignorance of Cuban frustrations played a major role in the eventual outcome of the conflict. For too long Washington had seen U.S. influence in Cuba as essentially benign and unproblematic. Such a perspective blinded U.S. analysts to the possibility that its country's own dominant presence on the island was the greatest barrier to independence. Growing out of this ignorance was an even more offensive arrogance that prevented the United States from conceiving of a genuine opposition to its influence. Thus Washington could only interpret Cuban opposition to its traditional dominance as immaturity or alien subversion. In the end, the confrontation between the United States and Cuba was all but inevitable, given the U.S. desire to influence Cuba and the Cuban desire to make real its dream of full independence (Benjamin 1990).

References

Aguilar, Luis E. "Cuba, c. 1860–1930," in *Cuba: A Short History.* Edited by Leslie Bethell. Cambridge: Cambridge University Press, 1993.

Aguilar, Luis E. *Cuba, 1933: Prologue to Revolution.* Ithaca, NY: Cornell University Press, 1972.

Alvarado Ramos, Juan Antonio. *La Ruta del Esclavo en Cuba.* Havana: Fernando Ortiz Foundation, 1998.

Baker, Christopher P. *Moon Handbooks: Cuba* (second edition). Emeryville, CA: Avalon Travel Publishing, 2000.

Bardach, Ann Louise, and Luis Conte Agüero. *The Prison Letters of Fidel Castro.* New York: Nation Books, 2007.

Barreiro, José. "Survival Stories," in *The Cuba Reader: History, Culture, Politics.* Edited by Aviva Chomsky, Barry Carr, and Pamela Maria Smorkaloff. Durham, NC: Duke University Press, 2003.

Benjamin, Jules. *The United States and the Origins of the Cuban Revolution: An Empire of Liberty in an Age of National Liberation.* Princeton, NJ: Princeton University Press, 1990.

Castro, Fidel. "History Will Absolve Me," in *The Cuba Reader: History, Culture, Politics.* Edited by Aviva Chomsky, Barry Carr, and Pamela Maria Smorkaloff. Durham, NC: Duke University Press, 2003.

Chibás, Eduardo A. "The Last Call," in *The Cuba Reader: History, Culture, Politics.* Edited by Aviva Chomsky, Barry Carr, and Pamela Maria Smorkaloff. Durham, NC: Duke University Press, 2003.

Cluster, Dick, and Rafael Hernández. *History of Havana.* New York: Palgrave Macmillan, 2006.

Dana, Richard. "The Trade in Chinese Laborers," in *The Cuba Reader: History, Culture, Politics.* Edited by Aviva Chomsky, Barry Carr, and Pamela Maria Smorkaloff. Durham, NC: Duke University Press, 2003.

DePalma, Anthony. *The Man Who Invented Fidel: Castro, Cuba, and Herbert L. Matthews of the New York Times.* New York: Public Affairs, 2006.

Domínguez, Jorge I. "Cuba since 1959," in *Cuba: A Short History.* Edited by Leslie Bethell. Cambridge, MA: Cambridge University Press, 1993.

Domínguez, Jorge I. *Cuba: Order and Revolution.* Cambridge, MA: Harvard University Press, 1978.

Farber, Samuel. *The Origins of the Cuban Revolution Reconsidered.* Chapel Hill: University of North Carolina Press, 2006.

Farber, Samuel. "The Political Gangster," in *The Cuba Reader: History, Culture, Politics.* Edited by Aviva Chomsky, Barry Carr, and Pamela Maria Smorkaloff. Durham, NC: Duke University Press, 2003.

Gott, Richard. *Cuba: A New History.* New Haven, CT: Yale University Press, 2004.

Guanche Pérez, Jesús. *Chinese Presence in Cuba.* Havana: Ediciones GEO, 1999.

Guevara, Ernesto. "Guerrilla Warfare: A Method," in *Che: Selected Works of Ernesto Guevara.* Edited by Rolando E. Bonachea and Nelson P. Valdés, pp. 89–103. Cambridge, MA: MIT Press, 1969.

Kuethe, Allan J. *Cuba, 1753–1815: Crown, Military, and Society.* Knoxville: University of Tennessee Press, 1986.

Martí, José. *José Martí: Selected Writings.* Edited and translated by Esther Allen. New York: Penguin Books, 2002.

Martin, Susan Taylor. "Can We Learn from Cuba's Lesson?" *St. Petersburg Times,* September 9, 2005.

Martínez-Fernández, Luis. "Geography, Will It Absolve Cuba?" *History Compass* 2:1 (2004): 1–21.

Martínez-Fernández, Luis, D. H. Figueredo, Louis A. Pérez, Jr., and Luis González, eds. *Encyclopedia of Cuba: People, History, Culture.* Two vols. Westport, CT: Greenwood Press, 2002.

Matthews, Herbert. "The Cuban Story in *The New York Times,*" in *The Cuba Reader: History, Culture, Politics.* Edited by Aviva Chomsky, Barry Carr, and Pamela Maria Smorkaloff. Durham, NC: Duke University Press, 2003.

Moreno Fraginals, Manuel. *The Sugarmill: The Socioeconomic Complex of Sugar in Cuba, 1760–1860.* New York: Monthly Review Press, 1976.

Ortiz, Fernando. *Cuban Counterpoint: Tobacco and Sugar.* Durham, NC: Duke University Press, 1995.

Pérez, Louis A., Jr. *The War of 1898: The United States and Cuba in History and Historiography.* Chapel Hill: University of North Carolina Press, 1998.

Pérez, Louis A., Jr. *Cuba: Between Reform and Revolution* (second edition). New York: Oxford University Press, 1995.

Pérez, Louis A., Jr. "Cuba, c. 1930–1959," in *Cuba: A Short History.* Edited by Leslie Bethell. New York: Cambridge University Press, 1993.

Pérez de la Riva, Juan. "A World Destroyed," in *The Cuba Reader: History, Culture, Politics.* Edited by Aviva Chomsky, Barry Carr, and Pamela Maria Smorkaloff. Durham, NC: Duke University Press, 2003.

Pérez-Stable, Marifeli. *The Cuban Revolution: Origins, Course, and Legacy* (second edition). New York: Oxford University Press, 1999.

Phillips, Ruby Hart. *Cuba: Island of Paradox.* New York: McDowell Obolensky, 1959.

Phillips, Ruby Hart. *Cuban Sideshow.* Havana: Cuban Press, 1935.

Scarpaci, J., and Annie Z. Hall. "Cycling in Havana: 'Green' Transportation by Policy Default." *Sustainable Transport* 6 (summer 1995): 4–6.

Schlesinger, Stephen, and Stephen Kinzer. *Bitter Fruit: The Story of the American Coup in Guatemala* (expanded edition). Cambridge, MA: David Rockefeller Center for Latin American Studies, Harvard University Press, 1999.

Sierra, J. A. "History of Cuba. 1898." http://www.historyofcuba.com/cuba.htm. Accessed November 26, 2006.

Stanley, David. *Lonely Planet: Cuba* (second edition). Melbourne: Lonely Planet Publications, 2000.

Staten, Clifford L. *The History of Cuba.* New York: Palgrave Macmillan, 2003

Sublette, Ned. *Cuba and Its Music: From the First Drum to the Mambo.* Chicago: Chicago Review Press, 2004.

Suchlicki, Jaime. *Cuba: From Columbus to Castro and Beyond* (fourth edition). Washington, DC: Brassey's, 1997.

Syrett, David, ed. *The Siege and Capture of Havana.* London: Navy Records Society, 1970.

Szulc, Tad. *Fidel: A Critical Portrait.* New York: Avon Books, 1986.

Thomas, Hugh. *Cuba or The Pursuit of Freedom* (updated edition). New York: Da Capo Press, 1998.
Thomas, Hugh. *Conquest: Montezuma, Cortés, and the Fall of Old Mexico.* New York: Touchstone, 1993

CHAPTER TWO
Economics and Development

INTRODUCTION

Like most subjects related to contemporary Cuba, accurate and unbiased data on the Cuban economy is hard to come by. Insiders are often hesitant to show poor performance, and outsiders are often reluctant to believe positive results. A significant but ultimately unknowable portion of the economy operates underground and exists off the books. Moreover, although the island has been led by the same "maximum leader" for the past half-century and has had ostensibly the same state socialist economic system in place for all that time, the sometimes drastic changes in its economic development policies can be confusing to outsiders not armed with a healthy sense of nuance, complexity, and apparent contradiction (Mesa-Lago 2000). Indeed, like many other areas of contemporary Cuban life, nothing concerning the Cuban economy is as simple and straightforward as it at first may seem.

A common joke heard on the streets of today's Cuba vividly illustrates the ironic and contradictory nature of many of the revolution's accomplishments. "What are the three greatest achievements of the revolution?" asks a curious foreigner of a Cuban national. "Universal access to education and health care, the eradication of poverty, and the defense of the home-land," responds the proud Cuban. However, when the inquisitive visitor asks about the revolution's three most prominent failures, the same Cuban sarcastically responds, "Breakfast, lunch, and dinner!" This bitterly humorous anecdote highlights the fact that the revolution's economic development policies have always been much more successful at redistributing the country's wealth and ensuring egalitarian access to basic social services than it has at creating wealth or implementing development policies that achieve economic growth.

As Manolo, a sharp-witted middle-aged Cuban observed to me on my first visit to the island in 1997, "In Cuba the revolution was fought and won in order to divide the wealth of the country evenly among all Cubans. Instead, what has been divided up and shared evenly is poverty." He then wryly pointed out the irony that he and his fellow Cubans were well educated, in good health, and ensured basic access to food and clothing, but at the same time, *Somos un país de pobres* ("We are a country of poor people").

This anecdote reveals the fundamental contradiction in the socioeconomic development of revolutionary Cuba. On the one hand, one of the revolution's top priorities has always been the leveling of the economic inequalities that plagued 1950s Cuba. Cuba has also successfully guaranteed universal access to many social services, including health care, education, and social security, as well as chipping away at the age-old inequities based on region and race. In sum, though already a regional leader in the provision of social services before 1959, Cuba's laudable and uncompromising commitment to universal access to a wide array of social services allowed for the achievement of enviable levels of social welfare between 1960 and 1990.

On the other hand, these social gains have always been achieved at the expense of economic growth, through the sacrifice of many civil and political liberties, and predicated on overdependence on the Soviet Union. Moreover, after the collapse of the USSR and the loss of its economic support, the island began to experience the precipitous erosion of many of its social development indicators, not to mention the drastic contraction of its already poor profile in the area of economic growth, efficiency, and productivity.

Drawing mainly on the work of a variety of Cuban and Cuban-American economists and sociologists, this chapter

provides a critical analysis of the Cuban government's changing economic development strategy over the last half-century.
Specifically, after describing the economic profile of prerevolutionary Cuba, I trace five overarching stages in the revolutionary government's economic policy. The first stage began
with economic experimentation and debate, culminating in
the eradication of nearly all private enterprise and an unsuccessful drive at economic independence symbolized by the
all-or-nothing failure to harvest 10 million tons of sugar cane
in 1970. This was followed by the gradual reintroduction of
market-oriented mechanisms, including the allowance of
small-scale private enterprise between 1971 and 1985. However, in reaction to the Soviet Union's reform policies of perestroika and glasnost, between 1986 and 1989 private markets
and material incentives were rolled back as part of the
"rectification of errors and negative tendencies."

The economic crisis brought about by the fall of the USSR
between 1989 and 1991 forced the Cuban government to
grudgingly enact a series of economic reforms, which included
the search for foreign investment, the rapid development of a
tourism industry, and the re-emergence of a domestic private
sector (in both its clandestine and legal manifestations) during
the first years of the "special period" (1990–1996). However,
starting in 1996 and increasingly thereafter, economic reforms
have stalled, and the incipient growth of private enterprise has
been gradually scaled back in favor of ever greater economic
centralization, crackdowns on corruption and the "new rich,"
and a newfound reliance on international tourism, nickel
export, oil exploration, and increased aid and trade from
China and especially Venezuela (1996–2006).

CUBA'S ECONOMIC HISTORY AND THE SOCIOECONOMIC PROBLEMS OF THE 1950S

Historically, Cuba has long suffered under a classic form of
economic dependence first on Spain and then on the United

States. The island was first developed by the Spanish as a roadhouse for gold coming from the Spanish Main and then, after the British occupation of 1762, as a factory for sugar. As a result, Cuba became an archetypically extractive and destructive monocultural, slave-based, export-oriented, agricultural economy that understood "economic development" as mere plunder of the island's natural resources. By the second half of the nineteenth century Cuba came face to face with the central contradiction of all economic colonies: the Creole (native-born) bourgeoisie found itself increasingly torn between a rising sense of nationalism and continued reliance on Spain for economic viability and social order.

This contradiction was exacerbated by the rapidly rising importance of the United States as the island's main trading partner leading up to eventual independence. In fact, over the course of the nineteenth century the proportion of Cuban exports going to the United States grew from 27 percent in the late 1820s to 84 percent in the early 1890s. During this same period, sugar grew from comprising just 35 percent of Cuban exports to the United States in the early 1820s to making up almost 80 percent of exports in the early 1890s (Moreno Fraginals 2001). Tragically, the result of U.S.-sponsored independence in 1901–1902 under the Platt Amendment was renewed economic dependence (now almost exclusively on the U.S. market) and insertion into the world economy as a monocultural sugar producer ruled by systematically corrupt and often illegitimate governments (Díaz-Briquets and Pérez-Lopéz 2006. The central economic contradiction of Cuba's republican period (1902–1958), then, was ostensible political independence coupled with the deep penetration of the Cuban economy by U.S. investors and its organization for the benefit of U.S. interests linked with a small, powerful native oligarchy (Warren 2005: 4–5).

Despite the great controversy that surrounds the socialist path eventually taken by the revolution, there is general agreement about the island's key socioeconomic problems during the 1950s. Paradoxically, on the eve of what would prove to be Latin America's most far-reaching revolution, Cuba ranked among the top two or three countries in the region in most social and economic development indicators. This contradiction was further exacerbated by the island's ongoing (if decreasing) economic dependence on sugar exports and the U.S. market. Hopes of political independence, stable economic growth, and social equality had given way to increasing economic insecurity and a growing sense of national frustration (Pérez 1999). Essentially, this frustration was rooted in two domestic imbalances that were all too clear to many Cubans, yet often overlooked by outsiders, especially by those in the U.S. government.

The first was the fact that while Cuba remained near the top of regional socioeconomic rankings, it had all but ceased comparing itself with its Latin American neighbors, having become fully incorporated into the U.S. sociocultural orbit (Pérez 1995; 1999). Thus, while standards of comparison were extremely high, Cuba lacked the domestic economic base to live up to such high expectations. Indeed, a report prepared in 1958 by the British development agency, the Royal Institute of International Affairs, captured this fundamental paradox by uncovering that while Cuba's standard of living was higher than that of any other "tropical" country, and among the highest in the hemisphere, it was just one-third that of the American Southeast, traditionally the poorest region of the United States (RIIA 1958: 22).

Dependent economic relations with the United States compounded this sense of frustration. For example, between 1955 and 1958, 64 percent of Cuban exports went to the United States, and 73 percent of its imports came from there. The asymmetrical nature of this relationship was highlighted by the fact that only 3.2 percent of U.S. trade was with Cuba. Thus, while many middle- and upper-class Cubans liked to think of themselves as the equal partners of their northern neighbors, the fact was that Cuba was completely dispensable to the United States, while the United States was all but indispensable for Cuba. Consequently, the economic costs of a break in such a lopsided relationship would be inestimably huge for Cuba, but relatively negligible for the United States (Ritter 1974: 51, 55–56).

The second domestic imbalance, hidden by high aggregate socioeconomic indicators, was the concentration of Cuba's great wealth and substantial middle class in Havana, with little of that success managing to "trickle down" to lower income groups or out to rural areas (Warren 2005: 5–6). Essentially, Cuba was one nation with two distinct socioeconomic realities. Skilled, urban, industrial workers benefited from high wages and were well protected by Cuba's strong labor unions, while isolated, rural, agricultural workers suffered from extremely low wages and chronic unemployment and underemployment especially harsh during sugar's eight-month "dead season" (Mesa-Lago 2000).

Furthermore, health and educational services, advanced for urbanites and especially so for those who could afford Havana's many private schools and hospitals, were notoriously absent from most rural areas. The 1953 census showed that illiteracy rates were 3.6 times higher in rural than in urban areas (41.7 percent vs. 11.6 percent). Such chronic regional inequities led to an increase in rural-urban migration during the decade. However, the insufficient growth of urban employment combined with high barriers to entry into skilled, unionized jobs transformed many migrants into shantytown dwellers and informal workers (ibid.: 172).

ECONOMIC EXPERIMENTATION AND COLLECTIVIZATION, 1959–1970

Given the revolution's ambitious goals of reducing income inequality, eradicating unemployment, raising the standard of living for all, ending chronic economic dependence on a single crop and a single market, promoting democratization, and creating a "new man" (Ritter 1974), there were a variety of economic developmental strategies open to the new government upon the revolutionary triumph in 1959. First, there were the radical (but not communist) measures announced by Castro in his well-known 1953 defense speech "History Will Absolve Me" (Castro 1967). A second, more specific development strategy was laid out in the "Economic Thesis of the 26th of July Movement," which was first published in 1958 and expressed the economic vision of the moderate wing of the 26th of July Movement (Ackerman 2004). While not openly socialist, this plan favored an increased role for the government in "democratically planning" the economy to ensure social justice, a greater redistribution of national income, and an increased participation of Cuban firms in the economy (Ritter 1974: 63–67, 226).

A third path, openly favored by Ernesto Guevara, was the institution of revolutionary communism, including not only nationalization of major U.S.-owned industries but also the collectivization of all the means of production under state ownership, an end to the private sector, and the replacement of the market by a central plan. Finally, there was the option likely expected by the majority of Cuba's moderate middle class: a return to pre-Batista business as usual, with a restoration of the 1940 Constitution and a focus on bringing honesty to public office, without attempting to alter significantly Cuba's economic base or external dependency (ibid.: 68–70, 226). It is likely that all but this final option would have been seen as a threat to U.S. economic interests and as such provoke an antagonistic response. However, it is equally likely that choosing the "business as usual" path would have made the achievement of nearly all of the radical nationalist goals outlined by Castro in his 1953 speech impossible.

Neither the radicalization of the revolution along the socialist path advocated by Guevara, nor its ultimate consolidation and survival, was at all clear in January 1959. Moreover, this ultimate outcome did not develop smoothly over the

In the wake of the failed U.S.-backed invasion of Cuba at the Bay of Pigs, President John F. Kennedy warned, "Those who make peaceful evolution impossible, make violent revolution inevitable." Mocking this sentiment, Cuban Economic Minister Ernesto "Che" Guevara delivers a famous speech denouncing Kennedy's Alliance for Progress with the words, "the Alliance for Progress is not for Cuba but against her... [It] is a vehicle designed to separate the people of Cuba from the other peoples of Latin America, to sterilize the example of the Cuban revolution, and then to subdue the other peoples according to imperialism's instructions." Guevara is flanked by other delegates to the Inter-American Economic and Social Conference of the Organization of American States (OAS) on August 8, 1961 in Punta Del Este, Uruguay. (Bettman/Corbis)

course of the 1960s. Instead, between 1959 and 1963 the revolution was consolidated politically, and Soviet-style central planning aimed at diversification and industrialization was instituted. A sharp change in development strategy (a return to sugar specialization) took place after mid-1963 and lasted until 1970, along with renewed debate and experimentation over just which kind of socialism would be built in Cuba. Finally, between 1966 and 1970, Cuba strove to achieve full collectivization, throwing all of its force behind Guevara's radical

The U.S. Embargo I—The beginning

While the particular political and economic direction that the Cuban Revolution would take upon coming to power in January 1959 remained unclear through most of that first year, the United States almost immediately recognized the new Cuban government and replaced its inflexible pro-Batista ambassador, Earl E. T. Smith, with the more experienced and cooperative career diplomat Phillip W. Bonsal. Despite Bonsal's efforts to work with Castro, diplomatic relations went from bad to worse because of the increasingly radical, unaccommodating direction the new government had chosen and the secret plans already incubating in Washington aimed at destabilizing and overthrowing the new Cuban regime.

The year 1960 saw the trading of economic blows between the two erstwhile economic partners beginning with the refusal of U.S. oil refineries to accept Soviet crude (at the direction of the U.S. State Department). That action was followed by Cuba's nationalization of those refineries, which was followed in turn by the suspension of the U.S. sugar quota—a veritable act of economic war. Sealing the acrimonious relationship was Cuba's decision to accept the Soviet offer to step in and purchase the remainder of the quota and then, later in the year, to announce the nationalization of all U.S. properties and companies. After that precipitous deterioration in relations between the two governments, Bonsal was recalled to Washington in late October with diplomatic relations definitively broken as 1961 dawned over a new Cuba.

In fact, on October 19, 1960, days before returning to the United States, Bonsal witnessed the implementation of the first elements of what became the infamous U.S. embargo, always referred to as the *bloqueo* ("blockade") by the Cuban government. Starting on that day, the Eisenhower administration began to prohibit all U.S. exports to the island except for non-subsidized food, medicine, and medical supplies. A little over a year later President John F. Kennedy made the embargo total, by prohibiting all exports and imports, with exceptions requiring a special license. By May of 1964 the U.S. Commerce Department had instituted an unofficial policy of henceforth denying all such requests, including food and medicine (Schwab 1999: 54).

vision of a new society peopled by selfless "new men." In the process, the last remnants of the private sector were subsumed under the "revolutionary offensive" of 1968.

Che Guevara, the "New Man," and the Great Debate

Largely a myth to the children (and grandchildren) of the revolution and an overcommercialized if still vaguely rebellious image to most of the rest of the Western world, Ernesto "Che" Guevara was one of the Cuban Revolution's most important and influential economic thinkers. Apart from being a major theoretician and practitioner of guerrilla warfare, Guevara was one of the main planners and protagonists in setting the economic goals and building the economic institutions of Cuban socialism before his departure from public life and re-entry into clandestine guerrilla struggle in late 1965.

While Guevara's economic ideas are complex, his most powerful, seductive, and influential idea was distilled in the concept of the "new man." Essentially, Guevara believed that the heroic self-sacrifice and moral motivation that were essential to the success of revolutionary triumph could be rekindled and powerfully applied to the day-to-day economic tasks of the new socialist society in the making. As he declared in his famous 1965 essay "Socialism and Man in Cuba," the challenge was "to find the formula to perpetuate in day-to-day life the heroic attitude of the revolutionary struggle," because "in the attitude of our fighters, we could glimpse the man of the future" (Guevara 1997).

In building the new economic base of socialism in Cuba, Guevara feared resorting to capitalist methods of individualism and material incentives. He argued against the capitalist idea of work as a means to personal enrichment, professional advancement, and social prestige. As such, he felt that it would be disingenuous to build socialism by using the tools of capitalism. For him, economic growth and development would be achieved only at the unacceptable price of sacrificing individual consciousness and revolutionary ideals. Instead, he argued that a new consciousness (the "new man") must be constructed, along with a new socialist society. It was thus impossible to create the "new society" without simultaneously creating a "new man."

As idealistic as it sounds today, Guevara believed that only moral incentives could engender what he considered to be the ultimate, socialist values of humanity: selflessness, altruism, sacrifice for the greater good, human solidarity, dedication to a cause, and a sense of duty—in short, a new revolutionary consciousness, what he and Fidel called simply, *conciencia.* Unfortunately for the Cuban economy of the 1960s, in practice, the ideals of moral incentives, work as a social duty, non-coercive voluntary labor (the three pillars of the consciousness of the "new man") often resulted in dramatic economic failures on a national scale

Hundreds of thousands of Cubans selflessly invested their lives, talents, and hopes in the revolutionary project by joining literacy brigades, volunteering for weekend sugar harvesting duty, signing up to go abroad on international or military missions. However, the individual moral transformation of thousands of people often against the dictates of both economic logic and human nature has always proven to be an unrealistic, even naive project of diminishing returns. Even worse, when revolutionary preaching and consciousness have proven insufficient to call into existence more than a handful of Guevara's "new men," political manipulation, opportunism, and coercion have been utilized to build socialism and save the revolution from economic ruin. This hypocritical cycle has produced a socialist version of alienation and disillusionment leading in turn to inefficiency, low productivity, systematic pilfering, and a duplicitous consciousness—what Cubans facetiously call *la doble moral.*

Because Cuba's initial attempt to establish central planning and industrialize its economy faltered, the Cuban leadership

The one peso bill (top) and coin (right) feature the likeness of José Martí. The three peso note (bottom) and coin (left) feature the visage of Ernesto "Che" Guevara, the first head of Cuba's Revolutionary National Bank. (Ted Henken)

decided to shift its priorities back to sugar production once again, starting in 1964 (Mesa-Lago and Pérez-López 2005; Ritter 1974: 167). This return to sugar was quite ironic, since monocultural dependence had long been blamed for Cuba's weak position vis-à-vis its international trading partners prior to the revolution. However, the costs of producing cane sugar in Cuba for its fraternal allies in the Soviet bloc were much lower than those incurred in Eastern Europe's beet sugar production. Furthermore, the very low input costs and high earnings that were ensured by access to large markets with stable prices, combined with the increase in world free market sugar prices at the time, convinced the leadership to return to sugar-centered development (Ritter 1974: 167). Thus, in a few short years revolutionary Cuba's development strategy shifted from rejecting sugar dependence as an obstacle to embracing it as a partial solution.

Unfortunately, the return to sugar monoculture was undertaken with the same overzealousness and lack of planning that had been characteristic of the failed industrialization campaign. Moreover, this return to sugar was combined in the latter part of the decade with an ideologically motivated march toward full collectivization, resulting in a ultimately disastrous belief that sugar production was both the material and symbolic salvation of the revolution. In the process, any pretense of following a moderate Soviet-style plan based on the selective utilization of material incentives and the private sector was abandoned.

Before he was to renounce his Cuban citizenship and depart the island to spread the revolution to other lands, Guevara led the domestic fight for the creation of a radical form of socialism that had at its base the belief in the malleability of human nature. In Marxian terms, he and his followers held that "subjective conditions" (the ideas, consciousness, and social morality of the "new man") could overcome Cuba's "objective conditions" of low natural resource endowments, weak productive forces, and lack of infrastructure. In Guevara's thinking, the transformation of consciousness would be achieved by consciousness raising, voluntary work, labor mobilization, and re-education on a massive scale, with patriotism and solidarity replacing greed and self-interest as motivating factors (Mesa-Lago 2000: 195–196). On the material and institutional level, the market and pricing would be abolished completely and replaced by full collectivization, highly centralized planning, and the rationed allocation of consumer goods (ibid.; Martínez Heredia 2003).

Staunchly opposed to the Guevarist model was a group of communists loyal to Soviet pragmatism in economic matters led by economist Carlos Rafael Rodríguez, one of the founders of Cuba's original Communist Party in 1925. Essentially, the pragmatists argued that Cuba, an underdeveloped country sorely lacking in the material conditions necessary for the immediate achievement of communism, must first develop a material base before embarking on the creation of the "new man." Toward that end, Rodríguez favored the implementation of a reform-minded socialism that made selective use of market mechanisms in the construction of Cuba's new socialist society. Only after objective, material conditions had been transformed could Cuba begin to transform subjective consciousness (Mesa-Lago 2000: 196).

This group also resisted full collectivization of the means of production, arguing that the premature elimination of all markets and the private sector would only lead to popular resentment and economic stagnation. They insisted that Cuba was not yet prepared to make the sacrifices and fill the gap left by the inevitable contraction of goods and services that the abolition of the market would engender. Rodríguez and his supporters advocated the distribution of goods based on work and were willing to accept a degree of inequality, which they considered the only way to enhance productivity and efficiency.

One historical anomaly of this important mid-decade debate over alternative socialist models is the fact that Castro, who had largely stayed out of this ideologico-economic imbroglio while it was going on, eventually threw his full authority behind the radical Guevarists and their arguments for full collectivization and total elimination of the market. Ironically, by mid-1966, when Castro publicly embraced

Guevara's radical economic policies, pushing them even further than Guevara himself had advocated, both Rodríguez and Guevara had already renounced their official posts and presumably no longer had any direct influence on policy making.

The Radical Experiment and the "Revolutionary Offensive," 1966–1970

What is often referred to as the "radical experiment" was an attempt to establish greater economic independence from the Soviets, while reintroducing the all-important element of *conciencia* (revolutionary consciousness) into the economy. In the summer of 1966, Castro announced the new radical direction that the economic organization of revolutionary Cuba would take. Over the next four years, Castro took Guevara's economic model and implemented it in a more radical and idealistic fashion than even Guevara had contemplated. As a result, the Cuban economy began to operate both beyond market principles and outside any bureaucratic central plan. Instead, economic decisions were based almost entirely on Castro's fervent belief in the power of *conciencia*. As with the against-all-odds guerrilla victory over Batista, economic challenges were to be conquered through the passionate application of revolutionary faith, struggle, and consciousness (Domínguez 1993: 108–109; Mesa-Lago 2000: 209–211).

Rules restricting rural-to-urban migration were strengthened, and excess urban employees were dismissed and reassigned to work in the countryside (Mesa-Lago 2000: 203). Voluntary weekend agricultural labor, as well as the use of students, soldiers, and convicts in the sugar harvest, became commonplace. Furthermore, starting in 1965 the infamous UMAP (Unidades Militares de Ayuda a la Producción) work camps were set up in an effort to re-educate "antisocial" elements through hard agricultural labor. Loafers, dissidents, religious believers, political prisoners, homosexuals, as well as youths who had decided to drop out of school or society were forcibly assigned to these camps (Pérez-López 1995: 72).

At the heart of the radical experiment lay two specific labor-related campaigns. Perhaps because it was such a colossal failure and led to the "taming" of the revolution during the 1970s, the best-known of these is the 10-million-ton sugar harvest of 1970. In his now patented, ad-hoc, charismatic style of leadership, Castro declared, quite arbitrarily, that producing anything less than 10 million tons of sugar in 1970 would be tantamount to a "moral defeat" of the revolution (Mesa-Lago 2000: 213). Thus the year 1969 was officially christened *El año del esfuerzo decisivo* ("the year of the decisive struggle"), while 1970 was baptized *El año de los diez millones* ("the year of the ten million"). For a period of eighteen months (folding part of the 1969 totals into 1970), every resource available was recklessly diverted toward the singular goal of achieving *los diez millones.*

However, Castro's attempt to free Cuba from economic dependency and political fealty to the Soviet Union and thus gain some economic freedom and maneuverability in the midst of the ideologically polarized Cold War was unsuccessful. Although a record 8.5 million tons of sugarcane were harvested, the elusive 10-million-ton goal was not achieved. The failure of this massive undertaking caused a major shift in Cuban socialism, leading to the institutionalization of a more strictly Soviet economic model in the country, with important implications for Cuban life during the 1970s. Despite the failure of the *esfuerzo decisivo* and the economic dislocation it caused, Cubans refused to be outdone by Fidel's constant mobilizations and revolutionary rhetoric. Instead, in a classic show of their own undying *choteo* (biting mockery of authority), they quietly rechristened the whole abortive effort, *El año del esfuerzo de si vivo* ("the year of the struggle to see if I'll survive") (Guillermoprieto 2004).

Coming during the lead-up to the push for a 10-million-ton sugar harvest in 1970 was a lesser-known economic campaign called the Revolutionary Offensive. Taking place in March and April of 1968 (just before Castro's endorsement of the Soviet's suppression of the Prague Spring), this offensive against the last remnants of private trade made crystal clear the Cuban government's antagonistic attitude toward the remnants of private enterprise. The stated objectives of the campaign were "to eradicate completely the individualism, selfishness, and antisocial behavior engendered by private ownership, to eliminate alienation and exploitation, to destroy the consumption privileges obtained by the private operators" (Ritter 1974: 237). In a single legislative act, the Cuban government banned self-employment, confiscated the country's still remaining 58,000 small private businesses, and eliminated farmer's markets and family gardens on state farms (Acosta 2003; Mesa-Lago 1969; Mesa-Lago and Pérez-López 2005: 10; Pérez-López 1995: 37–38; Ritter 1974: 238).

In the end the radical experiment failed, because human nature was not as malleable as the Cuban leadership had originally believed. The failure to achieve economic independence, create the "new man," and reach the 10-million-ton goal originated in the government's naive belief that self-interest could or even should be completely eliminated. First, the labor mobilization system put in place was one of absolutes. The capitalist man was to be completely eliminated and replaced by the "new (communist) man." In such a battle there would be no room for failure, and old selfish habits would not just be tempered but completely eradicated. Second, in such a process, work would become a social duty and be seen not only as a means toward greater production but also as an end in itself that would cleanse people of their selfishness. Such an all-or-nothing approach to the economy eroded personal freedoms. Third, when the objectives of the state become sacrosanct, civil society and political debate become unnecessary. The guiding truths of the revolutionary process had already been "revealed" to the leadership, and opposing or even questioning them was considered counter-revolutionary.

Part of the failure in achieving many of the stated goals of the radical experiment was surely the result of the autocratic and coercive methods of labor mobilization that were utilized. As it became increasingly apparent that *conciencia* alone was not enough to motivate Cuban workers, militarization of the labor force was used to fill the void. Conscripts, students, prisoners, declared emigrants, and weekend volunteers were all put to work under militarized labor arrangements (Pérez-Stable 1999). The "new man" was to be created in a schematic four-fold process that included political (re)education, the supervised practice of hard labor, following the example of the leadership, and working with the support of the party and the mass organizations (Ritter 1974). Despite massive re-education campaigns and government control of schooling and the mass media, Guevara's dream of transforming the Cuban population into a loyal cadre of new men and women bore little fruit. "Voluntary" manual work in agriculture for forty-five days a year became a duty for all true revolutionaries as part of their consciousness training. Furthermore, this same hard work, combined with political education, was also seen as a cure for all types of "antisocial behavior," including homosexuality, laziness, and decadent Western youth culture, exemplified by long hair, blue jeans, and rock and roll.

In the end, however, such methods tended to exacerbate antisocial and unproductive behaviors such as absenteeism, black market activities, loafing, and a general cynicism and distrust toward the revolution—the polar opposite of *conciencia*. Conceiving of the creation of the "new man" as an all-or-nothing project, in which individual self-interest and "the good of society" are necessarily mutually exclusive, led to a fundamental breakdown in Cuba's economic system. As a result of that breakdown, during the next decade and a half, Cuba introduced a moderate Soviet model that would make strategic use of the market and, especially after 1980, the private sector in self-employment, food markets, and housing construction. Indeed, after the catastrophic performance of the previous economic development model, the revolutionary government was left with little choice.

FROM RADICALISM TO SOCIALISM, 1971–1985

The end of the first stage of the revolution was signaled by three key events coming between 1967 and 1970. Externally, the ethic of exporting revolution to the Third World and "turning the Andes into the Sierra Maestra of Latin America," in Castro's provocative turn of phrase, died in Bolivia in 1967 with its greatest proponent, Che Guevara. A year later, upon Cuba's support of the Soviet invasion of Czechoslovakia, Castro signaled that Cuba's days of actively defying the USSR were temporarily over. Finally, on the domestic front, the catastrophic failure of the push for the 10-million-ton sugar harvest discredited the ethic of mass labor mobilizations and moral rewards, leading the regime to retreat to a more moderate version of socialism that would make strategic use of the market, institute material incentives, mechanize sugar production, and, after 1980, allow for private entrepreneurship in self-employment, farmer's markets, and housing construction.

During this fifteen-year period, Cuba's economic development model of export-led growth remained unchanged. Sugar was not abandoned, but its production was mechanized and modernized (Eckstein 1994). Also, Cuba's labor mobilization strategy shifted toward material rewards as an incentive for workers. This change had a positive effect on efficiency and productivity, but likely increased inequality and unemployment from previously low levels. Workers were paid according to the quality and quantity of work done, and some goods were distributed on the basis of productivity. At the same time, the 1971 vagrancy, or "Anti-Loafing," law signified that work was now understood not simply as a "sacred right" but as a "revolutionary obligation" (Ritter 1974: 333).

The state could not provide employment to everyone and allowed many small service-oriented businesses and self-employment activities to proliferate. The leadership also encouraged Cubans to grow, buy, and sell their own food, attempting to stimulate greater production, improve distribution, and at the same time undermine the black market and do away with rationing. These changes were implemented partly as a response to the economic stagnation provoked by the idealistic errors of the 1960s and partly because of the economic downturn in the second half of the 1970s caused by a drop in the world market price of sugar (after a price boom in the early 1970s). In short, the government found that it could not provide for all Cubans and was forced to open up the economy to allow them to provide for themselves.

Between 1971 and 1977, the Central Planning Board (JUCEPLAN) was revitalized and adopted a more market-oriented planning mechanism called the Economic Management and Planning System (Sistema de Dirección y Planificación de la Economía, SDPE). The SDPE extended some autonomy to state enterprises, eliminated voluntary labor, and allowed for the reintroduction of wage scales, work quotas, and material incentives. Although implemented slowly over the late 1970s and early 1980s, the SDPE also provided enterprise managers with more autonomy and independent authority with which to make economic decisions, and it allowed enterprises to keep a measure of profits to be distributed as work bonuses at the end of each year or reinvested into the enterprise itself. Along with these bonuses, overtime pay was used as a new and effective incentive for workers (Domínguez 1993: 113). Ideologically, the SDPE was oriented away from the spirit of revolutionary consciousness, which had supposedly won the revolution, toward a new way of problem solving that emphasized the "economic man" over the "new man" (Eckstein 1994).

Between 1971 and 1975, Cuba saw substantial economic growth brought about by the internal state sector reforms associated with the SDPE, as well as the formalization of

Soviet trade and aid relations. In the mid-1970s, Cuba joined the Soviet bloc's Council of Economic Mutual Assistance (CEMA). Also, a rise in the world market price of sugar and an opening to Western markets that had been closed during the 1960s were new factors that led to positive economic performance. By 1976, however, the price of sugar began to fall, Cuba's international debts were on the rise, and would, in the near future increase to support international commitments (such as Cuban troops in Africa). These changes provoked a downturn in the domestic economy and an increase in black market activity and state sector corruption.

Toward the close of the 1970s, two increasingly intractable problems resulted from the institution of the SDPE and its allowance of relatively decentralized and autonomous economic decision-making. These problems were unemployment and corruption. Unemployment was caused by the new emphasis on enterprise profitability and efficiency (Pérez-Stable 1998) and by entrance into the labor market of the mini–baby boom generation of 1959 to 1965 (Mesa-Lago 1988). Strategies aimed at absorbing unemployment included the allowance of early retirement, the barring of women from certain jobs, the expansion of the armed forces, and an increase in the number of professionals who were sent abroad on international missions. This process peaked with the unplanned exodus of 125,000 Cubans in the Mariel boatlift in 1980. A final strategy that helped pick up the slack of unemployment was the expansion of the private sector through the opening of free farmer's markets (*mercados libres campesions*, MLCs) and the acceptance of limited self-employment (Mesa-Lago 2000: 246–247).

Corruption was addressed with a two-pronged approach combining a crackdown on growing illegalities through the passage of new laws on "crimes against the national economy" (Pérez-López 1995: 62–75; Rosenberg 1992: 55) with a gradual opening of legal private enterprise. The hope was to eliminate the black market, increase productivity, and allow the private labor market to absorb some of the excess

The Soviet subsidy—size and importance

Between 1960 and 1990, Cuba received the equivalent of $65 billion from the USSR. That total does not include credits and aid received from the other sister socialist republics of the CEMA or the more than $6 billion in credits and loans from European and Latin American countries received before 1986 when Cuba discontinued payment on its foreign debt. The Soviet subsidy came in at an average of $2.17 billion per year over these thirty years. This aid was delivered in two ways. An estimated 40 percent came as non-repayable price subsidies, and the other 60 percent arrived as loans that were never repaid. In fact, during this entire thirty-year period, Cuba repaid just $500 million of the roughly $39 billion it borrowed from the USSR (less than 2 percent).

The U.S. embargo has cost Cuba dearly, and especially after being strengthened three different times since the economic crisis that began in 1990 (the Torricelli Act in 1992, the Helms-Burton Act in 1996, and the new regulations imposed by the Commission for Assistance to a Free Cuba in 2004 and 2006). However, the Soviet aid received during the first thirty years of the revolution more than compensated for the negative economic impact of the U.S. embargo (estimated by Cuba to be about $30 billion by the early 1990s). This balance places the onus for Cuba's economic problems on its inability to diversify its exports, its overdependence on and misuse of Soviet trade and aid, and its inflexible socialist economic system (Mesa-Lago 2000: 608–609; Mesa-Lago and Pérez-López 2005: 83).

workers. However the existence of *sociolismo* (camaraderie and favor exchange) among workers and between managers and workers made it difficult for managers to enforce strict labor discipline. Informal arrangements between workers and managers led to planned slowdowns, deals to easily exceed work quotas in half the workday, as well as illegal appropriation of state supplies and elite privilege-taking (Eckstein 1994: 56–57; Fernández 2000; Mesa-Lago 2000: 246; Pérez-López 1995: 97–105).

The U.S. Embargo II—The Carter thaw, family visits, and the Mariel boatlift

Beginning under the Gerald Ford administration and greatly expanded by Jimmy Carter (1976–1980), the United States attempted to soften the impact of the embargo without quite revoking it. First, at great personal risk, a number of Cuban-Americans including Bernardo Benes initiated a private "dialogue" with the Cuban government aimed at making possible family visits to the island for the first time since the early 1960s and at wining the release of more than 3,000 political prisoners languishing in Cuban jails (Levine 2002; Ojito 2005). Second, the Carter administration joined the talks to successfully win the release of the prisoners, and both governments agreed to allow more than 100,000 family visits in 1978 and 1979. Finally, the governments agreed to set up "interests sections" in each other's capitals to make possible diplomatic representation despite the continued lack of official diplomatic relations. However, these efforts at rapprochement were derailed by two major events: Cuba's entry into civil wars in Somalia and Ethiopia in the late 1970s, and the refugee crisis known as the Mariel boatlift (Mesa-Lago and Pérez-López 2005: 187).

Ironically, the exodus of 125,000 people from the port of Mariel in less than six months in the summer of 1980 was provoked in part by the demonstration effect of the visits of relatively happy, healthy, and wealthy Cuban-Americans during the two previous years. In short, Cubans on the island began to ask themselves exactly why they continued to sacrifice for a revolution that had not been able to provide a standard of living equal to that seemingly achieved in the United States in so short a time by their relatives, who en masse had been labeled counter-revolutionary worms by the Cuban government. Mariel also allowed for the release of a pent-up migration pressure building over the previous decade when very few Cubans were able to emigrate. While the boatlift did give many Cubans the opportunity to start over in the United States, it was achieved at the cost of contributing to the lopsided loss of Carter in the 1980 elections, throwing U.S.-Cuban relations into a deep freeze for more than a decade under Reagan and Bush, and giving the Cuban-American community both a black eye and a "scarred face," based on the negative portrayal of the *Marielitos* by the U.S. news media (think Al Pacino, a.k.a., Tony Montana).

In the summer of 1978, the Cuban government approved Decree-Law 14 on self-employment. This new law legalized parts of the underground economy and was aimed at absorbing unemployment, improving the supply and quality of goods and services, and shrinking the black market (Pérez-López 1995). The law permitted individuals to perform needed services in some forty-eight occupations, including hairdressers, tailors, taxi drivers, photographers, plumbers, electricians, carpenters, and mechanics (Mesa-Lago 2000: 230). Certain professionals—physicians, dentists, and architects—were also allowed to become self-employed if they had been in private practice prior to 1959 (Pérez-López 1995: 95–96). The self-employed were required to simultaneously hold down a state job, work alone or with unpaid family help, register with the government, and pay a monthly fee and taxes. Finally, these private workers had to obtain a certificate from their state work center attesting to a history of "proper conduct, diligence, and work discipline" (Pérez-López 1995: 93–96).

Despite this small opening in the early 1980s, these economic reforms were stymied by the government's repeated criticisms that lumped legal operators together with illegal profiteers (Mesa-Lago 2000: 230). In 1982, the government raised taxes and initiated a crackdown on self-employment, sending confusing signals to potential entrepreneurs. The legalization of self-employment in 1978 was followed on April 5, 1980, by Decree-Law 66, which opened private agricultural markets, the so-called free farmer's markets (MLCs). The MLC law allowed all private agricultural producers (private farmers and members of agricultural cooperatives) to set up retail agricultural markets throughout the island. Products like sugar, tobacco, coffee, and beef, thought to be vital in the state sector, were prohibited from these markets. Likewise, private farmers were first required to meet their *acopio* quota obligations to the state before being allowed to sell their surplus in these free markets. Finally, farmers were restricted to their local markets and prohibited from using intermediaries or hiring nonstate trucks to transport their produce (Marshall 1998; Pérez-López 1995; Rosenberg 1992). Although both the legalization of self-employment and the establishment of the MLCs were carried out with Castro's approval, these reforms never had his active support and continued to be viewed as anachronistic and somewhat illegitimate, despite their legality.

Already by 1982, private entrepreneurs were being accused of using state stores as sales points for their own products, secretly and illegally setting up their own shops, diverting raw materials from the state sector, hiring employees and middlemen, selling goods for which they had no authorization and in places that were prohibited, as well as making exorbitant profits (Mesa-Lago 1988: 78–81). As a result of these criticisms many self-employed workers were arrested, and raids were carried out against many workers in the MLCs. Finally, in 1986 the increasingly moribund private sector finally received its coup de grâce. That year saw a new crackdown on self-employment and the MLCs that all but eliminated private economic activity from Cuba once again.

THE RECTIFICATION PROCESS: FROM PERESTROIKA TO *LA ESPERA ESTOICA,* 1986–1989

In 1986, Cuba surprised many people both on and off the island by loudly shifting its policy gears once again and declaring a national campaign to rectify errors and negative tendencies (also known as the rectification process, RP). First announced publicly by Castro at the February 1986 inauguration of the Third Party Congress, this campaign was enacted in response to both rising domestic tensions and to external pressures coming from the rapidly changing Soviet bloc, accumulated debt to the Paris Club, and an emboldened U.S. embargo under the Reagan and Bush administrations. However, the RP lasted for only about four and a half years, because of the even more surprising and sudden collapse of the Soviet bloc between 1989 and 1991 and the subsequent onset of a depressionlike economic crisis on the island.

On the domestic front, the Castro regime did away with the SDPE and replaced it with a less constraining but also less economically successful Economic Development System (SDE) that gave Castro more flexibility to intervene in the economy as he saw fit. The government also rolled back many of the domestic policies that had liberalized Cuba's internal markets in the late 1970s and early 1980s, eliminating peasant markets, self-employment, and nearly all remaining private farms, as well as scaling back private construction and housing swaps (*permutas,* see below) considerably. However, new policies that seemed on the surface to be a return to the ideological purity of the radical experiment were accompanied by other moves that contradicted the espoused socialist values and radical aims.

For example, while the vast majority of Cuban workers were subject to stricter labor discipline and a loss of many union rights, the government simultaneously used selective market mechanisms and material incentives to stimulate labor in the housing construction sector. Cuba turned again to constructing "micro-brigades," which had been eliminated under the SDPE because of the inefficiency of the surplus labor force used in them. When the micro-brigade strategy again proved incapable of building large-scale infrastructural projects, in 1989 the government turned to "construction contingents," this time granting workers special access to higher pay, better foods, and nicer living quarters in exchange for longer hours and better-quality workmanship. Additionally, these workers were much more carefully selected based on experience and skill than their micro-brigade predecessors (Mesa-Lago 2000: 276–277).

Externally, instead of refusing to deal with Western economies, the government began to open up to tourism and foreign investment, transforming some state enterprises into semiautonomous capitalistlike corporations. However, due in part to the decision to suspend its payments of foreign debt to Western countries, little foreign investment or tourism development actually took place as a result of the lack of fresh financing credits from the Paris Club. Finally, relations with the USSR went from good to bad, while those with the United States went from bad to worse. Cuba exacerbated its already strained relations with the Soviets by criticizing Gorbachev's policies of glasnost and perestroika and by stepping up its military commitments in Angola. This led to the reduction of Soviet price subsidies and the freezing of new credits and trade flows. Finally, continued tensions with the United States over migration issues and African wars resulted in the emboldening of the trade embargo, which Castro continued to exploit expertly as a justification for ever tighter control and the stamping out of the capitalist Trojan horse of microenterprise (Mesa-Lago and Pérez-López 2005: 13–14).

In its original incarnation, the RP was intended as a middle road between the ideological errors of the 1966–1970 radical experiment and the "economicist" excesses supposedly committed under the SDPE. However, in practice the RP resembled the former much more than the latter. For example, the idea of a central bureaucratic plan to organize the economy was virtually abandoned, and control of the economy was placed back in Castro's hands. Thus, not only was the RP moving in an opposite direction vis-à-vis the rest of the socialist world at the time but, in addition, it did so not as an integrated, alternative economic organization plan but as an uncoordinated, ad hoc program based on charismatic leadership and the mobilization of voluntary labor based on revolutionary ideology. It seemed that the leadership was acting not from strength but based on fear of the fallout of domestic economic reforms: a loss of revolutionary consciousness, rising social inequalities and tensions, and a weakening of the leadership's tight grip on power. This fear was combined with an anxiety at the simultaneous and unsettling developments in the international sphere.

Se Permuta—House swapping in socialist Cuba

In 1983, one of Cuba's leading divas, Rosita Fornés, joined forces with first-time director and screenwriter Juan Carlos Tabío to produce the topical comedy *Se Permuta* (*House for Swap*). While largely apolitical (unlike Tabío's later, more critically minded coproductions with renowned director Tomás Gutiérrez Alea, *Strawberry and Chocolate,* 1994, and *Guantanamera,* 1995), the aim of *Se Permuta* was to make light of one of the most common and frustrating socioeconomic challenges facing Cubans under the revolution: finding a place to live in a context in which buying or selling housing is illegal. While Cubans generally do not have to worry about finding affordable housing, given the revolution's urban reforms, they do face a political context in which there is no private real estate market, no money can legally change hands, and parties are forced to set up a "swap" of two (or three or four . . .) apartments of roughly equal value.

While this may be the perfect premise for a cinematic comedy, it is also the exasperating reality for everyday Cubans who are often forced to live with parents and grandparents far into adulthood or remain under the same roof with a former spouse (even after remarriage) because there is simply no place else to go. One difficult if ingenious solution to this reality has been the infamous *barbacoa,* converting the grand, high-ceilinged homes of Havana into split-level studios by simply constructing a horizontal division between them, uncomfortably cramping one's headroom while effectively doubling one's floor space.

Another common solution to the housing shortage has been for an underground housing market to develop complete with down payments, large cash transfers, and peculiar security deposits, all normally arranged by speak-easy and often crooked housing brokers, known in Cuba as *permuteros, corredores de permutas,* or simply *intermediarios.* Because this market, like all underground markets, is subject to its own rules and based largely on a precarious balance between mutual trust and mutual fear, there are common abuses and often creative brokerage arrangements.

(continued)

A good friend of mine who is a fairly wealthy, up-and-coming musician explained how he has been able to "swap up" over the years, living in a better, more spacious, and more centrally located apartment on each of my periodic visits to his Havana home. Upon each housing "swap," he would pay an intermediary to locate an apartment that met with his new specifications. In each case, he would also transfer between US$1,000 and US$8,000 to the other party, to "even out" the transaction. However, once after having paid a substantial sum to the owner of his future apartment, the deal fell through, and he discovered that the guy had already spent his down payment. Because they were both knee-deep in illegality, they came up with an ingenious solution: the other guy gave him his prized 1963 red Czechoslovakian Škoda Felicia convertible as compensation. However, this was a Pyrrhic victory, since he had to keep the classic car in a garage; he neither had a license nor knew how to drive and feared trying to sell the car illegally to recoup his lost money.

In the more trafficked areas of Havana, it is common to come across postings for housing swaps like the one described above. However, in the age of the Internet a number of sites have appeared promising to aid in legal, hassle-free, not-for-profit *permutas*. For example, the website *www.SePermuta.com* offers free publicity and search service on the Internet for housing transfers with the stated goal of directly benefiting Cuban residents and undercutting the position of middleman brokers.

While the RP went to great lengths to tear down the supposedly corrupting influences of market relations and the private sector, it offered little in the way of alternative development or labor mobilization strategies that had not been tried before and found wanting (Mesa-Lago 2000: 264). As the months passed, it became increasingly apparent that no one in Cuba was really sure what the RP was all about. In fact, in a classic expression of Cuban *choteo*, the RP was given the popular nickname, *la espera estoica* (the stoic wait), in reference to Gorbachev's own perestroika (restructuring) then taking place in the Soviet world (Bengelsdorf 1994: 142). Castro justified the RP to his Soviet patrons by arguing that it was better suited to the characteristics of the Cuban Revolution: broad poplar support, relative youthfulness, and lack of significant ethnic divisions or a Stalinist period of terror. While they respected Cuba's right of independence, the Soviets were critical of the misuse of their economic aid, especially in Cuba's military commitments in Africa and what they saw as Castro's disregard for basic economic laws in the ordering of Cuba's internal economy (Mesa-Lago 1990).

Like the radical experiment of 1966–1970, the RP's overall performance was ultimately negative for the Cuban economy. This poor performance was exacerbated by the fact that it was attempted on the eve of what would prove to be the worst economic crisis faced by the revolution. The depths of the 1990s crisis were due primarily to the collapse of the Soviet Union and the repercussions that had for an overdependent Cuba. However, the RP's ideological approach to economic problem solving had likely exacerbated the proliferation of the economic "crimes" it was supposedly designed to eradicate. Moral and ideological exhortations are weak tools with which to motivate workers in a context of growing scarcity. Furthermore, such scarcity makes for fertile ground for robbery, corruption, and the growth of the black market. In the end, the RP generated a major recession in the Cuban economy, with nearly all economic indicators performing negatively. The rate of economic growth deteriorated, fiscal and trade deficits grew out of control, and unemployment began to climb (Mesa-Lago and Pérez-López 2005: 14–15).

FROM SOCIALISM TO SURVIVAL DURING THE "SPECIAL PERIOD," 1990–1996

Any attempt to come to terms with Cuba's current socioeconomic reality must begin with the dramatic changes brought to the island by the collapse of the Soviet Union. Between 1989 and 1993, foreign trade fell by 75 percent because as much as 70 percent had been concentrated with the USSR. Literally hundreds of Soviet-funded development projects were abandoned as thousands of Soviet technicians returned home. The life-sustaining two-way trade of Cuban sugar and other agricultural products (purchased by the Soviets at above-market prices) and Soviet crude, along with other consumer goods (sold by the Soviets at generously low prices), came to a sudden halt (ibid.: 15).

As a result, Cuba's internal gross social product (*producto interno bruto*, PIB) dropped 3.1 percent in 1990, followed by drops of 25 percent in 1991 and 14 percent in 1992, effectively throwing nearly 20 percent of the island's labor force out of work (Bengelsdorf 1994; Mesa-Lago 1994). Finally, the minimum wage shrank to an astounding $2 a month in real purchasing power, with monthly pensions for the elderly worth just over $1 on the black market (Mesa-Lago 1994). In sum, although the Cuban economy had begun contracting at least as early as 1986, it was the almost overnight loss of the traditionally massive amounts of Soviet trade and aid that initially triggered Cuba's economic tailspin.

Reacting to these macroeconomic shocks, President Fidel Castro declared a "special period in peacetime" (*período especial en tiempo de paz*) to begin on August 30, 1990. As if under siege of war, Cubans were forced to make major sacrifices in all areas. The sudden contraction of imports translated into increasingly deeper levels of austerity for most Cubans, as hundreds of basic goods disappeared from the shelves of the island's stores. Rationing of increasingly scarce resources took on a new urgency and soon came to include virtually all products. Workdays were cut back because of lack of energy, reliable transportation, and food for workers' lunches. Newspaper publication and circulation and television and radio broadcasts were cut severely to save on scarce material resources. Long electricity blackouts of up to eighteen hours a day became the norm (Bengelsdorf 1994).

Table 2.1 – Growth in Cuban Gross Domestic Product (GDP), 1990–2006

Year	Annual Growth Rate (%)
1990	−2.9
1991	−10.7
1992	−11.7
1993	−14.9
1994	0.7
1995	2.5
1996	7.8
1997	2.5
1998	1.2
1999	6.2
2000	5.6
2001	3.0
2002	1.5*
2003	2.6*
2004	5.0*
2005	11.8*
2006	12.5*

(Source: Mesa-Lago 2005; Mesa-Lago and Pérez-López 2005; Pérez-López 2006; Peters 2002b)

* Growth rates for 2002–2006 are not comparable to those for earlier years because of changes to computation methodology, which attempt to include the value of free social services.

The ration booklet—A Cuban staple

By 1962, the Cuban government had nationalized all major industries and was thus responsible for producing goods and services in sufficient quantity and at prices manageable for the mass of citizens who had supported the revolution. Also by 1962, most consumer prices were centrally fixed by the government and most consumer goods were henceforth distributed through rationing (as opposed to market allocation based on supply and demand). The rationale for this approach was based on the belief that if prices were allowed to float freely, the scarcity of goods and liquidity of cash in circulation

(continued)

would cause runaway inflation, making prices of basic goods out of reach for the weakest members of society. It was just these humble masses who were the revolution's greatest beneficiaries and supporters. Thus the logic of rationing was based on both socialist egalitarian ideology and political expediency (Mesa-Lago 2000: 186).

When begun in 1962, rationing provided all citizens with access to a basic minimum of subsidized goods and foodstuffs. The extent of rationing, as well as the need for it and the ability of the state to provide daily necessities, has fluctuated considerably over time. For example, during the 1960s, the basic monthly ration per person included 3 pounds of meat or chicken, 1 pound of fish, 6 pounds of rice, 1.5 pounds of beans, 14 pounds of tubers, 2 pounds of cooking oil or fat, between 5 and 15 eggs, 1 pound of coffee, and 6 liters of milk. An assortment of other basic consumer items were also included, including sugar, bread, cigarettes, gasoline, detergent, soap, toilet paper, toothpaste, cigars, and beer.

However, after the "special period" began in August of 1990, 28 foodstuffs and 180 consumer goods that had previously been widely available were added to the list of rationed commodities. Also, after that time many items simply disappeared from government *bodegas* (and the ration booklet) altogether. At the same time, the government has managed to maintain its laudable commitment to provide children under seven with a daily ration of 1 liter of fresh milk (even during the height of the "special period"), while those over sixty-five were provided with a ration of six cans of condensed or evaporated milk monthly until 1994, when the economic crisis led to its elimination (ibid.: 387).

Since 1994, rationing has remained a staple of Cuban life even while Castro began to hint at its abolition in late 2005. However, because of the economic crisis, monthly rations often run out in less than two weeks, forcing Cubans to become very "inventive," with a variety of other sources for their daily sustenance. Also after 1994, the Cuban government allowed two new food markets to open: *mercados agropecuarios* ("agros") and the dollar stores. The so-called

(continued)

agros are farmer's markets where surplus farm products are sold at market prices (in Cuban pesos) by private farmers themselves. The dollar stores are government-run grocery stores, supermarkets, and department stores that provide more upscale, usually imported goods sold at high dollar prices (or in convertible pesos after late 2004). These changes allowed many Cubans to break free from exclusive reliance on government rationing, while those without access to hard currency continue to struggle to survive on the ration booklet's dwindling offerings.

While the revolution surprised many outsiders by both surviving and struggling to maintain its vaunted social priorities of health, education, and literacy (Uriarte 2002), Cuba's touted social services were hurt by the crisis. Vital medical and school supplies became virtually nonexistent, while social security, pensions, and real wages lost much of their value. Perhaps most alarmingly, young people still in school or just beginning their education had little incentive to continue their studies aimed at work in state jobs, given the almost insignificant value of their future monthly salaries compared with what they could earn in emerging nonstate, underground, or tourism-related activities (Bengelsdorf 1994: 166–168). Given this shift in incentives, the labor market began to privatize rapidly during the 1990s, with joint ventures, cooperatives, and self-employed workers beginning to attract a higher proportion of the Cuban workforce because they could promise a marginally better return on the investment of time and hard work. In 1981 the state sector had accounted for 91.8 percent of all workers, with just 8.2 percent employed privately. By 2000 state employment had eroded to 77.5 percent, with private sector employment rising to account for almost a quarter of the workforce (not counting the burgeoning underground economy and black market) (Uriarte 2002: 26–27).

A Cuban ration booklet (top) used for basic food items. The set of coupons (bottom) allows the bearer to buy selected clothes in state stores on a rotating basis. (Ted Henken)

The Fall of Cuba's Sugar Kingdom

One major area of initial contraction in the state economic sector was in Cuba's big three agricultural/mineral exports:

tobacco, nickel, and sugar. While tobacco and nickel eventually rebounded after the worst of the economic crisis, sugar, the veritable engine of the Cuban economy since at least the late eighteenth century, experienced an unprecedented crisis during the 1990s and by 2002 had ceased being the main driver of the island's development. For example, the sugar crop dropped by half from 8.4 million tons in 1990 to a mere 4.2 million three years later (Mesa-Lago 1994). Moreover, between 1989 and 2002, sugar's role in the composition of export trade dropped steadily from 73 percent to just 32 percent. Crisis-induced shortages and the inability of Cuba to upgrade and compete internationally caused the average annual sugar production to fall to 3.7 million tons between 1994 and 2003, an amount equal to less than half of Cuba's average annual production during the 1980s (Mesa-Lago and Pérez-López 2005: 42).

What's more, by 2002 the Cuban government came to the difficult and previously unimaginable conclusion that producing sugar for the world market was becoming more of an economic liability than a rational development strategy. Instead of attempting to revive the industry with an outpouring of new subsidies and investments, the government chose to "cut its losses" and fundamentally restructure the sugar industry, aiming at making it both less costly and more efficient and profitable (Peters 2003: 1). In May of 2002, after the completion of the 2001–2002 harvest, Castro announced a major downsizing of the sugar industry, including the closure of 45 percent of Cuba's mills (71 of 156) and the laying off or retraining of as many as one-third (120,000) of industry workers. By 2003, Castro explained what he called the "rationalization" of the industry to a group of visiting Americans, saying, "It's crazy to make an effort to produce something that costs more to make than to import" (ibid.: 4).

Later that same year, Pedro Alvarez, the head of Cuba's food import company, *Alimport,* offhandedly commented to a group of U.S. business executives that Cuba had actually

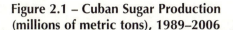

**Figure 2.1 – Cuban Sugar Production
(millions of metric tons), 1989–2006**

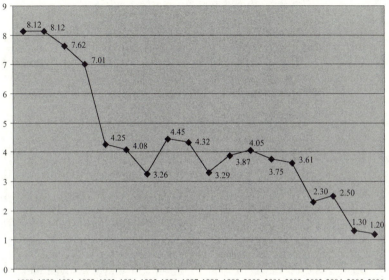

(Source: Mesa-Lago 2005; Peters 2003; Ritter 2006)

purchased "tens of thousands" of tons of sugar from the United States (ibid.: 1–4). As a result of this shift in economic priorities, Cuba harvested just 2.2 million tons of sugar in 2003, the lowest tonnage of any harvest since 1933, a year racked by unrest and governmental instability (Mesa-Lago and Pérez-López 2005: 66). Because of a series of fierce hurricanes and a devastating two-year drought, a new series of mill closures has begun since 2003, with depression and uncertainty seeping into mill towns across the country (home to 2 million of Cuba's 11 million inhabitants). As a result, the 2005 harvest was even more disappointing than that of 2003 and, at just 1.3 million tons, the lowest since 1908 (Frank 2005).

Because of the gradual disappearance of sugar as the developmental motor of the economy, Cuba has been

Boats, pigeons, camels, and Cuban "invention" "resolves" transportation crisis

My plane touched down at José Martí International Airport just after 9:00 P.M. on the last day of July 1997, at the peak of Cuba's sweltering summer. Then, as I left the airport and headed out into the Cuban night, I was met by a throng of boisterous, expectant Cubans who began to inundate me with offers for a ride. I was particularly struck when a slight man brushed past me, whispering, "*¿Taxi particular?*" ("Private taxi?"). He soon reappeared at the far back of the now thinning crowd, giving a sly glance that seemed say, "Well, what'll it be?"

I quickly assessed the situation and made a casual nod in his direction. Within minutes, he came to a screeching halt in front of me, sprang out of his small, Russian-made Lada, and began tossing my bags into his trunk, saying, *Rápido, rápido, para que no nos vean* ("Move quickly, so that they don't see us"). As we came out onto the main road, deserted except for an occasional car or, more commonly, a bicycle, my driver breathed a sigh of relief, explaining that he had once again successfully avoided an exorbitant fine for transporting a foreigner without a license. His relief was mingled with happiness, since his $10 fare (paid in U.S. dollars) was roughly the same as his monthly salary (in Cuban pesos) working as a meteorologist at the airport!

As never before, the 1990s were years when words like *inventar* ("to invent") and *resolver* ("to resolve") took on special coded meanings for Cubans. Nowhere was that more true than in the area of transportation, where Cubans prefer to leave unsaid exactly how they manage to use their unending "invention" creatively and often illegally, "resolving" their everyday problems. Like this resourceful *botero* ("boater," Cuban slang for a gypsy cabbie), the government has also been forced to develop its own inventive strategies to resolve the transportation crisis.

Two solutions have been harnessing the power of Chinese "pigeons" and Cuban "camels." First, between 1990 and 1992 as gas reserves dried up and Cuba's buses and cars were left idle in their garages, the government turned to China and

(continued)

brought in more than 1.2 million Flying Pigeon bicycles. Never one to miss a chance to turn a defeat into a revolutionary victory, Castro soon dubbed this the Bicycle Revolution, exhorting Cubans to use the bicycle as a healthy form of resistance against imperialism. In 1991 he even had the armed forces parade through the city on May Day atop their own bicycles, as an example for the people. Cuba soon had five of its own bike factories turning out lighter and more maneuverable brands, which were sold to the population at manageable peso prices (Baker 2000: 202–203).

A final, partial solution to Cuba's transportation crisis has been the appearance on Cuba's streets of the behemoth *supertrenbuses,* popularly known as *camellos* ("camels") for their distinctive double humped shape. Designed locally to save gas and provide transport to massive numbers of riders, these 20-ton *camellos* are designed to hold 220 passengers but normally are crowded with more than 300. In 2000 there were as many as 220 *camellos* roaming the streets of Havana each day, charging each rider the standard 20 centavo fare (equivalent to less than a penny). Cubans like to joke that riding on one of these metro-buses is like going to an R-rated movie, because of the likelihood of encountering violence, abusive language, and even sex (ibid.: 432)!

forced to turn to other, more market-oriented external and domestic mechanisms to reignite its failing economy and bring in foreign investment and hard currency. However, external and especially internal economic reforms have not been without their high prices in terms of ideological compromise and increasing social impacts in the area of socioeconomic inequality. In order to counteract that possibility, all laid-off sugar workers were ensured continuity of pay rates and full services in the *bateyes* (communities that surround sugar mills). They were also given the option of returning to school for retraining at full pay (Frank 2005; Peters 2003: 5).

The infamous Cuban camello, *a massive camel-shaped bus.* *(Ted Henken)*

External Economic Reform and Tourism

The special period has passed through three phases since it was first declared by Castro in August 1990. The first phase lasted from that initial declaration until the announcement of deeper, more socially jarring and contradictory internal economic reforms almost three years later, on July 26, 1993. As with previous promarket reforms in the 1970s and early 1980s, the economic reforms of the 1990s began with limited changes aimed at Cuba's external markets and internal "export" enclaves (foreign investment, joint ventures, and tourism). This external opening was combined with a set of state-enforced austerity measures that sought to utilize traditional popular mobilization strategies to confront the economic crisis.

During this first three years, the Cuban leadership made an attempt to bring in foreign investment in mineral extraction and the tourism industry, while exhorting the Cuban population to make greater sacrifices so that the revolution (and the regime) could survive the economic crisis without changing

As transportation became increasingly scarce during the 1990s, many trucks were converted into makeshift buses. This mode of transport is still common in Cuba's provinces. (Ted Henken)

its internal socialist economic policies or its authoritarian political structure. Only after initial external adjustments proved insufficient did the regime undertake a more fundamental economic restructuring of the island's internal economy. However, those economic changes were never intended to begin a transition toward capitalism. Instead, reforms were explicitly aimed at making possible the survival of socialism and "saving the revolution."

A principal area of economic growth arising from the needs of the special period has been tourism. Tourism has rapidly become the island's number one "export," recently pulling ahead of both sugar and hard-currency remittances. Tourist visits to the island have grown from a mere 275,000 in 1989 to almost 1.8 million in 2000, and the number of hotel rooms jumped from 5,000 in 1987 to more than 30,000 in 1999. Likewise, gross revenue from tourism jumped from just $243 million in 1989 to over $2 billion in 2000 (Peters 2002a). While Cuba's tourism economy did experience stagnation after 2000 because of the terrorist attacks of 2001, the

Table 2.2 – Cuban Tourism: Visitors, Revenue, and Countries of Origin, 1989–2005

Year	Visitors (thousands)	Gross revenues ($ million)	Leading source countries (2004 – thousands)	
1989	275	—	Canada	563
1990	340	243	Italy	179
1991	424	402	Spain	146
1992	461	550	Germany	143
1993	546	720	France	120
1994	619	850	Venezuela	86
1995	746	1,100	Mexico	80
1996	1,004	1,333		
1997	1,170	1,515		
1998	1,416	1,759		
1999	1,603	1,901		
2000	1,774	2,034		
2001	1,774	1,850		
2002	1,668	1,769		
2003	1,900	1,999		
2004	2,049	2,114		
2005	2,319	2,300 (estimate)		

(Source: Mesa-Lago 2005; Pérez-López 2006; Peters 2002a)

industry rebounded between 2002 and 2005 (Mesa-Lago and Pérez-López 2005: 42). In fact, Cuban tourism growth was back on track by 2005 with 2.3 million visitors arriving in that year (13.2 percent above the 2004 level). This new record number of tourists was combined with the fact that gross tourism revenue grew by 10.7 percent in 2004/2005, topping $2.3 billion.

These numbers do not include the tremendous effect that an end to the U.S. travel ban would have on Cuba's tourism industry. Ironically, the defiant nation that had once scoffed at foreign investment and decadent tourism from the capitalist West now finds itself forced to compete vigorously for hard-currency investment and to aggressively seek out partners for joint ventures in tourism. "Who would have thought," Castro asked in the summer of 1993, "that we, so doctrinaire, we who fought foreign investment, would one

The past and the future coexist in Havana. Standing on Calzada facing north toward the Malecón, this photo of the ultra modern Meliá Cohiba tourist hotel was taken through the massive window of a now ruined building. (Ted Henken)

day view foreign investment as an urgent need?" (Pérez 1995: 404). At the same time, the harnessing of tourism-led development in the context of extreme scarcity and

This photo of the tourist-friendly Plaza Vieja *in Old Havana shows both the renovations already completed and those still to be done.* (Ted Henken)

supposed socialist egalitarianism has forced Cuba to endure many of the social contradictions of Caribbean tourism, including ubiquitous prostitution and hustling, jarring inequalities between wealthy tourists and proud but poor natives, claims of "tourist apartheid," the cheap commodification of culture for tourist consumption, as well as concerns about environmental degradation.

Domestic Economic Reform, the "Second Economy," and Self-employment

Only after initial external adjustments proved insufficient between 1990 and 1993 did the regime undertake a more serious series of economic reforms in the island's internal economy. While never reaching the level of an all-out economic restructuring favored by some reformers, this second phase began with Castro's July 26, 1993, announcement of a host of internal economic reforms. Those reforms included the legalization of the dollar for use in the domestic economy (triggering a flood of Cuban-American travelers and remittances to the island), a reorganization of agricultural cooperatives, and the re-allowance of self-employment. Farmer's markets, now christened *mercados agropecuarios* (or agros) were reopened in 1994, further deepening the role of the island's private sector. Finally, in 1994/1995 the government sought to achieve greater fiscal flexibility and investment by creating a third, intermediary currency, between the U.S. dollar and the Cuban peso (MN). Called the "convertible peso" and popularly known as the *chavito,* this currency is pegged one-to-one with the U.S. dollar (Uriarte 2002: 23–25). At the same time, the government repealed previous bureaucratic investment rules by enacting a new foreign investment law in 1995 that, combined with new export processing zones (EPZs), sought to attract more outside investors (Mesa-Lago and Pérez-López 2005: 19).

Ironically, many of these economic reforms courted elements of capitalism and invited capitalists to help save Cuban socialism, admittedly running the risk of provoking new social tensions on the island. Also, many of these internal economic reforms were intended to decriminalize many of the very jobs, services, and transactions that were allowing Cubans to survive, and to strengthen the rapidly falling value of the peso. However, these significant reforms were enacted in a reluctant, piecemeal fashion, and were not integrated as a cohesive economic development plan (Fernández Peláez 2000; Mesa-Lago 2000: 293). Also, like the first series of external reforms, this internal opening to the private sector was justified as a necessary evil and never intended as the beginning of a move toward a mixed economy along the lines of the Chinese or Vietnamese economic models (Uriarte 2002: 26).

Although not new on the Cuban scene, Cuba's nonstate sector, or "second economy," has also expanded significantly during the special period. In fact, there is a consensus among government officials, analysts on the island, and scholars

Known to Cubans as the chavito, *Cuba's one peso note (top) (convertible peso, CUC) features the Cuban coat of arms with a key at the top center. In Cuba's other national currency (bottom) (moneda nacional, MN), which is what most Cubans earn their salaries in, a one peso note is worth just 1/26 of the chavito. This peso note from 2003 commemorates the 150th anniversary of Cuban independence leader José Martí's birth and features a rendering of the house where he was born in Old Havana in 1853. (Ted Henken)*

abroad that as the official, first economy has entered a major crisis since the early 1990s, the unregulated second economy has exploded in scope and size (Pérez-López 1995). An indicator of the growing economic importance of Cuba's second economy is the government's attempts to legalize and incorporate it into the official, first economy through the expansion of legal self-employment (*trabajo por cuenta propia*)

Casas particulares, *or privately run bed-and-breakfasts, have popped up all across the island catering to Cuba's many international tourists. They represent one of the few manifestations of legal private enterprise in socialist Cuba. (Ted Henken)*

(Henken 2002; Peters 2002b; Peters 2006b; Peters and Scarpaci 1998; Ritter 1998, 2000, 2004).

The size of the official self-employed sector has grown from 70,000 in December 1993 (just months after it was legalized) to 140,000 by May of 1994 (Jatar-Hausmann 1999; Peters and Scarpaci 1998; Smith 1999: 49). The unofficial government policy of alternately encouraging, repressing, and regulating self-employment has produced significant fluctuations in its size and composition since 1994. Although the sector reached its zenith in January of 1996 with 209,606 licensed operators, it shrank considerably thereafter as a result primarily of the institution of a quota-based, personal income tax later that same year. Likewise, the government's awareness that many of the self-employed either work without licenses or routinely "cut corners" to stay in business has caused the state to impose a law-and-order approach to the private sector. For example, in a March 1996, speech to the Party's Central Committee, Raúl Castro, observed,

> More than 200,000 citizens now engage in . . . self-employment . . . . It is evident that the real figure is much higher, since there are thousands more who engage in self-employment of some kind or another without the necessary authorization. . . . These [legal] self-employed workers should be the first to want to eradicate the new crop of speculators, thieves and violators of tax laws or health regulations—that is, those who wish to get rich off of the people's needs and hardships arising from the special period. . . . Severe punishment of those who break the law should serve to make everyone understand that crime has no future in a socialist country. (Castro 1996)

By April of 1997 official numbers of the self-employed sector had dropped to 180,919, falling further to 165,438 by April of 1998 (Jatar-Hausmann 1999; Peters 1997). Since then numbers have continued to drop, with the government marching out new offensives and obstacles to their growth and survival between 2003 and 2005 (Resolución No. 11 2004). Numbers had fallen to 153,800 by early 2001 (Espinosa Chepe 2002; National Office of Statistics 2001: 116), reaching 149,990 by 2003. Likewise, Cuba's famed speak-easy eateries, known as *paladares,* the one true example of private microenterprise allowed on the island, are reported to have dwindled from a peak of 1,500 in 1996 to just 150 by 2003 (Boadle 2003; Jackiewicz and Bolster 2003; Mesa-Lago and Pérez-López 2005: 52; National Office of Statistics 2003; Peters 2006b). My own interviews with both legal and clandestine *paladar* operators in Havana and Santiago between 2003 and 2006 confirm this downward trend. In fact, on a recent visit to Havana in April 2006, an anonymous government source confirmed that there were just 98 remaining licensed paladares in all of Havana.

La Guarida—strawberry, chocolate, and the Cuban *paladar*

Easily Cuba's most famous private *paladar* restaurant, La Guarida has served its delectable cuisine to a host of visiting dignitaries, including the king and queen of Spain, movie actor Jack Nicholson, and Nobel laureate Gabriel García Márquez. The reason for La Guarida's great success and popularity begins with the fact that it is located in the apartment in which the wildly successful, breakthrough Cuban movie *Fresa y Chocolate* (*Strawberry and Chocolate*) was filmed in 1993. Directed by Cuba's late master filmmaker Tomás "Titón" Gutiérrez Alea, the film treated the taboo subject of homosexuality in socialist Cuba in a sensitive and sympathetic way. Roughly translated as "The Hideaway," the restaurant's name originates with the nickname Diego, the homosexual character in the film, gave to his own third-floor apartment in the building.

The founder, owner, and operator of La Guarida, the affable entrepreneur Enrique Núñez, jumped on this opportunity after the film to become a worldwide success, converting a small part of what had been his parents' third-floor apartment in this truly impressive ruin of a building into what is now Cuba's most renowned *paladar*. In an interview, Enrique explained that following the international release and eventual worldwide popularity of the film, foreigners began to show up unannounced at the apartment to get a glimpse of the place where the film had been staged. "People came to the apartment because of the film," explained Enrique. "Again and again, they would tell us that the film changed their black-and-white image of Cuba, making Cuba real, close, and personal for them."

The tale of La Guarida's origin began when Enrique's brother-in-law, Andrés, showed him a copy of the screenplay to an upcoming film based on the Senel Paz short story entitled "The Wolf, the Forest, and the New Man." "As I read the screenplay, it occurred to me that the place Senel was describing was this very apartment. I suggested that they use it to shoot the film. Soon, Titón showed up and looked at the place and decided to do the film here." The rest, as they say, is history. However, Enrique admitted that at that point it never

(continued)

crossed his mind that he could later turn the apartment into a successful private restaurant.

The film was completed that same year and won best picture honors at the December 1993 Festival of New Latin American Cinema in Havana. In 1994, the film was released internationally and nominated for the best foreign film Oscar. It also won the award for best picture in many European festivals, including Cannes. During 1994 and 1995, the film's popularity spread across the globe. According to Enrique, this exposure led to a newfound interest in all things Cuban, giving a boost to the island's revitalized tourism industry. "No one can even calculate the amount of tourist dollars that have been brought to Cuba as a result of the film. I have witnessed it first-hand through this place," declared Enrique.

Thus the "House That Titón Built" became a mandatory stop on the tourist circuit for foreigners vacationing in Cuba. By mid-1995 uninvited knocks on the door became commonplace, with tourists from Japan, Scandinavia, and even the United States asking to tour their apartment. These never-ending visits gave Enrique what he called the "crazy" idea of transforming his parents' small apartment into a private restaurant. Since the possibility of opening such a business venture had just then been legalized, Enrique got his parents' approval and spent the next eight months pouring his savings and a number of loans into the apartment, turning his "crazy idea" into a reality. Friends chided him by reminding him that the apartment was on the third floor with no elevator, sat in the middle of a neglected and intimidating Cuban tenement, and was located in the middle of drab Central Havana, far from the usual tourist haunts. However, Enrique thought that it would be just those factors, mixed with the apartment's celluloid allure, that would ensure the venture's success. "Besides," he told me, "I had nothing else to do."

After much delay and anticipation, Enrique inaugurated La Guarida on July 14, 1996, inviting the entire cast of the film to the opening. In our interview, Enrique explained that the constant threat of fines from inspectors and the continuous search for hard-to-find supplies have been his biggest obstacles. Many times the items he needs are simply not avail-

(continued)

able in Cuba. He joked, "You should see my baggage whenever I return from a trip abroad. I pay a fortune in overweight charges!" However, he claimed that the best aspect of operating an independent business was the opportunity to meet people from around the world. Additionally, he admitted that he liked the challenge that the possibility of creating his own business presented. He joked, "Through this experience I realized that I was a born entrepreneur. However, the only problem is that I was born in the wrong country!"

ECONOMIC RETRENCHMENT AND RECENTRALIZATION, 1996–2006

Accompanying the economic reforms enacted between 1990 and 1996 was a brief policy debate over the extent and direction of economic reforms. Reformers favored deep structural changes in the island's socialist economy leading toward a more productive and efficient, if still fundamentally socialist, economy (Carranza et al. 1996). Hard-liners advocated the introduction of only limited market mechanisms that would halt the economic decline and save socialism, while avoiding the negative social consequences and loss of political control that would come from deeper structural changes in the economy. Although President Castro allowed this debate to take place within the party, his public statements during this period left no doubt that he backed the hard-liners and would halt the economic reforms if and when the economy recovered.

For example, in a 1992 interview, Castro stated, "We are trying to solve our problems without selling our souls" (Pisano 1992). A year later, when announcing a series of economic reforms on July 26, 1993, he reiterated his ambivalence, saying, "We must not do things that we will regret later because consequences were unforeseen" (Castro 1993). Likewise, in an interview with a French journalist in late 1994, Castro

Along with La Guarida, *the paladar* Gringo Viejo *is one of the most successful and colorful private restaurants in Havana today. Its motto,* El lugar adecuado en el momento oportuno, *translates roughly as "The right place at the right time." (Ted Henken)*

characterized the temporary market opening as "an unavoidable concession, . . . a long way [from] a march toward the market economy" (Mano 1994). Finally, in his annual

Moncada speech on July 26, 1995, he warned about the dangers of market reforms, reminding his listeners of the revolution's socialist principles:

> Several measures have been implemented in the past few months that constitute a major shift and focus on the economic sector . . . enabling our economy to adapt to the realities of today's world. . . . However, does this mean that we should abandon our socialist principles or our Marxist-Leninist convictions? On the contrary, we should continue to conduct ourselves as genuine Marxist-Leninists with all the courage and realism circumstances may demand. At any rate, this does not imply—as some would seem to believe—that this is a return to capitalism, or much worse, an insane and hysterical race in that direction. (Castro 1995)

In line with these priorities, deeper structural reforms that would transform the Cuban economy into a new kind of market socialism in line with the Chinese or Vietnamese models were rejected as unnecessary. In fact, the reforms already in place by 1996 were gradually scaled back over the next few years. Indeed, in March of that year, Raúl Castro signaled the end to the debate by publicly coming out against the market-oriented reform process. In the same speech to the party's Central Committee cited above, he criticized as potential fifth columnists a number of leading reform-minded economists associated with the Centro de Estudios sobre América (Center for American Studies, or CEA). As described in detail in Chapter 3, the CEA was subsequently reorganized, its reformers split up and farmed out to other agencies, and further discussion of a series of deeper economic reforms that had until then been on the table was scuttled (Castro 1996; Giuliano 1998; Gunn 1995; Pérez-Stable 1998).

The underlying goal of economic reforms in socialist states has everywhere been the same: to perfect and preserve socialism. As such, Eastern European economic reforms were a failure because they served only to pave the way for the end of socialism. Given that history, Castro's open rejection of the reform path taken in Eastern Europe is understandable. In other contexts, economic reforms accomplished few of their goals, destroyed leadership's control over workers and deprived leaders of a social base (Róna-Tas 1995). Learning from these lessons, the Cuban government has been able to squeeze enough benefits from its first (external) and second (internal) rounds of economic reforms to survive the worst years of the special period (Corrales 2004). It has also strategically utilized the newfound nationalist popular unity and resistance provoked by confrontational U.S. policies (from Helms-Burton, to Elián González, to the most recent antifamily U.S. travel restrictions). More recently, Cuba has gradually been able to scale back politically risky and ideologically contradictory internal economic reforms, such as self-employment, with little political cost.

At the same time, recent economic developments have lessened the urgency that initially made internal reforms necessary. Cuba has been adept at welcoming in increasing numbers of foreign tourists and attracting hard currency remittances from Cuban-Americans. It has also been able to recentralize the economy while simultaneously courting new, economically and politically strategic foreign partners, including a booming China and an oil-rich Venezuela (Corrales, Erikson, and Falcoff 2005; Erikson 2005; Yanes 2005). Finally, Cuba has benefited from the booming international market price of nickel, one of its leading mineral exports (Pérez-López 2006). However, it remains to be seen whether the triple threat of growing inequality, official corruption, and ubiquitous economic crime (significant problems in all failed state socialist regimes) can be remedied by Castro's age-old cocktail of preaching, policing, prohibition, and punishment (Ritter 2005, 2006), without resorting to deeper and perhaps more irreversible economic reforms.

Amid hard times, President Castro assures the Cuban people that "Everything's Okay." (Ted Henken)

Inequality and Social Contradictions in Today's Cuba

Although Cuba's reformers ultimately lost their battle for a greater economic opening, even they were hesitant to push too hard given the spotty experience of Eastern Europe. Transitions away from socialism toward a more mixed economic model that had taken place elsewhere showed that the private sector could be a positive complement to the state sector. However, Cuban reformers also feared that a Cuban transition might gather an uncontrollable momentum and challenge state authority, leading to social chaos and the sacrifice of the achievements and social protections that had become the pride of the revolution (Mesa-Lago 2000: 290–291).

Such fears were well-founded. The downside of an economic opening, at least in the short term, includes the high unemployment that would likely follow a contraction in the state sector, an increase in socioeconomic inequality that would inevitably accompany the growth of the private sector, price increases of nearly all products when inefficient state subsidies were scaled back, and a drop in Cuba's touted social services as privatization was introduced (ibid.: 291; Mesa-Lago 2007). Even with the limited market reforms and anemic growth of the private sector Cuba has seen since the early 1990s, many of these social problems have intensified anyway.

For example, the economic crisis and initial reforms brought along with them the social problems of income inequality, poverty, and unemployment, as well as an increase in economic crime and various forms of hustling and prostitution (Espina Prieto 2005; Espina Prieto et al. 1998). During the 1980s, Cuba had likely become one of the most egalitarian societies in the world. However, by all measures income inequality has risen precipitously since the crisis began in 1990. Cuba's Gini coefficient (a standard international measure of income inequality) rose from 0.22 in 1986 to 0.55 in 1995 by one estimate, while other measures have indicated a less significant but still substantial increase to 0.40 by the late 1990s. Likewise, real wages in the state sector have experienced a sharp decrease between 1989 and 2000, falling by 40 percent from 131 to 78 pesos ($19 to $5) per month. Added to that is a simultaneous increase in wages in the small but significant private sector (Mesa-Lago and Pérez-López 2005: 72–73).

Cuban-American economist Carmelo Mesa-Lago has compiled an estimate of various wage rates based on interviews conducted with recent Cuban emigres. For 1995, he estimated a wide differential of monthly wage rates (in U.S. dollars) for various state and private sector occupations in Cuba including the minimum wage worker ($4), average state

*One of Havana's many ruined buildings. Lack of resources and neg-
lect of an aging housing stock have made such scenes increasingly
common during the special period. (Ted Henken)*

worker ($6), teacher ($8–$9), doctor or college professor
($11–$12), driver of tourist taxi ($100–$467), private farmer
($187–$311), and *paladar* owner ($2,500–$5,000). This
range has only continued to widen since then, with the ratio
of the highest- to the lowest-paid occupation jumping from
4.5 to 1 in 1989, to 829 to 1 in 1995, reaching an amazing
12,500 to 1 by 2002 (ibid.: 73–75).

As the preceding list demonstrates, income inequality in Cuba arises mainly from the wide disparity between state and nonstate sectors, leading to the underutilization of talented and highly educated workers who follow the money into the tourism sector and underground economy. Many others have also chosen to emigrate to gain a return on their educational investment, make ends meet, and support family left behind in Cuba. This misuse of skills also provokes low worker morale, high labor turnover, low productivity, and disrespect for state sector rules against theft, as well as acting as a disincentive to staying in school.

Given the extent of free or heavily subsidized social services available to all Cubans even today (housing, education, health care, rations, and so forth), understandings of poverty and even uses of the word to describe Cubans who have limited access to certain goods must be qualified relative to measures of poverty elsewhere (Warren 2005: 1, 6–7). That said, poverty does exist in Cuba and, if defined as the "population at risk of not meeting some essential need," as is normally done by Cuban social scientists, it has been on the rise over the past fifteen years. Cuban studies estimate that the "at risk" population has risen from just 6 percent in 1988 to 14.7 percent in 1996, reaching 20 percent by 2000. Other econometric measures used in Cuban studies place the poverty incidence much higher, at between 61 and 67 percent, with surveys showing that between 41 and 54 percent of Havana's population considers themselves poor or nearly poor (Togores González 1999; Ferriol Muruaga 2003; Togores González and García 2004; Barberia, de Souza Briggs, and Uriarte 2004; Espina Prieto 2004).

The severe disconnect between wages earned in pesos and the equivalent of dollar prices for an increasing portion of consumer needs acts as a disincentive for Cubans to perform formal state-sector work, since it is no longer the fundamental source of family income. This fact has led to a number of disturbing social problems, including rising unemployment, lowered productivity,

The U.S. Embargo III—Torricelli ('92), Helms-Burton ('96), and CAFC ('04/'06)

After the onset of the "special period," the Cuban government legalized the possession of dollars. Cuban exiles responded by sending millions in remittances to their relatives in Cuba. Around that time Cuba's official news media began to refer to the Cuban-American community in more neutral terms, calling them simply *la comunidad* ("the community"), in place of the more derogatory *gusanos* ("worms") or *traidores* ("traitors") that had been standard previously. Cubans joke that this change in rhetoric was the result of the fact that these *gusanos* had now become all-important *mariposas* ("butterflies") flying back to Cuba with money that could be used to keep the revolution alive. In other words, the *traidores* ("traitors") of old had been transformed into *trae-dolares* ("dollar bringers") of the special period.

On top of that contradiction is the irony that the single most important group of organized and vocal supporters of the U.S. embargo against Cuba (Cuban-Americans) are the very same people who most consistently violate the spirit, purpose, and effectiveness of the embargo by sending upward of $800 million each year to their struggling relatives on the island. However, on an individual level most exiles can easily reconcile supporting an economic strike against Castro, while at the same time making sure that their relatives live marginally better during material scarcity and growing inequality of the interminable special period.

Prior to this much needed injection of hard currency from Cuban-Americans, the U.S. government (influenced by the powerful Cuban-American lobby) had sought to strengthen the stalemated embargo by passing the Torricelli Act (also known as the Cuban Democracy Act) in 1992. Prohibiting subsidiaries of U.S. companies from trading with Cuba and refusing docking rights to ships that had recently docked in Cuba, the act sought to make it harder for companies to thwart the embargo by working through a third party (Jatar-Hausmann 1999: 133). The Torricelli Act also included a "Track II" stipulation that promoted increased cultural and scholarly

(continued)

exchange with Cuba with the controversial aim of promoting change and "democracy building efforts" on the island. While many students, journalists, and scholars, including myself, were pleased to be able to travel to the island and collaborate with our Cuban counterparts as a result of this stipulation, the act was taken advantage of as a boondoggle by some exile organizations in Miami and attacked by the Cuban government as the equivalent of formalized spying (Castro 1996).

Combined with the catastrophic impact of the fall of the USSR, the Torricelli Act seemed to provoke just the chaos and desperation it was designed to create. In early August 1994, the government endured its first ever crisis-induced riots along Havana's Malecón, as unsafe departures on flimsy rafts exploded across the island. Forced to the bargaining table in order to put an end to the rafter crisis, the U.S. and Cuban governments eventually agreed to a migration accord that would allow a minimum of 20,000 Cuban immigrants per year to enter the United States, while future rafters would be returned to Cuba. Such an unexpected change in policy infuriated many exile leaders who emboldened their efforts to ratchet up the embargo through the Helms-Burton Act (Mesa-Lago and Pérez-López 2005: 17; Uriarte 2002: 30).

Helms-Burton, officially christened the Libertad (Liberty) Act, was essentially a thirty-nine-page law written by the political leaders of the Cuban-American community (Ileana Ros-Lehtinen and Lincoln Díaz-Balart of Florida, and Robert Menéndez of New Jersey) with a little help from their friends at the Cuban American National Foundation (CANF). The law's four titles required the United States to (1) oppose the admission of Cuba to any international lending organizations and revoke aid to any former republic of the USSR that provided economic assistance to Cuba, (2) draw up an assistance plan for a transition government that specifically did not include the Castro brothers and ensure the return of confiscated properties to Cuban-Americans, (3) allow these former property owners to sue third country parties who "traffic" in or profit from this property, and (4) deny U.S. visas to officers of any of those foreign companies and their family members. Given the unprecedented harshness of these measures, few

(continued)

expected the bill ever to become law. However, when the Cuban Air Force made good on its warnings to shoot down two exile-piloted Brothers to the Rescue planes in the spring of 2006, Clinton quickly signed the bill into law in a bid to outflank Bob Dole in the coming presidential elections.

Given the controversy surrounding the extraterritoriality of title 3 above, both Clinton and George W. Bush after him have consistently waived its application, as it imperils economic relations with many of the major trading partners of the United States. Apart from throwing a bone to the politically important Cuban-American lobby, Helms-Burton seems to have had little practical effect in Cuba. In fact, it has only served to further alienate U.S. policy toward Cuba in the eyes of the world, providing Castro another tool with which to rally a fearful Cuban population against the United States.

Ironically, while "democracy" and "libertad" are the code words used to name these acts, the fact is that the majority of the articles contained in them have more to do with recovering the lost property of exiles and dictating to Cuba what form its future government should take than actually promoting democracy or liberty on the island (Jatar-Hausmann 1999: 131–147). Perhaps Castro was indicating his preference for a politically useful enemy when he ordered the shoot-down of two planes in an election year, all but ensuring that Clinton would sign Helms-Burton.

Since 1996 a major movement by a host of grass-roots organizations and a collection of U.S. businesses has attempted to weaken the embargo. They scored a major victory in 2000 in the passage of the Trade Sanctions Reform and Export Enhancement Act (TSRA), which led to the first ever sales of U.S. food and agricultural products to Cuba since the revolution. Direct sales of these products continue to be fully legal, provided that they are conducted on a cash-only basis. Although rejected at first by a proud Castro, he decided to purchase these products starting in 2001 after a slump in tourism and the destruction caused by Hurricane Michelle. Since then Cuba has gradually increased its food imports from the United States from $4.4 million in 2001 to $470 million in 2005,

(continued)

making the island the twenty-fifth largest agricultural export market of the United States that year and making the U.S. Cuba's fourth most important supplier of imports after Venezuela, China, and Spain (Mesa-Lago and Pérez-López 2005: 38; Pérez-López 2006). Not one to miss an opportunity to wield his considerable political influence, Castro has required that all his U.S. business partners sign a memorandum declaring their opposition to and willingness to lobby against the embargo.

The latest battle in this ongoing economic war has been fought between Castro and President George W. Bush. After being the target of considerable criticism from an expectant exile lobby, the Bush administration announced new limits on the flow of foreign currencies into Cuba in May 2004, with the recommendations of the Commission for Assistance to a Free Cuba (CAFC). Realizing that remittances were neutralizing the effectiveness of the embargo, the commission targeted Cuban-American remittances and family visits. The various recommendations, accepted in their entirety by President Bush on June 30, 2004, confirmed the remittance limit of $300 per quarter, restricted the kinds of family members who could legally receive remittances, limited family visits to once every three years for a maximum of two weeks, and severely restricted the amount of luggage and money one can bring to the island (Mesa-Lago 2004).

Castro responded by raising prices in dollar stores across the island, instituting the equivalent of a 20 percent tax on anyone changing dollars into the convertible pesos, and removing U.S. dollars from national circulation (Mesa-Lago and Pérez-López 2005: 38, 188). Finally, in the summer of 2006, CAFC issued a second report that reiterated its refusal to accept a Cuban succession upon the death of Fidel Castro and included a secret annex that has given rise to much speculation. At the same time, a November 2006 GAO report criticized the USAID and many exile organizations for their inadequate oversight and misuse of some of the monies allocated by CAFC to spur the Cuban transition (GAO 2006; Ruiz 2006).

Finally, the U.S. embargo against the Cuban government obscures the two other more tangible embargos endured by the

(continued)

Cuban people. First, the collapse of the Soviet Union and the subsequent loss of massive amounts of trade and aid had the economic impact on Cuba equivalent to the original U.S. embargo, as imposed between 1960 and 1962. Overnight, Cuba was forced to radically shift its export markets, but this time both the global environment and the revolutionary resilience of the Cuban people had changed. Miraculously, Cuba has survived. However, the third embargo, that which the Cuban government imposes *internally* upon the creativity, entrepreneurship, and ambition of the Cuban people, continues.

The biggest irony and tragedy behind the continuance of the external U.S. embargo is that the threat it poses to the current Cuban government (both real and exaggerated) has made it easy for Castro to justify his continued internal embargo against any further economic or political reforms that might threaten his vicelike grip on power (Jatar-Hausmann 1999: 131–147). It is in this sense that the strengthening of the U.S. embargo under Helms-Burton and CAFC has only helped to entrench and embolden the regime it is presumably designed to weaken. Moreover, in practice, the embargo functions much like a new version of the hated Platt Amendment, dictating Cuba's future from abroad and arrogantly seeking to protect Cubans from themselves. Also like Platt, the embargo serves as the perfect imperialist symbol against which the Cuban government can easily rally nationalist unity and support.

and an increasing tendency for Cubans to turn to informal, unregulated labor arrangements and black market sources for consumer goods (Carranza 2001). This development has been coupled with a rise in prostitution, street hustling, high-level corruption, and small-time but systematic economic crimes (Castro 2005; Díaz-Briquets and Pérez-López 2006; Pérez-López 2004; Peters 2006a). In fact, the first pair of new regulations (Resolutions 187 and 188) approved under the leadership of provisional president Raúl Castro and set to take effect on April 1, 2007, and were aimed at reducing absenteeism and increasing productivity in state enterprises through a more rigorous vigilance of work schedules and time off (Encuentro 2006).

The disincentives against working in the state sector have also given rise to disguised unemployment. That is, while Cuban statistics show that the unemployment rate fell from 8 percent in the 1989–1995 period to 4.5 percent by 2001, reaching a low of 2.3 percent by 2003, this seems improbable given the massive dislocations caused by the economic crisis during those same years. Instead, these statistics likely reflect the fact that the Cuban government counts as employed hundreds of thousands of workers who have in fact been laid off but continue to collect their salaries while undergoing retraining. If displaced workers receiving compensation were added to those actually counted as unemployed, the "equivalent unemployment rate" would have been 35 percent in 1993 and perhaps 25 percent in 1998 (Mesa-Lago and Pérez-López 2005: 49–52).

CONCLUSION

On balance, the economic results of the reforms enacted between 1990 and 1996 were clearly positive. While commitments to equality and full employment were affected negatively, the growth rate rebounded, inflation fell sharply, the fiscal deficit contracted, and both exports and imports grew (Mesa-Lago and Pérez-López 2005). However, because of two unacceptable side effects further economic reforms were halted and many later reversed. First, the growth in inequality and the expansion of unemployment (along with other jarring social contradictions) were signs of the failure to uphold socialist egalitarian ideology. More important, on the political front, the economic reforms provided increased economic independence to a new class of state enterprise managers, private farmers, and self-employed workers (among others) to whom the state felt it was losing economic control. Essentially, the fear that economic independence inevitably leads to political independence caused the leadership to begin a slow rollback of reforms starting in 1996.

In 2006, when the U.S. Interest Section in Havana placed a ticker tape in its office windows broadcasting antigovernment propaganda, the Cuban government responded by erecting 138 massive flagpoles, each topped with a defiant black flag with a single white star; one flag for each year since the start of Cuba's first war for independence in 1868. The flagpoles are strategically positioned so as to effectively block the ticker tape from public view. (Ted Henken)

Caught between past policies of ideological repression of the private sector and the need for a pragmatic opening, during the special period the government found itself in a classic "catch-22" dilemma of economic reform under state socialism. It initially attempted to strike a balance between the economic growth that an expanded role for the market could provide and the political threat and ideological compromise that markets and an expanded private sector represents for the socialist system. However, after 1996 that tenuous policy balance has shifted away from the market reforms of the early 1990s toward a more centralized economy. New licenses for self-employment have been all but discontinued, and many licensed microenterprises have been forced out of business or underground by a predatory tax structure and stepped up public attacks on entrepreneurs as corrupt "new rich." The message is loud and clear: you may still be legal, but you are no longer legitimate (Castro 2005).

That same message combined with a stepped-up crackdown on more overtly political opposition has been reiterated time and time again since the late 1990s. First, in early 1999, Cuba's National Assembly passed the ominous Law for the Protection of Cuba's National Independence and Economy (Law No. 88). Popularly know as *ley mordaza,* or the "gag law," it set up harsh jail sentences for anyone convicted of spreading "subversive materials" or too closely associating with Cuba's foreign "enemies." That was followed by the Varela Project in 2002, which sought a referendum that would allow for a series of major political changes and permit the existence of small businesses. Even after former president Jimmy Carter publicized and supported the project on his historic visit to Cuba that summer, the government not only rejected the project but also launched a successful campaign to make socialism an "irrevocable" element of the Cuban constitution. The following spring, while the world's attention was focused on the Iraq war, seventy-five of Cuba's leading dissidents (including independent journalists, economists, human rights activists, union activists, and librarians) were rounded up, tried, convicted under the 1999 "gag law," and subsequently sentenced to long prison terms.

At around the same time, a new recentralization of the Cuban economy began and has lasted through the end of 2006. First, in 2003–2004, three of Cuba's still surviving reform-minded ministers were censured and replaced with hard-liners. At the same time, all operations in state enterprises were decreed henceforth to take place exclusively in convertible pesos, not dollars as in the past. The government also placed strict new controls on Cuba's supposedly "autonomous" enterprises, which prevented them from importing goods without prior approval. In October/November of 2004, new restrictions were placed on self-employment, and the dollar was officially removed from domestic circulation, replaced universally by the convertible peso, giving the central government more control over expenditures and forcibly channeling all foreign economic relations through the central government (Mesa-Lago and Pérez-López 2005: 22–25).

In 2005, the Cuban government moved to increase the minimum wage and pensions and began an ideological mobilization that included raising the prices of electricity and cracking down on corruption, theft, pilfering, and the "new rich." Specifically, in a November 17 speech delivered upon the sixtieth anniversary of his own entry into the University of Havana, Castro attacked the self-employed whom he considered part of the "new rich," singling out taxi drivers, bed and breakfast operators, and especially *paladar* operators. "In this battle against vice, nobody will be spared. Either we will defeat all these deviations and make our revolution strong, or we die," he declared. At the same time, Castro called for a return to an egalitarian society and hinted that the "total renewal" of Cuban society would include drastic moves to eliminate rising difference between Cuba's haves and have-nots (Castro 2005).

Finally, between 2004 and 2006, Cuba has developed a very public, defiant, and mutually beneficial relationship with Venezuela and its charismatic president, Hugo Chávez. Since Chávez was first elected in 1998, economic trade and aid have exploded between Cuba and Venezuela, with Cuban doctors serving Venezuela's poor and with beneficial oil agreements signed in 2000 and reconfirmed after Chávez survived an attempted coup in 2002. Even while concerns about Cuba's debt to Venezuela (estimated at nearly $1 billion by the end of 2004) worry some, both Cuba's Ministry of Foreign Trade and Venezuela's state oil company have brushed aside criticisms and actually increased oil shipments, which have climbed from 2.7 to 4.1 million tons per year (Mesa-Lago and Pérez-López 2005).

On an April 2005 visit to Havana, Chávez made clear that his growing relationship with Cuba went beyond mere economics to include strong links of ideological and political solidarity with Cuban socialism. Leaving no doubt as to his intentions, he declared publicly, "We call what we are doing in Venezuela '*Bolivarianismo,*' but I want you Cubans to know that it is really another word for '*So-ci-al-is-mo*' of the twenty-first century." The election of the Aymara Indian leader and former coca farmer Evo Morales as the new president of Bolivia in December 2005 further expanded this nationalist, socialist, anti-imperialist alliance in Latin America. Finally, even as it seemed increasingly unlikely that Fidel Castro would ever again be well enough to return to power given his absence at the December 2, 2006, celebration of the fiftieth anniversary of the start of the revolution, Chávez's lopsided re-election in Venezuela only a few days later confirmed for Cuba at least the short-term stability of its fruitful economic arrangement with Venezuela. Likewise, the resounding calm that has prevailed in Cuba during the first year of Raúl Castro's tenure as provisional head of state indicates that a stable succession (not transition) is well underway in Cuba and that expectations abroad of social upheaval, economic collapse, and rapid regime change upon the death of Cuba's "maximum leader" are based on imperial hubris and wishful thinking.

References
Ackerman, Holly. "Bibliography on Moderate Cuban Politics, 1952–1965." Miami: University of Miami, Otto G. Richter Library, 2004. Available online at: http://scholar.library.miami.edu/cubamoderate/index.html.
Acosta, Leonardo. *Cubano Be, Cubano Bop: One Hundred Years of Jazz in Cuba.* Translated by Daniel S. Whitesell. Washington, DC: Smithsonian Books, 2003.
Baker, Christopher P. *Moon Handbooks: Cuba* (second edition). Emeryville, CA: Avalon Travel Publishing, 2000.
Barberia, Lorena, Xavier de Souza Briggs, and Miren Uriarte. "Commentary: The End of Egalitarianism? Economic Inequality and the Future of Social Policy in Cuba," in *The Cuban Economy at the Start of the Twenty-First Century.* Edited by Jorge I. Domínguez, Omar Everleny

Pérez Villanueva, and Lorena Barberia, pp. 297–316. Cambridge, MA: David Rockefeller Center for Latin American Studies, Harvard University, 2004.

Bengelsdorf, Carolee. *The Problem of Democracy in Cuba: Between Vision and Reality.* New York: Oxford University Press, 1994.

Boadle, Anthony. "Cuba frena incipiente iniciativa privada." Reuters (Havana), June 16, 2003.

Carranza Valdés, Julio. "La economía cubana: Balance breve de una década crítica." Mimeograph provided by the author of a paper presented at the "Facing the Challenges of the Global Economy" workshop, University of London Institute of Latin American Studies, January 25–26, 2001.

Carranza Valdés, Julio, Luís Guitérrez Urdaneta, and Pedro Monreal González. *Cuba la reestructuración de la economía: una propuesta para el debate.* Havana: Editorial de Ciencias Sociales, 1996.

Castro, Fidel. "Discurso pronunciado por Fidel Castro Ruz en el acto por el aniversario 60 de su ingreso a la universidad." Havana, November 17, 2005. Available online in English at: http://www.cuba.cu/gobierno/discursos/2005/ing/f171105i.html.

Castro, Fidel. "Fidel Castro Speaks at Moncada Ceremony" (FBIS-LAT-95–145), July 26, 1995.

Castro, Fidel. "Castro Gives Speech at Moncada Barracks Anniversary" (FBIS-LAT-93–142), July 26, 1993.

Castro, Fidel. *History Will Absolve Me.* Havana: Guairas Publishing, 1967.

Castro, Raúl. "Informe del Buró Político al Comité Central." *Encuentro de la cultura cubana* 1 (1996), pp. 18–24. Available online in English at: http://www.marxmail.org/raul_castro.htm.

Corrales, Javier. "The Gatekeeper State: Limited Economic Reforms and Regime Survival in Cuba, 1989–2002." *Latin American Research Review* 39, no. 2 (June 2004): pp. 35–65.

Corrales, Javier, Dan Erikson, and Mark Falcoff. "Cuba, Venezuela, and the Americas: A Changing Landscape." Cuba Forum Working Paper, Inter-American Dialogue, Washington, D.C., and the Cuban Research Institute, Florida International University, Miami, Florida. December 2005. Available online at: http://www.thedialogue.org/publications/2005/winter/cuba_venez.pdf.

Díaz-Briquets, Sergio, and Jorge Pérez-López. *Corruption in Cuba: Castro and Beyond.* Austin: University of Texas Press, 2006.

Domínguez, Jorge I. "Cuba since 1959," in *Cuba: A Short History.* Edited by Leslie Bethell. Cambridge: Cambridge University Press, 1993.

Eckstein, Susan. *Back from the Future: Cuba under Castro.* Princeton, NJ: Princeton University Press, 1994.

Encuentro. "El gobierno introducirá una severa norma contra el absentismo laboral." *Cubaencuentro.com,* December 12, 2006.

Erikson, Daniel P. "Cuba, China, Venezuela: New Developments." *Cuba in Transition* 15, pp. 410–418. Association for the Study of the Cuban

Economy, Washington, D.C., 2005. Available online at: http://lanic. utexas.edu/project/asce/pdfs/volume15/pdfs/erikson.pdf.

Espina Prieto, Mayra Paula. "Structural Changes since the Nineties and New Research Topics on Cuban Society," in *Changes in Cuban Society since the Nineties*. Edited by Joseph S. Tulchin et al. Washington, D.C.: Woodrow Wilson International Center for Scholars, 2005.

Espina Prieto, Mayra Paula. "Social Effects of Economic Adjustment: Equality, Inequality and Trends toward Greater Complexity in Cuban Society," in *The Cuban Economy at the Start of the Twenty-First Century*. Edited by Jorge I. Domínguez, Omar Everleny Pérez Villanueva, and Lorena Barberia, pp. 209–243. Cambridge, MA: David Rockefeller Center for Latin American Studies, Harvard University, 2004.

Espina Prieto, Mayra Paula, Lucy Martín Posada, and Lilia Núñez Moreno. "Componentes y tendencias socioestructurales de la sociedad cubana actual—resumen ejecutivo." La Habana: Centro de Investigación Psicológica y Sociológica, March 1998.

Espinosa Chepe, Oscar. "Ofensiva contra el cuentapropismo en Cuba." Mimeographed article provided by the author. Havana, December 2, 2002.

Fernández, Damián. *Cuba and the Politics of Passion*. Austin: University of Texas Press, 2000.

Fernández Peláez, Neili. *Trabajo por cuenta propia en Cuba: Desarticulación y reacción*. Degree thesis, Department of Sociology, Universidad de la Habana, July, 2000.

Ferriol Muruaga, Ángela. "Acercamiento al studio de la pobreza en Cuba." Paper resented at the XXIV LASA Congress, Dallas, March, 2003.

Frank, Marc. "Cuba's Painful Transition from Sugar Economy." Reuters, August 17, 2005.

GAO (U.S. Government Accountability Office). "US Democracy Assistance for Cuba Needs Better Management and Oversight." November 2006. Available online at: http://www.gao.gov/new.items/d07147.pdf.

Giuliano, Maurizio. *El caso CEA: Intelectuales e inquizidores en Cuba. ¿Perestroika en la isla?* Miami, FL: Ediciones Universal, 1998.

Guevara, Ernesto Che. "Socialism and Man in Cuba," in *Che Guevara Reader: Writings on Guerilla Strategy, Politics, and Revolution*. Edited by David Deutschmann, pp. 197–214. Melbourne: Ocean Press, 1997.

Guillermoprieto, Alma. *Dancing with Cuba: A Memoir of the Revolution*. Translated by Esther Allen. New York: Pantheon Books, 2004.

Gunn, Gillian. *Cuba's NGOs: Government Puppets or Seeds of Civil Society?* Washington, D.C.: Georgetown University Caribbean Project, Briefing Paper #7, February 1995. Available online at: http://www.trinitydc.edu/academics/depts/Interdisc/International/ca ribbean%20briefings/Cubas_NGOs.pdf.

Henken, Ted. "Condemned to Informality: Cuba's Experiments with Self-employment during the Special Period (The Case of the Bed and Breakfasts)." *Cuban Studies* 33 (2002), pp. 1–29.

Jackiewicz, Edward L., and Todd Bolster. "The Working World of the Paladar: The Production of Contradictory Space during Cuba's Period of Fragmentation." *Professional Geographer* 55, no. 3 (August 2003), pp. 372–382.

Jatar-Hausmann, Ana Julia. *The Cuban Way: Communism, Capitalism, and Confrontation.* West Harford, CT: Kumarian Press, 1999.

Levine, Robert M. *Secret Missions to Cuba: Fidel Castro, Bernardo Benes, and Cuban Miami.* New York: Plagrave Macmillan, 2002.

Mano, Jean-Luc. "Castro: 'I will Go to Hell and Meet the Capitalists.'" *Paris Match,* October 27, 1994, pp. 92–93.

Marshall, Jeffery H. "The Political Viability of Free Market Experimentation in Cuba: Evidence from *Los Mercados Agropecuarios.*" *World Development* 26, no. 2 (1998), pp. 277–288.

Martínez Heredia, Fernando. "El Che y el gran debate sobre la economía en Cuba." Commentary upon the presentation of the book *Ernesto Che Guevara: El gran debate sobre la economía en Cuba, 1963–1964.* Havana: Ocean Press, Centro de Estudios Che Guevara, 2003. Available online at: http://www.nodo50.org/cubasigloXXI/economia/heredia_301104.htm.

Mesa-Lago, Carmelo. "Social Policy and Social Welfare," in *Looking Forward: Democracy in Cuba?* Edited by Marifeli Pérez-Stable. Notre Dame, IN: University of Notre Dame Press, 2007.

Mesa-Lago, Carmelo. "The Cuban Economy in 2004–2005." *Cuba in Transition,* vol. 15. Anuario Estadístico de Cuba, 2005. Available online at: http://www.cubagob.cu/ingles/otras_info/estadisticas.htm.

Mesa-Lago, Carmelo. "El reinado de la doble moral." *Encuentro en al red,* July 21, 2004. Available online at: http://arch1.cubaencuentro.com/sociedad/20040719/2a9420b525724927fe988fa580cb581a/1.html.

Mesa-Lago, Carmelo. *Market, Socialist, and Mixed Economies: Comparative Policy and Performance—Chile, Cuba, and Costa Rica.* Baltimore: Johns Hopkins University Press, 2000.

Mesa-Lago, Carmelo. *Are Economic Reforms Propelling Cuba to the Market?* Miami: University of Miami, North-South Center, 1994.

Mesa-Lago, Carmelo. "Cuba's Economic Counter-Reform (Rectification): Causes, Policies and Effects," in *Cuba After Thirty Years: Rectification and the Revolution.* Edited by Richard Gillespie. London: Frank Cass and Company, 1990.

Mesa-Lago, Carmelo. "The Cuban Economy in the 1980s: The Return of Ideology," in *Socialist Cuba: Past Interpretations and Future Challenges.* Edited by Sergio G. Roca. Boulder, CO: Westview Press, 1988.

Mesa-Lago, Carmelo. "The Revolutionary Offensive." *Trans-Action* 6, no. 6 (April 1969), pp. 22–29, 62.

Mesa-Lago, Carmelo, and Jorge Pérez-López. *Cuba's Aborted Reform: Socioeconomic Effects, International Comparisons, and Transition Policies.* Gainesville: University Press of Florida, 2005.

Moreno Fraginals, Manuel. *El ingenio* [The Sugarmill]. Barcelona: Crítica, 2001.

National Office of Statistics (Oficina Nacional de Estadísticas, ONE). *Anuario Estadístico de Cuba, 2002.* Havana, 2003.

National Office of Statistics (Oficina Nacional de Estadísticas, ONE). *Anuario Estadístico de Cuba, 2000.* Havana, 2001.

Ojito, Mirta. *Finding Mañana: A Memoir of a Cuban Exodus.* New York: Penguin, 2005.

Pérez, Louis A., Jr. *On Becoming Cuban: Identity, Nationality, and Culture.* Chapel Hill: University of North Carolina Press, 1999.

Pérez, Louis A., Jr. *Cuba: Between Reform and Revolution* (second edition). New York: Oxford University Press, 1995.

Pérez-López, Jorge. "The Cuban Economy in 2005–2006: The End of the Special Period?" *Cuba in Transition* 16, pp. 1–13. Washington, DC: Association for the Study of the Cuban Economy, 2006.

Pérez-López, Jorge. "Corruption and the Cuban Transition," in *The Cuban Economy.* Edited by Archibald R. M. Ritter, pp. 195–217. Pittsburgh, PA: University of Pittsburgh Press, 2004.

Pérez-López, Jorge. *Cuba's Second Economy: From behind the Scenes to Center Stage.* New Brunswick, NJ: Transaction, 1995.

Pérez-Stable, Marifeli. *The Cuban Revolution: Origins, Development, and Legacy* (second edition). New York: Oxford University Press, 1999.

Pérez-Stable, Marifeli. "El Caso CEA." *Encuentro de la cultura cubana* 10 (fall 1998), pp. 85–88.

Peters, Phil. "Who's to Blame for Corruption?" *Cuba Policy Report E-Newsletter #22,* Arlington, VA: Lexington Institute, October 22, 2006a. Available online at: http://lexingtoninstitute.org/1011.shtml.

Peters, Phil. "Cuba's Small Entrepreneurs: Down but Not Out." Arlington, VA: Lexington Institute, September 30, 2006b. Available online at: http://lexingtoninstitute.org/docs/cubas_small_entrepreneurs.pdf.

Peters, Phil. "Cutting Losses: Cuba Downsizes Its Sugar Industry." Arlington, VA: Lexington Institute, December, 2003. Available online at: http://lexington.server278.com/docs/cuba1.pdf.

Peters, Phil. "International Tourism: The New Engine of the Cuban Economy." Arlington, VA: Lexington Institute, December 2002a. Available online at: http://lexington.server278.com/docs/cuba3.pdf.

Peters, Phil. "Survival Story: Cuba's Economy in the Post-Soviet Decade." Arlington, VA: Lexington Institute, May 2002b. Available online at: http://lexington.server278.com/docs/cuba4.pdf.

Peters, Phillip. "Islands of Enterprise: Cuba's Emerging Small Business Sector." Arlington, VA: Alexis de Toqueville Institution, 1997. Available online at: http://adti.net/html_files/cuba/curpteml.htm.

Peters, Phil, and Joseph L. Scarpaci. "Cuba's New Entrepreneurs: Five Years of Small-Scale Capitalism." Alexis de Tocqueville Institution, 1998. Available online at: http://adti.net/html_files/cuba/TCPSAVE. htm.

Pisano, Isabel. "Castro on Economic Situation, U.S. Elections" (FBIS-LAT-92–203). *L'Espresso,* Rome, Italy, October 11, 1992.

Resolución No. 11. "Reglamento sobre el trabajo por cuenta propia." May 11, 2004.

RIIA (Royal Institute of International Affairs). *Cuba: A Brief Political and Economic Survey.* London: Chatham House Memoranda, Information Department, Oxford University Press, September, 1958.

Ritter, Archibald R. M. "Cuba's Economic Re-Orientation." Paper presented at the Bildner Center conference, "Cuba: In Transition? Pathways to Renewal, Long-Term Development and Global Reintegration," March 30–31, 2006. Available online at: http://web.gc.cuny.edu/bildner-center/cuba/documents/CITBookFMpdfbychapter_000.pdf.

Ritter, Archibald R. M. "Survival Strategies and Economic Illegalities in Cuba." *Cuba in Transition* 15 (2005). (Available under the title, "Economic Illegalities and the Underground Economy in Cuba." Available online at: http://www.cubasource.org/pdf/economic_illegalities.pdf.

Ritter, Archibald R. M. "The Taxation of Microenterprise," in *The Cuban Economy.* Edited by Archibald R. M. Ritter, pp. 121–145. Pittsburgh: University of Pittsburgh Press, 2004.

Ritter, Archibald R. M. "El regimen impositivo para la microempresa en Cuba." *Revista de la CEPAL* 71 (August 2000), pp. 145–162.

Ritter, Archibald R. M. "Entrepreneurship, Micro-enterprise, and Public Policy in Cuba: Promotion, Containment, or Asphyxiation?" *Journal of International Studies and World Affairs* 40, no. 2 (summer 1998), pp. 63–94.

Ritter, Archibald R. M. *The Economic Development of Revolutionary Cuba: Strategy and Performance.* New York: Praeger Publishers, 1974.

Róna-Tas, Ákos. "The Second Economy as a Subversive Force," in *The Waning of the Communist State: Economic Origins of Political Decline in China and Hungary.* Edited by Andrew G. Walder. Berkeley: University of California Press, 1995.

Rosenberg, Jonathan. "Cuba's Free Market Experiment." *Latin American Research Review* 27, no. 3 (1992), pp. 51–89.

Ruiz, Albor. "US fights Fidel—with Chocolates?" *New York Daily News,* November 26, 2006.

Schwab, Peter. *Cuba: Confronting the U.S. Embargo.* New York: St. Martin's Griffin, 1999.

Smith, Benjamin. "The Self-Employed in Cuba: A Street Level View," in *Cuba in Transition,* Volume 9, pp. 49–59. Washington, DC: Association for the Study of the Cuban Economy, 1999.

Stanley, David. *Cuba* (second edition). Melbourne: Lonely Planet Publications, 2000.

Togores González, Viviana. "Cuba: Efectos sociales de la crisis y el ajuste económico de los 90." In *Balance de la economía cubana a finales de los 90,* pp. 82–112. Havana: Centro de Estudios de la Economía Cubana, 1999.

Togores González, Viviana, and Anicia García. "Consumption, Markets, and Monetary Duality in Cuba," in *The Cuban Economy at the Start of the Twenty-First Century.* Edited by Jorge I. Domínguez, Omar Everleny Pérez Villanueva, and Lorena Barberia, pp. 245–295. Cambridge, MA: David Rockefeller Center for Latin American Studies, Harvard University, 2004.

Uriarte, Miren. "Cuba—Social Policy at the Crossroads: Maintaining Priorities, Transforming Practice." Boston: Oxfam America, 2002.

Warren, Cristina. "Governance and Social Justice in Cuba: Past, Present and Future—Policy Brief: Lessons for Cuba from the Latin American Experience." Miami: Cuban Research Institute, FLACSO-Mexico, and FOCAL, 2005 (the Canadian Foundation for the Americas). Available online at: http://www.focal.ca/pdf/cuba_brief.pdf.

Yanes, Hernán. "The Cuba-Venezuela Alliance: 'Emancipatory Neo-Bolivarismo' or Totalitarian Expansion?" Occasional Paper Series, Institute for Cuban and Cuban-American Studies, University of Miami, December 2005.

CHAPTER THREE
Institutions

INTRODUCTION

This chapter describes the origins and functioning of the many civil, political, social, and military institutions created in Cuba as a result of the revolutionary triumph in 1959. Specifically, I outline three distinct stages during the revolutionary period, beginning with a *charismatic* stage of government (1959–1970). During that stage, state institutions were relatively weak and the revolution's "maximum leader," Fidel Castro, was able to exercise unmitigated authority through his unique style of charismatic leadership. The *institutional* stage in state administration (1971–1989) saw the re-creation of the formal institutions of politics and government, including the Cuban Communist Party, the Central Committee, the Politburo, the Council of Ministers, the Council of State, and the Assemblies of People's Power.

Despite the relative institutionalization of the Cuban government after the mid-1970s, one cannot understand the exercise of political power in Cuba under the revolution without reference to the informal, personal authority of Fidel Castro. Indeed, according to Harvard political scientist Jorge Domínguez, "[F]ormal institutions manifest only one of the two 'faces of power' in Cuba" (2002: 229). Often trumping the power vested in formal institutions, Cuba's other "face of power" is founded on the personal stature of a small group of historic leaders, legitimized by the heroic triumph and social achievements of the revolution, and epitomized by Fidel Castro. Such authority has afforded Castro and his coterie of fellow leaders the unique ability to enact certain policies, while successfully resisting both internal and external challenges to their power.

Castro's ability to exercise political power is explained by two constants over the past half-century: defensive nationalism against external threat, and a respect, even reverence, for the powerful leadership, keen intelligence, missionary zeal, historic vision, untiring sacrifice, and uncommon bravery of the man himself. Indeed, many Cubans (both on the island and in exile, *Fidelista* revolutionaries and staunch counter-revolutionaries alike) relate to Castro not as a distant president (or dictator) but as an intimate father (or grandfather) figure, loved and hated in equal measure, often by the same people. Such a relationship is due in no small part to Castro's extraordinary charisma, his ubiquitous presence in the lives of generations of Cubans, and his staunch if often manipulative and always paternalistic defense of *la patria* (the homeland).

An old joke among Cuban-Americans has it that new immigrants to "the (banana) Republic of Miami" often wish that they had never left Cuba in the first place. "I left Cuba to get away from that man," they complain. "But here, all you do is talk about Fidel, Fidel, Fidel." As Domínguez has perceptively written, "Castro is still thoughtful, eloquent, inspiring, decisive, and charming. He is also ruthless, brutal, intolerant, egomaniacal, and manipulative. These and other traits make him a politician who is revered and feared, admired and loathed, but whom none take lightly" (ibid.: 268).

The most recent *emergent* stage of governance began in 1990 and is characterized by a relative weakening of state institutions, accompanied by a slight opening of public space. In this section, I describe a number of important institutional reforms and discuss the elusive concept of "civil society" as it has developed in socialist Cuba during the 1990s. I also describe the important institutional role of Cuba's military, the Revolutionary Armed Forces (FAR, Fuerzas Armadas Revolucionarias), and the state security apparatus, the Ministry of the Interior (MININT). I also highlight Cuba's education and health care systems, institutions distinguished by their high standards, impressive achievements, free access, and universal coverage.

CONSOLIDATION, RADICALIZATION, AND CHARISMATIC LEADERSHIP, 1959–1970

The brutality of the Batista dictatorship during the bloody two-year revolutionary war (1957–1958) culminated in the triumph of a loose coalition of rebel forces headed by Castro's 26th of July Movement. This left the old generation of Cuban political leaders discredited, along with their institutions and political parties. In fact, the constitutional democracy re-established in 1940 had proven deeply corrupt and easily gave way when Batista returned to the presidency in 1952, this time as a usurper and dictator. Thus, when Castro marched into Havana in January 1959 as the unmistakable leader of the future, he represented the long-frustrated aspirations of a new generation of Cubans (Domínguez 1993). Brimming with righteous indignation and contagious charisma, Cuba's new leader proved to be as persuasive and commanding as a public speaker as he had been audacious and effective as a military leader and political tactician during the war (ibid.: 95). Castro also benefited from the ideological and institutional vacuum left behind by the collapse of the Batista regime. Almost immediately, Castro's virtually unchallenged ascendancy revealed new rules of the game of Cuban politics.

First of all, the Cuban military was both discredited and destroyed, along with the political class in whose interests it had exercised its authority. Second, since Castro's movement was not a political party, it was not indebted to any established institutional interests when it gained power. Thus, upon victory the revolution easily swept aside all previous parties except the Communist Party (which had quietly begun to collaborate with Castro's movement during the last year of the guerrilla struggle). Third, Castro's refusal to seek approval from Uncle Sam for his political decisions, or financial aid for his economic projects, broke with a long tradition of Cuban dependency on U.S. approval and "generosity." Finally, Castro quickly responded to the power vacuum by creating a series of new decrees, laws, and institutions that could both channel the rising revolutionary effervescence of the people and stimulate social integration and national mobilization that would give weight to the meaning of revolution (Pérez 2002: 243).

Early Revolutionary Decrees

The new government's first major decree came in May 1959 with the announcement of the first Agrarian Reform Law. The law reduced individual land holdings to a maximum of 1,000 acres but extended exceptions in the key areas of sugar, rice, and livestock holdings, which were allowed to remain at a maximum of 3,333 acres. Despite the fact that the law was not as radical as many expected, it turned the U.S. government against Castro (Farber 2006). Along with the law, a vast, powerful state institution, the National Institute of Agrarian Reform (INRA), was created. The INRA had the authority to resolve labor-management disputes and grew to exercise extensive control over the economy during the first half of the 1960s.

The first nine months of 1959 saw as many as 1,500 revolutionary decrees, lowering postage, pharmaceutical, telephone, electricity, and tax rates. After agrarian reform, perhaps the most far-reaching reform measure was the Urban Reform Law of October 1960. That law reduced rents by up to 50 percent, gradually allowing renters to purchase their homes (Pérez 2002: 243). The law also socialized all commercially owned property, virtually eliminating the private real estate market (Domínguez 1993: 104). These first acts struck a balance between the rising demands of the people and the practical need to create order out of revolution (ibid.: 95). However, just as these new measures provided relief from

One of Vedado's many pre-revolutionary mansions, this home was divided and given over to those in need of housing after the Urban Reform Law was enacted in October 1960. (Ted Henken)

inequality and injustice and won the new government broad-based popular support, they also provoked powerful domestic and international enemies whose interests were directly affected by reforms (Pérez 2002: 243).

Although relatively modest in scope and in line with Castro's declared intentions in his programmatic defense speech of 1953, the May 1959 Agrarian Reform Law was interpreted as an assault on large-scale private property by the Cuban bourgeoisie, leading to a crisis in the revolutionary government's first moderate cabinet (Farber 2006). In June 1959, most of these moderates left the government. Prime Minister José Miró Cardona resigned in February, Pedro Luís Díaz Lanz, the head of the Cuban Air Force, left in June, and President Manuel Urrutia was forced out in July after publicly questioning the rising influence of communists in the government. He was replaced by Osvaldo Dorticós, who would serve until 1976.

For these exiting moderates, the issue of communism and what they saw as an emerging *caudillismo* (strongman rule) were crucial. However, Castro would have to continue to orchestrate a delicate balance of power between the communists (whom he secretly favored but attempted to control) and the many noncommunist members of the Rebel Army who now were becoming institutionalized as the new Cuban Revolutionary Armed Forces. In fact, while the communists were ultimately ascendant in politics, the military achieved a significant and lasting independence from the party early on. Their relative autonomy was enhanced by their greater legitimacy achieved during the war and by the leadership of the capable Raúl Castro, who was made Cuba's defense minister in October 1959 based on his distinguished service in the clandestine war. Over the next thirty years, he would create Cuba's single most coherent and effective revolutionary organization (Domínguez 1993: 104).

In late November 1959, two other prominent moderates were forced out of the cabinet, the minister of public works, Manuel Ray, and the president of the National Bank, Felipe Pazos. Thus, out of a total of twenty-one government ministers appointed at the start of the year, twelve had resigned their posts or been forced out by the close of 1959, signaling

the beginnings of an institutional shift toward the radical consolidation of the revolution. Four more ministers would leave
during 1960 (ibid.: 105).

The Consolidation and Radicalization of the Revolution

A number of major events enabled Castro to consolidate and
radicalize his rule into an overtly anti-American, communist
revolution. Three competing revolutionary organizations
remained intact and retained legitimacy upon the revolutionary triumph in January 1959. These were Castro's 26th of
July Movement (divided between the radical guerrillas who
had fought in the mountains and the movement's more moderate urban wing), the Revolutionary Directorate, which had
grown out of the University of Havana's Student Federation,
and the PSP (Popular Socialist Party), Cuba's traditional,
Soviet-aligned communist party. Ironically, though the PSP
was the organization least involved in the armed struggle, its
proven organizational capacity, clear political program and
ideological vision, and international links to Moscow made it
an especially attractive vehicle for consolidating power and
defending the revolution in the tense geopolitical atmosphere
of the 1960s. Furthermore, by repeatedly dissolving and
reconstituting the PSP during the first half of the 1960s,
Castro was able to purge its ambitious leaders, convert them
along with most of the country into *Fidelistas,* and create a
new Cuban Communist Party (PCC) under his unquestioned
leadership and vision.

Three major events during the early 1960s led to the eventual ascendancy of the Communist Party under Castro's
charismatic leadership as the central political institution of
the newly established revolutionary state. First were the 1959
trials of former Batista partisans aimed at achieving revolutionary justice. Next was the important step of melding the
three most prominent anti-Batista organizations into a single,

newly constituted communist party (1961–1965). Finally was the U.S.-backed Bay of Pigs invasion of April 1961, followed by the subsequent Missile Crisis of October 1962. Despite the deep political differences that existed both between and within the three leading revolutionary organizations, this single, seminal, externally induced event at the Bay of Pigs more than anything else allowed for the radical consolidation of the Cuban Revolution (Linger 1999).

In the months following Batista's fall in December 1958, the rebels faced the difficult task of establishing legitimate revolutionary institutions that could both defend the new regime and meet the rising expectations of the population after years of chaos and struggle. It was incumbent upon the rebels to establish the rule of law in their punishments of the old guard in order to be seen as legitimate and democratic by the Cuban people. However, the trials provoked an immediate conflict between the patronizing U.S. tradition of dictating to Cuba the liberal values of fairness and moderation, and the need for the new regime to enact revolutionary justice in response to the rising demands from an emboldened and traumatized populace (Domínguez 1993: 97). Reacting angrily to what he saw as hypocritical criticisms in the U.S. press of just punishments after turning a deaf ear to years of abuse under Batista, Castro flaunted U.S. concerns by holding trials in a huge sports arena and showing them to the anxious masses on live television.

Signaling his growing preference for revolutionary unity under communist leadership, Castro intervened in the fall of 1959 in the first postrevolutionary elections in two of the most important prerevolutionary institutions of civil society, the University Student Federation (FEU) and Confederation of Cuban Workers (CTC), Cuba's principal labor union. Although both institutions had already become thoroughly politicized before the revolution, Castro's open intervention on the side of what he called the "unity candidates" led to the victory in both cases of the less popular slate aligned with the

PSP and the loss of the coalition that grew out of Castro's 26th of July Movement. Castro argued that the defense of the revolution required unity above all. Thus, he catapulted the communists into positions of authority and undercut the cadres of his own movement, with the goal of preventing the 26th of July Movement from congealing into a real organization (ibid.: 104–105).

As the radical orientation of the new government became increasingly clear, Castro moved to orchestrate the elimination of the tension between the three leading prerevolutionary movements by doing away with the organizations themselves. In March 1962 he merged them all into a single new "unity" political party, to which he gave the name Integrated Revolutionary Organizations (ORI). However, this was an "integrated" party only in name, since both the 26th of July Movement and the Revolutionary Directorate had all but ceased to exist as organically independent groups.

Castro's initial effort at creating revolutionary unity, however, was largely unsuccessful because of the sectarianism of the old PSP, then led by Anibal Escalante. Members of the other groups argued that the PSP had not played an important role in opposing the Batista dictatorship and resented its growing dominance in the ORI and in the central government. In fact, the communists initially dominated the ORI in part because of their past experience in running an organized, disciplined party during the 1930s and 1940s. They were also key bridge builders to their deep-pocketed patrons in the Soviet Union. All personnel decisions were made with the approval of Escalante, who favored old party stalwarts for leadership positions and attempted to introduce political criteria in areas outside the party's traditional purview, including in the military.

This move erupted in a scandal that provoked Castro's personal intervention. He denounced Escalante and banished him to the diplomatic wilderness of Czechoslovakia. Castro then reorganized the ORI and renamed the party the United

Party of the Socialist Revolution (PURS). The name was changed one final time to the Cuban Communist Party (PCC) in 1965. Also in 1965, Cuba's three semi-independent daily newspapers, *Revolución, Hoy,* and *Combate,* were all closed down and replaced by a single daily, *Granma,* the official organ of the new PCC. Castro also made the first attempt to give the party some formal institutional responsibilities by creating a 100-member Central Committee, a Political Bureau responsible for making basic political decisions, and a Secretariat, which would carry out the administrative decisions of the Politburo. However, it was not until the major institutional changes of the mid-1970s that these three organizations had any real power or institutional influence to claim to represent the "will of the masses" beyond Castro's own exercise of "direct democracy" during his rousing and interminable speeches.

In 1961, the revolution's first structures of local governance, Coordination, Operations, and Inspection Boards (JUCEI) were set up. Aimed primarily at coordinating the many economic and social activities rapidly falling under state control, the JUCEI were disbanded in 1965 because they lacked proper coordination and structure. They were replaced in 1966 by a new system of governance, called Local Power. However, the various branches of Local Power rapidly degenerated into another layer of bureaucratic administration, since representatives lacked real power. Without proper resources to address local issues and lacking recognized administrative rules, these local structures only contributed to the growing governmental centralization that they were partly intended to alleviate. Finally, semiannual consultative meetings between Local Power delegates and citizens were abandoned and further elections canceled as the country threw itself into the 1970 sugar harvest (Roman 2003: 64–66).

As noncommunists and anticommunists were gradually removed from the government during 1959 and 1960, the way was paved for the complete transformation of Cuba's internal government and political institutions under centralized and authoritarian rule. Still, a trigger was needed to justify such a move to a nationalistic but still traditionally anticommunist populace. The radicalizing effect of the U.S.-backed invasion in April of 1961 cannot be overestimated. This watershed event in the consolidation of the revolution had the effect of undermining the position of the few moderates still left in positions of influence on the island at the time, while simultaneously strengthening the hand of the communists (Linger 1999). In the aftermath of the failed invasion, Castro could easily justify increased repression and stepped-up security measures, implanting a siege mentality in the country. Many moderates were jailed or fled the country, making space for the most radical elements of the revolutionary coalition, such as Che Guevara, to step in. Therefore, by 1962, power had been consolidated under socialist revolution, with Castro as the county's undeniable leader.

Mass Organizations

Although the revolution would not become fully institutionalized until the mid-1970s, the deepening rift with the United States, combined with other international and internal crises, led the government to begin to develop an incipient defensive, organizational, and institutional apparatus between 1960 and 1962. As a result, citizen participation in civic and political life became institutionalized under a number of formal mass organizations. While very popular during the early 1960s and sometimes described as "socialist civil society," these organizations are better understood as corporate control mechanisms used to channel popular mobilization into activities explicitly supportive of the government. Likewise, mass organizations seldom function as "interest groups" representing and promoting members' needs. Instead, they aim to subordinate members' interests to nationally defined goals, seeking to avoid conflict and enlist support for regime policies that affect members' lives.

While membership reaches well into the millions for the larger mass organizations, participation does not translate into effective influence or restraint on the behavior of the country's political leadership. While the popularity and effectiveness of mass organizations have waxed and waned over time, most Cubans participate to some degree in them, either because they freely choose to or because the cost of nonparticipation can be high. However, perhaps 20 percent of the adult population refuses to have anything to do with mass organizations, regardless of the consequences (Domínguez 2002).

The four most prominent mass organizations in terms of size, revolutionary integration, and external vigilance and internal control are the Committees for the Defense of the Revolution (CDR), founded in September 1960; the Federation of Cuban Women (FMC), first established in August of the same year; the Union of Young Communists (UJC), formed in 1962; and the Cuban Workers Federation (CTC), originally founded in the 1930s and reorganized under the revolution in 1959. Also a citizen militia with 300,000 members was created in 1960 to help defend the revolution from external attack. The year 1961 saw the formation of the National Association of Small Farmers (ANAP), which grouped together Cuba's remaining small farmers.

The CDRs are neighborhood-based organizations that span the entire breadth of the island. They are intended to monitor potential dissidents and pass information on to state security, further consolidating governmental power by turning the entire population into informants. Under the joint jurisdiction of the National Revolutionary Police (PNR) and the Ministry of the Interior, each CDR serves a variety of formal and informal functions, the most important of which is to stimulate political participation of neighborhood residents and guard against subversion of revolutionary principles. Led by a president who is popularly elected by all neighborhood residents based on his or her "revolutionary integration and commitment," each CDR maintains files on neighborhood residents and convenes monthly meetings aimed at political socialization in which revolutionary sloganeering, citizen complaint, and popular feedback on local issues take place.

The CDRs play a key role in stimulating mass participation in rallies and revolutionary offensives. They are also instrumental in effectively responding to natural disasters, such as rapid, coordinated evacuations during Cuba's frequent hurricanes. One regrettable example of the political function of the CDRs took place during the 1980 Mariel boatlift, when members were encouraged to participate in "repudiation meetings" (*mitines de repudio*) against those who had chosen to emigrate. Those public shaming sessions often included young school children and involved vicious insults, the throwing of eggs and tomatoes, and occasionally ended in violence. Such violent attacks are still selectively carried out today against regime opponents.

Other important functions of the CDR include drawing attention to needed neighborhood repairs, sponsoring community self-help missions, participating in government-initiated campaigns in the area of literacy and immunization, ensuring universal local participation in Cuban elections, as well as monitoring the activities of neighborhood residents. For example, despite the economic crisis of the 1990s and the general weakening of the role of the mass organizations since the start of the special period, the CDRs were a key element in combating selective and blank voting and ensuring that nearly 90 percent of voters approved of the official unity slate in the 1998 National Assembly elections. CDR members also take turns performing nighttime vigilance (*guardia*) of their building or neighborhood. Likewise, when neighborhood residents change residence, run for elected office, or apply for university admission, membership in other mass organizations such as the UJC or the party, promotions, special positions, or licenses (such as a self-employment license), other CDR members are questioned about that resident's proper revolutionary attitude and behavior.

The FMC actually began by merging as many as forty previously existing women's organizations, rapidly increasing its membership from just 17,000 in 1961 to 240,000 by 1962. The *federadas,* as members are known, have been led since the organization's inception by a single president, the recently deceased Vilma Espín, longtime member of the party's Central Committee, Rebel Army coordinator during the 1950s, and wife of Raúl Castro. By the 1990s, membership, which is virtually mandatory for all adult women, reached some 3.2 million women, or 81 percent of the female population over fourteen. Officially formed as a *feminine* organization (that is, non-*feminist* organization, officially considered an anachronistic, capitalist term), the FMC works to integrate women into the revolutionary process and labor force. The organization has also been recognized for improving living conditions for rural women and children and for defending the right of women to pursue higher education and ensuring their equitable treatment in the workplace. The FMC also runs an extensive network of daycare centers, called *círculos infantiles,* that allow women with children to enter the labor force. Sending one's children to these daycare centers is one of the privileges of FMC membership.

In the fall of 1960, the Association of Revolutionary Youth (AJR) was formed by collapsing the youth wings of the three most prominent revolutionary organizations—the old Popular Socialist Party (PSP), the Revolutionary Directorate (DR), and the 26th of July Movement. It would later become the Union of Young Communists (UJC). Like the FMC, this organization's goal is to promote revolutionary indoctrination among its members and to channel its activities toward the formation of new socialist men and women.

Members of the UJC must be under thirty years of age and are drawn from all sectors of society. In the early years of the revolution, noncommunists were expelled from the UJC, and membership dropped from 100,000 to just 18,000. There was also criticism in the early 1970s that the UJC had focused on

Featuring the triple profiles of Julio Antonio Mella, Camilo Cienfuegos, and Che Guevara, and the words Estudio *(Study),* Trabajo *(Work), and* Fusil *(Rifle), this is the official emblem of the Unión de Jóvenes Comunistas (UJC, Union of Young Communists). (Douglas Kirkland/Corbis)*

recruiting students and young professionals at the expense of urban workers and agricultural laborers. However, the UJC was eventually placed directly under the control of the Cuban Communist Party, and membership grew after the major institutional reorganization of the mid-1970s. The UJC eventually established its own newspaper, *Juventud Rebelde (Rebel Youth)*, and holds sway over Cuba's three student organizations: the elementary school Pioneers (Organización de Pioneros José Martí), the Federation of Middle School Students (FEEM), and the Federation of University Students (FEU). The UJC is an important grooming organization for ambitious and talented youth who hope to fill leadership positions as adults. While not a prerequisite, membership in the UJC strengthens one's candidacy for party membership after the age of thirty.

Unlike unions in most countries, the Cuban Workers Federation is not organized based on trades or professions but according to sectors of economic activity. Likewise, the role of the CTC is more that of assuring that labor discipline and the achievement of production goals in line with government priorities than of defending workers' interests. Strikes, for example, have been unknown in Cuba since the early 1960s. This does not mean, however, that workers have not developed an arsenal of resistance strategies. Absenteeism, off-the-books and after-hours work, and pilfering resources from one's state job for resale on the black market are a few of the many ways in which Cuban workers assert their autonomy. On the other hand, the revolution won workers a series of significant benefits including health care, periodic vacations, pension coverage, and a gradual increase in the role of material rewards (greater pay) over moral incentives.

The CTC also maintains a labor file on each worker that indicates occupational status, labor history, absenteeism, merits, special skills, and participation in voluntary labor brigades. These labor files are linked to the identity cards that each Cuban must always carry and produce upon request. Thus many Cubans seek to maintain an occupation not necessarily because of their need for a peso income (increasingly meager after 1990) but to gain access to state goods or out of the need to avoid the stigma that accompanies unemployment in a worker's state.

The 1990s has seen a slight increase in the autonomy of the CTC. On a number of occasions the federation has defended workers from proposed economic legislation interpreted to be harmful to their interests. For example, the CTC stalled a new law that sought to remove recalcitrant workers to other jobs, resisted the implementation of stricter sanctions on absenteeism, and objected to the increased use of material incentives that would lead to income inequality. The CTC also successfully modified legislation that would have included salaried workers in a new income tax law aimed at the self-employed (del Aguila 1994; Díaz-Briquets 2002; Domínguez 1993: 2002).

Castro as a Charismatic Hero

The lack of institutionalization during the first decade of the revolution was the result of Castro's charismatic style of leadership and staunch resistance to bureaucratic institutionalization under Soviet-style rule. In fact, Castro's rise to prominence from the early 1950s, through the triumph of the revolution in 1959, up to the end of the 1960s is a classic case study in the exercise of charismatic authority. The charismatic leader possesses distinct endowments of character allowing him or her to play the important role of a catalyst for social change. The charismatic hero typically emerges out of a widespread social crisis, is seen as the representative of an almost religious "mission," possesses special personal qualities, comes from outside normal channels, carries on an unorthodox pattern of life, and offers no set program or ideology except him/herself (Morton 1965).

Castro's gradual emergence as a national figure from Moncada to the Sierra Maestra during the late 1950s, as well as his idiosyncratic leadership style consistently exercised throughout the 1960s, mirrors the qualities of the charismatic hero. In fact, his long-standing authority and strength as a leader derive from his continued embodiment of those qualities. Indeed, while mechanisms would be set up in the mid-1970s to allow for formal election of Castro as Cuba's leader, early on it was clear that his preeminence did not depend on being elected by his followers, since he had already been "elected" in a sense by the force of his historical mission. In fact, "Castro's sway over his associates and many ordinary citizens," writes Domínguez, "has been the single most striking political fact of contemporary Cuban history" (1993: 125).

While his charismatic authority was somewhat constrained within formal, bureaucratic institutions after the mid-1970s,

Standing in front of Cuba's Plaza of the Revolution, this giant monolith is guarded by a statue of José Martí. Fidel Castro gave many of his spellbinding, if often interminable, speeches from here. Indeed, for more than forty years most national holidays have included hundreds of thousands of Cubans going a la Plaza con Fidel. (Ted Henken)

in the thirty years since then Castro has continued to embody nationalist sacrifice and convince the mass of Cubans to do the same. Such sacrifices have been justified with one eye on

For many years, this colorful and provocative billboard was set up directly across from the U.S. Interest Section. Recently moved down the Malecón *to make way for a new plaza, clumsily named, José Martí Anti-Imperialist Open Tribunal, the billboard features a brave Cuban cadet shouting at a monstrous Uncle Sam, "Hey imperialists, we have absolutely no fear of you!" (Ted Henken)*

the threatening enemy of the revolution just 90 miles to the north and another on the always unfinished work of the ongoing revolution. Partially because of consistently hostile U.S. policies, Castro has managed to convince or coerce enough Cubans that his retention of power is the best defense of Cuban sovereignty and the gains of the revolution.

If Castro is a classic example of the charismatic leader, then U.S. confrontational policies have worked only to strengthen his appeal (Morton 1965: 24). U.S. threats and actions (best exemplified by the Bay of Pigs fiasco, innumerable assassination and coup attempts, and the ongoing embargo) have allowed Castro's charisma to thrive and fully justified his demand for continued popular sacrifice, loyalty, and revolutionary unity. Washington would do well to remember the old saying: that which does not kill me only serves to make me stronger. In other words, "Charisma operates on the idealistic and sensational level. Material sacrifice for the cause, short of complete collapse, bolsters and strengthens it" (ibid.: 25). That is, U.S. actions during the first years of the revolution had exactly the opposite of their intended effect. Rather than undermining Castro's leadership and destabilizing his communist regime, the U.S. policy of confrontation and punishment strengthened Castro's charisma and nationalist popularity and helped him to consolidate his hold on power.

BUREAUCRATIC AUTHORITY, INSTITUTIONALIZATION, AND PEOPLE'S POWER, 1970–1989

Because of the charismatic nature of revolutionary authority, upon victory and consolidation Castro faced the danger of becoming obsolete. However, in the late 1960s he made the creation of a new, selfless, socialist man and the achievement of all-or-nothing economic goals the new battles around which to rally the nation. Continued U.S. hostility also provided him with a threatening Goliath against which to call for revolutionary unity and focus nationalist resistance. From 1959 to 1976, no national elections took place in Cuba. Instead, Castro's legitimacy as Cuba's maximum leader (though hardly unquestioned) stemmed from the four pillars of charisma, political deliverance, redistribution, and nationalism (Domínguez 1993: 126).

However, the failure of the 10-million-ton sugar harvest in 1970 called that arrangement into question. Built as it was on Castro's charismatic preaching, his all-encompassing faith in the new man, and the revolutionary consciousness of the masses, the failure of the *Gran Zafra* signaled the bankruptcy of personal charisma and revolutionary consciousness as the basis for long-term institutionalization of the revolution. Starting in 1970 and culminating in the First Congress of the Cuban Communist Party (PCC) in 1975 and the subsequent constitution approved by popular referendum in 1976, Castro reluctantly moved toward the institutionalization of the revolution under the guidance of the Soviet Union (Blanco and Benjamin 2003; Guillermoprieto 2004; González 1974; Halperin 1972, 1981, 1994).

Prior to the First Party Congress, Cuba gradually began to make important adjustments in international alignments and governmental organization. First, in July 1972, Cuba became a member of the Soviet bloc's Council of Mutual Economic Aid (CMEA) and initiated a process of fashioning Cuban government institutions in the image of the Soviet Union. For example, in November 1972, Cuba's Council of Ministers was reorganized to create an executive committee, headed by a prime minister and composed of a handful of deputy ministers who oversaw the various state ministries. This change made the executive committee of the Council of Ministers the government's central decision-making body. In 1974, communist Cuba's first experiment in local government was begun in Matanzas, later formalized in the 1976 Constitution and applied nationwide in the form of the Organs of People's Power (especially in the National Assembly of People's Power, or ANPP).

The Cuban Communist Party (PCC)

It was not until the First Congress of the PCC, held in 1975, more than fifteen years after the start of the revolution, that the party began to exercise a central institutional role in governing. For the first time, party members worked together to draft platforms affecting national policy. Specifically, the party helped to draft the new 1976 Constitution (which was largely modeled after the Soviet Constitution of 1936) and approved the first five-year plan, as well as other economic policies (del Aguila 1994). The new constitution also designated the party as the "guiding force of society and the state," leading the effort to build socialism.

While powers of governance are formally separated among the party, the Council of Ministers, and the Council of State (which represents the supposedly all-powerful National Assembly), in practice the top leadership of all three of these organs is largely the same. Moreover, the PCC exercises great informal power through party cells, which are found at all levels of society. For example, the First Party Congress set up party committees in each of the country's fourteen provinces and all 169 municipalities, with formal party representation in the military, schools, neighborhoods, and workplaces. Furthermore, because municipal elected officials in Cuba have little effective clout, the party has focused its influence on the selection process of appointed officials. Thus, while the PCC does screen electoral candidates for the national and provincial assemblies, all appointed officials, as well as central government agency heads, state enterprise managers, hospital administrators, and military leaders, must be cleared and endorsed by party commissions (Domínguez 1993).

At the time of the First Congress, in 1975, the Central Committee was expanded to 112 members. The party's more exclusive Political Bureau was also vested with new authorities. Party membership gradually increased from 15,000 in 1962, to 50,000 in 1965 when its name was changed, to about 100,000 in 1970, reaching 203,000 on the eve of the First Congress in 1975. After the institutionalization of the party in 1975, membership shot up to more than 400,000 by 1980, reaching beyond 500,000 by the Third Congress in 1986.

Since party membership provides the opportunity for preferential access to some material goods, membership actually grew during the economic crisis of the early 1990s, reaching 780,000 by 1997 (Domínguez 2002). This growth was aided by the decision to drop the long-time ban on religious believers becoming party members and to shorten the waiting period for UJC members to apply for consideration from three to two years. Not all who desire to become *militantes del partido* (party "militants," or members) can do so. Membership must be sought out, and there are typically two paths to consideration for membership: having been selected as a "vanguard worker" or having distinguished oneself previously in the UJC.

The PCC is organized in a strictly hierarchical structure, with the periodic party congresses formally governing its decisions and policies. However, given the unwieldy nature of large organizations and the long period that typically passes between congresses (though slated for every five years, the last one was held in 1997), the Central Committee's much smaller and more exclusive Political Bureau (PB) actually holds effective power and makes day-to-day decisions. The Central Committee meets annually, and its size increased from just over 100 members in 1975 to 225 after the Fourth Party Congress in 1991. However, by 1997 the Political Bureau decided to shrink the Central Committee to just 150 members, ending the experiment of making it broadly representative of the population.

In contrast to the Central Committee, the Political Bureau meets weekly and is composed of Cuba's most powerful leaders. It has been presided over by the same three men since its inception in 1965: first secretary Fidel Castro, second secretary Raúl Castro, and chief of party discipline Juan Almeida. In the fifteen years between 1965 and 1980, it doubled in size, growing from eight to sixteen members. At the time of the Fourth Congress in 1991, however, the PB dropped six members (through death or retirement), adding a total of seventeen new members, increasing total membership in this elite group to twenty-five. By 1997 it had dropped to twenty-four members, but apart from José Ramón Machado, who joined in 1975, and Abelardo Colomé Ibarra and Esteban Lazo who joined in 1986, eighteen others had joined in the 1990s, rejuvenating Cuba's top decision-making organ during the nation's most difficult time. Thus, contrary to popular assumption, apart from the Castro brothers and their closest advisors, the revolution's political baton has already begun to pass to a new generation of leaders (ibid.; Corrales 2004). Most recently in 2006, after having been abolished decades earlier, the party Secretariat was reconstituted, signaling the party's emergence as Cuba's central power base, as Fidel Castro receded in prominence.

The National Assembly (ANPP)

The creation of the National Assembly of People's Power in 1976 coincided with the political and geographical reorganization of the island that transformed the six traditional provinces into fourteen (with the Isle of Pines, renamed the Isle of Youth, made a special municipality). Old municipal divisions were abolished, and 169 new municipalities were created in their place. At the same time, municipal and provincial governments (Assemblies of People's Power) were established within each province through elections for the first time (see figure 3.1).

The 1976 Constitution formally vested the ANPP with legislative and judicial powers, naming it the ultimate repository of all power and authority in the socialist state. These functions had been exercised exclusively by the Council of Ministers before 1976. Henceforth, the members of the National Assembly would represent the people in law-making and governance, have the power to declare war, and make all international and domestic policies. The ANPP also elects the members of the Council of State, Council of Ministers, the president and vice president, and the judges of the People's Supreme Court. In practice, however, the ANPP meets just twice each year for brief periods and rarely initiates original legislation. Instead, most day-to-day legislative and policy-making authority (which includes all of the above functions) is relegated to the Council of State. In fact, the Council of State is the real decision-making institution in the Cuban government, ruling largely through decree laws that are usually later ratified unanimously and perfunctorily by the National Assembly.

Figure 3.1 – Organizational Structure of the Cuban Government

Fidel Castro   →→→→   Grupo de Apoyo y Coordinación
Commander-in-Chief   del Comandante en Jefe
President of the Council of State   (Fidel Castro's inner staff)
Prime Minister of the Council of Ministries
First Secretary of the Central Committee of PCC
↑

Raúl Castro   →→→→   Grupo de Apoyo y Coordinación
Second-in-Command   (Raúl Castro's inner staff)
Head of the Armed Forces
Second Secretary of the Central Committee of PCC
↑

POLITBURO
↑   ↑   ↑

POLITICAL
EXECUTIVE   **LEADERSHIP**   **LEGISLATIVE**   **JUDICIAL**
↑   ↑   ↑   ↑

Executive Committee (7)   Central Committee   Council of State (31)
↑   ↑   ↑

Council of Ministries (27) Organization Secretariat National Assembly   Supreme People's
↑   Departments   of People's Power (609)   Court
↑   ↑   ↑

Provincial Governments   Provincial Committees Provincial Assemblies Provincial Courts
(14)   (14)   (14)   (14)
↑   ↑   ↑   ↑

Municipal Governments   Municipal Committees Municipal Assemblies Municipal Courts
(169)   (169)   (169)   (169)
↑   ↑   ↑   ↑

Public Enterprises   Party Committees   Local Delegates
↑   ↑

Party Core Members   Voters
↑

Party Membership
↑   ↑

Militantes del Partido (PCC)   Union de Jovenes Comunistas (UJC)
↑

MASS
ORGANIZATIONS
↑   ↑   ↑   ↑   ↑   ↑

Committees   Federation   National   Confederation   Federation   Federation of
for the   of Cuban   Association of Cuban   of Secondary University
Defense of   Women   of Small   Workers   Students   Students
the Revolution **(FMC)**   Farmers   **(CTC)**   **(FEEM)**   **(FEU)**
(CDR)   **(ANAP)**

(Sources: Cuban Transition Project 2007; Domínguez 2002; Sagás 2002.)

Thus, on the one hand Cuba's institutions of governance formally passed from the exclusive realm of Castro's personalistic charisma to various representative and administrative bodies. Moreover, the new constitution formally separated the powers of Cuba's three institutional branches of government. The executive committee of the Council of Ministers led the government (executive branch). The Political Bureau represented the Central Committee of the party. And the Council of State stood in for the National Assembly when the latter was not in session (legislative branch).

On the other hand, while Cuba's People's Supreme Court is the county's foremost judicial unit, it does not in fact constitute an independent branch of government, with the leverage and autonomy to act as a check on potential excesses of the executive, legislative, or Communist Party branches. Such "adversarial" relations among different branches of government are a threat to the overriding principle of national "unity." In short, Cuban courts are not designed to limit the power of the government and protect individual rights and liberties (del Aguila 1994: 165). Likewise, the formal separation of powers and the investing of legal, institutional preeminence to the National Assembly cannot hide the fact that it does not exercise de facto rule.

In sum, the delegation of some responsibility to incipient institutions has not fundamentally changed the oligarchic character of Cuban state institutions. A small group of two or three dozen trusted, historic leaders made up the majority of members in the Council of Ministers, the Political Bureau, and the Council of State well into the 1980s. By law the head of government (the prime minister of the Council of Ministers) and the head of state (the president of the Council of State) are the same individual. In Cuba, this individual is also the first secretary of the Communist Party, Fidel Castro (Domínguez 1993). This cross-cutting, interlocking membership pattern between the party (and especially the Political Bureau) and the top posts in governmental institutions and ministries ensures a commanding role in policy making and governance to historical leaders. Those leaders are often two or three steps removed from having to face voters directly, despite the existence of an institutionalized system of representative government known as People's Power. Despite its name, many Cubans have long concluded that as currently organized the system of popular power is in fact neither "popular" nor very "powerful" (Bengelsdorf 1994).

Cuban Elections and the Organs of People's Power

Elections for the 609 National Assembly deputies take place every five years simultaneously with provincial assembly elections, while midterm elections for municipal assemblies occur every two and a half years. Victory is based on simple majority. Voting is by secret ballot but is not mandatory. However, since voting is considered a fundamental revolutionary duty, failing to do so repeatedly can brand a citizen politically suspect and impact his or her social standing and career aspirations. In order to avoid the creation of a self-interested political class, all delegates and deputies serve on a part-time, nonprofessional basis, retaining their day-to-day occupations. However, there are no term limits.

Between 1976 and the electoral and constitutional reforms of 1992 (discussed below), only the members of municipal assemblies were directly elected by the voters. Those elected as delegates to the municipal assemblies became empowered then to elect the delegates for each provincial assembly and the deputies who would serve in the National Assembly. However, these municipal delegates do not freely elect those who serve on the provincial or national assemblies. Instead, lists of candidates (along with alternates) are drawn up by candidacy commissions after consultation with mass organizations, and then these lists are presented to municipal delegates for approval (Roman 2006, 2003, 1993).

Entreating all Cubans to go to the polls, this billboard reads, "ELEC-TIONS: VOTE for the BEST and the most CAPABLE." (Ted Henken)

While the Constitution of 1976 created a new system of People's Power, the new electoral law, passed in the same year, placed significant obstacles on the flexibility, strength, and autonomy of the National Assembly. For example, self-nominations were prohibited. Instead, all municipal nominations took place in public assemblies through a show of hands. Also, electioneering was outlawed, and campaigning did not include the discussion or debate of national issues. The party and government simply published candidate biographies, to which candidates had no input. Thus, while neither money nor negative campaigning plays a role in Cuban elections, the electoral system and governmental structure limit candidate autonomy and effectiveness (Domínguez 1993).

In fact, the electoral law of 1976 indirectly strengthened the power of the party over popularly elected representatives, since nominating commissions led by the party representatives prepared lists of nominees for provincial delegates, municipal and provincial executives, and national deputies (ibid.). Also, prior to 1992, National Assembly candidates had to be approved by the party's Central Committee before they could stand for election. Consultation in drawing up these lists was greatly broadened after 1992 to include input from all the major mass organizations, except the PCC and the UJC, which were removed from formal consultation (Roman 2006, 1993).

While elected officials need not belong to the party, in practice these procedures resulted in more than 90 percent of National Assembly members being party members in the 1976 elections. In fact, there is only one legally recognized political party, the Cuban Communist Party, and no freedom of political association exists outside that entity. While slightly over half of those elected to the first 1976 National Assembly had indeed been previously elected directly by the voters to their own municipal assemblies, more than 40 percent of the National Assembly was nominated for office by party-controlled nominating committees without ever having gone before the voters in direct elections.

Finally, as is true in any parliamentary system, there are no direct elections for the offices of president and vice president in Cuba. Instead, in Cuba those offices are filled by internal, indirect, noncompetitive elections within the National Assembly itself. Likewise, all top officers of the National Assembly, as well as the leadership cadre of the Council of State and the Council of Ministers, are elected by the National Assembly, not by popular vote. Furthermore, as with president and vice president, all candidates for these top posts are preselected by the party leadership. Thus, unlike elections at the municipal level, internal elections in the National Assembly provide deputies no choice among candidates (Roman 1993: 19).

Cuban authorities openly admit that only municipal elections are open and competitive, in the sense that candidates are chosen by constituents at neighborhood meetings and voters have a choice among two to eight different candidates at election time. However, even after the 1992 electoral and constitutional reforms, which made elections for National Assembly direct, elections for both the provincial and national assemblies remained closed and noncompetitive. Voters now vote directly for their National Assembly deputies (who do not have to live in or be from the district they represent), but they are presented with a closed list of preselected candidates and encouraged to vote for the entire slate rather than for individuals. Thus, the number of candidates is equal to the number of posts to be filled: nomination by the municipal assembly is the equivalent to being elected, since there is just one candidate per post (Roman 2006, 2003). As a result of these structural conditions, no candidate who ran for office in the 1993, 1998, or 2003 National Assembly elections failed to be elected (Domínguez 2002: 243).

National Assembly president Ricardo Alarcón has explained that these procedures are a way to ensure "pluralistic" representation in the National Assembly. Thus, while the 1992 electoral reforms stipulate that up to 50 percent of National Assembly delegates must be previously elected in open, competitive elections at the municipal level, the rest are selected by candidacy commissions to ensure the election of those who already hold important government or party jobs, as well as to promote the representation of all sectors of society (women, youth, religious leaders, workers, doctors, farmers, teachers, and so forth). Thus, unlike municipal elections in which voters are given a ballot of competing candidates, National Assembly elections feature a ballot with a list of preapproved candidates. Voters can approve of the candidates as an entire slate, choose individual candidates, or vote "blank" in protest (Roman 2006, 2003, 1993).

Thus, the Cuban electoral system functions under a different logic than that common to most Western democracies, where open, competitive elections of candidates from two or more opposing parties are the hallmark of the electoral process. Moreover, in countries like the United States, political parties choose candidates with limited feedback from the electorate, and the competing war chests of campaign contributions often decide elections. In Cuba, in contrast, the problems of campaign finance abuse and partisan demagoguery have been eliminated. The principles of consultation, consensus, pluralism, and local representation on the country's highest legislative body have replaced those of interest group lobbying, party conflict, and competitive debate (ibid.).

However, the Cuban electoral system has achieved high levels of consultation and consensus, while reducing the number of real political alternatives. The fact that candidacy commissions are empowered to nominate candidates through consultation in order to achieve pluralistic representation seems based on state paternalism and distrust of the voters. The fact that these commissions have the power to choose final lists of candidates, as well as all alternates, weakens the role of municipal committees that must answer directly to voters. Furthermore, the practice of closed nominations and noncompetitive elections at the provincial and national assembly levels emasculates the effectiveness and autonomy of the National Assembly and of the candidates themselves under the façade of revolutionary unity. Finally, there is a tendency to relegate the National Assembly to a ratification role, while the party and party-controlled government posts hold sway over the commanding heights of national, economic, and foreign policy.

ECONOMIC CRISIS, REFORM, AND EMERGENT CIVIL SOCIETY, 1990–2006

The 1990s were years of major transformations in Cuban social and economic life. The economic crisis that began in the late 1980s led to a series of economic reforms, including the promotion of foreign investment and international tourism and the allowance of domestic microenterprise and exile remittances. Such reforms are best understood as calculated adjustments *within* the existing socialist political system aimed at ensuring its survival, not changes of the system itself necessarily leading to transition or regime change (Domínguez 1997). Still, reforms led to the emergence of new domestic and international dynamics that directly affected the way state institutions had traditionally interacted with Cuban society.

Specifically, the economic crisis allowed the emergence of a host of new civil, cultural, intellectual, and economic actors. The presence of these actors has indirectly and unintentionally challenged the hegemony of existing revolutionary state institutions. Likewise, the presence of new national and especially international nongovernmental organizations (NGOs), the renewed profile and presence of organized religion, and the boom in both exile visits and emigration have affected Cuban society and especially the composition and role of the Cuban family in important ways. In short, the vast array of civil, political, and cultural institutions originally created by the Cuban government in the 1960s and 1970s to serve and promote, as well as to channel, coerce, and control, the broad-based revolutionary consensus of the Cuban population were confronted by a new economic and sociopolitical environment, challenging their effectiveness and legitimacy as representatives of the Cuban people.

The Fourth Party Congress of 1991 and the Constitutional Revisions of 1992

One major result of the collapse of the Soviet Union was the series of institutional adjustments proposed during the Fourth Congress of the PCC in 1991, most of which were approved as part of the revised constitution in July 1992. On the one hand, party leadership underlined its desire to make no ideological concessions and rejected outright the errors of openness and flexibility (glasnost and perestroika) that had led to the "political disaster" in the communist regimes of Europe. On the other hand, the Congress ratified the repatriation of

Cuban troops from Africa and sought to work within the UN system in the future. Likewise, while the Congress reiterated the socialist nature of the revolution under the principles of Marxism-Leninism, it also recognized that ideology "should not be applied dogmatically" (Domínguez 2002: 246) and that the nationalism of José Martí was as important to the revolution as the socialism of Karl Marx.

This ambivalent opening to the realities of a changing world was exemplified by the often contradictory policies approved of by the Fourth Congress and later added to the revised constitution. For example, the Congress endorsed the development of an international tourism industry, the liberalization of self-employment, and the promotion of foreign investment. It also committed itself to real dialogue with Cuba's various religious denominations and permitted believers to join the rank and file of the party for the first time. However, the main thrust of the 1991 Congress was to resist any far-reaching political change and preserve the socialist character of the revolution at all costs.

Similarly, while the party issued a call for open discussion and debate in the run-up to the Congress and subsequent constitutional revisions, final changes were tightly controlled by party and National Assembly committees, and the final text was never submitted to a national plebiscite. Still, a few changes in the constitution and the functioning of the institutions of governance are noteworthy. First, all references to the Soviet Union and to Cuba's membership in the "socialist community" of nations were removed from the constitution and replaced with a greater emphasis on the nation's "solidarity" with its Latin American and Caribbean neighbors. Second, the declared commitment to advocate and support "internationalist" missions and wars of national liberation was stricken from the constitution.

Third, the open advocacy of a "scientific materialist conception of the universe" was replaced by a new emphasis on the freedom of religion. In fact, the PCC's requirement that all members be strictly "atheist or agnostic" was replaced by a declaration of the party's "secular" orientation. This change indicated that religious belief and revolutionary commitment were no longer incompatible, presaging a religious revival in Cuba during the 1990s. Fourth, the ineffective National Assembly was brought back to life through the appointment of rising star and Castro confidant Ricardo Alarcón as its new president. Included in the renovation of the National Assembly was the initiation of the first ever direct elections for its deputies (mentioned above). Finally, the constitution limited state ownership to the "fundamental" means of production, theoretically opening the economy to limited forms of foreign investment, privatization, and private entrepreneurship.

Despite these formal constitutional changes, few far-reaching economic reforms and no real political liberalization took place after initial adjustments proved sufficient for ensuring regime survival. In fact, privatization never took place, private entrepreneurship has been regulated almost out of existence (or at least driven underground), and foreign investment has dropped off significantly since 2000. The character of the Cuban government continues to be deeply authoritarian, with a single legal political party and extensive limits on the exercise of most individual political and civic freedoms. Freedom of expression is theoretically guaranteed in the constitution, but only as long as it supports the "goals of a socialist society," and no freedoms can be exercised "against the existence and purposes of the socialist state."

Despite the emergence of a lively and at times vigorous intellectual, social, and cultural debate and criticism in the arts, in popular music, in cinematic production, in some semi-independent think tanks, and in the pages of specialized journals and some magazines, all mass media (radio, television, and newspapers) remain under strict state control. Indeed, mass media comes across like a series of government press releases and remains essentially a tool of the party, faithfully performing a clearly propagandistic, cheerleading function. Finally, the new constitution grants the president of the Council of State (Castro) the unchecked ability to declare a state of emergency, modifying or revoking the rights and duties outlined in the constitution.

Human Rights, Political Prisoners, and Opposition Groups

Despite the initial broad-based popular support for the revolution, active opposition existed from the very beginning. However, in the aftermath of the Bay of Pigs fiasco (April 1961) and the eventual routing of the remaining armed opposition groups by the mid-1960s, most significant antigovernment activity was organized from abroad and thus had little impact or resonance with the Cuban people. Those who openly criticized the direction that the revolution took were routinely sentenced to long prison terms. Many who criticized the regime but were unwilling or unable to fight sought to emigrate in one of the many exile waves since 1959. In short, with the unwitting help of the United States in welcoming exiles "with open arms," the Cuban government succeeded in controlling internal dissent by externalizing it.

In fact, many of Cuba's most prominent political prisoners have been released on the condition that they immediately leave the country. Such was the case of most of the 3,600 political prisoners released from Cuban prisons after the tireless efforts of some Cuban-Americans working in conjunction with the Carter administration in 1979. Those who opposed the regime but could not go into *exilio* ("exile"), had to resign themselves to living in what Cubans call *insilio* ("internal exile," or "insile"). That is, these citizens opted to unplug as much as possible from public life and develop a strategic double personality or duplicity (*doble moral*), wearing one, false face in public and another, more authentic face in private.

The economic, moral, and existential crisis of the special

period, however, has made it more difficult for all Cubans to maintain such a delicate ideological balance. This new environment led to the strengthening of an increasingly vigorous and legitimate opposition movement from within the island's alienated professional middle class. That movement had begun to emerge at the end of the 1970s under leaders such as Ricardo Bofill and the brothers Gustavo and Sebastián Arcos Bergnes, who advocated nonviolent change from within. Unlike early counter-revolutionaries who saw socialism as a betrayal and used violence and often terrorism to undermine and overthrow the revolution, most emerging dissidents had been lifelong revolutionaries and thus directed their objections against the widespread lack of intellectual freedom, authoritarian centralism of state power, and absence of any real opportunity for internal debate. As such they have generally rejected solutions coming from Washington or Miami, including the embargo, and instead have attempted to work within the socialist structure to bring about nonviolent change and national reconciliation (Sánchez Santacruz 2003).

The first significant dissident movement of the 1990s to provoke repression from the Cuban government and gain international recognition was a coalition of more than 140 tiny opposition groups led by Leonel Morejón. The Cuban Council (Concilio Cubano), as the group called itself, was founded in October 1995 and called for amnesty for political prisoners, respect for the current socialist constitution, respect for all human rights as recognized by the United Nations, freer markets and ownership rights, and a more open and direct electoral system. However, before the group could hold its first major meeting, the government unleashed a wave of repression against it, jailing its leaders and banning any future meetings.

The second high-profile effort to bring about nonviolent changes from within was led by a small nucleus of four economic specialists, one of whom, Vladimiro Roca, is the son of a founder of Cuba's Communist Party. Known as the Internal Dissidents' Working Group, this group, which also included

Félix Antonio Bonné Carcasses, René Gómez Manzano, and Martha Beatriz Roque Cabello, published a scathing critique of the government's economic strategy and political system, entitled "The Fatherland Belongs to Us All" ("*La patria es de todos*"), demanding that the government go beyond tentative economic reforms and embrace a full democratic opening. Criticizing the total lack of space in which to develop an authentic Cuban civil society where alternative voices, policies, and visions could be developed, the declaration argued, "The Cuban government ignores the word 'opposition.' Those of us who do not share its political stance, or who just simply don't support it, are considered enemies" (Bonné Carcasses et al. 1997). The government responded by arresting the four authors of the declaration and holding them without a trial for almost two years. They were charged with sedition and endangering the national economy in September 1998 and were finally tried and convicted in March 1999. Roca, the last dissident to be released from prison, was not freed until 2002. However, he has continued to work for change from within, a stance eventually landing him in prison again in 2003.

An even higher-profile effort to widen the political playing field and bring about major changes in the country's institutional structure grew out of the Catholic Church and has been led by the long-time dissident Osvaldo Payá. Named the Varela Project, after the famous nineteenth-century Cuban priest and independence advocate Félix Varela, Payá's effort also worked from within, using nonviolent means. After effectively (if only temporarily) quashing the Varela Project, even after Jimmy Carter lauded it during his historic May 2002 visit to the island, Castro led an unprecedented crackdown on Cuba's growing dissident movement. In the spring of 2003, while the United States moved to invade Iraq, Castro stoked the nationalist fear of a simultaneous invasion of Cuba, using the rising popular anxiety to justify his harsh measures.

With the help of a number of well-placed Cuban agents who had been masquerading as dissidents, including Manuel David

Portrait of Father Félix Varela, Roman Catholic priest, abolitionist, and advocate of Cuban Independence, ca. 1853. (Library of Congress)

Orrio, who had become a well-known independent journalist and frequent visitor to the home of the chief of the U.S. interest section in Cuba, a total of seventy-five opposition leaders, economists, and independent journalists were arrested.

Convicted of collaborating with the country's "enemies" against Cuban independence, these activists were sentenced to prison terms averaging twenty years each. These dissidents joined the roughly 350 political prisoners already in Cuba's jails, according to Elizardo Sánchez Santacruz, the leader of the island-based Cuban Committee for Human Rights and National Reconciliation. As a result of this episode and other similar incidents over the past forty-five years, Cuba's poor record in upholding universally recognized civil and political freedoms continues to be condemned by the leading human rights organizations around the world, including Amnesty International, the United Nations, and Human Rights Watch.

The Emergence of Civil Society

Cuban political sociologist Haroldo Dilla, who now lives in the Dominican Republic, has argued that the economic crisis of the 1990s has "accelerated the bankruptcy of the state socialist economic-growth model" (Dilla and Oxhorn 2002: 16). As a result, the vertically integrated and highly centralized system of state institutions has begun to erode, ceding space to a wide variety of new actors and organizations, which together constitute an emergent civil society. This civil society includes the strictly private fraternal, cultural, and sports associations, which have little impact or social profile beyond the local level. We could also include the many state-sanctioned mass organizations themselves, given their embeddedness in many people's lives.

Raúl Castro declared as much in a March 1996 speech to the party's Central Committee. "Our concept of civil society is not the same as the one they refer to in the United States," he explained. "Rather, it is our own Cuban socialist civil society, encompassing our strong mass organizations, namely the CTC, the CDRs, the FMC, the ANAP, the FEU, the FEEM, and the Pioneers" (Castro 1996). However, the limited autonomy of these government-operated "nongovernmental" organizations prevents them from successfully resisting subordination to the state as they normally function as mere "transmission belts" for top-down state policies.

Civil society can be defined as "the social fabric formed by a multiplicity of self-constituted, territorially based units which peacefully coexist and collectively *resist subordination* to the state, at the same time that they *demand inclusion* into national political structures" (Dilla and Oxhorn 2002: 11, emphasis in the original). By this definition, institutions of civil society need not be absolutely independent from the state, nor have an antistate agenda. However, they must exercise significant autonomy from the state, have some organic, sui generis base, appeal to or derive from elements within the national territory, seek to impact national issues, and accept nonviolent coexistence with other civil and political organizations. While such criteria clearly exclude some, it would also include a wide spectrum of actors and organizations that make up the emergent civil society of today's Cuba.

This group is constituted by a variety of churches and religious congregations, including the many traditional Afro-Cuban communities of faith, the Catholic Church and its many lay organizations, Cuba's many mainline and evangelical Protestant denominations, as well as a small but vibrant Jewish community. There are also a series of community-based social movements clustered around environmental and self-help issues. Furthermore, Cuba's many new economic actors, including the members of cooperatives and farmer's markets, the foreign and domestic technocratic-entrepreneurial sector, and the more than 100,000 registered self-employed workers (along with their more numerous underground counterparts) are perhaps the domestic leaders in transforming their growing economic power and independence into civic and social influence, if not yet into a formal political presence (Dilla 2006, 2005, 2003, 2001, 2000; Dilla and Oxhorn 2002). Finally, there are an assortment of domestic and international think tanks and nongovernmental organizations, of which the Centro de Estudios sobre América (CEA) was once the most renowned and representative.

Given the fact that Cuba is a "divided nation," with a significant portion of its intellectual, artistic, cultural, and political leaders and movements operating outside the national territory, any understanding of Cuban civil society must reflect this transnational character. In fact, most of the important political, civil, and cultural movements in the nation's history have been incubated to some degree abroad. Cubans who spent significant portions of their professional and political lives abroad, demanding inclusion in the debate over the island's future, include Félix Varela, Narciso López, Cirilo Villaverde, José Martí, Tomás Estrada Palma, Alejo Carpentier, Fernando Ortiz, Julio Antonio Mella, Ramón Grau San Martín, Fulgencio Batista, and Fidel Castro, to say nothing of the many members of the post-1959 Cuban diaspora who have continued this long tradition. In fact, Cuba's civil and political history can be understood as an often antagonistic dialogue with the island's own diaspora, with the losers of today's political battles choosing exile, only to return to fight again tomorrow.

In the spirit of this tradition, the wide variety of exile organizations in the expatriate community certainly influence Cuban civil society. The last forty-five years have seen every conceivable kind of exile movement and activity, including innumerable invasion and assassinations attempts aimed at bringing down the Castro regime; a less well-known series of Cuban-American solidarity organizations, including Areíto and the Antonio Maceo Brigade; an increase in family visits and remittances, both in the late 1970s and again during the 1990s; as well as new efforts after 2000 to broaden the monolithic and often inflexible political stance of the earliest generation of exile leaders. However, their history of using violence (and occasionally terrorism), as well as their close historical association with the U.S. government, has traditionally disqualified the most vocal and visible elements of the

The case of the Center for Studies of the Americas (CEA)

The case of a once renowned Cuban think tank, the Centro de Estudios sobre América (CEA), is especially illustrative of the difficulty of finding the delicate balance necessary to exist as a vital and autonomous, if not exactly independent, part of Cuba's emerging civil society. The CEA was an institute founded in the late 1970s at the direction of the PCC in order to develop research expertise on the Americas as a region, with special focus on the United States (Castro 1996). Over time this think tank managed to attract some of the more innovative and daring young scholars in the country and began to distinguish itself both for the increasing independence of its perspective and the quality and sophistication of its analysis.

By the early 1990s, the center had begun to focus its attention on Cuban domestic issues and led many successful workshops and conferences, which were attended by government officials and visiting international scholars. In fact, these qualities won the center powerful advocates throughout the government and among many progressive Cuba watchers abroad. Such support would later prove crucial to the survival of the center's individual scholars when the center itself was targeted for investigation and closure (Domínguez 2002; Giuliano 1998; Pérez-Stable 1998).

Much of the work of the CEA was published in its journal *Cuadernos de Nuestra América*. Likewise, the center's researchers put out a number of widely circulated monographs that challenged the economic and political structure of the country. The best-known of these, *The Restructuring of the Cuban Economy: A Proposal for Debate* (1995), by Julio Carranza, Pedro Monreal, and Luís Gutiérrez, began an intense debate about the nature, direction, depth, and breadth of the economic reforms enacted in the first half of the 1990s. The book challenged the government to go further with some market-oriented economic reforms while preserving the overall socialist character of the economy.

Other books written by center scholars (Haroldo Dilla and Rafael Hernández, for example) took on the topics of the

(continued)

health of Cuban civil society and the quality of Cuban democracy and elections. Some of these publications included foreign authors who were not to the liking of the party leadership (Giuliano 1998). Finally, a preliminary analysis of Cuban NGOs published in the United States in 1995 and provocatively entitled "Cuba's NGOs: Government Puppets or Seeds of Civil Society?" provoked the ire of the PCC and particularly of Raúl Castro (Castro 1996; Gunn 1995). A year later, in March 1996, Raúl Castro attacked Cuba's NGOs, singling out the CEA for special criticism in a scathing speech to the Central Committee (Castro 1996).

Vice President Castro labeled CEA researchers "fifth columnists" whose work served U.S. interests and who were, wittingly or not, undermining revolutionary ideology. "The enemy does not conceal its intention," he declared, "to use some of the so-called NGOs established in Cuba in recent times, as a Trojan horse to foment division and subversion" (ibid.). All CEA scholars were suspended and subjected to a seven-month investigation-cum-witch-hunt. This episode took place in the immediate aftermath of the Cuban shoot-down of two exile-piloted U.S. planes and the subsequent passage of the Helms-Burton Act, which included the infamous Track-Two provision. Track-Two allowed for greater "person-to-person" contacts between the United States and Cuba under the assumption that exposure to U.S. ideals would undermine the revolution. The Cuban government interpreted this as a veiled threat and justified its crackdown against the CEA based on its long record of hosting American academics.

exile community from playing a more legitimate role inside Cuba.

The organized internal opposition (described above) is perhaps a leading element of civil society, except that it still is internally divided and continues to suffer from the problem of invisibility on account of its total lack of access to the news media. The government holds that this opposition is illegitimate, arguing that members join only in order to qualify for U.S. refugee status so they can emigrate. Another common accusation is that dissidents are merely "lackeys of imperialism" whose nationalist aims are compromised by the considerable moral, material, and financial support they supposedly receive from the U.S. government. Furthermore, the government claims that they lack any internal following or organic popular support.

While these criticisms are indeed true of some of the more opportunistic elements of the opposition, in my own conversations with dissidents I have found that most actually oppose the U.S. embargo and maintain a political line quite independent from that promoted by Washington. Furthermore, in my estimation the only real difference between their opinions and those held by the population at large is that they have decided to cease being silent (and complicit) in a system with which they have fundamental disagreements. They bravely overcome their considerable and legitimate fears of state retribution, seeking to exercise their rights as citizens to share their opinions openly about the significant issues that face their embattled homeland.

Finally, there are many outstanding academic and cultural centers and publications both inside Cuba and abroad. These organizations constantly attempt to balance their valued autonomy with political or economic support from broader interests and institutions. Perhaps the four leading elements of this civil-intellectual current today are the journals *Temas* (published in Havana since 1995 and directed by Rafael Hernández), *Encuentro de la cultura cubana* (published in Madrid and founded in 1996 by the now deceased Jesús Díaz), *Cuban Studies* (founded in 1970 by the Cuban-American economist Carmelo Mesa-Lago and published by the University of Pittsburgh Press), and *Cuba in Transition* (published since 1990 by the U.S.-based, nonpartisan but promarket Association for the Study of the Cuban Economy). Significantly, all four publications defend the independence of their editorial policy and celebrate the diversity of views presented in their pages. Unfortunately, the distrustful and often intolerant atmosphere that dominates Cuban life both on the island and abroad has a direct impact on intellectual dialogue and debate, making the publication and wide dissemination of each of these important journals extremely difficult.

DEFENSE, SECURITY, EDUCATION, AND HEALTH

The Ministry of the Revolutionary Armed Forces (MINFAR) and the Ministry of the Interior are each distinguished by their great power, proven effectiveness, extreme secrecy, hierarchical structure, and controversial and at times adversarial natures. On the other hand, Cuba's public education and health care systems are social-developmental institutions distinguished by their high standards, great achievements, universal coverage, and free access, yet are increasingly under threat from the twin ravages of lack of supplies and insufficient material rewards.

The Revolutionary Armed Forces (FAR)

Like every other major governmental institution in the country, MINFAR is headed by the Castro brothers, who have held the institution's top two positions since 1959. Fidel Castro is the FAR's commander-in-chief, a post he carried over from the Rebel Army. His younger brother, Raúl Castro, is the acting head of the FAR, having held the post of minister of the armed forces since the organization's inception in October 1959. The FAR has four central missions: ensuring external defense, maintaining internal order, engaging in "internationalist" military support, and periodically performing various domestic economic tasks. While the first two of these missions have been constant priorities throughout the revolutionary period, the second two have waxed and waned over time, with international engagement (mainly in Africa and Latin America) prioritized between 1976 and 1991 and economic duties becoming vital to the institution's mission only during the special period after 1991.

The FAR was formed during 1959 out of the remnants of the Rebel Army. Thousands of Batista rank-and-file soldiers and even some lower ranking officials were also incorporated into the FAR initially, while most officers who had not gone into exile were jailed or removed from military service to avoid conflict with their former adversaries in the Rebel Army. Originally, the MINFAR aimed at forming a lean force of 15,000 to 25,000 well-trained troops. However, the political costs of discharging the thousands of journeyman soldiers who had joined the Rebel Army in the final year of the fight against Batista led to the decision to organize a larger army that numbered as many as 40,000 soldiers and officers by 1961.

The FAR did not have to wait long to establish its reputation and legitimacy as an effective and loyal fighting force. In April 1961, it successfully beat back a CIA-sponsored invasion force of Cuban exiles at the Bay of Pigs. The FAR's reputation was further consolidated during the first half of the 1960s through the eventual defeat of the various counter-revolutionary bands (many of whom were also supported and supplied by the CIA) operating in the Escambray Mountains. By the close of this military effort in 1966, euphemistically termed the "fight against bandits," the FAR had grown to nearly 300,000 troops.

Given the definitive defeat of internal subversion and Kennedy's promise not to mount another invasion, the second half of the 1960s saw the FAR shift its focus to tasks of economic development. The two most important military operations during this period were the organization and operation between 1965 and 1968 of the infamous forced-labor and re-education centers known as the UMAP camps (Military Units to Aid Production, Unidades Militares de Ayuda a la Producción), and the "revolutionary offensive." Begun in the late 1960s and culminating in 1970, this radical economic offensive included military participation in the effort to

Revolutionary militias and the war of all the people

At the FAR's inception in 1959, the institution separated professional soldiers and administrators from a less formal network of citizen-soldiers known as the National Revolutionary Militias (MNRs). While they have been periodically reorganized under different names, citizen's militias and civil defense forces have continued to play an important part in the revolution's defense strategy, known as the *Guerra de Todo el Pueblo* (Doctrine of the War of All the People). This doctrine calls on the population itself to take up arms when necessary to defend the revolution. This strategy is designed to convert the entire civil population of "noncombatants" into reservists under the assumption that such a tactic would both strengthen conventional forces and make the costs of an invasion unacceptably high in terms of casualties.

The MNRs were disbanded in 1963 and replaced by the Popular Defense Forces, which in turn were replaced in 1966 by a national system of Civil Defense. Since 1980, when the FAR established the Territorial Troops Militia (MTT), the system of Civil Defense was entrusted with an operational focus distinct from that of the MTT. Whereas the perhaps 1-million-strong MTT took over the task of backing up the FAR's professional soldiers with civilian-based defense, Civil Defense came to concentrate its efforts on preparing the civilian population for effectively responding in the event of a peacetime natural disaster. The system of Civil Defense has been recognized as especially adept at protecting lives and property (including livestock, pets, and major appliances) during Cuba's frequent bouts with hurricanes (MINFAR 1981; Walker 2002: 312–315).

achieve a 10-million-ton sugar harvest in that fateful year. As with the UMAP camps, this effort included the use of "voluntary labor," which was often at least partly coerced from young military recruits in the Youth Labor Army (EJT, Ejército Juvenil de Trabajo) aimed at achieving higher levels of agricultural production.

As part of the process of overall institutionalization, professionalization, and "Soviet-ization" of Cuban life during the 1970s, the military undertook a major administrative reorganization beginning in 1973. Changes included a stepped-up training regimen for officers and enlisted soldiers alike. Especially promising recruits were rewarded by being sent to military schools in the Soviet Union. Also, a new military conscription law required three years of military service of all males between sixteen and fifty years old. The mid-1970s were also the beginning of the FAR's more than fifteen-year military odyssey on the continent of Africa.

Cuba's most important African military mission began in 1975, when Castro answered a call for military support from Angolan president Agostinho Neto (the leader of MPLA, the Popular Movement for the Liberation of Angola). Tens of thousands of Cuban soldiers served in Angola's civil war over the next sixteen years, successfully defending the MPLA from the constant attacks of the U.S.-funded and South African–backed UNITA forces (National Union for the Total Independence of Angola) led by Jonas Savimbi. In 1988, the final, decisive year of the war, the FAR flooded Angola with as many as 50,000 Cuban reinforcements, support that proved crucial in preserving MPLA rule against the South African/UNITA final assault on Cuito Cuanavale in February. The successful Cuban defense of the city forced South Africa to abandon Angola and withdraw its forces from occupied Namibia, leading to a U.S.-mediated peace treaty in 1988 (Gott 2004: 277–278).

As part of the Tripartite Agreement between Angola, Cuba, and South Africa, the independence of nearby Namibia was recognized and Cuban forces were gradually withdrawn from Angola. The last Cuban troops departed African soil in May 1991, ending Cuba's military involvement on the African continent (Walker 2002: 292–293). At the same time, Castro's commitment to the MPLA, Cuban support for Namibian independence, and the FAR's staunch resistance against the fearsome South African Defense Forces, earned Cuba and its charismatic leader wide popularity throughout Africa. In fact, the Cuban victory at Cuito Cuanavale symbolized that the days of apartheid rule in South Africa were numbered (Gott 2004: 278). Three years later, in July 1991, South Africa's newly released freedom fighter and soon-to-be president, Nelson Mandela, personally delivered his thanks to a proud Castro in Havana, calling Cuba's defeat of the South African army "a victory for all Africa [that] destroyed the myth of the invincibility of the white oppressor [and] served as an inspiration to the struggling people of South Africa" (quoted in ibid.: 279).

Apart from the Angolan engagement, Cuban troops spent considerable time in Ethiopia, as well as being dispersed throughout the African continent in a half-dozen other countries. Later, after socialist revolutions succeeded in gaining power during the 1980s in Nicaragua and Grenada, the Cuban military sent them considerable technical and material support, as well as military advisors. The FAR, along with the more secretive Ministry of the Interior, also provided extensive clandestine military support and training for various Latin American guerrilla forces throughout much of the 1960s and early 1970s.

These Latin American and Caribbean commitments grew out of Castro's vision of "turning the Andes into the Sierra Maestra of Latin America." That is, Castro believed that the military success of the Cuban revolution in overthrowing a U.S.-backed dictator and establishing an anti-imperialist socialist republic could be repeated across the continent. This vision of irregular armed struggle on a continental, even global scale, was most vociferously popularized and most clearly exemplified by the iconic guerrilla fighter Che Guevara. In fact, after an unsuccessful foray into the African Congo, Guevara met his death in 1967 attempting to spark a guerrilla war in Bolivia.

Cuba's UMAP camps

Intended as much as punishment and behavior-modification centers as units of agricultural production, the UMAP camps were part and parcel of the larger effort, most emphasized during the late 1960s, of turning Cuban youth into a new generation of socialist men in line with the ideals of Che Guevara. Thus these camps, all of which were located in Camagüey province, were filled with an assortment of young Cubans who did not fit into the narrow mold of a true revolutionary. For that reason, anyone not clearly and unquestionably dedicated to the revolution and reflective of traditional masculine values of virility, hard physical labor, and conformity was a potential target.

Outright dissidents and counter-revolutionaries were not typically sent to the camps. Instead, those who could reasonably be expected to accept re-education, such as suspected homosexuals, religious believers, and vaguely defined "anti-social elements" were the camp's main residents. Ironically, countercultural types, rock aficionados, hippies, and others who exhibited insubordinate attitudes and the unmistakable traits of "corrupting Western decadence," such as long hair and a preference for blue jeans, were singled out. Although it is doubtful that the camps were created with homosexuals in mind, they tended to be the most common targets of "re-education." Ironically, alongside some of Cuba's most flamboyant gays, members of the notoriously homophobic Christian sects Jehovah's Witnesses and Seventh Day Adventists were also commonly interned in these camps for their conscientious objection to performing mandatory military service.

Most observers agree that conditions in the camps were rustic at best, with hard labor in the fields mandated from 7:00 in the morning to 7:00 at night. Reports from some camps indicate that workdays went even longer, from twelve to sixteen hours, and that workers were often enclosed within high barbed-wire fences as they worked. Furthermore, residents were not allowed to leave the camps without military escort. Indicative of the dual mission of punishment and re-education was the slogan plastered at the entrance to at least one camp,

(continued)

El trabajo os hará hombres ("Work will make men of you"). A significant number of Cubans who would later distinguish themselves in the arts and culture were one-time camp residents, including the writer Reinaldo Arenas, the musician Pablo Milanés, and Cuba's current Roman Catholic cardinal Jaime Ortega (Almendros and Jiménez-Leal 1984; Díaz-Briquets 2002; Lumsden 1996: 65–71).

In the aftermath of the Ochoa Affair, Cuba's military remained one of the largest and best equipped conventional armies in all of Latin America, if not the entire developing world. However, given the subsequent Soviet collapse and military pullout that began in 1991, the FAR would never be the same. A single statistic illustrates this change. In 1990, the FAR counted 180,500 active duty troops. A decade later, that number had been cut by two-thirds to just 65,000 (Walker 2002: 311). Moreover, during the 1990s, the portion of Cuba's national budget given over to military expenditures dropped by half, from 10 to 5 percent. Of course, this general weakening of the Cuban military's size and capability was a direct result of the collapse of the Soviet Union and its discontinuance of any military aid, technical support, or resident troop presence on the island.

In fact, after Castro reacted to the failed coup against Soviet president Mikhail Gorbachev in August 1991 with what can only be described as "resounding silence" (after decades of almost bottomless Soviet generosity), the Russians had little qualms about implementing its long-feared exit strategy in Cuba. In September 1991, without prior warning or consultation, Gorbachev announced the unilateral withdrawal of the Soviet "special training brigade," ending its uninterrupted presence on the island since 1962. Russia also unilaterally decided to mothball its high-tech listening station at Lourdes, further provoking the ire of the Cuban leadership. The last of the 2,800-member brigade exited the island in 1993, bring-

The Ochoa Affair, 1989

As a result of his distinguished service in Angola in the mid-1970s, as well as a long and successful military career, FAR officer and division general Arnaldo Ochoa was recognized with MINFAR's highest decoration, Hero of the Republic, in the 1980s. Thus, when Ochoa returned to Cuba freshly victorious from Angola in 1989, he expected to take over as the newly appointed chief of the Western Army that June. Nevertheless, the scandal that erupted during that summer proved that no one, however distinguished or decorated, is untouchable in Castro's Cuba—that is, except Castro himself.

In his public trial in 1989, Ochoa was accused of having directed an intricate scheme of contraband and corruption during the 1980s, including international clandestine trade not only in sugar, ivory, and diamonds (between Cuba and Angola) but also in Colombian cocaine smuggled through Panama and Cuba into the United States with the aid of Cuba exiles. The person who was actually in charge of implementing these operations in Angola, Cuba, and elsewhere, through the Ministry of the Interior was Lieutenant Colonel Tony de la Guardia. De la Guardia firmly believed that Castro approved of their contraband activities. In fact, it seems that the minister of the interior, Division General José Abrantes, had given him his approval, with the understanding that Castro knew everything.

Ochoa was arrested in mid-June on charges of corruption and illegal use of economic resources. In short order, he and his three codefendants found themselves before a court martial composed of forty-seven of their fellow generals facing charges of high treason, punishable by death, instead of drug trafficking charges that called for a maximum sentence of eight years in prison. Starting on June 30, 1989, the trial played itself out dramatically over the next few weeks, with the entire proceedings broadcast on state television. As each new detail was revealed, Cubans were forced to ask themselves if it was possible that such an intricate, high-reaching scheme could have been orchestrated without the knowledge and participation of the Castro brothers.

(continued)

The verdict to execute the four former officers by firing squad was handed down in early July and approved unanimously by the Council of State. Before the end of the year, the Ochoa Affair, as the episode has come to be remembered, would grow into a wide-ranging purge of at least ten other leading officers in the MINFAR and MININT, scores of lower intelligence operatives, and the minister of the interior himself, Division General José Abrantes. Abrantes was the only man who could say for sure if Castro had known everything. However, despite a good health record, he died only a few months after being sent to prison (Walker 2002: 295–298; Gott 2004: 279–286).

ing to a close one of the most lucrative, symbolic, and controversial foreign relationships in Cuba's 500-year history (Walker 2002: 299–300).

As a result of this downturn, the Pentagon issued a 1998 report that characterized the Cuban military as "weak" and declared that it no longer posed "a significant military threat to the U.S. or to other countries in the region." In one sense, the end to the Soviet relationship and the overall weakening of Cuba's military capability allowed the country to shift much of its considerable military budget, personnel, and infrastructure to other areas, reaping a badly needed "peace dividend" in the darkest years of the special period. In fact, the crisis forced the military to begin to self-finance a portion of its budget in 1991, and by the end of the decade it had largely achieved self-sufficiency in food production and managed to cover as much as 80 percent of its own budget through its growing revenues (Walker 2002: 300).

The FAR's new economic role has been carried out primarily in three industries: agriculture, manufacturing, and tourism. Many active duty and retired military personnel have taken over positions of great responsibility as government ministers and managers of state-owned corporations. Major General Ulises Rosales del Toro, the presiding general at Ochoa's trial, was appointed head of the military's business operations, which included Almacenes Universales, responsible for warehousing and free trade zones; Antex, which focused on construction and real estate projects; and Banco Metropolitano, the military's financial holding company (Gott 2004: 295). The FAR even has its own chain of hundreds of "dollar stores," called TRD Caribe, which sell hard-to-get imported consumer goods across the country for hard currency. Perhaps the clearest and most successful example of the FAR's foray into business is its development of a number of joint tourism ventures formed by the military-run corporation Gaviota Tourism Group, S.A. Originally formed in the late 1980s to provide holidays to officers in the Cuban and Soviet militaries, Gaviota transformed itself during the 1990s into Cuba's most adept enterprise at partnering with leading European tourism multinationals (Sol Meliá, Tryp, and Club Med) and successfully attracting upward of 2 million international tourists annually (Walker 2002: 300–301).

The FAR's economic role is only expected to grow now that ailing Fidel Castro has passed the day-to-day administration of the government to his brother Raúl. This power shift makes Raúl all the more powerful, since he is now Cuba's de facto commander-in-chief, as well as its CEO-in-chief, given the depth of the military's involvement in the economy. For more than forty years Raúl has earned the loyalty of all the top uniformed and retired military brass, many of whom now operate in the highest echelons of the government and military, often more as business executives than as soldiers. For example, five of the nineteen-member Communist Party Politburo are active-duty generals along with retired commander Juan Almeida. Retired military officer José Ramón Fernández is a vice president of the Council of State. Also, Lieutenant-General Abelardo Colomé Ibarra is the minister of Cuba's domestic security and intelligence apparatus and the ministry of the Interior, and Major General Rosales del Toro has most recently been named minister of the sugar industry. Generals and other military officials also head up the fishing and transportation ministries, Habanos S.A., a joint venture in charge of marketing Cuban cigars abroad, and Grupo de Electrónica de Cuba, a computer and electronics importer run by a former commander, Ramiro Valdés. Overseeing all of these operations is the FAR's Business Administration Group, which periodically sends its deputies to earn business degrees in European universities and is run on a daily basis by Raúl's aide-de-camp, Lieutenant General Julio Casas Regueiro (Hitchens 2006; Latell 2005; Snow 2006).

The Ministry of the Interior (MININT)

The institutional home of Cuba's infamous state security apparatus, the Ministry of the Interior, is a large, bureaucratic organization with a wide range of security-related responsibilities not unlike the newly formed, controversial, and quite unwieldy U.S. Department of Homeland Security. The MININT has six separate vice ministries, each of whom oversees a series of departments and directorates. Included under the first vice ministry are perhaps the most important of the MININT's responsibilities, including the General Directorate of Personal Security, responsible for safeguarding the president; the General Directorate of Special Troops, which constitutes the MININT's own highly trained paramilitary force; the General Directorate of Border Guards; and the Directorate of Immigration. Other vice ministries include the Vice Ministry of Counterintelligence, the Vice Ministry of the Economy, and the Vice Ministry of Internal Order, which oversees the Cuban police force (NRP), prisons, firefighters, and the issuance of national identification cards (Walker 2002: 336–337).

The MININT was officially established on June 6, 1961. However, its origins go back to the guerrilla struggle in the Sierra Maestra. Juan Almeida, fellow guerrilla fighter and future member of Castro's inner circle, recommended the creation of a special force to protect Castro after a plot to assassinate him was uncovered in 1958. This new secret intelligence organization was called the Organización de Observación Campesina (Rural Intelligence Organization). Simultaneously, fellow insurgent Ramiro Valdés was tapped to head a separate intelligence organization with cells both in the Rebel Army and in the larger 26th of July Movement. The main incubator of what later would become the Ministry of the Interior, this secret organization sought to prevent the infiltration of the revolution by enemy agents, to shore up those within the revolution suspected of being vulnerable to outside recruitment, and to penetrate government military and police forces.

Valdés continued as head intelligence operative into the 1960s, when the new government appointed him chief of the Rebel Army's new Department of Information (DIER). The DIER had the responsibility of capturing Batista henchmen and other war criminals, as well as infiltrating organizations deemed potential threats to the new revolutionary government. Soon thereafter, Castro decided to remove the DIER from the army's jurisdiction and place it under his direct control as the Department of State Security (DSE). Now directly answering to the chief of state himself, the DSE continued its intelligence work, eventually penetrating all major civil and political organizations nationwide. At that point, the DSE also set up a number of special departments including Sections Q and K, which were aimed at identifying and monitoring those suspected of being enemy agents and conducting electronic surveillance, respectively. Eventually, the DSE was folded into the Ministry of the Interior when that organization was formally created in June 1961 as a response to the failed invasion at the Bay of Pigs (Cancio Isla 2002: 235–236).

Since its inception, the MININT has coexisted in a state of antagonistic rivalry with the MINFAR. The relationship between these two institutions is somewhat like the territorial antipathy that has characterized relations between the CIA and the FBI in the United States. However, in the case of Cuba, this clash of powers is exacerbated by the fact that each ministry is directly identified with each one of the Castro brothers. As minister of the FAR, Raúl has worked especially hard to keep his ambitious, often free-wielding generals humble after the successes of their foreign exploits brought them into direct conflict with the equally ambitious officers of the MININT.

After serving as minister of the Interior for more than fifteen years, Valdés handed power over to trusted revolutionary Sergio del Valle Jiménez, who is known to have made efforts to curtail some of the ministry's more egregious abuses. Then in 1986, Division General José Abrantes, who had served as the ministry's longtime vice minister, took over as head of MININT. Abrantes's tenure, however, was short-lived. In July 1989, as part of the larger scandal involving General Ochoa, Abrantes was stripped of his office, arrested, and charged with negligence, corruption, and tolerance of corruption for his knowledge and apparent approval of Ochoa's activities. Sentenced to twenty years in prison, Abrantes died of a heart attack in prison just two years later.

Abrantes was not replaced by someone from within the intelligence service itself. Instead, Army Corps General Abelardo Colomé Ibarra, the MINFAR's second in command under Raúl, as well as a member of the Cuban Council of State and the Politburo, was placed atop the MININT, clearly indicating the Castro brothers' intent to put an end to the long-standing intraministry rivalry. During the early 1990s, hundreds of other MININT career officers were purged or forced into retirement, and replaced by officials from the FAR, effectively neutralizing any ministerial autonomy developed during the 1980s. At the turn of the twenty-first century Colomé Ibarra remains at the helm of MININT, with the apparent full support of the Castro brothers (Cancio Isla 2002: 235–236; Walker 2002: 295–298, 335–336).

Education and Health Care

By almost any measure, Cuba has one of the world's most educated populations. For example, in the late 1990s, Cuba's literacy rate stood at 96 percent, and roughly 95 percent of children from ages six to sixteen were attending school. Already relatively advanced in educational attainment in the 1950s, since 1959 the revolution has introduced a new set of more practical and equitable educational priorities based on the country's developmental needs and on the principles of open access, equity, and conscientization (some would say ideological indoctrination). The revolution also took over a highly unequal educational system that prioritized wealthy, urban dwellers who attended private, often parochial schools, introducing in its place a comprehensive national educational system that focused on making education available to traditionally underserved groups including the rural population, the poor, blacks, and women (Ripton 2002: 280).

This system began with preschool, primary, and secondary education, followed by a tracking system that based one's advancement on academic and political criteria. Some students were channeled into vocational/technical training schools, while others entered the preuniversity educational system during their teens, preparing for a higher education and a professional career (Díaz-Briquets 2002: 145–146). The revolution also sought to correct the imbalance of the prerevolutionary educational system in which available training did not respond to the labor needs of the country and administrative corruption had become chronic.

For example, in the 1940s and 1950s, administrative costs absorbed as much as 20 percent of the educational budget, while only 4 percent was set aside for vocational and technical training. Moreover, in 1956, despite pouring 23 percent of the national budget into education, only 6 percent of the population had received a secondary education and just 2 percent had attended college. In the mid-1950s, more than half of the population had less than a fourth-grade education, and just 1

Dating from 1977, this third-grade class photo shows a young pionera *posing beside a bust of the Cuban* apóstol *José Martí, with the Cuban flag and coat of arms in the background. (Ted Henken)*

percent held a university degree. Finally, among those with degrees, there was a vast overemphasis on law, while scientific, technical, and engineering were relatively neglected. In fact, the 1953 census counted just 309 engineers, 355 veterinarians, and 294 agronomists, while the country was flooded with 6,500 lawyers (Ripton 2002: 279).

With the goal of open access in mind, massive educational reforms were begun in 1959, including the building of at least 1,100 new schools and the development of training programs to prepare new teachers. As part of the educational reforms, the government decreed a new Law on the Nationalization of Education, which outlawed all private and religious education, confiscated schools and property, and deported scores of foreign teachers, especially the parochial schools' many Spanish priests and nuns. As a result of these and other reforms, between 1959 and 1971 primary school enrollment jumped from 811,000 to 1.7 million. More startling was the jump in the badly neglected secondary and higher educational

Patria potestad, "Pedro Pan," and the fight over Elián González

Given the fact that the educational priorities of the revolution emphasized both social justice and political indoctrination, Cuban families reacted differently to the ways the island's new educational system affected the lives and futures of their children. Some embraced the new educational opportunities, believing that the revolution would provide their children the educational opportunities they had been denied. Other parents reacted with alarm, fearing that the government would seek to socialize their children in communist ideals, sowing division within their families. Some of these parents' fears were justified by the effects (intended or not) that the new system of countryside and boarding schools had on their children.

Working with limited resources offset by generous aid from the USSR, the Cuban educational system sought to ensure equal access, erase socioeconomic distinctions, and combine the ideals of work and study even for the youngest of students. As such, the revolution set up countryside schools (*escuelas del campo*), where children would go for thirty to forty-five days each year to perform agricultural labor, and boarding schools (*la beca*), where children would spend their entire school year, provided with education and meals, allowing their parents to enter the workforce and dedicate their free time to the tasks of building the revolution.

While these schools were a boon for many poor, rural families, other parents saw them as a direct attack on their parental rights (*patria potestad*) to raise their children as they saw fit. As a result of this objection, as well as the unfounded rumor that Castro planned to round up Cuban children and ship them off to be educated in the Soviet Union, thousands of parents decided to send their children into exile in the United States with the help of the Catholic Church and the U.S. embassy. These parents feared that the state would gain the ability to inculcate political values in conflict with parental preferences (Díaz-Briquets 2002: 146; Torres 2003).

Dubbed operation *Pedro Pan*, after the storybook character Peter Pan, more than 14,000 children were sent into exile

(continued)

in the early 1960s. While most parents were later reunited with their children, some were never able to rejoin their families in the United States. The experience was traumatic for parents and children alike (Conde 2000; de la Campa 2000). While few North Americans could understand their rage, it was partly the memory of this aspect of the Cuban educational system that motivated members of the Cuban-American community to campaign so vociferously against the repatriation of Elián González in 1999. On the other hand, most Cubans on the island (communists or not) were insulted by the implication that they were incapable of imparting positive values to their children within the context of the revolution.

enrollments. Between 1959 and 1986, secondary enrollment grew from just 88,000 to 1.2 million. Likewise, university enrollment grew from 26,000 in 1966 to 269,000 by 1986 (Díaz-Briquets 2002: 145).

Perhaps the most significant and certainly the most symbolic educational achievement in the revolution's early years was the literacy campaign of 1961. The mass mobilization that drove the campaign began in December 1960, when the new government announced an all-out "war on illiteracy," officially christening 1961 the Year of Education. Although as optimistic as President Lyndon Johnson's similarly named War on Poverty, Cuba's literacy campaign truly captured the imagination of the country's idealistic youth. By April of 1961, as many as 120,000 young, idealistic literacy workers, known as *brigadistas*, began to penetrate the long-neglected reaches of the island, armed with the catechism of reading and writing. These literacy volunteers wore uniforms and carried with them signature blue and red oil lamps to light their way through the countryside, chanting the campaign's slogan, *Alfabetizando Venceremos* ("through literacy we shall overcome"). However, a number of *brigadistas* were killed in the line of duty. In fact, they were often sent into the same remote rural areas where various anticommunist forces had gained a foothold, successfully holding out against the government.

While Cuba could already boast a literacy rate of perhaps 70 percent (relatively high for the time), the *brigadistas* managed to affect the lives of perhaps 1 million illiterates. As prorevolutionary influences on their peasant pupils, *brigadistas* encouraged their newly literate students to pen "Dear Fidel" letters to the revolution's *comandante en jefe,* thanking him personally with their newly acquired literacy skills. The government followed up by building more than 10,000 rural schools throughout the country and launching an ongoing *biblioteca movil* ("traveling library") project. Ever since, education has been recognized as one of the crowning achievements of the revolution (Gott 2004: 188–189).

As in the area of education, the Cuban Revolution achieved significant progress in the provision of health care between 1960 and 1990. While already a regional leader in 1958, Cuba established a National Health System (NHS) in 1960 under the new revolutionary government. Part of the Ministry of Public Health, the NHS instituted universal, free health services and built an expansive network of urban and rural local outpatient clinics (*policlínicos*) starting in 1964, which now number 440 islandwide. The revolution also improved access to primary health care further in the 1980s through its innovative family doctor program, which located doctors and nurses in patients' neighborhoods and focused attention on primary care, prevention, and regular checkups. Finally, an extensive network of health centers was set up across the island, which today number 276 hospitals and 700 clinics, providing 76,500 beds to the Cuban population.

In terms of focus, the revolution has prioritized the reduction of infectious diseases, promoted maternal and child health, and begun to develop a modern biotechnology industry. More recently, Cuba has sought to bring in hard currency by catering to paying customers in its network of tourist-oriented health clinics (Díaz-Briquets 2002: 138–139).

In mocking reference to an ambitious plan drawn up by President George W. Bush's Commission for Aid to a Free Cuba in the summer of 2004, this new billboard facing the U.S. Interest Section features a group of Cuban children intoning, "Thanks Mr. Bush, but we already have our shots." (Ted Henken)

Finally, as part of this effort to build a comprehensive system of public health, the revolution trained a new generation of health care professionals to replace the doctors who left. Indeed, fully half of Cuba's 6,300 physicians went into exile between 1959 and 1964 (Martínez-Fernández 2002: 288). Today, the only physicians permitted to perform private practice are those few remaining doctors who received their medical training in prerevolutionary Cuba. However, an underground market for medical services does exist for those with personal connections or hard currency.

Cuba has become renowned worldwide for its extensive network of medical professionals stationed in developing countries across the globe. In the 1990s, the government even set up an international medical school in the western suburbs of Havana to train needy students from a wide array of developing countries, including a group of underprivileged medical students from the United States. Although originally begun as a form of international solidarity, Cuba's international medical program has also benefited the regime politically and economically. In many cases the Cuban government has begun to charge receiving countries in hard currency for its medical services. The most recent and controversial example of this political and economic tradeoff has been the massive deployment of Cuban medical professionals in Venezuela in exchange for access to President Hugo Chávez's nearly unlimited reserves of petroleum.

As a result of these innovations, virtually all health indicators improved during the first thirty years of the revolution. Cuba's per capita number of physicians rose from 9.2 to 33.1 per 10,000 inhabitants; its infant mortality rate fell from 33.4 to 11.1 per 1,000 live births; many contagious diseases such as diphtheria, malaria, tuberculosis, and polio were eradicated (while others, especially venereal diseases, increased); and the gap in access and standards between rural and urban regions was significantly reduced. Unfortunately, because of the economic crisis that began in 1990, this trend of steady improvement has been interrupted and in some cases drastically reversed. While the infant mortality rate continued to improve, dropping to under 6 by the late 1990s, most other health indicators worsened between 1993 and 1995, recovering slowly since then. Most recently, the rate of physicians to patients has begun to worsen as a result of the expansion of Cuba's internationalist health missions to Venezuela and other countries.

One major obstacle to maintaining the high health standards achieved by the late 1980s was the contraction in nutritional levels accompanied by the severe scarcity of medicine, medical equipment, lab tests, drugs, and basic inputs of all kinds, including vaccinations, prophylactics, and anesthetics. Exacerbating this material crisis was an intensification of stratification in medical care in a context of desperation and

This billboard near the Plaza of the Revolution welcomes Venezuelan president Hugo Chávez to Cuba for the celebration of May Day, 2005. (Ted Henken)

scarcity. Theft of materials and medicines at pharmacies and medical centers became commonplace. Reliance on impersonal rules, contacts, and bribes increased. Finally, preferential treatment for members of the elite (the armed forces, state security, top government functionaries, and Communist Party cadres) and hard currency–paying foreigners became a frustrating symbol of inequality in a context of crisis and supposed commitment to social egalitarianism (Mesa-Lago and Pérez-López 2005: 83–87).

CONCLUSION

These most recent transformations in state-society relations reflect a long-incubating contradiction at the heart of Cuba's political and institutional life. On the one hand, the revolution succeeded in defending itself against constant U.S. hostility while simultaneously ensuring egalitarian well-being devoid of consumerism, built upon a vigorous political culture and deep wellspring of popular participation and mobilization (Dilla 2000: 34). The vast majority of Cubans gave themselves over to the revolutionary project as their own, channeling their participation through an extensive network of "grass-roots" mass organizations, such as the Federation of Cuban Women and the Committees for the Defense of the Revolution, and projects such as the 1961 Literacy Campaign.

The creation in the early 1960s of these organizations and mobilizations was aimed at both defending the revolution and transforming an alienated, corrupt (if still liberal democratic) political and civic culture into a participatory socialist democracy arranged in an increasingly vertical, monolithic structure. Later, in the mid-1970s, an attempt was made to institutionalize this system into a series of constitutionally recognized organizations that would project an image of formal representation of the will of the people through elections within a one-party political system. These were the municipal, provincial, and national Organs of People's Power (Bengelsdorf 1994; Roman 2006, 2005, 2003, 1995, 1993).

On the other hand, the siege mentality provoked by U.S. aggression, combined with a deep authoritarian paternalism on the part of the Cuban revolutionary political class and a constant struggle against economic underdevelopment, gradually led to a centralizing, bureaucratizing tendency in state institutions (Bengelsdorf 1994). Over time, the demand for absolute loyalty and unquestioning revolutionary unity slowly circumscribed citizen autonomy and turned many once popular and vital revolutionary institutions into mere "conveyor belts" of top-down political control (Bengelsdorf 1994; Dilla and Oxhorn 2002: 16). Civic and political institutions that were intended to embody nationalist self-defense and self-determination were institutionalized under such extreme conditions of external threat, centralizing will, and internal rigidity that periodic grass-roots efforts to create marginally autonomous and effective mechanisms of a genuine socialist democracy have been obliterated, leading to a closed political culture, the harsh repression of any dissent, and permanent ideological mobilizations (Dilla 2005: 45; Dilla 2006: 42).

References

Almendros, Nestor, and Orlando Jiménez-Leal. *Improper Conduct* [*Conducta Impropia*]. Madrid: Playor, 1984.

Bengelsdorf, Carollee. *The Problem of Democracy in Cuba: Between Vision and Reality.* New York: Oxford University Press, 1994.

Blanco, Juan Antonio, and Madea Benjamin. "From Utopianism to Institutionalization," in *The Cuba Reader.* Edited by Aviva Chomsky, Barry Carr, and Pamela Maria Smorkaloff, pp. 433–442. Durham, NC: Duke University Press, 2003.

Bonné Carcasses, Félix Antonio, René Gómez Manzano, Vladimiro Roca Antúnez, and Martha Beatriz Roque Cabello. "The Homeland Belongs to Us All." *Havana,* June 27, 1997. Available online at: http://www.cubanet.org/CNews/y97/jul97/homdoc.htm.

Cancio Isla, Wilfredo. "Ministry of the Interior," in *Encyclopedia of Cuba: People, History, Culture.* 2 vols. Edited by Luís Martínez-Fernández, D. H. Figueredo, Louis A. Pérez, Jr., and Luís González, pp. 235–236. Westport, CT: Greenwood Press, 2002.

Carranza Valdés, Julio, Pedro Monreal González, and Luís Guitérrez Urdaneta. *Cuba la reestructuración de la economía: una propuesta para el debate.* Havana: Editorial de Ciencias Sociales, 1995.

Castro, Raúl. "General of the Army Raúl Castro Ruz to the Central Committee of the Communist Party of Cuba," March 23, 1996. Available online at: http://www.marxmail.org/raul_castro.htm.

Conde, Yvonne. *Operation Pedro Pan: The Untold Exodus of 14,048 Cuban Children.* New York: Routledge, 2000.

Corrales, Javier. "The Gatekeeper State: Limited Economic Reforms and Regime Survival in Cuba, 1989–2002." *Latin American Research Review* 39, no. 2 (June, 2004): 35–65.

Cuba Transition Project, Institute for Cuban and Cuban American Studies, University of Miami, "Organizational Charts." Available online at: http://ctp.iccas.miami.edu/main.htm. Accessed on May 4, 2007.

Del Águila, Juan M. Cuba: Dilemmas of a Revolution. (third editon) Boulder, CO: Westview Press, 1994.

De la Campa, Román. *Cuba on My Mind: Journeys to a Severed Nation.* New York: Verso, 2000.

Díaz-Briquets, Sergio. "The Society and Its Environment." In *Cuba: A Country Study.* (fourth edition) Edited by Rex Hudson. Washington, D.C.: Federal Research Division, Library of Congress, 2002.

Dilla Alfonso, Haroldo. "Cuban Civil Society: II. Future Directions and Challenges." *NACLA Report on the Americas* 39, no. 4 (January/February 2006), pp. 37–42.

Dilla Alfonso, Haroldo. "Larval Actors, Uncertain Scenarios, and Cryptic Scripts: Where Is Cuban Society Headed?" In *Changes in Cuban Society since the Nineties*. Edited by Joseph S. Tulchin, Liliam Bobea, Mayra P. Espina Prieto, and Rafael Hernández, pp. 35–50. Washington D.C.: Woodrow Wilson Center Report on the Americas #15, 2005.

Dilla Alfonso, Haroldo. "Civil Society," in *The Cuba Reader*. Edited by Aviva Chomsky, Barry Carr, and Pamela Maria Smorkaloff, pp. 650–659. Durham, NC: Duke University Press, 2003.

Dilla Alfonso, Haroldo. "Local Government and Economic and Social Change in Cuba." FOCAL Background Briefing (Canadian Foundation for the Americas, RFC-01–1). Ottawa, Ontario, May, 2001. Available online at: www.cubasource.org.

Dilla Alfonso, Haroldo. "The Cuban Experiment: Economic Reform, Social Restructuring, and Politics." *Latin American Perspectives* 27, no. 1 (January 2000), pp. 33–44.

Dilla Alfonso, Haroldo, and Philip Oxhorn. "The Virtues and Misfortunes of Civil Society in Cuba." *Latin American Perspectives* 29, no. 4 (July 2002), pp. 11–30.

Domínguez, Jorge I. "Government and Politics." In *Cuba: A Country Study*. (fourth edition) Edited by Rex Hudson. Washington, DC: Federal Research Division, Library of Congress, 2002.

Domínguez, Jorge I. "¿Comienza una transición hacia el autoritarismo en Cuba?" *Encuentro de la cultura cubana* 6, no. 7 (fall/winter 1997).

Domínguez, Jorge I. "Cuba since 1959," in *Cuba: A Short History*. Edited by Leslie Bethell. Cambridge: Cambridge University Press, 1993.

Farber, Samuel. *The Origins of the Cuban Revolution Reconsidered*. Chapel Hill: University of North Carolina Press, 2006.

Giuliano, Maurizio. *El caso CEA: Intelectuales e inquisidores en Cuba*. Miami, FL: Ediciones Universal, 1998.

González, Edward. *Cuba under Castro: The Limits of Charisma*. Boston: Houghton Mifflin Company, 1974.

Gott, Richard. *Cuba: A New History*. New Haven, CT: Yale University Press, 2004.

Guillermoprieto, Alma. *Dancing with Cuba: A Memoir of the Revolution*. Translated by Esther Allen. New York: Pantheon Books, 2004.

Gunn, Gillian. *Cuba's NGOs: Government Puppets or Seeds of Civil Society?* Washington, DC: Georgetown University Caribbean Project, Briefing Paper #7, February, 1995. Available online at: http://www.trinitydc.edu/academics/depts/Interdisc/International/ca ribbean%20briefings/Cubas_NGOs.pdf.

Halperin, Maurice. *Return to Havana: The Decline of Cuban Society under Castro*. Nashville, TN: Vanderbilt University Press, 1994.

Halperin, Maurice. *The Taming of Fidel Castro*. Berkeley: University of California Press, 1981.

Halperin, Maurice. *The Rise and Decline of Fidel Castro: An Essay in Contemporary History.* Berkeley: University of California Press, 1972.

Hitchens, Christopher. "The Eighteenth Brumaire of the Castro Dynasty: Cuba's Military Coup Marks the End of the Revolutionary Era." August 8, 2006. Available online at: http://www.slate.com/id/2147243/.

Latell, Brian. *After Fidel: The Inside Story of Castro's Regime and Cuba's Next Leader.* New York: Palgrave Macmillan, 2005.

Linger, Eloise. "From Social Movement to State in Cuba, 1952–1966." Unpublished Ph.D. dissertation, New School for Social Research, New York, 1999.

Lumsden, Ian. *Machos, Maricones, and Gays: Cuba and Homosexuality.* Philadelphia, PA: Temple University Press, 1996.

Martínez-Fernández, Luís, D. H. Figueredo, Louis A. Pérez, Jr., and Luís González, eds. *Encyclopedia of Cuba: People, History, Culture.* 2 vols. Westport, CT: Greenwood Press, 2002.

Mesa-Lago, Carmelo, and Jorge Pérez-López. *Cuba's Aborted Reform: Socioeconomic Effects, International Comparisons, and Transition Policies.* Gainesville: University Press of Florida, 2005.

MINFAR (Ministerio de las Fuerzas Armadas Revolucionarias). *Manual básico del Miliciano de Tropas Territoriales.* Havana: Editorial Orbe, 1981.

Morton, Ward M. *Castro as Charismatic Hero.* Kansas City: Center of Latin American Studies, University of Kansas. Occasional Publications No. 4, 1965.

Pérez, Louis A., Jr. "The Cuban Revolution," in *Encyclopedia of Cuba: People, History, Culture.* 2 vols. Edited by Luís Martínez-Fernández, D. H. Figueredo, Louis A. Pérez, Jr., and Luís González, pp. 242–246. Westport CT: Greenwood Press, 2002.

Pérez-Stable, Marifeli. "El Caso CEA." *Encuentro de la cultura cubana.* Volume 10 (fall 1998), pp. 85–88.

Ripton, John. "Education in Cuba." In *Encyclopedia of Cuba: People, History, Culture.* 2 vols. Edited by Luís Martínez-Fernández, D. H. Figueredo, Louis A. Pérez, Jr., and Luís González, pp. 279–280. Westport, CT: Greenwood Press, 2002.

Roman, Peter. "Electing Cuba's National Assembly Deputies: Proposals, Selections, Nominations, and Campaigns." Paper presented at the Latin American Studies Association Conference, San Juan, Puerto Rico, March 15–18, 2006.

Roman, Peter. "The Lawmaking Process in Cuba: Debating the Bill on Agricultural Cooperatives." *Socialism and Democracy* 19, no. 2 (July 2005): 1–20.

Roman, Peter. *People's Power: Cuba's Experience with Representative Government.* (revised edition) Lanham: Rowman and Littlefield Publishers, 2003.

Roman, Peter. "Worker's Parliaments in Cuba." *Latin American Perspectives* 22, no. 4 (autumn 1995), pp. 43–58.

Roman, Peter. "Representative Government in Socialist Cuba." *Latin American Perspectives* 20, no. 1 (winter 1993), pp. 7–27.

Sagás, Ernesto. "Government Structure," in *Encyclopedia of Cuba: People, History, Culture*. 2 vols. Edited by Luís Martínez-Fernández, D. H. Figueredo, Louis A. Pérez, Jr., and Luís González, pp. 224–226. Westport, CT: Greenwood Press, 2002.

Sánchez Santacruz, Elizardo. "A Dissident Speaks Out.," in *The Cuba Reader*. Edited by Aviva Chomsky, Barry Carr, and Pamela Maria Smorkaloff, pp. 664–665. Durham, NC: Duke University Press, 2003.

Snow, Anita. "Cuba's Military Men Loyal to Raúl Castro." *Houston Chronicle*, August 9, 2006. Available online at: http://www.chron.com/disp/story.mpl/ap/world/4103708.html.

Torres, María de las Ángeles. *The Lost Apple: Operation Pedro Pan, Cuban Children in the U.S., and the Promise of a Better Future*. New York: Beacon Press, 2003.

Walker, Phyllis. "National Security," in *Cuba: A Country Study*. (fourth edition) Edited by Rex Hudson. Washington, DC: Federal Research Division, Library of Congress, 2002.

CHAPTER FOUR
Culture and Society

At the start of British historian Hugh Thomas's monumental 1,700-page historical classic, *Cuba or the Pursuit of Freedom* (1998 [1971]), the following surreal scene unfolds in the Plaza of the Revolution. As Castro began to tire after railing nonstop against the Kennedy administration for more than four hours (it was July 1961, just three months after the failed Bay of Pigs invasion), the immense crowd began to drown him out singing the Cuban National Anthem, and then as if on cue, the socialist hymn, "The Internationale." This already super-charged scene took on a surreal quality when the motley crew of Cubans surrounding Thomas "began to sing and dance the Internationale to a cha-cha-cha rhythm."

An imposing Afro-Cuban woman belted out the lyrics to which the laughing crowd that encircled her responded with the song's chorus. In a classic mimicry of traditional Afro-Cuban call-and-response structure, the words came over with bizarre new melody, but fully Cuban syncopation, *arriba hijos, de la tierra* . . . ("arise children, from the earth" . . .). This experience prompted Thomas to recall the comment French surrealist writer André Breton once made to Cuban painter Wilfredo Lam: *Ce pays est vraiment trop surréaliste pour y habiter* ("This country is truly too surreal a place to live"). In response, Thomas was forced to reassess what he had originally planned as a brief project about the then youthful and buoyant revolution, and his "short" book on Cuban history was not published for another ten years.

Forty-five years and a famous "90 miles" later in early August 2006 on Calle Ocho in Miami's Little Havana, a surprisingly similar scene unfolded. With news of Fidel Castro's failing health spreading through South Florida, a live cable television feed from a hovering news helicopter broadcast to the world the scene of throngs of jubilantly expectant Cuban-Americans parading down the street waving Cuban flags. Even from high above, one could clearly make out a circle forming around two figures, one a young woman and the other an elderly man, playing out a seductive pantomime of a classic Cuban guaguancó with the cheering crowd chanting *¡libertad!* ("liberty") to the beat of an improvised rumba rhythm. Watching this equally surreal scene unfold, I wondered if any of the revelers on Calle Ocho that August night had also been in the Plaza with Fidel forty-five years earlier. The lesson here, of course, is that nothing in Cuba concerning culture, society, or politics (and especially the combination of the three) is as simple or straightforward as it may seem at first.

I begin this final chapter of the book's narrative section by focusing broadly on Cuban society in the areas of religion and the family, national identity, race and ethnic relations, and the Cuban diaspora. Then, in order to highlight the extraordinarily broad and prolific cultural production that has emanated from Cuba during the course of the twentieth century, I will chronicle the nation's cultural achievements in the arts with a particular focus on the areas of music, filmmaking, and literature. I will emphasize the contradictory governmental policies of institutionalization and encouragement of art and culture, describe the various "gray" periods of cultural and artistic censorship and self-censorship, and highlight the gradual yet incomplete growth of tolerance in the dynamic, ongoing relationship between art and revolution.

FAITH AND FAMILY

As social organizations, the intimate, personal, and affective institutions of religion and the family are both distinguished by paradox. For example, to different degrees, Cubans engage in a wide variety of informal religious and spiritual practices yet are notorious for their reluctance to participate in formal, organized religious institutions. This contradiction arises in part from the revolution's repression of religion. However, Cuba's failure to internalize religious formalism predates socialism and is rooted in the long history of a weak, elite-oriented Catholic Church in both colonial and republican Cuba. Although Cuba is often considered the "most Spanish" of all Latin American countries, it is simultaneously the "most African," leading to a syncretic mixing of formal Spanish Catholicism with a wide array of less rigid spiritual practices introduced by African slaves. This mixture produced what is popularly referred to as santería, a diverse group of Afro-Cuban religious beliefs and rituals that has essentially become the popular religion of today's Cuba. Likewise, while the Cuban family continues to be the island's strongest and deepest social institution (despite geographic separations and antagonistic political divisions), the strength and stability of marriage has slowly eroded over the past forty-five years—both on the island and in exile.

During Pope John Paul II's historic visit to Cuba in 1998, Castro decided to take him on a tour of the city along the Malecón, the famed seaside drive that runs the entire length of Havana. En route to Habana Vieja, the capital city's colonial quarter, Castro decided to stop in order to show the pope the famed Hotel Nacional, as well as to point out the unmistakable headquarters of his archenemy's diplomatic mission, the U.S. Interests Section. However, just as they emerged from their vehicle, a powerful wind whipped John Paul's cap off his head and out into the Gulf Stream. The elderly Castro surprised the even older John Paul by springing to his feet, vaulting over the sea wall, and striding across the top of the water, effortlessly retrieving the pope's cap.

The next day, three different newspapers reported the extraordinary news, but with three very different spins. *Granma,* Cuba's party-run national daily, led with the bold declaration, *Nuestro Comandante Es Inmortal! Viva La Revolución! Venceremos!* ("Our Commander Is Immortal! Long

Live the Revolution! We Shall Overcome!"). In contrast, the Vatican newspaper, *L'Osservatore Romano,* confidently reported: "With God's Help, Pope Performs Miracle Allowing President Castro to Walk on Water." Not to be outdone, *El Nuevo Herald,* the Spanish-language counterpart to the *Miami Herald,* printed this triumphant headline: "Fidel's Days Are Numbered—Now We Have Definitive Proof That the Dictator Can Not Swim!" Perhaps the only element missing from this apocryphal tale is a *babalao,* a santería priest, reacting to the news with a ceremony of thanks to the Afro-Cuban orishas Yemayá and Ochún (the sister goddesses of the seas, identified, respectively, with the Catholic Virgin of Regla and the Virgin of Charity, Caridad de Cobre, Cuba's patron saint) for aiding Fidel in his daring undertaking.

Cuba is perhaps the most secular of all Latin American and Caribbean countries. That is due to the shallow penetration of organized religion during the island's history. Also, given the militant anticlerical orientation of the revolution, organized religion faded from public view after 1959, with the older generation either rejecting its practice or practicing it in secrecy, and the new generation being socialized as if organized religion simply did not exist. However, most Cubans on the island (even if they have never been inside a church) exhibit a deep cultural spirituality that manifests itself in the practice of different forms and degrees of syncretic religion.

For example, before my wife emigrated from Cuba a few years ago, she felt the need to call not only on an Afro-Cuban *babalao* but also on a card-reading fortune teller, as well as an astrologist. At the same time, she would have considered it absurd to pay a similar visit to a Catholic priest. Moreover, as an immigrant in the United States, she routinely lights candles of devotion to San Lázaro (Saint Lazarus, syncretized with the Afro-Cuban orisha Babalú-Ayé) whenever she has an exam or begins any new undertaking. However, she wouldn't dream of joining an organized religion, considering the whole enterprise inhibiting and ridiculously superstitious.

Among Cuba's most important pilgrimage sites (even for communists), this is the shrine of Our Lady of Charity (Caridad de Cobre, patroness of Cuba, syncretized with the Afro-Cuban orisha Ochún). Cobre is a town on the outskirts of Santiago de Cuba, in the foothills of the Sierra Maestra. (Ted Henken)

These two anecdotes indicate the complexity of Cuban spiritual practice and religious belief. They also highlight the degree to which religion has become mixed with culture, tradition, and nationalism. Still, in today's Cuba, organized religion plays a relatively minuscule role in the public sphere and focuses most of its energy on nonconfrontational evangelical and social welfare activities. Unlike the role of organized religion in other national contexts, where it has often become wedded to nationalism (as in Poland or Colombia), in Cuba, Catholicism was long associated with Spanish colonialism and later in the republican period with urban middle-class whites, while Protestantism was associated with the United States. "In Cuba," by contrast, "it is the state that has had a greater identification with the assertion of nationalism. Given this," argues Margaret Crahan, "any religion that criticizes the government can be attacked as unpatriotic" (Crahan 2003: 2).

To the extent that Cubans are religious, they have creatively hedged their (religious) bets by rejecting the typical Western either-or approach to organized religion. Instead of highlighting religious exclusivity, Cubans have typically embraced a wide spectrum of religious beliefs, spiritual practices, and Afro-Hispanic cultural traditions. As Ned Sublette has wisely observed in his recent history of Cuban music, "You do not have to disavow Catholicism to practice santería, though the priest might tell you that you must disavow santería to be a Christian" (2004: 213). Even before the revolution, religion was understood as more personal than institutional. For example, a 1954 survey carried out by a group of Catholic university students revealed that while 96.5 percent of those Catholics polled claimed to believe in God, just 17 percent of them actually attended church regularly (Fernández 2002: 526).

Despite a long history of repression from church and state officials, African religion, African deities (orishas), and especially African-influenced musical forms survived during the 400-year colonial Spanish-Catholic period of Cuba's history by "hiding in plain sight" under the catch-all term *santería* (literally, the worship of the saints) (Sublette 2004). In order to avoid detection and harsh punishment, African slaves and their descendants in Cuba would mimic and feign fealty to

Catholic symbols and saints, when in fact they were keeping their long-repressed traditions and beliefs alive. However, after hundreds of years of simulation, few Cubans today know (or care) where Catholicism starts and santería begins. Moreover, the Catholic Church typically neglected its religious obligation to instruct Africans in the faith, rarely going beyond baptizing them and providing them with a Christian name (Thomas 1998).

Such neglect, however, opened the door for both slaves and free coloreds alike to blend their varied and rich traditional beliefs with Spanish Catholicism. The need to hide one's religious practices in a context of repression and violence certainly motivated slaves to quickly adapt a feigning and duplicitous display for their masters and priests, while secretly preserving authentic traditions. However, over time it is likely that many Africans and certainly their descendants could think of themselves as Christian while continuing to worship and pay homage to African deities. Indeed, Cuba's blacks could easily reconcile being adherents of two or more belief systems at once. Take, for example, Cuban novelist Alejo Carpentier's description of religious syncretism in Cuba:

> From the outset, the Christian church exercised a powerful attraction for the blacks brought to the Americas. . . . Deep down, of course, it did not mean that the ancient gods of Africa were renounced. Ogún, Changó, Elegguá, Obatalá, and many others continued thriving in the hearts of many . . . . But the African transplanted to the New World never believed that these two worlds, Catholic and African, could not be shared in admirable harmony. . . . In this fashion, Saint Lazarus became Babalú-Ayé; the Virgin of Regla is Yemayá; Saint Barbara is associated with Changó; and so forth. (2001: 81–82)

While generally grouped under the term *santería*, there are in fact a handful of African-derived religious/cultural traditions still alive in Cuba today. The first of these is popularly known as santería, but more properly called Regla de Ochá. That religious group is perhaps the most widespread throughout the island and has been the most adept at absorbing new influences and syncretizing itself with Catholicism. Ethnically, practitioners of santería were originally known to Europeans as *lucumí* (apparently from the Yoruba greeting *Oluku mi*, meaning, "my friend") and hailed from the great African civilization of Oyó in what is now Nigeria. Today, the term *lucumí* has lost prominence to the more general term *Yoruba* to describe not only the language but also the people and their religion, though the catch-all term *santería* is more commonly used to describe their religion.

The second Afro-Cuban religious tradition is known as *palo monte*, the adherents of which are referred to as *paleros*, or more generally, *Congo*. The tradition originated in central and southwestern Africa in what is today the Democratic Republic of the Congo (formerly Zaire) and Angola. The third major religion is called *abakuá*, and its practitioners are known as *Ñáñigos* or, alternately, *Carabalí*. It comes from a region of Africa once called the Calabar, but divided today between Nigeria and Cameroon. Three other, less widely diffused and practiced Afro-Cuban rites in Cuba are the Dahomeyan tradition known as *arará*, the transplanted Haitian religion *vodú* ("voodoo"), and the legacy of the blacks who came to Cuba directly from Spain, known in colonial times as the *negros curros* (Sublette 2004: 171–172; 207).

Although Cuban slaves originated from many African "nations" and thus brought a diverse array of gods and beliefs with them on the slave ships, they generally shared animistic belief systems that endowed natural objects with supernatural power and meaning. They also brought with them their own pantheon of orishas, each of which possesses a particular personality. Though often called *santos* ("saints") in Spanish, these orishas are not particularly saintly and, indeed, can frequently act quite deviously. Each orisha also has favorite foods, songs, rhythms, dances, an earthly realm, special symbolism (colors, vestments, and so forth), and sacrificial animals.

Each practitioner of santería is connected to a particular orisha, who in turn serves the believer as the equivalent of a guardian angel. Initiates are distinguished by dressing all in white for an entire year prior to their acceptance as practitioners, a process known as *hacerse santo* ("becoming saint") that includes the performance of many costly rites and rituals. As an orisha's "son" or "daughter," an initiate will frequently make an offering of the blood of a sacrificed animal in order to contribute to the life force, or *aché,* of the orisha. In this sense, the orishas are not the dead saints of old but alive today, constantly intervening in the lives and affairs of human beings. As such, these orishas are frequently consulted for knowledge about the past or future through a process of divination usually involving the reading of cowry shells by a *babalao.* Of course, these many rituals gave themselves easily to mixing with Spanish Catholicism, which has always had its own elaborate tapestry of processions, rituals, idols, stories, signs, omens, and saints (Luis 2001: 27–32; Sublette 2004: 213).

Derived in their majority from the Yoruba practices of the *lucumí,* some of the most commonly celebrated of these orishas include:

Olodumare: The supreme but indifferent and rarely mentioned creator deity, also known as Olofi.

Obatalá: Olodumare's son and the god of the mind and thought. A peacemaker often represented by a dove,

Obatalá is syncretized with Jesus or the Virgin of Mercy, and, like Jesus, is considered cocreator of the world and humankind with Olodumare. Given the centuries of Muslim monotheistic influence in ancient Yorubaland (in northern Africa), it is thought that the name Obatalá, often used interchangeably with Orisha 'lá or Orishanlá, derives from the practice of considering the Muslim one-and-only God, Allah, the supreme deity in the Yoruba pantheon.

Thus, Orisha Allah became Orishanlá, which in turn became Obatalá. It is presumably for this reason that Obatalá's color is pure white, that he represents law, justice, and purity, and that his followers or "children" are expected to be peacemakers and abstain from alcohol (Sublette 2004: 209).

Elegguá: Being the god of the crossroads, Elegguá is always the first and last to be addressed in any santería ceremony. He is the equivalent of the African-American figure Legba, to whom blues master Robert Johnson supposedly sold his soul in order to learn to play the guitar. Syncretized with Saint Martin of Porres or San Benito, Elegguá's trickster ways have often led to his being compared with the Devil.

Ochún: The Yoruba Aphrodite, Ochún is the goddess of the waters, love, beauty, and prosperity. She is syncretized with Our Lady of Charity, also known as Caridad de Cobre, the patron saint of Cuba.

Changó: The god of thunder and fire, Changó is syncretized with Santa Barbara and very important in Afro-Cuban sacred and popular music because he is the keeper of the drums, specifically the triple set of two-headed *batá* drums used to beat out the "rhythms of the saints."

Ogún: The blacksmith god of metals. Ogún is often depicted wielding a machete and bathing in blood and is syncretized with Saint Peter.

Yemayá: The mother of the world, Yemayá is Ochún's sister, with whom she shares the waters. She is syncretized with Our Lady of Regla, the Black Madonna of the Havana suburb.

Orula: Keeping the oracle of divination, known as the Ifá, Orula is the orisha first addressed when a *santero* goes to visit a *babalao* to seek information on his or her fortunes.

Babalú-Ayé: Famously syncretized with San Lázaro, Babalú-Ayé is the god of sickness and is always depicted as a thin leprosy-stricken man on crutches followed by dogs licking his open wounds. Cuba's sick and infirm often turn to him for comfort, as does anyone in need of good luck on a special occasion. I have a friend who lit a candle to San Lázaro recently when Fidel Castro underwent life-threatening surgery (ibid.: 212–219; Luis 2001: 27–32).

During the special period that began in 1990, Cuba underwent what can only be described as a spiritual revival. Many Cubans, especially the young, have found themselves confronted with a moral crisis as the institutions and beliefs that had sustained them for three decades began to disintegrate. Family and community solidarity have begun to erode, provoking a sense of alienation and anomie in many youth (Crahan 2003). As a result, churches of many faiths have become more popular than ever. During the 1990s, many Cubans joined Protestant and Catholic churches, sought to rediscover their Jewish roots by visiting the island's few synagogues, and deepened their practice of Afro-Cuban rituals in search of answers to spiritual questions. For many Cubans, this quest was mixed with a more immediate search for accessing the material goods that many churches and synagogues could provide. Also, since spiritual belief and public practice of religion had long been punished by the government and associated with counter-revolutionary attitudes, some people joined churches to make explicit their rejection of what they saw as the bankrupt values on which the revolution was predicated.

It was within this context that Castro extended an invitation to Pope John Paul II to visit Cuba, which he accepted in February 1998. Among the many repercussions of the late pope's visit to Cuba was his call for "the world to open up to Cuba and Cuba to the world," hinting at his rejection of the U.S. embargo. This statement was a crucial turning point for many Cuban-American Catholics who felt called by their religious leader to set aside their pain and resentment and work toward reconciliation (de Aragón 1998). Also, Protestant churches, both mainstream and evangelical, have begun to attract greater numbers of believers in Cuba, reflecting the explosive growth of evangelical sects throughout Latin

This is the largest of Havana's three surviving synagogues, Temple
Beth Shalom (House of Peace). Built in 1957 and renovated in 2000,
Beth Shalom also houses an expansive Jewish community center
known as the Patronato. *(Ted Henken)*

America. In fact, a year and a half after the Pope's historic
visit to Cuba, 100,000 Protestants turned out for a massive
public religious service in the Plaza of the Revolution.

Vitral Magazine and the Center for Civic and Religious Formation

In November 2006, the President of Cuba's National Assembly, Ricardo Alarcón, responded to a question about the lack of an independent press in Cuba by pointing to the existence of the magazine *Vitral*. "Read the magazine *Vitral*," Alarcón suggested, "unlike the moderate posture of the Catholic Church, the magazine is harshly critical of the Revolution. Still the government has not interfered with its circulation nor have we sanctioned those Cubans who subscribe to it" (Montoya 2006). *Vitral* has, indeed, remained independent and uncensored, but due more to the tenacity of its staff than to the tolerance of the Cuban government.

The magazine's director, Dagoberto Valdés, an agronomist who was once the director of a Cuban state tobacco company, was ordered to cease his involvement with the publication in the mid-1990s. When he refused, he was punished by being reassigned the unenviable job of spending his days collecting tobacco leaves. Undaunted, Valdés patiently performed this new task each morning for ten long years, continuing to direct the magazine after hours. Vindication came recently when he was reinstated to his previous management position. If you visit him at his office, he is likely to proudly show you his tobacco collector's pouch that still hangs on the wall.

This helps explain the quote pasted across the door to the magazine's headquarters: "Don't ask for a light load; ask instead for a strong back." This is precisely what the magazine's staff did when they founded the Center for Civic and Religious Formation as part of the Catholic Diocese of Pinar del Río and soon thereafter began to publish *Vitral*. The aim of the magazine is as straightforward as it is audacious. In a country where a single party holds monopoly control over the media and where independent associations and businesses are illegal, *Vitral* aims to plant the seed of a vigorous, pluralistic, civil society in the shell of postrevolutionary Cuba.

While such a vision has clear political implications in the Cuban context, *Vitral's* project is not primarily political. Whereas most government critics seek immediate institutional

(continued)

change in the country's economic and political system, *Vitral* seeks to create independent ways of thinking. The magazine's very title (meaning "stained glass") denotes Cuba's colonial era stained-glass windows that filter light through a prism, refracting the full spectrum of colors. Thus, the magazine seeks to serve as a critical medium where Cuba's multiple points of view are reflected. Indeed, ordinary Cubans have grown tired of the so-called *doble moral* (double morality), forced to live one life in public and another in private. To them, the open debate found in the pages of *Vitral* is a welcome relief.

The magazine offers a humanistic, grass-roots approach to Cuba's many problems, aimed at the formation of truly free persons who recognize their rights and responsibilities as citizens, not subjects. It seeks to replace the mutual fear and suspicion that underlies relations among Cubans in the public sphere with the seeds of hope and trust, leading to the rebuilding of civil society. In order to achieve these goals, the Center offers a host of courses and workshops on provocative subjects like economics, ethics and values, political pluralism and participation in Cuba, human rights, and starting a small business.

While visiting *Vitral's* headquarters in Pinar del Río, I found Valdés to be a wise and good-humored survivor driven by a progressive Christian faith and a strong sense of Cuban nationalism—in the tradition of Cuba's nineteenth century patriot, Father Félix Varela, who fought for Cuba's independence from Spain. Valdés is often quite critical of the Cuban government, but his criticisms betray no trace of hatred; rather, they issue from tolerance and hope—two values sorely lacking in Cuban circles on both sides of the Straits of Florida.

Valdés has also been uniquely consistent in his opposition to U.S. policies like the embargo and travel restrictions that only serve to further insulate Cubans from the free flow of ideas while strengthening the government's control over them. In fact, when chief U.S. diplomat Joseph Sullivan visited *Vitral* back in 1995, Valdés had to exercise caution and preserve his hard-won independence. Clearly impressed, Sullivan declared: "This is just the kind of independent voice that the U.S. should support. What we can do to help?" To which Valdés replied, "If you really want to help us, I ask you not to help at all."

(continued)

Finally, *Vitral* is especially unique in that it refuses all financial support coming from the U.S. government, including the many antiregime organizations in South Florida, which distribute funds to dissidents. It has survived to date by successfully navigating an autonomous path between the two shoals of cooptation by the Cuban government and control from regime opponents. However, on Easter Sunday, 2007, the magazine sent out a cryptic e-mail message that read, "Due to a lack of resources, *Vitral's* editorial board informs its readers that it can no longer guarantee the future publication of the magazine" (Vitral 2007).

Behind this purposely euphemistic announcement lies the fact that the magazine has always existed at the pleasure of Cuba's conservative Catholic hierarchy and under the protection of Pinar del Río's progressive Bishop José Siro González Bacallao who retired in December 2006. However, fears that his replacement, Jorge Enrique Serpa Pérez, named by Rome with the support of Havana Cardinal Jaime Ortega, would follow a less prophetic line, more accommodating to the Cuban government, seem to be born out by the tragic announcement of the magazine's impending closure. It is still an open question whether this crucifixion means the end of *Vitral*, or is only the first act of a struggle that will be followed by the magazine's vindication and eventual resurrection (Alfonso 2007).

As with religion, family relations in Cuba exhibit a deep paradox. The Cuban family is seemingly beset by extremely high rates of divorce. Many children have been educated in countryside boarding schools, spending long, often traumatic periods of their youth away from their parents. Others were sent into exile without their parents so as to "save" them from the revolution as part of the controversial *Pedro Pan* program run by the Catholic Church with collaboration from the U.S. government (Conde 2000; de la Campa 2000). Other families have struggled with the trauma of separation, sacrifice, and struggle, as parents often gave themselves and all their free time over to the never-ending task of building (or fighting against) the revolution. Moreover, many families have been tragically divided between the United States and Cuba by the politics of the revolution, as well as by the bureaucratic, intractable, and often inhumane orientation of each country's migration laws.

Nonetheless, the family is truly the heart of daily life in Cuba and in Cuba's extensive diaspora, regardless of the distances between one's family members or the orientation of one's politics. While North Americans like to claim that American society is based on "family values," the fact is that in the United States family constitutes one's roots (where one comes from), not normally the essence of one's intimate daily activities (what one lives for). For Cubans, however, family is often one's very raison d'etre. That is, for most Cubans, the members of the extended family (including not only one's parents, siblings, and children but also one's cousins, aunts and uncles, grandparents and great-grandparents, nieces and nephews, and grandchildren, as well as one's many in-laws) constitute a network of the most intimate, heartfelt, and consuming relationships in one's life.

That is not to say that Cuban families are uniformly happy and well-adjusted. On the contrary, highly charged emotions, disagreements, and conflicts are often aired openly, loudly, and passionately among family members. Still, family unity and solidarity normally override individual privacy and independence, and family loyalties are often stronger than all others. Decisions that would be personal and individual elsewhere are in Cuba endlessly discussed and debated by family members. Indeed, because of current U.S. restrictions my wife has been forced to endure three long years without seeing her family in Cuba. For her, not being able to share in her family's daily struggles and joys and the difficulty of maintaining such a close, intimate relationship from afar amounts to *el amor que te mata* ("the love that kills you").

NATIONAL IDENTITY AND FRUSTRATED NATIONALISM—CUBANÍA AND INTRANSIGENCIA

Growing out of its long frustrated struggle for sovereignty and self-determination, Cubans have developed a fierce, sometimes defensive, and always proud sense of national identity. As an indication of the depth of that feeling, Cubans have coined not one but three different words, all of which roughly translate as "Cubanness": *cubanidad, cubaneo,* and *cubanía* (Pérez Firmat 1997). Ironically, because of the deep North American penetration of the newly independent Cuban nation during the first three decades of its existence under the Platt Amendment after 1902, many of the elements of this Cubanness derive from common North American notions of modernity, prosperity, individual rights, consumption, pragmatism, and lifestyle. As Louis A. Pérez argues in his history of the emergence of a distinctly Cuban identity, *On Becoming Cuban: Identity, Nationality, and Culture* (1999), U.S. economic and political influence was the foundation upon which was laid a host of other lasting cultural (music, sports, movies, and so on), linguistic, and religious characteristics that were all gradually absorbed by Cubans in the crucial years of the formation of their national identity.

As a result of this deep penetration, Cuban Spanish is filled with Anglicisms (nearly all of which are derived from American English), such as *blúmer* ("bloomers"), *pulóver* ("T-shirt"), and *cake* ("cake") (for more see the reference section on language in Part II). Also, as in the United States (and largely because of U.S. influence), there is nothing so Cuban as a game of *pelota* ("baseball"), for which nearly all of the terms for positions, plays, and equipment come from American English. Finally, any visitor to Havana today (especially during the first two weeks of December, when the International Festival of New Latin American Cinema takes place) will be astounded at the wealth of large, U.S.-style movie houses that blanket the city.

José Martí, Cuba's leading poet and founding father, foresaw the tension surrounding the birth pains of Cuban national identity in his famous 1891 essay "Our America." For him, Cuba both admires the United States as a land of liberty and fears it as a land of imperialism. For that reason, he argued that Cuba can never become part of the United States—that "other America." Instead, Martí celebrated his homeland as a guiding light of what he called *nuestra América* ("our America"), Latin America. This sense of national identity and frustrated nationalism, is a helpful paradigm with which to explain the entire turbulent history of the island following the first stirrings of independence at the start of the nineteenth century, through the major independence wars of 1868 and 1895, and especially during the republican period, 1902–1952.

Furthermore, the idea of frustrated nationalism is useful in understanding the Cuban Revolution of 1959, which was initially nationalist (not socialist) in character. However, that rising nationalism was wedded to three separate struggles that became fused together by 1962: the struggle against corruption and dictatorship; the struggle against foreign domination and imperialism; and the struggle for social justice and, eventually, socialism. Thus, as Cuban nationalism became increasingly identified with socialism through Castro's leadership, it also came to be understood as anti-American to the extent that U.S. policy in the context of the Cold War was seen as an obstacle to the achievement of national sovereignty and socioeconomic development. This chronically frustrated nationalism was temporarily overcome through a break with the United States and the establishment of a series of social rights long denied the majority of the population. At the same time, the defense of socialist nationalism led to the gradual entrenchment of a siegelike mentality, top-down command structure, and political intransigence that inflicted many costs, the most obvious of which were long-term economic dependency on the Soviet Union and the sacrifice of many essential political, civil, and economic rights of the Cuban people.

Because of its elongated shape, Cuba is often referred to by its inhabitants as *el caimán* ("the alligator"). "People say we are a dinosaur, but Cuba is shaped like an alligator," Cubans are wont to correct outsiders. And, like that still surviving prehistoric animal, the island and its people have survived by learning to adapt. That's why they are still around. Today in Cuba, this ability to change with the times is often facetiously referred to as *resolver* ("resolving" problems) or *inventar* ("inventing" creative and often illegal solutions to the seemingly insurmountable challenges of everyday life). While the key junctures in Cuban history are clearly European conquest and settlement in 1511, the achievement of independence from Spain in 1898, and the revolution of 1959, there is as much continuity as change in the island's history. There are a number of distinctly Cuban characteristics that are surprisingly consistent over time, despite major changes during the colonial, republican, and socialist eras.

These national characteristics include the following: economic dependency on outside powers and on sugar monoculture; emigration, exile, and the fight to recover the homeland; a patrimonial state in which the government directs national economic development; the cultural trait of lightheartedness and mockery of authority (known among Cubans as *choteo*); Cuban exceptionalism (an exaggerated sense of national pride and accomplishment that has been referred to as the Cuban "superiority complex"); and a winner-take-all political culture influenced by machismo, the preservation of honor, and lack of negotiation, dialogue, and compromise.

In fact, the word *compromise* itself is not easily translated into Cuban Spanish, with *compromiso* usually understood to mean unwavering commitment to a principle or cause. That is the direct opposite of the American ideal of compromise:

the pragmatic art of negotiation. Such give-and-take is often ridiculed by Cubans as weakness or unprincipled flexibility. Any Cuban on the island who attempts to establish political options that challenge the supposedly irrevocable socialist character of the government is automatically labeled a traitor and accused of collaborating with the enemy against the integrity of the homeland. Likewise, at various points in the history of the Cuban diaspora, most notably in the late 1970s in Miami, anyone who engaged in "dialogue" with the Cuban government was attacked as a *dialoguero,* considered a traitor to the goal of a *Cuba libre,* and terrorized with intimidation and violence.

RACE AND SEXUALITY—BETWEEN PROGRESS AND PATERNALISM

Afro-Cubans and women (and to a lesser extent homosexuals) benefited greatly from the many socioeconomic achievements of the Cuban Revolution. This was especially so in the early years, when legal discrimination was abolished and the institutional mechanisms of racism and sexism were destroyed. However, because these groups were never empowered to advocate for their own liberation as blacks, women, or gays, their liberation (to the extent that it has existed and still exists) has always been channeled through and contingent upon their acceptance of and incorporation into the larger project of top-down state socialism. Specifically, the revolutionary mass organizations described in Chapter 3 have been the means for citizens to participate in society and build socialism—always under the guidance (and control) of the government.

This has been the case for at least four reasons. First, as a revolution that has prioritized the goals of economic equality, social justice, and national sovereignty, Cuban socialism has consistently pursued its goals through an approach that sees class exploitation and foreign imperialism as the root causes of injustice. Other discriminatory practices against blacks or women (discrimination against homosexuals was not targeted as a problem to be solved) were considered to derive from capitalism and would disappear when class privilege was eradicated. Likewise, the constant threat of U.S. invasion created a siegelike mentality among the Cuban leadership that prioritized revolutionary unity above the claims of any particular group. Indeed, under the ideal of national revolutionary unity the socialist government has consistently avoided the implementation of any "affirmative action" policies to equalize opportunities for specific aggrieved groups (blacks and women). Instead, the eradication of the private economic sphere permitted the government to enact policies that would uplift all members of previously oppressed classes, regardless of race or gender (Casal 1989).

Second, Cuban culture is imbued with a deep machismo that celebrates male virility, aggressiveness, and fearlessness, while simultaneously devaluing men who cannot or will not live up to the macho stereotype—foremost among those being homosexuals. By extension, in revolutionary Cuba there was very little space in which homosexuals could participate in the socialist project as homosexuals, since their very homosexuality was often considered a decadent perversion or sickness, anathema to the ideal of the new socialist man. Most were faced with a stark choice: remain closeted as most had been under the previous system, disengage from society and become a nonperson, or go into exile.

Third, socialist Cuba inherited from the island's cultural history a deep prejudice against all forms of African culture and religion—most of which were long considered primitive witchcraft or outright criminality. Thus, while the revolution cleared the playing field, giving unprecedented opportunities to blacks, it left largely unchallenged whites' deeply imbedded prejudices against Afro-Cuban traditions. On top of that, Cuban socialism attacked all forms of religious belief and ritual as superstition to be eradicated in the building of socialism. This meant that expressions of Afro-Cuban religion that ran deeper than mere folklore had to be "hidden in plain sight" once again. Indeed, after the revolution's initial focus on eradicating institutional forms of discrimination, especially in the areas of employment, education, and access to health care and public services, by the mid-1960s it was clear that religions of Afro-Cuban origin were deemed obstacles to the construction of socialism and the formation of the "new man" (De la Fuente 2001).

Finally and perhaps most important, from the start the revolutionary leadership sought to achieve its often laudable and popular goals in a classically paternalist manner. This top-down command structure had the benefit of establishing an effective government apparatus that accomplished more in the first five years for Cuba's dispossessed and disenfranchised than had been achieved over many preceding decades. However, after those unprecedented efforts by the new government to eradicate past racial and sexual discriminatory practices, any further debate on the issues of racism and sexism (not to mention homophobia) quickly became taboo, since the problems were deemed already to have been solved. The lack of discussion of these issues as ongoing social problems made it impossible to go beyond the eradication of institutionalized discrimination and begin to address the more intractable racist, sexist, and homophobic attitudes and orientations rooted in Cuban culture. That is, "the lack of a public debate about race and racism facilitated the survival and reproduction of the very racist stereotypes that the revolutionary leadership claimed to oppose" (ibid.: 295).

This difficulty has been exacerbated by the outlawing of any autonomous organizations that aimed at the self-empowerment of these social groups. In most Western states, subordinated groups are controlled through their marginalization from the centers of power. However, in Cuba, Afro-Cubans and women have been controlled through their very incorporation. While their inclusion in the revolutionary project has brought them many benefits as Cubans, in practice it has also served to demobilize them as political or social interest groups, with the expectation that they feel forever indebted to the revolution for having given them their freedom.

A good example of one of the negative side effects of this paternalistic approach to women's liberation is abortion. While the revolution has made abortion legal and readily available to all women regardless of class position, it has completely failed to educate women (or men) about the risks of unprotected sex or empower them with contraceptive knowledge. As a result, condom use is rare and abortion is routinely used as a form of birth control. It is not uncommon for Cuban women in their twenties and thirties to report having had two abortions or more. Furthermore, to prevent a second or third unwanted pregnancy, doctors have been known to insert IUDs in young women against their will or without their knowledge during an abortion.

In turning to a more detailed examination of race relations in Cuba, it is necessary to underline the significant differences between North American and Caribbean notions of racial identity. First, it is unclear whether we can speak of "Afro-Cubans" as a distinct social or ethnic group with its own separate racial identity, as is normally done in reference to African-Americans. In Cuba blacks often think of themselves as Cuban first and foremost, with their racial designation playing a decidedly secondary role in their identity. However, when immigrating to the United States, black Cubans quickly learn that in North America their racial designation as blacks easily trumps their national/ethnic identity as Cubans or Hispanics, often influencing where they live, what they can aspire to do for a living, and who their friends are (Ojito 2000). Furthermore, since the onset in 1990 of a major economic crisis in Cuba itself, race has re-emerged with a vengeance as a significant social and economic cleavage. That is due in part to the unequal racial distribution of cash remittances sent by (mostly white) Cuban-Americans to their

These three young women from the traditional Afro-Cuban dance troupe, Conjunto Folklorico Nacional, highlight the mixed racial and ethnic heritage common among Cubans. (Ted Henken)

relatives back home and to the under-representation of Afro-Cubans in the island's booming tourism industry (De la Fuente 2001).

Despite becoming a leading importer of African slaves to labor in its many sugar plantations during the nineteenth century, during the course of the twentieth century Cuba has gradually redefined itself as a "transculturized" nation that combines both Spanish and African elements. Coined in the 1940s by eminent Cuban anthropologist Fernando Ortiz, the key concept of transculturation celebrates Cuban national identity as a unique meld of a number of diverse cultural elements similar to the American notion of the "melting pot." However, the Cuban version of this melting pot, known as the *ajiaco* (a tropical stew), is not based on the dominance of a single mainstream group (whether white, Anglo-Saxon Protestant or white, Spanish Catholic). Instead, the Cuban *ajiaco* reflects a more fully transculturalized national identity that recognizes African and European (as well as Indian, Chinese, Jewish, English, French, and American) cultural elements as cocontributors, without claiming any single one as the mainstream.

Unfortunately, the notion of a shared, transculturalized national identity has led to the simplistic belief that Cuba is a "racial democracy" where racism is rare and racial discrimination has been mild (Pérez Sarduy and Stubs 1993; 2000). On the positive side, the ideal of racial equality has been employed by blacks as a way to claim full and equal rights *as Cubans.* However, on the negative side, the myth of racial democracy has made it difficult for Afro-Cubans who have suffered from systematic discrimination to mobilize *as blacks* (De la Fuente 2001). This dilemma was exacerbated by the well-meaning but idealistic writings on race by Cuban patriot and independence leader José Martí. In his most important essay on the subject, "My Race," Martí made the antiracist claim: "To insist upon the racial divisions and racial differences of a people naturally divided is to obstruct both individual and public happiness." Engaged as he was in a fight for independence based on national unity, Martí's point about the irrelevance of the very concept of race was as practical as it was idealistic. For him, the term *Cuban* meant "more than white, more than mulatto, more than Negro" (Martí 2002: 319).

Likewise, in his famous essay "Our America," he reiterated this idealistic aphorism, writing: "There is no racial hatred, because there are no races" (ibid.: 295). However, Martí was well aware that racial animosity and fear *did* exist in Cuba, and perhaps the fact that he was not around in the early twentieth century to rearticulate his claims allowed Cuba's white politicians easily and cynically to manipulate that animosity and fear to the detriment of the very blacks who had sacrificed so much for Cuban independence and emancipation. Thus, while perhaps appropriate for his 1890s project of bringing together Cubans of all racial and ethnic backgrounds, Martí's utopian approach to race relations in Cuba proved impractical as an actual policy that could ensure equal rights and promote the full participation of blacks in a newly independent nation whose economy had been based on slave labor for most of the previous century.

During the first half of the twentieth century, the Cuban republic betrayed the egalitarian ideology of Martí. First, a mixed-race liberation army was replaced by an exclusively white U.S.-organized police force and rural guard. Those and other common exclusions based on race led some Afro-Cuban leaders to begin organizing defensive movements around their common racial identity. However, the mobilization of groups around racial identity or ideology was criticized and repressed as itself a racist act. In 1910 the Cuban Congress approved the Morúa Amendment that outlawed political parties based on race, directly leading to the 1912 massacre of the Independent Party of Color (PIC). This "nationwide extermination of Blacks of quasi-genocidal proportions" had the long-term effect of eliminating the leadership of Cuba's Afro-Cuban community, leading to a generation of black under-representation in politics and systematic occupational discrimination (Casal 1989: 474). As a result, discrimination against Afro-Cubans as second-class citizens during the first half of the twentieth century was the norm. Civil and social rights taken for granted by white, urban Cubans were systematically denied to blacks. Discrimination was especially egregious in access to housing, education, health care, and employment.

In response to the desperate economic and social situation of Afro-Cubans on the eve of the revolution, the new government made the eradication of racial discrimination one of its highest priorities. On March 22, 1959, Castro specifically threw down the gauntlet over the issue of racial discrimination, singling out the routine discrimination that took place at work centers and in the social sphere. In an open assault on the structures of institutionalized racial discrimination, the revolution opened up Afro-Cuban access to employment and integrated most of the previously segregated clubs, parks, and beaches. These policies legitimized Afro-Cubans' claims about the pervasiveness of racism and discrimination and had the effect of making racial discrimination tantamount to a counter-revolutionary act (Casal 1989; De la Fuente 2001).

While these egalitarian and redistributive moves made a point never to single out blacks as the exclusive beneficiaries, such measures benefited blacks the most since they were the most oppressed sector in prerevolutionary Cuba. Also, Castro's very public declarations against racism and discrimination led to a sea change in the perception of such attitudes. Now, not only was discrimination illegal, but it was also considered anti-Cuban. Thus, while old racist attitudes, habits, and preferences would take a long time to die out, even among the most ardent of revolutionaries, now racists would have to pay a tremendous price when expressing such attitudes publicly. Moreover, given the rapid efforts to eradicate all legal forms of discrimination, it became much more difficult for an individual's private prejudices to translate into systematic institutional discrimination (Casal 1989; De la Fuente 2001).

In response to these revolutionary reforms, Cuba's poet laureate, Nicolás Guillén, a mulatto activist and longtime communist who often decried racial and class inequalities in his poetry, penned the poem "Tengo" ("I Have," 1964), perfectly capturing the jubilant hope now unleashed in the hearts of many Afro-Cubans. In part, the poem reads:

Tengo, vamos a ver:	I have, let's see:
Tengo el gusto de andar por mi pais,	I have the pleasure to walk about my country,
Dueño de cuanto har en él,	Owner of all I see,
Mirando bien de cerca lo que antes	Looking closely at what before
No tuve ni podía tener.	I didn't, nor could I have had.
[...]	[...]
Tengo, vamos a ver:	I have, let's see:
Que siendo negro	That being Black
Nadie me puede detener	I can be stopped by no one at
A la puerta de un dancing o de un bar.	The door of a dancing hall or bar.
O bien en la carpenta de un hotel	Or even at the desk of a hotel
Gritarme que no hay pieza	Have someone yell at me there are no rooms.

Clearly expressing a boundless happiness and pride at having gained a new lease on life, the poem celebrates the achievements, hope, and possibilities that the revolution has afforded to Juan, a former lowly black laborer. The poem also expresses a strong sense of nationalism, as Juan rejoices at being able to walk freely about his homeland without interference from wealthy, privileged foreigners. Finally, the poem ends with these signature lines: "I have, let's see; I have what I had to have" (*Tengo, vamos a ver; Tengo lo que tenía que tener*), expressing elation at the end to class, racial, and nationalist discrimination and the beginning of national equality for all.

After 1962, however, the rapid and effective initial efforts of the revolutionary government to do away with racial discrimination were accompanied by the outlawing of all previously established Afro-Cuban organizations. While the government did not single out these black cultural, civic, or religious organizations, all such independent associations (black or white, civic or political, cultural or religious) were now subsumed under new revolutionary organizations that stressed national unity above all else. In fact, the insistence upon revolutionary unity had the effect of demobilizing any independent activity on the part of blacks themselves. Under the assumption that Cuba's traditional racial divisions had been solved by decree, the new government tended to view Afro-Cuban leaders as ungrateful malcontents whose revelations of ongoing racial problems served only to divide a nation under siege. Alejandro de la Fuente, one of the leading scholars of race relations in Cuba, sums up this paradoxical impact of the revolution on racism, indicating that "the ultimate irony is that the same government that did the most to eliminate racism also did the most to silence the discussion about its persistence" (ibid.: 338).

When Cuba's economic crisis that began in 1990 forced the socialist economy to open up to foreign investment, remittances from Cuban-Americans, and international tourism, many Cubans began to feel relegated to second-class citizenship in their own country once again. As dollars flooded parts

These four smiling children share the same father but each has a different mother. It is not uncommon for Cuban siblings, even those with the same parents, to reflect the many elements that make up the Cuban ajiaco *(tropical stew). (Ted Henken)*

of the socialist economy, inequality expanded. However, this new inequality emerged with a marked racial profile, leading to renewed social tensions and accusations of racial discrimination. Because roughly 85 percent of Cuban-Americans are white, few blacks on the island benefit from remittances.

Likewise, Afro-Cubans are often indirectly (but not accidentally) excluded from jobs in the booming tourism industry under the requirement that potential employees possess a "pleasant aspect" (that is, white skin). Effectively excluded from the most lucrative sector of the economy, many Afro-Cubans have turned to the island's ubiquitous underground economy for survival. However, their conspicuous presence among the ranks of Cuba's hustlers and prostitutes has led other Cubans to condemn them based on long-dormant notions of blacks' supposedly "natural" criminality (De la Fuente 2001). Commenting on the bitter resentment felt by many Cuban youths (blacks and whites alike), Spanish anthropologist Isabel Holgado Fernández has written:

> One of the facts that has caused the most resentment among the Cuban population, especially among the youth, has been the impossibility of gaining access to areas of tourism and entertainment. . . . The development of tourism and the corresponding exclusion of Cubans from the enjoyment of its infrastructure contradicted the revolutionary axiom of social egalitarianism. Cubans had the bitter sensation that they were being demoted to second-class citizenship in their own country: Foreigners had access to beaches, hotels, restaurants, nightclubs, to all those places where they, the builders and beneficiaries by right of all that exportable paradise, could not even touch with their Cuban pesos. (Holgado Fernández 2000: 208, my translation)

This change gives the once eloquent and evocative words of Guillén's "Tengo" a biting irony when read today, since blacks are routinely turned away from most Cuban hotels. More ironic still is that they are denied entry not because they are black, but because being black they are assumed to be Cuban and are therefore prohibited access to spaces reserved for dollar-paying tourists. In fact, Alden Knight, one of Cuba's leading black actors, who has made his reputation reciting Guillén's poetry, has recently refused to recite "Tengo" with this explanation: "*Tengo* is the sum total of what was achieved in this country for blacks, for the poor . . . and now it's been lost. I have said that when that poem can be read again in all honesty, we shall have regained what we had won by the end of the 1960s when we were poor but equal" (Pérez Sarduy and Stubs 2000: 114).

In a more satirical vein, the wildly popular Cuban timba group La Charanga Habanera came out with a song entitled "El Temba" ("The Sugardaddy") in the mid-1990s that poked fun at Guillén's ode to what Cubans "have" because of the revolution. Given the fact that many young Cuban women were actively seeking out foreigners as boyfriends in order to gain access to material goods, the song advises its young female listeners to "Look for a sugardaddy who can maintain you; So that you can enjoy, so that you can have [things]" (*Búscate un temba que te mantenga; Pa' que tú goces pa' que tú tengas*). Building on this ironic use of the words "maintain" (*mantenga*) and "have" (*tenga*), the song closes with a repeated chorus that directly mocks the signature line in Guillén's famous poem: "So that you have, what you had to have; A rich sugardaddy, with a lot of cash" (*Pa' que tengas, lo que tenías que tener; Un papirriqui, con güaniquiqui*) (K. Moore 2001; R. Moore 2006).

CUBAN-AMERICANS—FROM EXILES TO IMMIGRANTS

Fixed as they were on this image of the melting pot, of immigrants fleeing a disruptive revolution to find a place in the American sun, Anglos did not on the whole understand that assimilation would be considered by most Cubans a doubtful goal at best. Nor did many Anglos understand that living in Florida was still at the deepest level construed by Cubans as a temporary condition, an accepted political option shaped by the continuing dream, if no longer immediate expectation, of a vindicatory return. *El exilio* was for Cubans a ritual, a respected tradition. (Didion 1987: 57–58)

The existence of a diasporic Cuban community in the United States is a respected tradition indeed. Beginning with

Father Félix Varela who escaped to exile in New York on December 17, 823, the nineteenth century saw a succession of other prominent political exiles including Father Félix Varela, filibusterer Narciso López, novelist Cirilo Villaverde, and patriot José Martí all come to live in the United States for extended periods. Likewise, the first sixty years of the twentieth century saw small but significant Cuban immigrant communities develop in Key West, Tampa (Ybor City), New Orleans, and New York (Pérez 2000). During that time, a small portion of these Cubans came as political exiles fleeing the repression of the Machado (1925–1933) and Batista (1952–1958) dictatorships. Ironically, Fidel Castro himself toured the United States during the mid-1950s in search of support from the then very small Cuban-American communities in South Florida, New York, and New Jersey.

However, it was not until the revolution of 1959 that Cubans began to come to the United States in large numbers. Upon the revolutionary victory, many new émigrés began to descend upon Miami and New York, crossing paths with those already in exile from the Batista dictatorship who began to return to Cuba in the early months of 1959. Unlike the bulk of the Cuban immigrant generations that had preceded them in the United States, however, these newcomers saw their stay in America as temporary. For these émigrés, their sojourn in the United States was an emergency measure that would end only when the political crisis that necessitated it also ended. In short, these new arrivals did not think of themselves as immigrants at all, but as *exiles*.

Both sides in the ideological war between Cuba and the United States have attempted to manipulate the meanings and identities of post-1959 Cuban émigrés in line with their own geopolitical interests. On the one hand, between the 1960s and 1980s, the Cuban government consistently sought to politicize emigration as a threat to the revolution and to stigmatize emigrants as worms (*gusanos*) or traitors (*traidores*). However, in response to economic need, during the 1990s (and occasionally before then) the Cuban government began to give nuance to its image of Cuban-Americans. While some exiles were labeled members of the "Miami mafia," the émigré group as a whole was often referred to as the Cuban *comunidad* abroad. It seems that the Castro regime realized that the *gusanos* of old had been magically transformed into today's valued *mariposas* ("butterflies"). That is, instead of being stigmatized as *traidores,* Cuban-Americans are now counted on to be the *trae-dolares* ("dollar-bringers") whose remittances help to maintain the Cuban economy.

U.S. federal, state, and local governments have a similarly schizophrenic, love-hate relationship with Cuban-Americans. The first waves of Cuban émigrés were initially given wide welcome as freedom-loving "exiles," "heroes," and "refugees from communism." Essentially, the United States sought to use this exodus to fulfill its strategic goal of overthrowing the regime (draining off its professional class and enlisting them in an invasion attempt) and its ideological goal of embarrassing Castro by welcoming Cuban émigrés who were ostensibly "voting with their feet" against the regime by leaving (Domínguez 1992). However, such a strategy had the unintended consequence of actually helping Castro consolidate his rule by allowing him to externalize dissent. Subsequent waves, however, beginning most notably with the Mariel boatlift of 1980, have often been portrayed as unsavory criminal elements and social charges: Castro's bullets aimed at Miami. As such, new Cuban arrivals are increasingly treated as just another group of unwanted and unwelcome immigrants (notwithstanding the fact that virtually any Cuban who manages to arrive on U.S. soil is allowed to stay legally).

Despite the early exiles' expectation of an eventual return to their homeland, they remained in the United States and were joined by four successive waves of new arrivals, each of which would gradually alter the overall orientation and identity of the émigré community at large. Typically, these five waves of Cuban émigrés are grouped into cohorts based on time of exit/arrival and their common social extraction

(Pedraza 2002). First, there are the so-called "golden exiles" who arrived in the United States between 1959 and 1961. Pedraza has characterized that group as "those who wait," in the sense that they were made up largely of Cuba's prerevolutionary elite who came to the United States awaiting a rapid regime change to the status quo ante back home. After the revolution had entered a new, more radical phase and was attacked by the United States at the Bay of Pigs in April 1961, there ensued a new phase of emigration characterized by "those who escape." This cohort was more middle class in social composition, included families, unaccompanied children, and others who resorted to escaping the island on boats and rafts when exit flights from Cuba were discontinued after the October 1962 missile crisis.

These first two waves of Cuban exiles shared a number of characteristics that both distinguished them from other Latinos and enabled them to achieve unprecedented socioeconomic mobility and political influence in the United States. First of all, these Cubans were not simply a new ethnic minority in the American mosaic. Nor were they just another group of impoverished refugees. Instead, they were "the displaced elites of their former country with considerable resources of education, organizational skills, and entrepreneurship" (Portes 2005: 189). As such, many of them came with business skills, managerial experience, and, occasionally, financial capital. Many were also already knowledgeable about the United States from having previously attended U.S. colleges or worked with U.S. firms. Finally, their common experience of dispossession, expulsion, and (in their minds) betrayal turned them into implacable anticommunists and helped them to create strong bonds of social solidarity that were quickly utilized in the formation of a powerful ethnic enclave (Portes 1998; 2005).

By 1965, with the break with the United States hardened and the radical turn of the revolution firmly consolidated, emigration from Cuba took on a somewhat routine quality. In that year, the United States and Cuba arranged for regularly scheduled flights for those wanting to leave the country as a solution to a brief, chaotic boatlift from the port of Camarioca. However, Pedraza has labeled this cohort "those who search" (2002), in the sense that it was neither easy nor automatic to get permission to leave the country through these so-called freedom flights. First, most potential émigrés had to be claimed by relatives already living in the United States. Then, after being approved for emigration by the Cuban authorities, many were required to perform undesirable labor in the countryside and endure the humiliating experience of being stigmatized as persona non grata before leaving. Still, by 1973, more than 250,000 Cubans had arrived in the United States via the airlift, joining the arrivals of the early 1960s and driving the U.S. Cuban exile population up to 665,043 by 1977.

After 1973 exit routes for potential emigrants were few. That changed drastically when a spontaneous occupation of the Peruvian embassy in April 1980 led President Jimmy Carter and Castro to engage in a dangerous game of rhetorical one-upsmanship, resulting in the historic exodus of more than 125,000 refugees through the port of Mariel during a six-month period that summer. In fact, what became known as the Mariel boatlift was in part the unintended consequence of a series of efforts at reconciliation that took place between Havana and Miami in the late 1970s. This thaw in relations included a controversial dialogue between progressive members of the exile community and the Cuban government that succeeded in winning the release of more than 3,000 political prisoners from Castro's prisons. More important, perhaps, was the demonstration effect of the first ever family visits of Cuban-Americans back to their homeland since the early 1960s (Ojito 2005).

Although the regime could benefit from the image of flexibility and the injection of needed hard currency brought by the exiles, it did not calculate the unrest that these more than 100,000 visitors would sow among the Cuban population.

Many Cubans reconnected with family abroad and began to question their continued sacrifice for a revolution that had been unable to provide the material rewards that their supposedly traitorous *gusano* relatives had obtained in the United States. Given that the *marielitos* who began to pour out of Cuba in 1980 were largely young, single men of working-class origins (veritable children of the revolution, with a more marked Afro-Cuban component than ever before), Pedraza has labeled them "those who hope" (2002). Also, given the fact that they were by and large formed by the revolution, their social composition and mix of motivations to leave began to reflect more closely that of traditional immigrants rather than that of their exile forebears, making a warm reception from their compatriots in Miami unlikely.

The final cohorts of Cuban émigrés are those who came to the United States during the economic crisis that began in the late 1980s, officially labeled the "special period" by President Castro in 1990. Because these Cubans began leaving in increasing numbers on makeshift rafts as a result of the socioeconomic upheaval that resulted from the collapse of the Soviet Union, they have been characterized as "those who despair" (ibid.). However, while "desperation" may be an apt term to capture the complex and contradictory motivations of this cohort, Cuban immigration since 1990 has actually been composed of a number of different, complementary streams. While the late 1980s and early 1990s saw upward of 30,000 to 40,000 Cuban rafters (*balseros*) arrive in the United States, after the 1994–1995 bilateral migration accords between the two governments, that stream split in two different directions.

First, since 1995 well over 200,000 Cubans have benefited from the guaranteed minimum yearly quota of 20,000 immigrant visas (the bulk of which are granted through a visa lottery), as stipulated by the accords. Second, unable to "win" one of these much-sought-after visas, a rising number of Cubans have again resorted to taking to the sea as a means of exit. However, they have largely abandoned the dangerous and unreliable method of coming as *balseros* (rafters) and instead have opted for the more reliable method of emigrating on speedboats. With the aid of a network of professional smugglers, these newest immigrants take conscious advantage of the infamous loophole in U.S. immigration law that interdicts and repatriates most Cubans caught at sea (wet-foot), while granting legal status to those who successfully make it to U.S. shores (dry-foot). Elián González is the most prominent example of the more than 20,000 Cubans who have attempted to emigrate from Cuba by irregular maritime means since 1995.

In fact, official U.S. Coast Guard numbers for 2005 and 2006 show that more Cubans are taking advantage of this opportunity now than at any time since the rafter crisis of 1994. In no single year since 1994 has the number of inter-dictions surpassed 2,000. However, fiscal year 2005 saw a total of 2,712 sea interdictions and 2,530 arrivals on South Florida coasts, while the number of interdictions in 2006 reached 2,754 and arrivals numbered 3,075. At the same time, Cubans are finding ever more inventive routes into the United States, with more than 700 arriving in Puerto Rico via the Dominican Republic, and another 350 rafters landing in Honduras en route to the U.S.-Mexico border in 2006. Another 1,000 undocumented Cubans were detained in Mexico in 2006, while an estimated 6,000 have crossed the Rio Grande and claimed political asylum once in U.S. territory (Cancio Isla 2006; Goodnough 2005).

All told, the 2000 census counted 1,241,685 Cubans living in the United States. Some 73 percent (906,430) of that total were immigrants, while the other 27 percent (335,255) made up the growing U.S.-born Cuban second generation (Díaz-Bri-quets 2006; Pedraza 2002). According to a recent report by the Pew Hispanic Center (2006), the U.S. Cuban population had reached 1,448,684 by 2004. Although still predominant, the Cuban-born portion of that total had dropped to 63 per-cent (or 912,686 persons), while the U.S.-born portion had

risen to 37 percent (or 535,998 persons). Further disaggre-
gating the Cuban-American population shows a clear growth
in the segment of the Cuban immigrant population to have
arrived after 1980. That is, out of a total population of
1,448,684, 30 percent (431,429) arrived in the United States
before 1980, another 12 percent (171,798) came between
1980 and 1990, and 21 percent (309,459) have arrived since
1990 (table 4.1).

Cuban-Americans are heavily concentrated in South
Florida, with a full 67 percent living in the state (more than
half of whom reside in Miami-Dade County). Other important
states of Cuban settlement include New Jersey (6.2 percent),
California (5.8 percent), and New York (5.0 percent). They
have also defied trends by tending to concentrate more
densely in South Florida over time rather than dispersing
across the region or nation. The continued arrival of a large
group of new immigrants since 1995 has only strengthened
this tendency, which may continue as long as Cuba's socialist
system survives (with or without Fidel Castro). Apart from
this pronounced demographic density, the Cuban émigré population is distinguished by its racial composition (overwhelm-
ingly white), advanced age, high average income, and low

Table 4.1 – Cuban Population in the United States by Nativity, Time of Entry, Percentage, and Citizenship, 2004

	Total Population	Percentage of Cuban Population in U.S.	Percentage of Group with U.S. Citizenship	Yield of Potential Voters
Cuban immigrants	912,686	63.0	60	547,068
Pre-1980 arrival	431,429	29.8	90	388,286
1980-1990 arrival	171,798	11.9	60	103,079
Post-1990 arrival	309,459	21.4	18	55,703
Children of immigrants	535,998	37.0	100	535,998
Total	**1,448,684**	**100.0**	—	**1,083,066**

(Source: Pew Hispanic Center 2006)

poverty and unemployment rates (Martínez-Fernández 2002: 601–602; Pew Hispanic Center 2006).

Finally, while Cuban-Americans consistently registered and voted Republican during the 1980s and 1990s, the influx of new immigrants and the growth of the second-generation have resulted in a shift away from this single-minded political focus. Today, while 28 percent of Cubans say that they consider themselves Republicans (a considerably higher percentage than for other Hispanics), another 20 percent are Democrats, with a full 27 percent considering themselves Independents (Pew Hispanic Center 2006). This indicates a growing division among Cuban émigrés between the dwindling number of old guard exiles on the one hand, and the growing number of new immigrants on the other. The continued addition of at least 20,000 new immigrants directly from Cuba each year has constantly renewed the Cuban-born portion of the Cuban-American population.

The arrival of new immigrants along with the gradual increase in the size of the Cuban second generation competes with the demographic (as well as economic and political) strength of the pre-1980 exiles in determining the overall orientation and identity of the Cuban émigré community (Grenier and Pérez 2003). That is, while *exile* identity and politics have predominated among the Cuban-American community historically, a new *immigrant* identity and politics have more recently emerged. However, relatively few of these more recent Cuban immigrants have become citizens, limiting their political voice and impact on U.S. policy toward Cuba.

Whereas the raw numbers of Cuban immigrants who arrived before 1980 (431,429) is now overshadowed by those who have come since (481,257), the newer immigrant group's relatively low rate of citizenship has allowed the traditional exiles to continue to exercise significantly greater political power. For example, the 431,429 pre-1980 Cuban-Americans have a naturalization rate of 90 percent, while only 60 percent of the 171,798 Cubans coming between 1980 and 1990 have become citizens. Even lower is the naturalization rate of those Cubans arriving in the United States since 1990. Though they number 309,459 persons, only 18 percent (55,703) have naturalized. Thus, the 431,429 pre-1980 Cuban-Americans yield 388,286 potential voters, while the more numerous 481,257 post-1980 Cuban-Americans yield just 158,781 voters (see table 4.1).

The importance of these numbers was illustrated in the most recent Cuba Poll conducted jointly by the Institute for Public Opinion Research (IPOR) and the Cuban Research Institute (CRI) of Florida International University. On the one hand, the poll showed the continued erosion of a unified hard-line policy approach toward Cuba among Cuban-Americans. For example, when the IPOR/CRI "Cuba Poll" was first conducted among Cuban-Americans in Miami-Dade county in 1991, it revealed that 86.6 percent was in favor of the embargo. However, by 2000 that number had dropped to just 62.4 percent, reaching a new low of 57.5 percent in March 2007. Similarly, the same March 2007 poll indicated that now a clear majority of Cuban-Americans in Miami-Dade favor establishing diplomatic relations with the Cuban government (57.4 percent) and support unrestricted travel from the United States to Cuba (55.2 percent). On the other hand, among those Miami-Dade Cuban-Americans registered to vote, 57.7 percent opposed allowing unrestricted travel, clearly indicating the fact that older exiles are much more likely to be U.S. citizens, be registered to vote, and hold hard-line positions relative to their more recently arrived brethren (Bachelet 2007; FIU 2007).

It remains to be seen whether the newfound diversity of political opinion and policy approach within the Cuban exile community can overcome the three enduring paradoxes of Cuban-American life: resistance to assimilation, political intransigence, and the legitimacy dilemma (Portes 2005). In order to achieve success, immigrants usually feel the need to integrate into the mainstream of the host society. In contrast, Cubans remain proudly separate and have even created a distinct political and moral economy in South Florida (ibid.). That is, unlike virtually every other immigrant group, Cubans in Miami have rewritten the standard rule of American immigration, which says that assimilation equals success. Instead of assimilating into the mainstream in order to succeed, they have largely redefined the mainstream by taking it over (in South Florida) and forcing others to acculturate to Cuban(-American) culture (Portes and Stepick 1993). As with Northeastern Jews, Cubans' tremendous socioeconomic and political success in the United States has not been based on assimilation, but predicated on the preservation of their ethnic social networks and a distinct ethnic identity. It remains to be seen, however, whether this resistance to assimilation is but a generational lag that will dissipate over time, especially after inevitable regime change in Cuba puts a definitive end to Cubans' exile identity.

The second paradox is the focused, intransigent, and conservative orientation of Cuban-American politics. Over time in the host country strident political attitudes tend to mellow under the pressure of external influences. However, in the Cuban case, the historic exile leadership has remained an unbending foe both of the Castro government and of any U.S. policy approach other than absolute isolation. While this approach has earned Cuban-Americans the reputation of being extremists who are willfully out of touch with the post–Cold War world, it has served them well as perhaps the most successful immigrant/ethnic lobby in U.S. political history. This Cuban-American political machine originated out of a common perceived experience of dispossession, expulsion, and betrayal. However, it was consolidated only beginning in 1980, with the election of President Ronald Reagan and the ascendance in South Florida of Miami businessman and lobbyist Jorge Más Canosa, the founder of the Cuban American National Foundation (CANF).

Modeling itself on the Pro-Israel PAC, CANF came into being just as Cuban-Americans were gaining citizenship and voting in U.S. elections for the first time. Given its laserlike focus on the issue of U.S. foreign policy toward Cuba under Reagan during the Cold War, CANF could be counted on to line up block votes for both Democratic and Republican candidates and consistently generate campaign donations from its Cuban-American followers. In short, under CANF's leadership the exile lobby had a simple, powerful, and extremely effective three-pronged strategy based on message, money, and votes. Its anticommunist message was clearly consistent with U.S. foreign policy interests during the Cold War. No other political lobby had an interest in challenging its goals by funding dialogue-minded politicians. And no other group could deliver such disciplined, focused, and reliable voter turnout (Zamora 2005).

These abilities resulted in CANF's success in having three Cuban-American members of congress elected, two Republicans from South Florida (Representatives Ileana Ros-Lehtinen and Lincoln Díaz-Balart) and one Democrat from New Jersey (former representative and now Senator Robert Menéndez). After 2000 three other Cuban-Americans were elected to national office with CANF's help, Representative Mario Díaz-Balart (Lincoln's younger brother), Senator Mel Martinez (both Republicans), and Representative Albio Sires (a New Jersey Democrat who filled Robert Menendez's seat in the House). These politicians were elected as much as the voice of the Cuban nation in exile and to defend an intransigent U.S. policy toward Cuba, as they were to represent the more mundane domestic concerns of their constituents.

CANF's influence extended across the partisan divide, with Más Canosa routinely consulted by both Republican and Democratic administrations. Likewise, CANF was always willing to support the candidacies of non-Cuban and non-Republican politicians with money and votes, as long as they supported a hard line against Castro. That was the case in the 1980s in Florida with Democratic representatives Dante

Fascell and Claude Pepper (both of whom were succeeded by Cuban-Americans upon retirement), and again in the 1990s with Republicans Jesse Helms and Dan Burton, and Democrats Robert Torricelli and Joe Lieberman (Portes 1998).

The final paradox is one of legitimacy. In short, while the Cuban-American political machine has successfully elected politicians and influenced (even at times dictated) U.S. policy toward Cuba, it increasingly suffers from a legitimacy crisis, given the fact that its tactics of aggression, embargo, and isolation have been supremely unsuccessful at achieving regime change in Havana. In fact, if anything it is likely that CANF's confrontational tactics have only fueled Castro's thirst for power and control, allowing him to stoke the coals of Cuban nationalism and manipulate fears of foreign invasion (Portes 1998; 2005). Indeed, one oft-cited irony of the historic Cuban exile community is that though they never came with the intention to stay, they have enjoyed unequalled success among Latinos at what they say they are not (immigrants) and continued failure at what they say they are (exiles). In the end, exiles succeed only if and when they can return triumphantly to their homeland (Grenier and Pérez 2003).

This paradox of legitimacy gradually deepened during the 1990s as the interests of the exile lobby and the U.S. government began to diverge. In short, after the end of the Cold War the exile lobby's message began to lose its focus and come into conflict with U.S. interests. Moreover, both the U.S. farm and tourism lobbies began to challenge the generous political donations of the exile lobby, competing for the attention of U.S. politicians. Finally, as the Cuban-American population began to diversify with new immigrants (not exiles) arriving from Cuba by the tens of thousands, the exile lobby gradually lost its effectiveness at getting out a unified Cuban-American vote. What had been the lobby's strengths, a unified message that coincided with U.S. interests, well-placed political donations with no competition, and command of a disciplined voting bloc, began to unravel, fatally undermining its effectiveness (Zamora 2005). Partially as a result of this paradox of legitimacy, CANF experienced an internal debate over its traditional isolationist approach and identification with the Republican Party. That debate led to a rift within the organization and the departure of many CANF hard-liners, who formed the Cuban Liberty Council in 2001.

Thus, are Cubans in America still exiles, and not immigrants? As with Castro's own legendary longevity in Havana, the exile identity is subject to "the biological solution" (death from old age). At the same time, Más Canosa's death in 1997, the pope's visit to Cuba in 1998, and the outcome of the Elián González affair in 1999–2000 have combined with some negative fallout from new restrictions on remittances and family travel to Cuba since 2003, leading to the emergence of many new, more moderate voices and organizations within the Cuban-American community that are beginning to challenge the monolithic image of Cuban-Americans. Some of these more moderate groups include the Cuban Committee for Democracy, founded in 1993; the Cuban-American Alliance and Education Fund, founded in the late 1990s; the Cuba Study Group, a group of Cuban-American business leaders founded after 2000 who seek alternatives to current U.S. isolationist policy; and ENCASA/US-CUBA (Emergency Network of Cuban American Scholars and Artists for Change in U.S.-Cuba Policy), founded in 2006.

CUBAN MUSIC

Cuba has developed and successfully exported a long succession of musical styles and infectious rhythms, many of which have gone on to conquer the hemisphere and circle the globe. In this section, I describe the development of a variety of Cuban musical genres over the course of the twentieth century, including son and rumba; danzón, canción, and punto guajiro; "rhumba," conga, mambo, Latin jazz, and cha-cha-chá; bolero, trova, nueva trova, songo, timba, Cuban hip-hop, and, of course, salsa itself, whose Cuban paternity is universally recognized by the mostly "Nuyorican" (Puerto Rican New Yorker) musicians who brought it into existence in New York City in the late 1960s (see figure 4.1 on page 324). In presenting these various genres, I focus on the two most unique and outstanding characteristics of Cuban music: *absorption* and *diffusion* (Padura Fuentes 2006: 205). These traits have allowed Cuban music to take on a multitude of diverse influences and cross borders to the United States and beyond, constantly reinventing itself while remaining both vital and "authentic" in the process. As famed Cuban anthropologist and ethnomusicologist Fernando Ortiz once observed, the son itself, the sine qua non of authentic Cuban "roots" music, was born out of an impure "love affair between the African drum and the Spanish guitar."

The Son

Best compared to American blues as Cuba's central, most widely influential musical genre, son was essential to the development of popular Cuban dance music between 1920 and 1940. The son began as relatively "simple" country music from the highlands around the Sierra Maestra played by wandering groups of musicians armed with maracas, a standard acoustic guitar, a *tres* (an acoustic guitar with three sets of double strings), a *güiro* (a dried, elongated calabash with ridges that are scraped with a stick), a set of bongo drums, and sometimes a *marimbula* (a "finger piano," or rudimentary bass instrument). The *claves*, a pair of hard wooden pegs, were added after the son arrived in Havana around 1910 (Sweeney 2001: 45–52). Carried to the capital city by young black army recruits from Oriente, the son rapidly displaced the danzón and grew into the most popular dance music of Cuba, later becoming the source of most forms of modern Latin American and Caribbean dance music.

After 1910, the entire vast history and innumerable genres of music on the island converged through the crystallization of son into a national musical style, producing a synthesis that for the first time posed an effective, brilliant musical resolution to the age-old tension between classically inspired European salon music (such as the contradanza, danza, and danzón) and popular Afro-Cuban percussive styles emanating from the street (such as the rumba) (Manuel 2006: 43–44). In his book *Music in Cuba,* first published in Cuba in 1945, Cuban writer Alejo Carpentier argues that, "Thanks to the *son,* Afro-Cuban percussion, confined to the slave barracks and the dilapidated rooming houses of the slums, revealed its marvelous expressive resources, achieving universal status" (2001: 228).

Specifically, it was son's African-inspired 2–3 "rhythmic key," known as the clave, that made it unique. *Sin clave, no hay son* ("without clave, there is no son") is how Cuban musicians emphasize the central importance of the clave. The powerful and penetrating rhythmic crack of the two wooden pegs (also called the *claves*) both distinguished the son from other types of Cuban music and allowed it to meld together the floating melodies and harmonies of European instruments based on strings and horns (especially the Spanish guitar) and the driving percussive rhythms and call-and-response vocals based on the African drum. Ethnomusicologist Ned Sublette's gloss of the term is helpful:

> The ships were held together not with nails but with wooden pegs, called *clavijas,* made of hard, dense wood that wouldn't rot when wet. . . . The word *clave* has several meanings in Spanish. . . . One of the meanings of the word is "key" . . ..
> Just as the hardwood claves once held ships together, when they are clicked together as instruments, the rhythm they play holds the melody line and percussion parts together. . . . So the claves locked the black and white together in song—the process of creolization in action. (Sublette 2004: 94–96)

Three key instruments in a typical modern son/salsa band: a young boy plays the güiro (front, center), while his father plays the bongos (back, right). Another man plays the larger tumbadora (conga) drums (back, left). (Ted Henken)

Carpentier made much the same point, focusing his attention on the clave's previously mentioned ability to bring a variety of previously incompatible instruments together, giving birth to a new, singular musical genre.

The great revolution of ideas instigated by the *son's* percussion was in giving us *the sense of a polyrhythm subjected to a unity of time.* Up until then, one spoke of *the* rhythm of the *contradanza,* the rhythm of the *guaracha, the* rhythms of the *danzón.* . . . The *son,* on the other hand, established new categories. Within a general tempo, each percussive element assumed an autonomous existence. (Carpentier 2001: 229, emphasis in the original)

Early popularizers of the son include Miguel Matamoros, who composed a veritable catalogue of songs that have since become tropical standards such as "Son de la Loma" for his group Trio Matamoros, and Ignacio Piñeiro who infused the son with an urban feel derived largely from the rumba most evident in numbers like "Échale Salsita," recorded with his group Septeto Nacional. Such is the omnivorous power and open nature of son, what Cuban ethnomusicologist Radamés Giró called "a force capable of digesting everything it borrows" (Fernández 2000: 275), that it was later transformed, most famously by the composer and blind *tres* guitar player Arsenio Rodríguez and his conjunto orchestra (a dance band with a piano, large horn section, and a Conga drum) in the late 1940s and 1950s, into the many different styles we know today: son guaguancó, son montuno, son pregón, son afro, guaracha-son, guajiro-son, bolero-son, and modern-day salsa—which is essentially son played with new musical arrangements, Caribbean and North American influences, a Latino/Latin American consciousness, and a more aggressive New York urban sensibility. Although the son is perhaps the most powerful symbol of Afro-Hispanic cultural fusion and Cuban nationalism, it was "re-Africanized" by Rodríguez in the late 1940s when he enriched its rhythmic base by introducing the piano, double trumpets, a stand-up base, and, most importantly, the conga drum (*tumbadora*) for the first time, creating the conjunto arrangement. These instrumental additions added a fiery dynamism to Rodríguez's musical arrangements that combined the musical world of the son septet with the swing of the North American jazz band (Sublette 2004).

Of Rodríguez's many musical innovations, perhaps his most important was the son montuno, the final, more open-ended "jam" section of a son arrangement that follows the initial verse section. Although the son montuno had been played for years already, Rodríguez's conjunto breathed new life into it by dividing it into sections that highlighted the horns, pumping more energy and excitement into it until it climaxed and "broke." This final montuno section, which Rodríguez renamed *diablo* ("devil") (and to which many attribute the origin of the later wildly popular mambo), was characterized by a cyclic, African-derived formal structure, constant improvisation (with lyrics and instrumental solos), and a typically African call-and-response interaction between the main *sonero* (singer) with either the chorus or one or another instrumental soloist (ibid.).

In his own highly original development of the son montuno, Benny Moré, a contemporary of Rodríguez's and perhaps the most gifted Cuban *sonero* of the twentieth century, clearly demonstrated the difference between *cantar* ("singing") and *sonear,* the ability to improvise lyrics "in a manner that fits rhythmically and melodically with the accompanying *coro* ['chorus'] of the *son montuno*" (Fernández 2000: 269, 276). This arrangement closely mimics the structure of a traditional rumba, described below.

After 1960, the son's central importance in Cuban popular music waned. Still, the transformation of the son into the songo by the wildly popular dance band Los Van Van, kept Cuban audiences dancing to the basic clave rhythm through a new series of modernizations, miscegenations, and mutations. Also, during the 1970s and 1980s a number of son "revival" groups, including Sierra Maestra and Alberto Álvarez y Son 14, succeeded in keeping classic son alive. In fact, it was Sierra Maestra's bandleader, Juan de Marcos González, who was the main producer and musical arranger in Cuba behind the formation and worldwide success of the 1990s son revival sensations Buena Vista Social Club and the Afro-Cuban All Stars (Robinson 2004; Sweeney 2001).

The Rumba

While the son is normally understood as the root of all modern Cuban (and Caribbean) dance music, the influence of the instrumentation and structure of the equally "rootsy" rumba is ubiquitous in modern "tropical" dance music. Strictly speaking, the classic rumba can be described as a combination of vocals, percussion, and dance performed together in any one of three styles—the yambú, the columbia, or the guaguancó—often referred to as the "rumba complex." However, the term *rumba* itself can refer to this specific group of traditional music-dance performances or to a variety of other tropical musical forms and even social gatherings (*rumbear* is a Cuban-Spanish verb that means "to party"). Carpentier once famously quipped, "Everything can be labeled [a rumba]. . . . More than a genre, [it] represents an 'atmosphere' or feeling; . . . in Cuba there is no single 'rumba,' but various 'rumbas' [all] synonym[ous] for revelry, lascivious dance, carousing with loose women of the street" (quoted in Moore 1997: 169). It is perhaps for this reason that when son music was first marketed in the United States in the 1930s it was not labeled son, but the more Africanized, seductive rumba, often misspelled "rhumba" (Sublette 2004: 258).

Much like jazz, blues, and hip-hop in the United States, tango in Argentina, merengue in the Dominican Republic, samba in Brazil, and reggae in Jamaica, historically the rumba was rejected by polite, middle- and upper-class Cuban society as vulgar music fit only for the black underclass (Manuel 2006: 16). As such, it was constantly repressed by both colonial and republican authorities. Nor has the revolutionary government been immune to that Eurocentric attitude. In fact, during the 1960s and 1970s many battles were fought

This famous alleyway, known as the Callejón de Hamel, *hosts frequent public performances of traditional Cuban rumba by some of Havana's leading groups. (Ted Henken)*

between promoters of Afro-Cuban musical styles and the socialist authorities over the provision of public spaces for the development and performance of rumba (Moore 1997: 169).

As a secular artistic expression with roots in sacred ritual, the rumba has a number of precursors. First, its form and purpose are surprisingly similar to those of the *areíto,* a sacred ceremony of Cuba's indigenous peoples that involved percussive music, communal dancing and singing, and the ritual consumption of tobacco and alcohol. Second, the Afro-Cuban bembé is an even more direct influence on the modern rumba. As an informal devotional event common to many Afro-Cuban religions in Cuba, the bembé is a ritual organized around music and dance performances in praise of the orishas. For that reason a bembé is often casually referred to in Cuba today as a *toque de santo*—that is, a festival in which the rhythm that calls forth each orisha is ritually performed on the three sacred two-headed batá drums, the smallest okónkolo drum, the mid-sized itótele drum, and the largest "mother" drum, the iyá. During this devotional drumming ceremony, the lead singer, known as the *akpwon,* engages in a musical dialogue with the chorus, called the *ankorí* (Sweeney 2001). As with the areíto, during a bembé food and drink are ritually offered to the orishas and then consumed by participants at the conclusion of the ceremony. Other influences on the development of the rumba were the yuka and makuta, a pair of dances from the Congo commonly performed in nineteenth-century Cuba, as well as the more aggressive baile de maní, often performed on Cuban slave plantations (Alén Rodríguez 1992; Sublette 2004: 258–262).

Rumba, however, is a nonsacred, secular music/dance complex that emerged in Cuba's western provinces of Havana and Matanzas in the mid-nineteenth century. That is, the rumba is neither African nor Spanish, but a Cuban invention synthesized from both African and Hispanic elements. The rumba was developed by lower-class free black and poor white dockworkers and stevedores in the tenements (*solares*) and ports of Havana and Matanzas. Whichever of the three aforementioned types of rumba is being played, the performance amounts to a profane festival with each "song" sharing a similar, very specific structure. All rumbas begin with an opening, nonsensical melodic fragment called a *diana.* While the diana has no "text" as such, it acts as an opening call that sets the musical tone, instructing the chorus how to respond during the rumba that follows. It is likely that this element derives from the vocal wails common in the flamenco singing of Spanish Andalucía and the Canary Islands (themselves influenced by both Gypsy music and the Moorish/Arabic chants common in medieval Spain) (Sublette 2004: 267).

Immediately after the diana comes the rhythmic sound of the clave (similar to the son clave, but done in 3–2 time), which continues to echo throughout the entire song. Now the "lead singer," called a *decimista,* begins an energetic call-and-

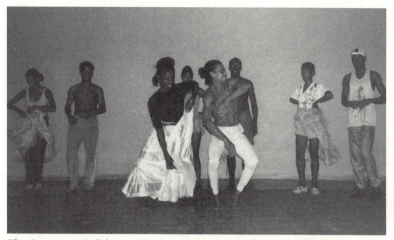

The Conjunto Folklorico Nacional rehearses a guaguancó. (Ted Henken)

response exchange with the accompanying chorus of voices that includes a *censor* (who provides the texts), a *clarina* (a female singer with a high voice), and a *tonista* (a *rumbero* with a good ear who acts as a listener and guide). A rumba usually begins with a relatively slow tempo, building up speed and power as it progresses. This gradual strengthening normally takes up the first third of the song, at which time the rumba reaches an energetic climax and "breaks" (*se rompe la rumba*) (ibid.). At this point the entire performance enters a kind of controlled but ecstatic chaos in which the chorus and various percussion instruments join in the fun (and oh is it fun!).

The most important of these percussion instruments are the three *tumbadoras* (better known as conga drums when used in popular dance music). Inherited from a combination of the *cajones* (packing crates) used by dockworkers (and similar to the *cajon* used in flamenco music) and the *mula, caja,* and *cachimbo* used in the nineteenth-century Congo yuka dance, these three drums are known as the *tumbadora conga,* the *salidor,* and the *quinto* in their modern incarnations. The *tumbadora conga* and the *salidor* are both low-pitched drums, which carry the rhythm of the rumba, while the *quinto* is a high-pitched drum used for "talking"—that is, communicating with the singer and dancers. In addition to the clave and these three *tumbadoras,* the rumba percussion section is completed by the *catá* (a clavelike instrument also known as the *guagua,* as in guaguancó), which locks together with the clave producing the rumba's rhythmic structure (ibid.: 266–267). As the three *tumbadoras* join in the rumba, with the clave and *catá* wailing away in the background, a complex three-way call-and-response interaction begins to take place between the *decimista,* the *quinto,* and the various dancers whose strangely stiff movements can suddenly turn smooth, seductive, graceful, and acrobatic.

As a dance, the rumba can take one of the three afore-mentioned basic forms, the yambú, columbia, and guan-guancó, of which the guaguancó, a seductive couple dance, is easily the most common and influential on the way modern salsa is danced (figure 4.1). Rarely danced today, the yambú is a mimetic dance that re-enacts household chores as performed slowly by an elderly couple with the movements devoid of sexual content. In contrast, the columbia is an impossibly rapid, even convulsive dance, which involves the interaction of a group of male dancers in a kind of physical dialogue with the beat of the *quinto* drum and the voice of the *decimista.* The columbia also involves the high-speed handling of various props such as a machete, knife, bottle, glass of water, or plate (ibid.: 268). As such, every movement of the columbia is designed to show off the dancers' skills and acrobatic abilities in competition with one another, with improvisation, speed, wit, and grace the most highly prized qualities.

Finally, the guaguancó is a rumba danced by a couple at an intermediate speed involving an often explicit sexual pantomime of the interaction of a rooster and a hen. Playing hard-to-get, the female dancer uses a colored kerchief, which she occasionally drops to the ground and with which she feigns bashfulness, coquettishly, hiding her private regions from her dance partner. Meanwhile, the male dancer slyly moves ever closer to her, waiting for his opportunity to pounce. Her moves to variously avoid, deflect, or reject his advances are known as the *botao* (from the Spanish *botado,* or "rejected"), while his attempts at conquest are called the *vacunao* (from the Spanish *vacunado,* or "vaccinated"). The guaguancó concludes when the goal of the symbolic sexual possession of the female by the male dancer is achieved (ibid.; Alén Rodríguez 1992).

The Danzón, Canción, and the Punto Guajiro

Three other principal genres of Cuban music straddle the turn of the nineteenth century, when Cuba ceased being a Spanish colony and entered the community of (semi-) sovereign republics. These are the danzón, the canción, and the punto guajiro (figure 4.1). Prior to the ascendance of the son as Cuba's premier national style of dance music, the danzón was king. The danzón grew out of two more European styles of ballroom dance music, the contradanza and the danza. The Cuban version of the contradanza was usually called the contradanza francesa because its most immediate influence came from the group of nineteenth-century ballroom "square" dances (bailes de cuadros) that included both the courtly French contre danse and the English country dance. Popularized in Cuba in the late eighteenth century by French-Haitian colonists fleeing the 1791 slave insurrection that became the Haitian Revolution, Cuba's contradanza is based on the cinquillo, a five-beat rhythmic pattern also found in the later danzón. This "square" dance quickly passed through a danza phase, where it broke down into a couple dance before crystallizing into the Cuban danzón in the 1870s.

The first danzón known to be composed, performed in public, and later recorded was Miguel Faílde's "Alturas de Simpson," named after the neighborhood of Simpson Heights in Matanzas. Like the contradanza and danza before it, the

Figure 4.1 – From Son to Salsa: The Origins and Development of Cuban Music

Fernando Ortiz: "Cuban music is a love affair between the African drum and the Spanish guitar" (chorus and percussion) (melody and harmony)

1850–1920

Europe	SON	Africa
DANZÓN	**SON**	**RUMBA**
(HAVANA)	*(ORIENTE / SANTIAGO)*	*(HAVANA / MATANZAS)*
Ballroom/salon music	Sp. and African guajiros	Free colored and poor whites
Contradanza (Spain)	Montuno (mtns./improv.)	1. Yoruba/Lucumí (Santería/Nigeria)
Danza (Habanera)	Changüi (Guantánamo)	2. Bantú/Palo Monte (Congo)
Danzón	Sucu-sucu, Parranda	3. Abakuá/Ñáñigo (Carabalí/Calabar)
Danzonete	Guaracha, Pregón	4. Arará (Dahomey/Benin)
Cha-cha-chá	**PUNTO GUAJIRO**	**"Rumba Complex"**
	Punto Libre vs. *Punto Fijo*	Combo: song, percussion, and dance
	a. Tonada espirituana	1. *Yambú* (slow couple dance)
	b. Punto cruzado	2. *Columbia* (fast male dance)
	c. Seguidilla	3. *Guaguancó* (fast couple dance)
	Terms: *Décima, Guajira,*	Terms: *Vacunao* and *Botao*
	and *Controversia*	

1920–1960

Cuba		United States
CANCIÓN Cubana	**Son** (1910-1950s)—Matamoros, Piñeiro, Rodríguez, Moré (CU)	
Canción (Ital./Sp. origins)	**"Rhumba"** (1930s)—Azpiazu and "El Manicero" (Peanut Vendor)	
Habanera (nineteenth cent.)	**Conga** (1930s–1940s)—Xavier Cugat and Desi Arnaz (U.S.)	
Vieja Trova (troubadour)	**Mambo** (late 1940s)—Pérez Prado and Beny Moré (MX/CU)	
Clave and Criolla	Bauzá/Machito (NY) ➔	**AfroCuban/Latin Jazz**
Guajira	**Cha-cha-chá** (1950s)—E. Jorrín	**Cu-bop** (Gillespie/Pozo)
Bolero (romantic ballad)		C. Valdés and *Irakere*
Fílin (Feeling)		Paquito D'Rivera
		Arturo Sandoval

1960–2006

Nueva Trova (Protest music)   **Descarga**—1950s–1960s ("Cachao" López)
Guaracha, Pachanga, Doo Wop, Boogaloo

SALSA: "Cuban Music played by Puerto Ricans in New York City" (1960s–1980s)
Nuyorican/Fania All-Stars; Puerto Rico, Colombia, Venezuela, Panama, Dominican Republic

Novísima Trova (Protest rock)
New styles of popular music developed since 1960 in Cuba:
Songo, Mozambique (Pello El Afrokan), **Pilón, Timba, Cuban Hip-Hop**
          Timba (1990s—a.k.a. Cuban "salsa"): Modern Cuban dance music
          Leading Cuban "timba" dance bands of the 1990s:
          "NG" La Banda, Manolín "El médico de la salsa," Isaac Delgado, David
          Calzado and La Charanga Habanera, and Los Van Van

musical structure and sound of the danzón is primarily derived from European traditions and is an instrumental dance music for couples. Although it sounds virtually identical to its predecessors and features couples holding each other in a loose embrace, it was originally controversial because of its association with Afro-Cubans and Haitians (who were among the form's first composers and performers).

Another innovation of the danzón that would allow it to continue to morph in later years, was its start-and-stop structure that allowed couples to rest and chat between the song's various sections, or danzones. Each time the danzón restarted, a new instrument played a solo, now the clarinet, now the violin, and so forth. Responding to the needs of the dancers, these various sections would prove to be fertile ground for later innovation in the 1930s, 1940s, and 1950s, when dancers became bored and demanded vocals (the *danzonete*), fast-paced frantic convulsions (the *mambo*), and finally less movement but more syncopation (the cha-cha-chá). One still popular danzón, composed by Israel "Cachao" López in the 1940s, appears on and gave its name to the wildly popular recording of the mid-1990s, "Buena Vista Social Club."

The Cuban canción (literally meaning "song") is a Caribbean descendant of the Spanish romance, Neapolitan song, and the operatic aria. Along with the contradanza, the canción is the only European form developed in Cuba. Important in the late nineteenth century as a vehicle for the first strains of Cuban nationalism in the form of the anthem "La Bayamesa," the canción typically waxes philosophical or romantic over the beauty of the Cuban landscape. Taking its rhythmic form from the contradanza, the canción produced one subgenre (called alternately the contradanza habanera or the canción habanera) that grew into a hugely influential genre in its own right, the habanera, the rhythm of which was later reborn in Buenos Aires as the tango (Alén Rodríguez 1992).

Within Cuba, the canción also had a fertile role as the principal musical influence on the subsequent development of a series of highly lyrical, melodic, and romantic styles. These include the canción trovadoresca, also known as the vieja trova, trova tradicional, or simply the trova. This is the music of roving troubadours and is associated with the legendary Cuban composers José "Pepe" Sánchez and Sindo Garay. There are also the canción criolla and canción guajira, which, like the canción, specialize in idyllic representations of the Cuban countryside. Finally are three more modern musical derivations of the canción: the bolero, fílin, and nueva trova. The bolero is a romantic, often melodramatic ballad, while the subgenre of the bolero, known as fílin, is more a style of singing than a musical form as such. "Feeling" got its name from the sentimental way American jazz singers sang and is most associated with the Cuban singer-songwriters José Antonio Méndez and César Portillo de la Luz, and divas Elena Burke and Omara Portuondo. Also influenced by the canción is Cuba's answer to the "protest" music of the 1960s and 1970s, nueva trova, which is described more fully below (figure 4.1).

Under the general heading of punto guajiro fall a number of related but stylistically distinct forms of sung poetry derived most directly from Iberian forms of country music. The first of these is guajira music (aka, música guajira), a rural music closely associated with Cuba's Spanish roots and usually composed by nonprofessional farmers. (In Cuba, a *guajiro* is a Spanish-descended dweller of the island's interior. The term is alternately used as a point of pride and a distinction of true, unadulterated Cubanness or a derogatory epithet for a backward, provincial hick or "country bumpkin.") The core structural feature of this and all forms of the punto guajiro is the décima, a form of sung poetry (either formally composed or improvised on the spot) based on ten eight-syllable lines with an *espinela* rhyme scheme (abbaaccddc). While the melodies of the décima are often formulaic and feature little variety, the often witty or humorous lyrics are of central importance and based on a long improvisational Spanish tradition. Like the son, of which some consider it a subgenre, guajira music has hybrid qualities and is dominated by the acoustic guitar, *tres,* maracas, and *cencerro* (cowbell) (ibid.).

Easily the most famous example of música guajira is the song "Guajira Guantanamera," a kind of alternate Cuban national anthem, first popularized on the island in the 1930s by the radio personality Joseíto Fernández. One of many guajira songs composed or improvised over the same basic structure, the world famous "Guantanamera" features a repeated refrain that alternates with a series of changing *coplas,* or verses. These coplas are simple, yet often witty and inventive two-line phrases of text improvised by the soloist. They typically share gossip about some local event or comment on national affairs with political overtones. The song was popularized internationally by the American folk singer Pete Seger (using lines from José Martí's poetry, *Versos sencillos*—"Yo soy un hombre sincero . . ."). An excellent example of how the song can be employed to narrate a story in a humorous or satirical way is its use in the 1995 Tomás Gutiérrez Alea movie *Guantanamera,* in which the endless bureaucratic hassles of moving a woman's dead body across the island are chronicled in song throughout the film.

Finally, the punto cubano (also known as the punto guajiro) features the strongest Iberian origins of all Cuban musical styles. Growing out of a kind of sung poetry known as *el ay,* this style becomes "punto" when it is put to music. Like the previous styles, the punto cubano features lyrics derived from a classical Spanish strophic form called the décima espinela (described above). The melodic line of the punto is known as the *tonada,* and can be divided into two distinct forms: the punto libre (free) and the punto fijo (fixed). The punto libre is defined by an almost complete independence between the poet/singer (called a *repentista*) and the musical instrumentation, which almost ceases when the poet begins to improvise (*a piacere*). On the other hand, the punto fijo follows clear metric pattern and is sung from memory (*tempo giusto*). Additionally, the punto fijo is performed in three varieties known as the tonada espirtuana, the punto cruzado, and the seguidilla. One final feature of the punto guajiro as a general style is its development into a well-known and much loved form called the *controversia humorística,* in which two veteran repentistas engage in a poetic duel as each one attempts to improvise the sharpest décimas without flubbing a syllable or repeating the same word twice (ibid.).

Authenticity and Crossover: The "Rhumba," Conga, Mambo, and Cha-cha-chá

Together, the son and rumba form the backbone of all popular Cuban dance music, with lesser influences coming from the other musical genres described above. However, the son has been more successful than the rumba (through absorbing many of its characteristics) at achieving popular crossover success both in Cuba and abroad. This success at having, in the vivid phrase of Fernando Ortiz, "the dances of the rabble accepted by aristocrats in their palaces" was accomplished through an ambivalent process of "nationalizing blackness" (Moore 1997). In fact, as ethnomusicologist Robin Moore argues in his recent monograph, *Nationalizing Blackness: Afrocubanismo and Artistic Revolution in Havana, 1920–1940* (1997), a strange mix of pride and embarrassment accompanied the gradual embrace of son as Cuba's national music par excellence. During these pivotal twenty years, a host of mostly white, conservatory trained Cuban composers and musicians including Alejandro García Caturla, Amadeo Roldán, Eliseo Grenet, Moisés Simons, Ernesto Lecuona, the mulatta Rita Montaner, and the black Ignacio Villa, better known as Bola de Nieve ("Snowball"), participated in the simultaneous "purification," popularization, and "universalization" of the son first in Cuba and then abroad.

Notwithstanding the fact that most of Cuba's white nation-alist leaders of the time denounced the raw, syncretic musics of working-class blacks as unfit to represent Cuba to the world, these musicians together with leading progressive middle-class Cuban intellectuals such as Alejo Carpentier, mulatto Nicolás Guillén, and Fernando Ortiz began to tentatively accept Afro-Cuban culture as their own, succeeding in making it Cuba's own in the process (ibid.: 116–118). Likely the most positive spin on what Ortiz called the "chaotic transplantation" of African religion, music, and culture to Cuba was given by Carpentier in a 1929 article he wrote after seeing Rita Montaner perform Cuban music in Paris:

> Let us protect our *guajira* music, our Afrocuban music! Let us defend it against its detractors! Let us praise the *son,* the noisy *solar,* the *güiro,* the *décima,* the lithography on cigar boxes, santería drumming, the picturesque *pregón,* the *mulata* with rings of gold, the light sandals of the *rumbero* . . . . Blessed be the lineage of *Papá Montero* and *María la O!* . . . When one sees things from abroad, the value of these popular treasures is understood as never before! (Quoted in ibid.: 176)

Hovering somewhere between nationalist valorization and racist stereotype, this movement to advocate and legitimize the traditionally despised music of Cuba's slums frequently engaged in a complex process of appropriation and cooptation of Afro-Cuban musical forms in order to achieve popular and commercial success both in Cuba and abroad (ibid.; Manuel 2006 38). While this process modifying Cuban "roots" music produced some of the best known popular "hits" of the golden age of Cuban music (1920–1960), such as Moisés Simons's "El manisero" ("The Peanut Vendor"), it also frequently degenerated into a bastardization of Cuban styles as "exotic" products refined for the American consumer involving the exploitation of Cuban musicians. That is, the success of son in Cuba and later of the Cuban son as "rhumba" in the United States and elsewhere did not always translate into success for Cuban musicians themselves (Pérez 1999: 198–218).

The Son Afro

An early example of this process is a musical subgenre of the son, called the son afro or simply the afro. First popularized in Cuba in the 1920s (prior to the son's crossover U.S. success in the 1930s), this style of son makes overt lyrical and musical references to Afro-Cuban culture, including allusions to santería, the orishas, and slave life. Lyrics were often written in faux-*bozal* speech, the "broken" Spanish spoken by Cuba's African slaves and their descendants. The three (white) Grenet brothers, Eliseo, Emilio, and Ernesto, were perhaps the leaders of this afro trend. Emilio and Eliseo set a number of the mulatto poet Nicolás Guillén's works from the 1930 *Motivos del son* to music, and Ernesto composed the famous faux-*bozal* lullaby "Duerme negrita." The prolific Eliseo composed the standard afros "Lamento esclavo," "Negro bembón," and most famously, "Ay, Mamá Inés," later made famous as the signature song of the Afro-Cuban composer and piano virtuoso Bola de Nieve (Sublette 2004: 406–408).

Perfectly capturing the racial ambivalence of the Afrocubanismo movement, Emilio Grenet made this clarification: "[T]he music of the black which becomes popular is always an interpretation by a white musician who poses as a *dilettante* of [Afrocuban] music, a spectator or commentator at most but never a protagonist" (quoted in Moore 1997: 135). Still, while most of these stylized afros had little in common with traditional Afro-Cuban "roots" music, they were often inspired by black working-class street culture and composed from an aesthetic position that valorized Afro-Cuban culture as truly Cuban. Unlike later crossover "rhumba" hits in the United States, these were popular

Cuban reworkings of an element of Afro-Cuban culture previously denigrated as primitive. They were not foreign bastardizations, nor were they at this stage diluted for American ears (and eyes) (ibid.).

Two Afro-Cuban musicians played key roles as mediators between the Afro-Cuban "street" and the white/Hispanic "elite": Bola de Nieve and Rita Montaner. Like their white counterparts, they performed and popularized the various stylized genres of Afro-Cuban music. However, they often did so in a way that was simultaneously more authentic and ironic than the performances of their white colleagues. The career of black pianist Bola de Nieve especially highlights the irony of this ambivalent embrace of Afro-Cuban musical culture.

Born Ignacio Villa in the Havana suburb of Guanabacoa, Bola de Nieve was given his graphically ironic stage name (Snowball) by his close friend and collaborator Rita Montaner because of his dark black skin and his rounded head (Sublette 2004: 387). Bola became famous in Cuba for his highly original versions of the stylized afros of white composers. Being black himself, however, he was distinguished as the one-and-only successful Afro-Cuban performer of this *afrocubanista* salon music (Moore 1997: 137). Alternately derided for being a kind of Cuban Uncle Tom or celebrated as the incarnation of authentic afro son, Bola de Nieve was neither. Instead, his unique position as a kind of translator of Afro-Cuban culture allowed him simultaneously to celebrate Afro-Cuban popular culture and parody the often simplistic renditions of it created for popular consumption by white composers.

According to Moore, Bola's signature self-parodying performances "overtly reflect the tensions between racism, populism, and elitism so prevalent in Cuban works" of the 1930s (ibid.: 138). Bola's songs would typically poke fun at the figure of the *negro catedrático,* the humble Afro-Cuban who put on airs by dressing up and singing in English, Catalan, French, Italian, and Portuguese (sometimes within a single song).

Indeed, his live shows have been called "mini-docudramas of Cuban social/racial everyday life" (Fernández 2000: 268). However, because of the effectiveness of his stage persona, it was never clear whether he was engaging in sophistocated mockery, humorous self-deprecation, or had internalized racist stereotypes. Combining the extravagance and flamboyance of Liberace and the talent and authenticity of Louis Armstrong, Bola was a complex and talented figure (Moore 1997: 137–138). His recordings of "Messié Julián," "Ay, Mamá Inés," and "Chivo que rompe tambó" are the best examples of his originality as an interpreter of the afro son form.

The "Rhumba"

As mentioned above, what was labeled "rhumba" by 1930s America was in fact a highly stylized version of Cuban son music, often modified to appeal to the musical tastes (or lack thereof) of American tourists in Cuba, and later to the U.S. consumer in general. First, Cuba satiated American appetites for alcohol during American prohibition (1920–1933) becoming a major tourist destination. At the same time, it served as an oasis for the exotic and erotic pleasures unavailable stateside. Among those pleasures were the son and rumba, described disapprovingly by some Americans as "writhing African jungle dances" and celebrated by others as a kind of drug that allows the tourist to "forget that he is a bald-headed businessman from Manitowoc, [and believe that] he is part of something young and strong and fierce and ageless . . ." (quoted by Pérez 1999: 199–201).

Following this prologue, Cuban music began to enter the United States in 1930. As it did so, a stylization and commercialization process took place leading to a series of Cuban music "crazes" that overtook American popular music between 1930 and the late 1950s. This succession of Americanized Cuban musical styles began with the "rhumba" in the early 1930s, was followed by the conga in the late 1930s, was overtaken in the 1940s and 1950s by the mambo, and culminated in the early 1950s with the cha-cha-chá (see figure 4.1) (ibid.: 198–218). This thirty-year influence went underground in the middle to late 1950s when rock and roll (itself a stylized version of African-American blues music) began simultaneously to push aside and incorporate Cuban music in the United States. However, the irrepressible rhythms of that music would only burst forth once again in the late 1960s and early 1970s, this time under the generic, catch-all label for Cuban-inspired Latin dance music: salsa. But first, the "rhumba."

What can accurately be described as the "son heard 'round the world," marking the beginning of Cuban music's conquest of American airwaves and ballrooms, took place on Saturday, April 26, 1930, at New York City's Palace Theater, then located at 47th and Broadway. On that night Cuban bandleader Modesto "Don" Azpiazu and his Havana Casino Orchestra inaugurated the "rhumba" era in the United States by performing first "Ay, mamá Inés" and then, most famously, "El manisero," which became better known in the United States as "The Peanut Vendor" (Roberts 1999). The song became so popular over the next decade that it sold a record 1 million copies in sheet music and was recorded no fewer than thirty times by everyone from Louis Armstrong and Duke Ellington to Woody Herman, Dean Martin, and Xavier Cugat. As a result, 60 percent of the business of Arthur Murray dance studios was composed of "rhumba" lessons (Pérez 1999: 203–204).

During the 1930s, "rhumba" came to be understood in the United States as a generic label for Latin America–influenced musical composition. In actual form, most so-called "rhumbas" were conflations of Cuban son with big band jazz music. As popularized in the United States (and presumably as taught at Arthur Murray), the ballroom "rhumba" dance had virtually nothing in common with the traditional form of rumba described above. In fact, there were few nonblacks even back in Cuba in the 1930s familiar with authentic rumba. Still, when Cuban musicians collaborated with American big band jazz orchestras, the result was anything but a simple foreign bastardization of "authentic" Cuban music. There were collaborations and then there were collaborations.

For example, American jazz arranger and trumpeter Dizzy Gillespie's work with Luciano "Chano" Pozo, and later with Frank "Machito" Grillo and Mario Bauzá in the formation of Machito and his Afro-Cubans, led to the creation of the truly original CuBop/Latin Jazz genre. This indicates that the line between "pure" adaptations and "adulteration" is not always so clear (Moore 1997: 189–190). The issue of authenticity is an important one given the tensions over racial, class, and national control and commercialization of Cuban music during the twentieth century. However, as we chronicle and analyze the ongoing process of absorption and diffusion in Cuban music, we should not confuse authenticity with purity. *New Yorker* music critic Alex Ross had it right when he wrote: "Purists of all genres can never stand the fact that the genealogy of music is one long string of miscegenations and mutations" (2003).

This is not to say that all collaborations and miscegenations have been unqualified aesthetic successes, and this is especially true for those that became commercially successful in the United States. Perhaps the single most important crossover figure in "translating" Cuban music into a form that was both appealing and accessible to North Americans was the Spanish-born, Cuban-raised U.S. bandleader Xavier Cugat, affectionately known to U.S. audiences as Cugie. Unabashedly frank about his formula for success, Cugat once famously declared, "Americans know nothing about Latin music. They neither understand nor feel it. So they have to be given music more for the eyes than for the ears" (Roberts 1999: 87). When this second stage of adaptation and stylization of

Cuban music began during the 1930s in the United States, where ignorance of Cuban music reigned, the result was often criticized in Cuba as an adulteration or foreign bastardization.

Such was the case with the most commercially successful collaboration of all, between Cuban Moisés Simons and American Marion Sunshine. The original Spanish lyrics of the son-pregón "El manisero" were "translated" by Sunshine for American audiences into an English version ("The Peanut Vendor"). However, seeking to evoke the tropical and exotic for her American listeners, Sunshine's new version included frightening rhyme schemes such as, "If you're looking for a moral to this song / Fifty million monkeys can't be wrong." Of course, "Cuba didn't see itself as a nation of peanut vendors," or monkeys, for that matter. But being seen as "a novelty, with cutesy ethnic stereotyping" (Sublette 2004: 398) was often the price Cuban musicians had to pay in order to gain access to the American market. And sometimes the quality and authenticity of the music suffered as it was made presentable to the American public. Sadly, this ethnic exoticism has anything but disappeared today, even if it has perhaps become more sophisticated since 1930.

> "The Peanut Vendor" was Exhibit A of a tradition of two parallel Cuban musics: one for domestic consumption; the other for export. Don Azpiazu's record wasn't the revelation in Cuba that it was in the United States. This would be a permanent feature of the Cuban music economy. Azpiazu, Machín, Xavier Cugat, Desi Arnaz, Machito, Gloria Estefan, and the Buena Vista Social Club all found success outside of Cuba and had little or no presence on the island. (Ibid.: 399)

The novelty status of Cuban music in the United States is part of the reason that Americans are so unaware of the deep influence it has had on American music historically. That also explains why Americans seem to "rediscover" Cuban music every twenty or thirty years, each time as something new.

The Conga

Like its cousin the son, the conga got its start in Cuba's Oriente. The conga is a version of the often spontaneous Afro-Cuban neighborhood parades, or *comparsas,* that were first celebrated in Santiago de Cuba. Growing out of the now-defunct Afro-Cuban mutual aid societies known as *cabildos de nación,* comparsas are most common during carnival season (which takes place in July in Santiago). Although often used interchangeably, historically the term *comparsa* was used to describe more formal affairs featuring a uniformed troupe of choreographed marchers, while the word *conga* denoted a more spontaneous percussion-driven dancing parade open to all comers, not unlike the famous "second line" parades that often erupt out of New Orleans African American neighbor-hoods (ibid.: 370). Though long repressed during colonial times and the early twentieth century, these Afro-Cuban congas caught on by the 1930s and 1940s, growing into major civic events with corporate sponsorship by the 1950s.

Derived from the Bantu word *maconga,* meaning "song," the term *conga* was first applied to the *tumbadora* drum commonly played in the comparsas and then to the parade itself. While a Cuban comparsa or conga is normally com-posed of a street full of sweaty Cubans in various states of ine-briation gyrating wildly to the sound of conga drums, spoons rattling against frying pans, and, most characteristically, the high-pitched whine of the *corneta china* ("Chinese coronet"), stateside the conga has become formalized into a "conga-line," with a long line of people snaking through a dancehall all simultaneously doing the dance-step "1–2–3-kick." Of course, the popularity of the conga in Cuba and abroad is due to its simplicity, its mobility, the novel use of drumming, and the fact that everybody can join in (ibid.: 408–409).

Desi Arnaz, the man most associated with the conga in the United States (and virtually unknown in Cuba today), is a strange keeper of the conga flame, given his class, racial, and political origins in Cuba (ibid.: 534). In fact, Arnaz fled Cuba for Miami in 1933 after his pro-Machado father was jailed in the wake of the overthrow of Cuban dictator president Gerardo Machado. Ironically, while mayor of Santiago in the early 1930s, Arnaz's father (also named Desiderio Arnaz) passed a law banning the public playing and dancing of the conga, given its association with "immoral gestures," "epileptic, ragged, and semi-naked crowds," "lubricious contortions and brutal movements" that could "contaminate by example the minors of school age who are carried away by the heat of the display" (ibid.: 370–371).

Despite his father's edict, it seems that Arnaz, Jr., himself was just such an impressionable child, easily "contaminated" by the street congas of Santiago, since upon arriving in the United States, he quickly established himself as a leading Latin musician, bandleader, and "Conga Man," playing with the wildly successful Spanish-Cuban bandleader Xavier Cugat. Arnaz's success in the United States was partially made possible by the trailblazing performances and recordings of the innovative musician and singer Miguelito Valdés, who had also got his start in the United States with Cugat's band in the 1940s and was the first to use the stage name later made popular by Arnaz, "Mr. Babalú" (ibid.: 321–322; Moore 1997: 72; Pérez 1999: 205–206; Sweeney 2001: 29–31). As an increasingly talented comedic showman, touring across America and appearing on both television and Broadway, Arnaz helped to ignite a new "conga craze" in the United States, picking up where the "rhumba" had left off.

The Mambo

In 1948 the mambo, a new up-tempo, horn-driven dance music performed by big band jazz orchestras, quickly eclipsed both the "rhumba" and the conga in the United States, reaching its peak of popularity by 1953. The mambo was a Cuban musical style that for the first time managed to achieve crossover success in both the United States and Latin America, with Afro-Cubans as its most famous and sought-after composers and performers. Originally the term for the faster, more syncopated section at the end of a danzón, the origins of the mambo are most commonly attributed to the brothers Orestes and Israel "Cachao" López, who composed a danzón called "Mambo" in 1938 as members of Antonio Arcaño's orchestra. Essentially, Cachao modified the second section of the slow-paced danzón into a more syncopated, driving, danceable rhythm. He did this by transforming his instrument, the double bass, into a more percussive instrument by emphasizing the downbeat (often referred to as the *bajo anticipado* or, more popularly, the *tumbao*). Arsenio Rodríguez, who often referred to the final section of his son montuno as a mambo, or *diablo,* is also understood to be a key contributor to the birth of the genre. However, pianist, arranger, and bandleader Dámaso Pérez Prado is clearly the single figure most responsible for refining and popularizing the mambo into an internationally recognizable sound.

Essentially, the mambo is a musical hybrid that was born in Cuba in the late 1930s and developed there during the 1940s. However, because it was considered too experimental even in Cuba, it had to wait almost ten years for its eventual consolidation and popularization in Mexico, Latin America, and the United States, between 1948 and 1953. A Bantu word meaning "communication (with the gods)," *mambo* can also refer to an improvisational percussive section of a son or salsa composition. Lyrically the mambo is uninspiring, since the texts of most mambos are composed simply of the word *mambo,* endlessly repeated, interchanging with shouts and loud gruntlike sounds such as "Ungh!" or "Dilo!" (an especially typical feature of Pérez Prado's recordings). Often working in collaboration with sonero Benny Moré in Mexico in the late 1940s, Pérez Prado developed the mambo into a distinct style of Cuban dance music by adding vibrant, driving rhythms, a fast tempo and pulsating flow, blaring trumpets, and a signature reckless dissonance to his compositions. Although his compositions are often criticized by purists for their lack of the complex polyrhythms more common in the work of Machito's Afro-Cubans or Arsenio Rodríguez, Pérez Prado was an undeniable musical innovator who continued to create new rhythms and experiment with ambitious compositions throughout his long career. In fact, his performances openly embraced popular and commercial success, while never abandoning daring experimentation. He also was immensely popular with his audiences, since his numbers invariably pushed dancers to the very limits of human endurance.

Pérez Prado was able to join forces at the height of his popularity with Benny Moré, allowing him to balance his angular, taut, and technical approach with Moré's more smooth, easy-going, and intuitive side (Sublette 2004). Nicknamed *El bár-baro del ritmo* ("The Wizard of Rhythm"), Moré first traveled to Mexico in 1945 with the son sensation Miguel Matamoros, but he soon surpassed Matamoros first as a big band singer and later as a bandleader himself. Moré left the Conjunto Matamoros to join Pérez Prado's mambo orchestra, quickly becoming as popular as Pérez Prado himself. After a number of years of traveling back and forth from Cuba to Mexico, changing bands constantly, Moré finally formed what was to be the ultimate dance band in Cuban musical history, in many ways the culmination of the long evolution of Cuban popular dance music, Benny Moré and his *Banda Gigante*.

Although Moré had no formal musical training, he commanded this enormous orchestra with an exacting precision and typically Cuban flair, making the band's performances an unforgettable spectacle. During his rise to superstardom, he developed a signature style of singing, dressing, and performing that always included a wide-brimmed hat, cane, baggy pants, and long coat. As he sang and directed his orchestra, he often danced wildly across the stage in much the same way as James Brown, "The Godfather of Soul," would do later in the United States. Although less of a composer than a performer, before his death from alcoholism in 1963, Moré composed a number of his own hit songs that have since become standards, including the smash hit and signature Moré number "Castellano, que bueno baila usted," which he cowrote with his trombonist and arranger Generoso "El Tojo" Jiménez.

From the Mambo to Afro-Cuban Jazz (Latin Jazz)

Before being partially supplanted by the cha-cha-chá in the mid-1950s, the mambo took on a new life as the most popular dance music of New York City's vibrant music scene. That was due to the combination of a variety of "Latin" musicians (primarily Cubans and Puerto Ricans) living and working in close and constant collaboration with the two centers of black and white American jazz: the hot jazz in Harlem and the big band jazz of the more exclusive (and racially segregated) downtown hotels like the Waldorf-Astoria. Thus, by the late 1940s the downtown club known as the Palladium became a musical mecca of sorts where Cuban, Puerto Rican, African-American, Jewish, Italian, and other musicians would constantly mix and compete for the distinction of being king of the mambo for a night. The mainstays in this scene, the original "mambo kings" as it were, were the bands of Nuyorican Tito Puente, Puerto Rican Tito Rodríguez, and Machito and his Afro-Cubans, founded by the Cuban brothers-in-law Mario Bauzá and Frank "Machito" Grillo (figure 4.1).

Bauzá and Grillo's collaboration was especially fruitful, since it went beyond mambo and began to experiment with a Cuban-jazz fusion known as Afro-Cuban Jazz (also called Latin Jazz or CuBop), inadvertently laying the groundwork for the later blossoming of salsa in New York twenty-five years later. Unlike the mambo, Latin Jazz is a nondanceable and almost exclusively instrumental genre that is heavily improvisational (like jazz itself, especially bebop). Starting in 1940, when the band formed, Machito played the role of the charismatic front man with the voice and maracas, while Bauzá was the behind-the-scenes innovator skillfully integrating the two "musical languages" of American jazz and Cuban son.

Since the Afro-Cubans were both black and Latino, they were pioneers in breaking down the racial barriers that had previously prevented "black" orchestras from playing on Broadway. This "in-between" position also allowed them to come up with an original, authentic sound that appealed to both blacks and whites, Latinos and Americans, and hard-to-please jazz aficionados, as well as the most demanding mambo dancers (Acosta 2003). Beyond the benefits of a commercial market and booming dance scene in New York, the Afro-Cubans had the luck of landing in the middle of an exceptionally fertile polyglot environment in the New York of the 1930s, 1940s, and 1950s. The massive Puerto Rican immigration of the 1920s had already begun to transform East Harlem into El Barrio. As the invention of salsa would later confirm, these Puerto Rican musicians were especially adept at assimilating Cuban rhythms and black American jazz with their own home-grown musical styles.

The Cha-cha-chá

The final Cuban music craze to take the United States by storm was actually an attempt by Cuban composer and violist Enrique Jorrín to give dancers a break from the fast-paced calisthenics of the mambo. In his famous "La engañadora" ("The Trickster"), Jorrín inserted a one-two-three accent on the fourth beat of the bar, thus breaking the mambo in half and allowing dancers to move two steps and then slowly, gracefully shuffle their feet three times before the next one-two punch. The sound of hundreds of shuffling feet gave the new rhythm its name, cha-cha-chá (Sweeney 2001: 98).

Although it was first developed for Cuban audiences in Havana, the cha-cha-chá took the United States by storm starting in 1954, allowing dancers a respite from the brassy and technically complicated mambo.

Easy to dance and based on strings and the flute, the cha-cha-chá was the opposite of the mambo and as such gave itself easily to simplification and "Americanization" by U.S. composers. As a result, in the following years everyone from Lawrence Welk and Tommy Dorsey to Sam Cooke, Richard Berry, and the Kingsmen put out their own versions of the cha-cha-chá, often shortened to cha-cha. In fact, the musical structure of the 1950s party tune "Louie Louie" is derived directly from an obscure cha-cha-chá. Indeed, listening to the opening bars of René Touzet's arrangement of Rosendo Ruiz, Jr.'s, "El loco cha chá" will convince any American where Richard Berry, and later the Kingsmen, got the inspiration for the "1–2–3, 1–2" lick that opens "Louie Louie" (Sublette 2004: 527).

Cuban Music in Revolution and Exile: From Salsa to Songo, and Trova to Timba

The long series of Cuban dance crazes that had periodically overtaken the United States came to an abrupt halt in the late 1950s. In those years, the upstart child of the blues that called itself rock and roll dealt a fatal blow to American social dancing and at the same time neutralized the crossover appeal of Cuban music in the United States Simultaneously, Cold War isolationism and hostility cast a dark shadow over the two-way musical collaboration between Cuba and the United States that had existed since the end of the nineteenth century. Cuban music and musicians in the United States suddenly found themselves cut off from their musical roots, and, unable to constantly reconnect and renew, were increasingly relegated to the margins of the American musical mainstream. Meanwhile, back in Cuba, new cultural policies that eradicated the economic backbone of the island's music industry—tourism, hotels, casinos, and independently owned bars and night clubs—sent many leading musicians into permanent exile (Celia Cruz, Pérez Prado, Cachao, Arsenio Rodríguez), while others, like Moré, died before their time (Moore 2006). This series of cultural, economic, and geopolitical shock waves sounded the death knell to what had been the golden age of Cuban popular music (Padura Fuentes 2003a: 186).

Salsa

The permanent exile of many of Cuba's leading musicians in New York combined with the unprecedented surge of Caribbean immigration into New York City began to create a new mixture of urban musical styles based on the kernel of the Cuban son that had long since been internalized by Big Apple musicians and universalized throughout Latin America and the Caribbean. The result of this new mixture would simmer and mature underground during much of the 1960s only to burst forth in the late 1960s and 1970s as salsa. Partly for the same reasons of novelty and marketing that had previously given birth to Cuban music in the United States as "rhumba," salsa was unique in that it became identified as a pan-Latino banner of cultural pride not just for Cubans but also for Puerto Ricans, Colombians, Dominicans, Panamanians, and the host of other displaced Latin Americans and Caribbeans residing in *Nueva York* (Fernández 1994). For this reason, despite the initial rejection of the term as a simplistic and confusing commercial tag by many of its leading practitioners, salsa is an appropriate label for this new tropical urban sound in that it describes a synergic musical product that is more than the sum of its parts.

Just as the term *rhumba* was given to a wide variety of son-based rhythms once stateside, salsa is a catch-all label that means different things to different people. First of all, salsa music shares much with its most important musical ancestor, Cuban son, itself a "transculturalized" hybrid with its own rural sensibility. Thus, while salsa is clearly an appropriation of Cuban musical tradition, it is a truly "creative appropriation," the rightful heir to Cuban son, since it is "a miscegenation of the already mestizo Cuban *son*" (Padura Fuentes 2003a: 198). Many Latinos in the metropolis celebrate salsa as their collective cultural patrimony and as a form of resistance to cultural marginalization. In essence, it has become a sign of cultural heritage as "natural" as the equally constructed and problematic term "Hispanic." On the other hand, for a time many Cubans interpreted salsa as a cultural looting: "another instance of Yankee imperialism taking advantage of musical sources for purely commercial purposes" (Fernández 1994: 112).

For the sake of simplicity and in order to recognize its three central characteristics, it may be best to define salsa as: *Cuban* music, played by *Puerto Ricans,* in *New York City* (notwithstanding the fact that many leading salseros were honorary Nuyoricans, like Panamanian Rubén Blades and Brooklyn jew, Larry "el judio maravilloso" Harlow—born Lawrence Ira Kahn). That is, nearly all of the participants in the salsa movement including Nuyorican Tito Puente, Dominican Johnny Pacheco, and Cuban-born Celia Cruz have gone on record as recognizing Cuba as the transcendent musical inspiration for the basic rhythms and arrangements of the salsa phenomenon (López 1997). At the same time, upon this Cuban foundation was erected a sound that owes as much to the traditional *Boricua* rhythms of bomba and plena, given the overwhelming demographic presence of Puerto Ricans in New York City at the time salsa was brought into being.

"If salsa exists (and at least I'm sure it does)," declares Leonardo Padura Fuentes, one of Cuba's leading contemporary novelists, "there's a name without which one cannot even conceive of its existence. And that name is Johnny

Pacheco" (2003a: 51). Dominican-born Pacheco, who immigrated to New York with his family in 1946 at the age of eleven, is so central to the birth of salsa because he cofounded the famed record label Fania with the Brooklyn-born lawyer Jerry Masucci in 1964. It was under Pacheco's tutelage over the next twenty years that Fania Records almost single-handedly discovered, recorded, produced, and promoted the musicians who would come to embody the classic verdadera salsa sound: Willie Colón, Héctor Lavoe, Charlie and Eddie Palmieri, Larry Harlow, Rubén Blades, Santos Colón, Bobby Valentín, Ray Barreto, Celia Cruz, and Tito Puente. (In the cases of Cruz and Puente, these were clearly rediscoveries.)

Less well-known, but perhaps equally as important as Pacheco's role as cofounder of Fania, is the fact that his long career allowed him to act as a bridge linking Cuba's greatest soneros and danzoneros (Benny Moré, Arsenio Rodríguez, Antonio Arcaño, and Celia Cruz) from the 1940s and 1950s, the veritable "golden age" of Cuban music, to his New York salsa of the 1960s and 1970s. For example, only a few years after arriving in New York in 1946, Pacheco was already filling in first as *timbalero* and later as flautist in bands that included such standout Cuban bandleaders and musicians as Gilberto Valdés, José Fajardo, Mongo Santamaría, Richard Egües, Pérez Prado, Xavier Cugat, and Enrique Avliés, as well as the Puerto Rican mambo kings, Tito Puente and Tito Rodríguez.

Indeed, the Cuban seed of the salsa phenomenon as created by Caribbean immigrants on the island of "Nueva York" in the late 1960s was planted in him even before he left Santo Domingo. Pacheco's own father directed Orquesta Santa Cecilia, the Dominican Republic's leading big band of the late 1930s, which played not Dominican merengues, then still considered vulgar and unrefined, but Cuban danzones. Moreover, like hundreds of thousands of other future immigrants to New York City from all across the Caribbean, Pacheco grew up at his mother's knee listening to the danzones, sones, and guarachas that traveled as if by magic across the waters of the

Caribbean from radio stations in Cuba. "At that time," he explained in an interview, "the music I most enjoyed listening to, and that ended up having a lifelong influence on me, came through the radio . . . from Cuba every afternoon" (ibid.: 53).

Asked about the origins of "salsa" music, Pacheco elaborates:

> Well, salsa is, and always has been, Cuban music. The thing is that we put a New York influence into it. We made the arrangements a bit more aggressive, but the name "salsa" came from the fact that we began touring to an infinity of locations around the world where people don't speak Spanish. To avoid confusing these people by trying to explain the difference between a "guaguancó," a "guaracha," a "son montuno," and so on, we decided to put all tropical music under the same roof—"salsa." What's more, the musicians featured in our orchestras were also from all around the world. Well, this is exactly how you make a "salsa" in the kitchen, from a variety of different condiments and spices. (Johnny Pacheco, *Yo soy del son a la salsa*, quoted in López 1997)

Ironically, the salsa phenomenon did not come to fruition in Cuba's other capital, Miami, until the mid-1980s. However, it did so with a mainstream crossover success unmatched by perhaps any group before or since: Gloria Estefan and the Miami Sound Machine. After having fled Cuba with her family as a child, Gloria Fajardo met Emilio Estefan, then the musical director and percussionist of a Spanish-language group, the Miami Cuban Boys, in the mid-1970s while attending a wedding. Called up on stage to sing with the group, Gloria eventually joined them in 1976 under the new name Miami Sound Machine. Although the group played mostly Spanish-language numbers, recording four Spanish-language albums between 1981 and 1983, by 1984 the band had begun to add English lyrics to their Cuban-based rhythms and immediately won great popular success with hit songs like "Dr. Beat" and "Conga." The band was one of the first and most successful groups in the United States to fuse Cuban rhythms with American rock, virtually inventing what became known as the "Miami sound."

In the late 1980s, Gloria Estefan went solo, still backed by the Miami Sound Machine, and in the early 1990s she reinvented herself once again, recording a number of albums in Spanish, including the powerful and evocative *Mi Tierra* (Epic, 1993), for which she won a Grammy. These albums were wildly successful across Latin America and especially in Spain, where *Mi Tierra* became the best-selling album of all time. Although often criticized by purists or those who disagree with her politics, Estefan's Spanish-language albums include a number of true musical gems, especially the stunning modern version of what can best be described as a salsa/rumba/conga, "Tradición," on *Mi Tierra*. A true tour de force, this track includes solo performances by a veritable hit parade of Cuban and Latin musicians, such as Arturo Sandoval, Israel "Cachao" López, Paquito D'Rivera, and Tito Puente.

Nueva Trova

After 1960, the break in commercial, cultural, and tourism-related exchange with the United States effectively eliminated Cuba's recording industry and the pool of American visitors who had patronized Havana's cabarets and hotels. These drastic changes, combined with constant political mobilizations, were more than many leading musicians could bear. And when those musicians chose exile, as many did throughout the 1960s, their disappearance from the scene further damaged the ability of others to make music (Acosta 2003).

With the end to Cuban tourism and subsequent disappearance of most live music venues, the state began to subsidize music schools and offer a systematic artistic education to many musicians for the first time. Music production was reorganized with new, noncommercial goals in mind. These included safeguarding the island's cultural roots and national traditions, promoting the education of amateur musicians in an effort to discover new talent, training professional musicians through upgrading Cuba's musical education system, and creating bureaucratic structures that would allow for musical experimentation. However, those goals quickly ran up against a number of obstacles, including chronic shortages of musical equipment, the primacy of the ideological (revolutionary) struggle over purely creative, aesthetic, or market criteria, and the rise of a new class of bureaucrats (most of whom were nonmusicians) who controlled funding and often arbitrarily withheld state support of any musical initiatives not clearly in line with revolutionary principles (Moore 2006).

For example, a new emphasis on the revival of "folk" traditions led to the creation of a number of *conjuntos folkloricos.* However, that laudable achievement was neutralized by an open discrimination against "popular" music such as big band son, mambo, or rumba orchestras, equating them with the prostitution and decadence of the capitalist past. Even the past contributions of standard bearers of Cuban musical culture such as Celia Cruz, Cachao, and Pérez Prado, were now officially considered Yankee corruptions of authentic Cuban culture and associated with vice, casinos, and organized crime (Guillermoprieto 2004). Despite its laudable efforts in the areas of cultural promotion and musical education, the Cuban Revolution fell like a bucket of cold water on the musical world of 1950s Havana, filled as it was with lavish, lascivious cabarets and new luxury hotels, each having its own night club and casino. In fact, one of the reasons that Cuban popular music in general and jazz specifically suffered so much during the 1960s was that they were associated in the minds of many revolutionaries with the imperialist control of the island since at least the 1930s (Acosta 2003).

The revolution ushered in a series of "idiosyncratic" crackdowns on jazz by "extremist, opportunist, and Neanderthal" apparatchiks who ignorantly tried to portray jazz as "imperialist music." The transformation of Cuban society during the 1960s included the closure of most music venues (cabarets and hotels) in the early 1960s and the elimination or nationalization of all bars, small privately owned clubs, bodegas, and the all-important "holes-in-the-wall" in the "revolutionary offensive" of 1968. Because of its disruption of the normal flow of social life and spontaneous musical exchange and innovation so essential in musical creation, the 1968 ideological crackdown on the last vestiges of independent entrepreneurial space amounted to "the most disastrous year for Cuban popular music . . . whose negative consequences [Cuba is still] suffering thirty years later" (ibid.: 202). These various measures either bureaucratically reassigned cabaret models, chorus girls, and thousands of musicians, or simply left them at home on unemployment, striking a blow against both musical culture and the national economy. Likewise, Havana's famed nightlife, show business, musical reviews, and the great tradition of marathon popular dances were left in ruins for at least the next twenty years (ibid.).

At the same time, certain government cultural institutions, including the ICAIC (Instituto Cubano del Arte e Industria Cinematográficos), began to promote experimentation with new revolutionary and nationalistic forms of musical and filmic expression, including what became known as the nueva trova, as well as a number of danceable "new rhythms" such as the songo, the batanga, the mozambique, and the pilón (figure 4.1). Except for the songo, none of these rhythms caught on for very long among the dancing public. However, after experiencing a period of repression caused by its association with the "decadent" youth culture of 1960s America, nueva trova began to find a protected space of its own and win a public following in the early 1970s. Best described as Cuban "protest" music performed by young Cuban singer-songwriters on acoustic guitars in the poetic and often political mold of Bob Dylan, nueva trova was also inspired by the politically progressive Latin American "new song" movement.

Unlike most other forms of Cuban music (but like its immediate Cuban predecessors, vieja trova and canción), nueva trova is music more for the head and heart than for the hips and feet. Likewise, unlike the often raunchy, macho lyrics of the rumba, son, mambo, or guaracha, nueva trova approached the topic of love from a poetic, sentimental perspective. Calling it "protest" music, however, is a bit confusing, since nueva trova clearly celebrates the Cuban Revolution and expresses solidarity with leftist, anti-imperialist struggles throughout Latin America. Given those political concerns, though some of the genre's leading musicians were harassed and even jailed before 1971, afterward they were increasingly identified both in Cuba and abroad as standard bearers of the revolution, becoming international symbols of a new Cuban culture.

The clear leaders of the nueva trova movement are Silvio Rodríguez and Pablo Milanés. Rodríguez's deeply poetic lyrics have been committed to memory by many a Cuban, and his strong tenor voice is among the most recognizable of any in the Spanish language today. Among his most famous compositions are "Unicornio" and "La maza" Minlanés' musical style is rich in harmonies, engaging melodies, and palpable symbolism. He is also an expert at integrating folkloric elements into his modern compositions. During the 1980s and 1990s, Milanés became instrumental in promoting many younger Cuban musicians through his foundation. Some of his better-known works include the political anthems "A Santiago" and "Yo pisaré las calles nuevamente," as well as the romantic ballads "El breve espacio en que no estás" and "Yolanda."

Other leading nueva trova singer-songwriters include Carlos Puebla (famous for his rustic odes to revolutionary leaders such as "Y en eso llegó Fidel" and "Hasta Siempre"), Sara González, a kind of "official" protest singer, and the more independent and critical minded Pedro Luis Ferrer. Finally, since 1990 a new generation of singer-songwriters has emerged on the island, often cultivating a more critical stance vis-à-vis the government and infusing their songs with more elements from rock music. Sometimes referred to as novísima trova, the leaders of this movement are Carlos Varela in Cuba, Juan-Carlos Formell in exile in New York, and the groups Habana Abierta and Buena Fé.

Irakere and Cuban Jazz

Because of the revolutionary credentials and personal connections of its longtime director Alfredo Guevara, the Cuban Film Institute (ICAIC) enjoyed a bureaucratic latitude and relative creative autonomy unlike that of other state institutions. That fact allowed classical guitarist Leo Brower to set up the Grupo de Experimentación Sonora (GES, Musical Experimentation Group) in the late 1960s. Like many nueva trova singer-songwriters, a host of aspiring jazz musicians enjoyed protection under the ICAIC's auspices. The GES produced soundtracks for Cuban cinema, promoted politically oriented song, worked to protect and renew Cuban musical traditions, and provided a space for limited musical experimentation.

It was through the auspices of the GES that the Orquesta Cubana de Música Moderna (OCMM) was created in 1967. The core of this bureaucratically created supergroup had begun their musical odyssey in 1963, when pianist Jesús "Chucho" Valdés, guitarist Carlos Emilio Morales, and saxophonist Paquito D'Rivera, took part in an experimental jazz orchestra known as Teatro Musical de La Habana. As a jazz ensemble called into existence by the decree of the National Council of Culture, the OCMM constantly suffered from bureaucratic obstacles that hindered the artistic spirit that music such as jazz is supposed to embody. As a result, these three musicians struggled constantly for creative autonomy during their tenure in the OCMM. Finally, in 1973 they broke off to form what would become Cuba's premier Latin Jazz band, Irakere (figure 4.1).

A central plaza at one of the five Cuban Art Schools (Escuela Nacional de Arte, ENA). One of the greatest architectural achievements of the revolution, the ENA complex was built after 1959 on the grounds of the old Country Club in western Havana to house new schools for ballet, music, theater, fine art, and modern and folkloric dance. Ironically, some of the schools were criticized for their "flamboyance" and aesthetic "indulgences," and abandoned to ruin after the mid-1960s (Loomis 1999). (Ted Henken)

Although Valdés was able to gain a significant measure of autonomy in the formation of Irakere, he has constantly had to maneuver bureaucratic obstacles since the band's incep tion. This kind of negotiation is especially evident in the band's dual repertoire. From the start, it sought to push th limits of experimentation and fusion in jazz and Afro-Cuban music, but also successfully produced a stream of popular danceable music—a must for any Cuban band that wants to connect with the dancing Cuban public. This skill has also been instrumental in allowing the group to stay alive for mor - than thirty years and spawn a series of virtuosos who themselves would go on to stellar solo careers and form a new genf eration of jazz fusion groups. The most prominent alumni o Irakere include Paquito D'Rivera and Arturo Sandoval (both of whom have since established themselves as leading "Latin Jazz" musicians in the United States), Valdés himself, as well as two of the most talented and innovative Cuban jazz fusion musicians of the 1990s, Orlando "Maraca" Valle and his group Otra Visión, and the popular timba sensation José Luis "El Tosco" Cortés and his group NG (Nueva Generación) La Banda (Acosta 2003).

Songo, Timba, and Cuban Hip-Hop

A third type of "new music" to emerge in Cuba after the revolution was the popular dance music that became known as songo. Most associated with what is easily Cuba's leading popular dance orchestra, Los Van Van, songo is a musical fusion developed by the group's leader, Juan Formell, that successfully combines the rhythms and instrumentations of big band Cuban dance music of old with rock, jazz, funk, bolero, and, in the 1990s, hip-hop. Formed in 1969 during the abortive nationwide struggle to harvest a record 10 million tons of sugarcane, Los Van Van has consistently ranked among Cuba's most popular musical groups, in part because its rhythms are aimed at giving the people something to dance to and because the lyrics to its many, many songs directly relate to and comment with humor on the ironies and struggles of daily life as lived by Cubans under the revolution.

Neither revolutionarily orthodox nor dissident, the most popular of Los Van Van's songs take note of Cuban society's failings not with combativeness or aggression, but with a lighthearted irony that most Cubans share. Los Van Van constantly perform concerts in Cuba and around the world, having toured across Latin America, Europe, Africa, and even on rare occasions in the United States. Some of the most popular songs from the group's many albums are "Marilú," "Chirrín Chirrán," "Sandungera," "Soy todo," "El buey cansao," "Se acabó el querer," "La Habana no aguanta más," "Temba, Tumba, Timba," "Somos Cubanos," and "Muévete." Neither a traditional son conjunto nor a salsa band, Los Van Van has been in many ways Cuba's own original answer to American salsa music. During the 1990s, however, the original rhythms of songo have been modified by Cuban bandleaders under the influence of a variety of new national and international styles, becoming timba in the process.

Originally a rumba term, timba is used today to denote modern Cuban dance music. While based on the basic rhythm of the son and similar to international salsa, timba incorporates influences from a wider variety of international and Cuban folkloric sources. For example, jazz, rock, and funk are all clearly evident in most timba compositions, as are many styles of Afro-Cuban ritualistic music, including batá drumming and authentic neighborhood rumba. Also, timba bands have incorporated American-style drum sets, synthesizers, and rapped vocals, giving their numbers a more innovative, experimental, and modern feel than is typical of other Cuban dance music. Finally, timba is both unapologetically raw in its use of often vulgar street language and often harshly critical of the growing social and economic cleavages that have descended upon Cuba during the special period of the 1990s. As such, timba bands commonly celebrate the semilegal black market "inventions" of young Afro-Cubans from marginal neighborhoods in their lyrics. They also often demand respect for Afro-Cuban traditions of worship and rituals.

"More generally," writes Maya Roy, commenting on the leading ensemble NG La Banda, timba "targets everything smacking of hypocrisy or of any variance between revolutionary discourse and reality. It does not wave the flag of revolt, but proclaims its wish that young people may be and may live as they see fit" (2002: 172). This hard urban edge has both given timba its unique flavor and provoked official criticism of it as over-the-top and disrespectful of authority. In one incident, NG La Banda was criticized as disrespectful of women for its song "La Bruja" ("The Witch"), which derided Cuban women who abandon their Cuban men in order to leave the country with foreigners. Also, because a timba ensemble normally incorporates a wide variety of instruments and singing styles, the music and lyrics are often dense and somewhat inaccessible to non-Cubans, making the successful marketing of the genre outside of Cuba difficult. While the most recent work of Los Van Van could easily fall into the timba mode, other singers and bands more representative of this new genre include Issac Delgado, Manolín—El Médico de la Salsa, and La Charanga Habanera (ibid.; Orovio 2004: 210; Perna 2005).

While timba groups frequently incorporate rap modalities in their songs, a number of undiluted hip-hop groups have emerged on the island since the early-1990s. Perhaps the leading Cuban hip-hop group (now based in France) is Orishas. As their name indicates, on their debut album, "A lo cubano," they created a powerful and authentic synthesis of hip-hop and Afro-Cuban spirituality. They also successfully use the hip-hop technique of musical "sampling," paying homage in their songs to their musical forebears. That is especially evident in the nostalgia-filled song "537 C-U-B-A," the musical structure of which is clearly based on Compay Segundo's "Chan Chan" (537 is the international access code for the city of Havana). Another group that has caused a more recent splash goes by the name Clan 537. Although not nearly as successful or prolific, this group gained widespread notoriety in 2002 with the hip-hop anthem "¿Quién tiró la tiza?" ("Who Threw the Chalk?"), a strident denunciation of growing racial and economic inequality in contemporary Cuba (Robinson 2004). Other prominent hip-hop groups active in Cuba today include Obsesión and Doble Filo, who have joined forces to produce the collective La Fabri-K (The Cuban Hip-Hop Factory), whose brief U.S. tour was chronicled in the 2005 documentary film of the same name by Cuban-American filmmaker, Lisandro Pérez-Rey.

Unfortunately, Cuban rap has increasingly been debilitated by official recognition and support, leading to the control and cooptation of the grassroots hip-hop movement by the Cuban government since 2000 (Fernández 2006; Robinson 2004). Starting in August 1995, the first International Festival of Rap Cubano was held in Alamar, a suburb in eastern Havana, with support from the non-governmental Asociación Hermanos Saíz. In 2002, a state-run Cuban Rap Agency was created along with a hip-hop magazine, *Movimiento*. However, after a brief period where artists and promoters used the increased support and attention to their advantage, the window of opportunity seemed to close with state oversight only serving to stifle the freedom and creativity sought by the rebellious and frustrated hip-hop artists. Likewise, the Alamar rap festival seemed to reach its peak between 2002–2004, with the 2005 festival flopping and the 2006 follow-up being cancelled.

Apart from struggling against government cooptation, Cuban hip-hop artists have found themselves up against the commercialization of what they see as authentic social protest and competing against the explosively popular but much less socially conscious musical form known as reggaetón, derived in part from rap music (Acosta 2007a; Lacey 2006). Another major obstacle confronted by the founders of the Cuban hip-hop movement has been the tendency for the leading promoters and groups to choose exile abroad in reaction to both bureaucratic and political frustrations and economic necessity (Fernández 2006). Hip-hip promoters saw themselves as the vanguard of a truly revolutionary grassroots movement giving voice to the concerns of some of the most marginalized sectors of Cuba's population (Afro-Cubans and young people). These concerns include the growth in social and economic inequality, police brutality, racial profiling and discrimination, domestic violence, and prostitution. However, these promoters soon found themselves in the frustrating position of having to enforce government censorship of their fellow rappers if their lyrics strayed too far from the party line.

In fact, only nine rap groups are officially recognized by the Cuban Rap Agency, while more than 500 others exist under-

ground. While many of these groups purposely reject association with the state agency in order to preserve their autonomy
and artistic freedom, they pay a high price in terms of low
media visibility and little or no access to recording studios or
performance venues (Acosta 2007a; Lacey 2006). Some of the
leading underground groups and artists include Papá Hum-
bertico, Explosión Suprema, Mano Armada, Alto Voltaje,
Amenaza, Krudas Cubensi, La Rapandula, Kumar y Tekma,
100% Originales, Hermanos de Causa, Anónimo Consejo, Los
Aldeanos, and Los Paisanos (Fernández 2006).

This back-and-forth struggle is vividly chronicled in the
recent documentary film *East of Havana* and by the *Washington Post* journalist Eugene Robinson in his penetrating
2004 book, *Last Dance in Havana: The Final Days of Fidel
and the Start of the New Cuban Revolution.* Robinson's book
chronicles the central role of music and dance in today's Cuba
with a focus on Afrocentric forms of expression such as timba
and hip-hop. On the other hand, *East of Havana* (the title is
a reference to the humble, largely black neighborhood of Alamar located in the eastern Havana suburb where Cuban rap
was born in the 1980s), directed by Cuban-American
filmmakers Jauretsi Saizarbitoria and Emilia Menocal, cap-
tures the daily struggles and cutting-edge artistic expression
of a group of musicians collectively known as El Cartel during
the lead-up to the 2004 International Festival of Rap Cubano
(Seitz 2007).

REVOLUTIONARY CUBAN CINEMA

Socialism is a great script, but with poor directors.
—Tomás Gutiérrez Alea (Chanan 2004: 12).

In one of the revolutionary government's first decrees, on
March 25, 1959, it created the Instituto Cubano del Arte e
Industria Cinematográficos (better known as ICAIC, the
Cuban Film Institute). Realizing that Cubans had become

avid moviegoers during the previous sixty years of American influence, Castro sought to use this very important art form to communicate with the masses. Over the next twenty-four years, under the leadership of Castro's college friend, Alfredo Guevara, Cuba developed one of Latin America's most prolific and vital film industries, producing, distributing, and exhibiting films of high aesthetic quality and deep intellectual content, if often simultaneously used as a tool of propaganda. Under Guevara, the ICAIC successfully made 112 feature-length films, an astounding 900 documentaries, and more than 1,300 newsreels by 1983 (Luis 2001).

During this period, the production of documentary films was prioritized, with Santiago Álvarez emerging as Cuba's foremost documentary filmmaker. There were political documentaries that aimed to explain government policies and encourage popular participation in the revolutionary process. There were also films that sought to delve into Cuban history and help viewers understand the formation of Cuban national identity. Other films focused on disseminating knowledge about Cuban culture or chronicling Cuba's role in world affairs. Finally, a number of films were made with the didactic purpose of teaching technical and scientific skills to Cuban workers (ibid.). In both its documentaries and its feature-length films, the ICAIC was able to achieve its goal of creating a national, self-reflective cinematic art form despite the revolution's constant attempts to over-regulate and control culture. That was possible because the revolutionary process, for all its mistakes and abuses, "unleashed among a new generation of filmmakers a furious creative energy as they turned the cameras on the process they were living, and told the Cuban people—and anyone else who was interested—who they were and what they were doing" (Chanan 2004: 4).

However, during the 1980s and especially after 1990, the Cuban film industry entered a crisis because of the collapse of the socialist bloc and the evaporation of its material resources. Still, since that time the country has been able to make a virtue of necessity and continue producing films of high quality—often with funding from abroad. Moreover, given the tense political atmosphere and traditional restrictions on artistic freedoms in Cuba, it is impressive that the Cuban Film Institute has managed to engage viewers in a critical dialogue about the socioeconomic crisis in which they live. Perhaps the three best examples of films made since 1990 that achieve that delicate balance are *Fresa y chocolate* (*Strawberry and Chocolate*, 1993), *Guantanamera,* and *Suite Habana,* all discussed below. In fact, the history of film under the revolution can be described as a series of movements between openness and creativity on the one hand, and rigid cultural orthodoxy on the other.

One reason that the ICAIC has succeeded in preserving both its relative autonomy and its aesthetic quality is that it has functioned over the years as a "quasi-autonomous nongovernmental organization." This means that, unlike the press, radio, and television, which the state has made into governmental mouthpieces, filmmaking in Cuba "came to occupy a unique cultural space as a major site of public discourse that at the same time enjoyed a de facto autonomy because of a privileged relation to the source of power and authority" (ibid.: 17). The impeccable revolutionary credentials of ICAIC director Alfredo Guevara and leading director Tomás Gutiérrez Alea, combined with their personal relationships with Fidel Castro, afforded them the space in which to develop a national cinema that answered to artistic and intellectual criteria without being forced to spout a simplistic revolutionary line.

In Cuban cinema, politics do not dictate the contents of cinematic art but constitute a space in which the two engage in an ambivalent, sometimes adversarial, but often fruitful dialogue. As Michael Chanan argues in his study of revolutionary Cuban cinema:

This dialogue allows the cinema screen to become more than
either propaganda or a diversionary space, but a crucial preserve of public speech, a space that engages large sectors of
the population in debate about the meaning and quality of
their lives; a vicarious role that is negatively reinforced by the
much tighter control exercised by the party over broadcasting
and the press. (Ibid.: 18)

That adversarial but fruitful dialogue has been evident at
various key junctures over the past half-century, especially
during the *P.M./Lunes* crackdown in 1961, the *quinquenio
gris* ("gray five years") from 1968 to 1976, the *Cecilia* scandal of 1981, the political fallout over Daniel Díaz Torres's *Alicia en el pueblo de maravillas* in 1991, and the criticism surrounding the release of Tomás Gutiérrez Alea's final film,
Guantanamera, in 1998 (ibid.: 1–22).

Perhaps the best way to chronicle the history of filmmaking in Cuba under the revolution is to describe the prolific,
fifty-year career of the most acclaimed filmmaker of the revolutionary period, Tomás Gutiérrez Alea. Better known by his
nickname Titón, he succeeded like no other in making movies
that were both entertaining and intellectually stimulating:
"committed" to the revolution and critical of its errors; satir-
ically humorous and deeply emotional; and catering to Cuban
idiosyncrasies, while at the same time appealing to international audiences. Titón began making films at a very young
age, producing three films before he turned twenty-one. In
the late 1940s he became involved in the Cine Club de la
Habana, later renamed the Cinemateca de Cuba, which
showed classic art films for its members, most of whom were
filmmakers or critics. After studying filmmaking in Rome at
the Centro Sperimentale de Cinematografía, Gutiérrez Alea
coproduced a short, neorealistic film about Cuban coal scav-
engers with Julio García Espinosa called *El mégano* (*The
Charcoal Worker,* 1954–1955). A few years later, upon the triumph of the revolution, the two directors collaborated once

again on a film about agrarian reform in Cuba, *Esta tierra nuestra* (*This Land of Ours,* 1959).

Gutiérrez Alea successfully avoided the controversies that led to the banning of the documentary on Cuban nightlife *P.M.* and the eventual closure of the vital cultural magazine *Lunes de Revolución* at the end of 1961. Starting in the early 1960s he began to focus more intensively on feature-length films, producing a succession of movies considered by critics and the public alike to be of the highest artistic quality. Among his work are what have become five of the most powerful and popularly successful films associated with revolutionary Cuba. First, he produced a slapstick comedy called *La muerte de un burócrata* (*The Death of a Bureaucrat,* 1966), which simultaneously managed to be a penetrating commentary on the maddening frustration felt by Cubans faced with the new system's sometimes mindless bureaucracy. Two years later he made what many consider his masterwork, *Memorias de subdesarrollo* (*Memories of Underdevelopment,* 1968), winning him acclaim at home and abroad for this complex chronicle of the difficult choices faced by an intellectual who chooses to remain in Cuba after his bourgeois wife and family leave for the United States.

In the 1970s, Titón made a powerful historical film about Cuban slavery, entitled *La última cena* (*The Last Supper,* 1974). He also aided in the completion of Sara Gómez's *De cierta manera* (*One Way or Another,* 1977), after the director's untimely death. This was an experimental film about the culture of marginal communities and die-hard male chauvinism (sometimes jokingly referred to in Cuba as "Machismo-Leninismo"). After the controversy that surrounded a big-budget flop, Humberto Solás's *Cecilia* (1981), Guevara stepped down as head of ICAIC, leading to a long period of mediocrity and bureaucratic control in the film industry. Few important films were made during this decade as a result, with Gutiérrez Alea all but silent. The one bright spot during this period for Cuban film was the inauguration of the annual New Latin American Film Festival at the beginning of the decade, in December 1979.

As the special period began to ravage Cuba, at the start of the 1990s, the young director Daniel Díaz Torres released *Alicia en el pueblo de maravillas* (*Alice in Wonderland*, 1991–1992). The film amounted to a "scatological satire on bureaucratic mismanagement" (Chanan 2004: 10) and rigid socialist attitudes, provoking a sustained attack on the ICAIC as an institution. Fortunately, Cuba's filmmakers met the attack with a rigorous defense of the film industry and managed to avoid being folded into the state broadcasting company. The ICAIC also managed to preserve its three previously established Grupos de Creación (creative groups), one of which was headed by Titón.

As Cuba entered the dark and uncertain years of the special period, Gutiérrez Alea responded with what were to be his final two films (both codirected with Juan Carlos Tabío). The first was the international sensation *Fresa y chocolate* (*Strawberry and Chocolate,* 1993), an emotionally and politically powerful film about Cubanness, homosexuality, and the search for tolerance within the revolution. Nominated for an Oscar in 1995, the film humanized Cuba for many foreigners as the Cold War receded into history. However, the film was far from a denunciation of the socialist project, and in fact it managed to "channel a powerful plea for tolerance and a cogent defense of the autonomy of critical thinking into what was in many ways an old-fashioned film of political commitment to the socialist ideal" (ibid.: 11).

Gutiérrez Alea's final film, *Guantanamera* (1995), was made as he was slowly dying of cancer. The film is a black comedy that makes a strong parody of officialdom and bureaucracy and can be understood as a newer, more biting version of his earlier movie on socialist bureaucracy, *La muerte de un burócrata.* As with *Fresa y chocolate,* Titón's final film did not take issue with the socialist project itself but with the often inflexible and dogmatic methods of day-to-day socialist rule. As he put it in a conversation with Chanan: "Socialism is a great script, but with poor directors" (ibid.: 12). However, this time his thinly veiled criticisms provoked a negative reaction from President Castro, who, though he hadn't seen the film and didn't realize that Titón had directed it, expressed the opinion that in times of crisis artists needed to call on the public for revolutionary unity rather than satirize the nation's problems.

Since Gutiérrez Alea's death in 1996, Fernando Pérez has emerged as Cuba's most talented filmmaker. While his early films *Clandestinos* (1987) and *Hello, Hemingway* (1990) were well received, it was not until he began to chronicle the decay and contradictions of life during the 1990s that he gained widespread critical acclaim. He did this first with *Madagascar* (1994) and later with *La vida es silbar* (*Life Is to Whistle,* 1998). However, his most innovative and heartfelt film to date is his poetic, melancholic ode to the city and people of Havana, *Suite Habana* (2003). In this film, Pérez manages to achieve the near-impossible feat of making a successful feature-length docudrama that almost completely dispenses with dialogue, while at the same time portraying the everyday struggles and joys in the lives of a series of real Cubans without embellishment, preaching, or spin.

CUBAN LITERATURE—THE AVANT-GARDE VS. THE VANGUARD
Colonial Literature

Throughout Cuban history, writers and intellectuals have coalesced into a series of intellectual and literary movements. This tendency was first established in the nineteenth century during the triple struggle to achieve the abolition of slavery, gain political independence from Spain, and form a distinctly Cuban national identity. The five leading writers and intellectuals who did the most to advance those causes were José María Heredia (1803–1839), Domingo del Monte (1804–1853), Gertrudis Gómez de Avellaneda (1814–1873), Cirilo Villaverde (1812–1894), and José Martí (1853–1895).

Born in Santiago de Cuba at the start of the nineteenth century, José María Heredia's short life belies his importance as the most prominent Cuban Romantic poet of the nineteenth century. Because his father was a Spanish governmental official, Heredia's childhood was spent in various parts of the Caribbean basin, including Pensacola, Florida; Santo Domingo; and Venezuela. Later, because of his proindependence political activities, he spent a good deal of his short adult life in exile in the United States and Mexico. While living in Mexico, he served the newly independent Mexican government in multiple capacities and collaborated in a number of Mexican literary magazines. After publicly renouncing his conspiratorial beliefs, he was allowed to return to Cuba in 1836, only to be met with the scorn of his former friends, including one former mentor, Domingo del Monte. Rebuffed, he returned to Mexico almost immediately and died there a few years later in 1839 (Padura Fuentes 2003b).

Because of his untimely death in exile, Heredia's life and work was among the first to establish the recurrent theme of nostalgia for a lost homeland in Cuban poetry. During his lifetime, he published two editions of his collected poems, *Poesías*. His most well-known works are his odes. The first, "En el Teocali de Cholula" (1820), is a reflection on the passage of time after viewing the ruins of an Aztec temple in Mexico. The other, "Oda a Niágara" (1824), was composed after visiting Niágara Falls (Padura Fuentes 2001).

Domingo del Monte was the leader of the most important literary salon of nineteenth-century Cuba, which served also as an important incubator of abolitionism and protonationalism. From his home first in Matanzas and later in Havana, del Monte hosted a weekly *tertulia* (literary salon) where he mentored an entire generation of Cuban intellectuals, writers, and abolitionists, many of whom called themselves *delmontinos* in his honor. Included among these writers were Heredia, the novelist Cirilo Villaverde, and the poet and former slave Juan Francisco Manzano. Because of his abolitionist activities and friendship with the British antislavery crusader David Turnbull, del Monte was forced into exile in 1842. Thereafter, he was tried in absentia as part of the Escalera conspiracy and died in exile in Madrid.

Del Monte's role as the main intellectual force incubating Cuban protonationalism was furthered by his disciple Cirilo Villaverde. Like del Monte, Villaverdre was forced to spend much of his life in exile because of the political content of his writings, especially his novel *Cecilia Valdés,* which has come to be seen as Cuba's "national" novel and founding myth. The novel, subsequently made into a play, operetta, and film, features a rivalry between sugar-planting and coffee-growing families set in the early decades of the nineteenth century. Also prominently featured is a complicated cross-racial and cross-class romance between the star-crossed lovers, Cecilia, a free mulatta, and Leonardo, a wealthy white planter (who turn out to be half-brother and -sister). Although originally written in Cuba in 1839, the novel was not completed and published until 1882 in exile in New York.

Together with José María Heredia, Gertrudis Gómez de Avellaneda, often referred to simply as "La Avellaneda," was one of the most important figures of nineteenth-century Cuban Romanticism. This literary movement was characterized by hostility toward Spanish rule in the Caribbean, support for political freedom for Spain's remaining colonies, a marked sense of Cuban identity and nationalism, and a commitment to exposing the social, political, and economic conditions as lived on the island. Though born in Camagüey to a Spanish father and a Cuban mother, Avellaneda departed for Spain at twenty-two years of age after rejecting an offer of a "good marriage" from a Cuban suitor. As a writer and thinker, Avellaneda can be described as an abolitionist and protofeminist who enjoyed tremendous success in Madrid's literary circles as a playwright between 1846 and 1858. Prior to this success, Avellaneda bore a child out of wedlock to her Spanish lover, the poet Gabriel García Tassara. The child later died, and a subsequent marriage to another Spaniard ended after only three months when her new husband also died. Despite her strong literary qualifications, Avellaneda was denied membership in the Spanish Academia in 1853 because she was a woman. She is best known in Cuba for her 1841 novel that attacked slavery, *Sab.*

Finally, apart from his constant political activities and writings on behalf of Cuban independence, Cuban patriot José Martí distinguished himself as one of the leading journalists and literary figures in the Spanish-speaking world of his time. As a poet, Martí was a cofounder with Nicaraguan Rubén Darío of what was perhaps Latin America's first wholly unique literary movement, Modernismo. Although Martí published only two slim volumes of poetry during his lifetime, *Ismaelillo* (1882) and *Versos sencillos* (1891), together with Darío he revolutionized the way poetry was written in American Spanish, in the same way that Walt Whitman and Edgar Allan Poe had done with poetry in American English. Two other volumes of Martí's poetry were published posthumously, *Versos libres* (1913) and *Flores del destierro* (1933). Finally, as a journalist and essayist Martí had no equal. He wrote voluminously about every subject under the sun, but perhaps his greatest journalistic achievement was as an observer of life in North America and its relationship to Latin America and Cuba. Usually written in a "letter to the editor" format for a wide group of leading Latin American newspapers, his many essays and dispatches in the series "Escenas norteamericanas" provided information and analysis on the life, culture, and politics of the United States for his many readers across the region (Luis 2001; Martí 2002).

Literature of the Republic

The first literary and artistic movement to coalesce around a particular theme in an independent, republican Cuba was known as Afrocubanismo. Lasting roughly from 1920 to 1940, Afrocubanismo was like the Harlem Renaissance in its celebration of black art and culture. However, it was more apt than its New York counterpart to be led by white intellectuals, more politically radical, and more concerned with the project of building a national identity and culture independent from both Spain and the United States. Ironically, while the promoters of Afrocubanismo celebrated some aspects of black Cuban culture (especially in music and literature), a central characteristic of the movement was its ambivalence toward the more authentic expressions of Afro-Cuban culture that came from the street. For example, some of the movement's main protagonists, including the writer Alejo Carpentier, the painter Eduardo Abela, the popular musicians Ernesto Lecuona and Eliseo Grenet, and the classical composers Alejandro García Caturla and Amadeo Roldán, both took pride in and exhibited embarrassment toward black-derived cultural forms (Moore 1997).

The leading light of Afrocubanismo, Alejo Carpentier (1904–1980), would go on to become one of Cuba's most distinguished novelists of the twentieth century. Carpentier's early involvement in the radical anti-Machado politics of the late 1920s landed him in prison, where he wrote the first version of what would later be published as his first novel, the Afro-Cuban themed *¡Ecue-Yamba-O!* (*Praised Be the Lord!*, 1933). During this period, Carpentier also began to collaborate with the Cuban composers Roldán and García Caturla, putting together a series of concerts of "new music," culminating in the Afrocubanismo artistic movement.

The excitement of this moment is evident in Carpentier's breathless declaration in his 1946 book, *Music in Cuba:*

[We] began to notice, that in Regla, on the other side of the bay, there were rhythms as complex and interesting as those created by Stravinsky to evoke the primitive rituals of pagan Russia. . . . The possibility of expressing what was local with a new conception of its values became ingrained in the minds of artists. . . . Suddenly, blacks were at the center of everything. . . . Thus, the Afro-Cuban tendency was born. (2001: 268–269)

Carpentier admits that in their effort to exasperate the old guard and establish a new, more authentically Cuban cultural identity, he and his colleagues had a tendency to exoticise Afro-Cuban culture with superficial stereotypes such as the "black man under palm trees drunk on the sun." Despite these immature flourishes, he asserts that "Afro-Cubanism was a necessary step in better comprehending certain poetic, musical, ethnic, and social factors that had suffused all contours of what it meant to be uniquely Cuban" (ibid.: 269).

What distinguished Carpentier from the host of other progressive white Cuban intellectuals of his time was the life-altering and artistically fertile trip he made to Haiti in 1943. That trip allowed him to understand Cuban and Latin American culture in a deeper and more fantastic way, leading to his coining the term, *lo real maravilloso* (later popularized as "magical realism"). His most famous works from that period include *The Kingdom of This World* (1949) and *The Lost Steps* (1953), both of which he wrote in exile in Venezuela. Upon the triumph of the revolution, he returned to Cuba and was appointed Cuban ambassador to France. His later works include *The Chase* (1956), *Explosion in the Cathedral* (1962), and *Baroque Concert* (1974). In 1977, he was awarded Spain's Cervantes Prize. He completed his final novel, *The Harp and the Shadow* (1978), before succumbing to cancer in Paris in 1980.

Together with Afrocubanismo, 1920s Cuba saw a veritable boom in progressive political, artistic, and literary movements, including the *Protesta de los trece* ("Protest of the

13"), the establishment of the Grupo Minorista, and the founding of what would become the period's leading literary magazine, *Revista de Avance* (1927–1930). In a public protest against the corruption of the Zayas administration (1921–1925), a group of thirteen writers, artists, and lawyers, including Rubén Martínez Villena, Jorge Mañach, Juan Marinello, and José A. Fernández de Castro, boycotted the Academy of Science in May of 1923. In that same year a group of leftist nationalist writers and artists, which included some of the "13," began to meet in *tertulias* in cafes around Havana, issuing increasingly strident calls for social, political, and cultural reform. Given their small number, they labeled themselves the Grupo Minorista.

In 1927 this group published a manifesto, written by Rubén Martínez Villena, in which it expressed its principles and goals, including the economic independence of Cuba, an end to personalistic dictatorships, a revision of nationalist values, and an artistic renovation in music, literature, and painting. While not a formal organ of this group, *Revista de Avance,* published between 1927 and 1930 and edited by Carpentier, Mañach, and Marinello, was in many ways the voice of the progressive intellectual and artistic generation of the 1920s. Its voluntary closure in 1930 after the publication of its own anti-Machado manifesto was caused by the editors' rejection of a new law that would subject all mass media to government censorship (Martínez 1990).

The beginning of the poetic work of mulatto Cuban poet Nicolás Guillén (1902–1989) can also be traced to the sociopolitical upheaval and renovation of the 1920s and 1930s. In fact, Guillén was a guiding light of the emerging pan-Caribbean "Negrista" literary and cultural movement. In 1926, Guillén moved to Havana and began to dedicate himself full-time to poetry and politics. During the late 1920s and early 1930s, he began to publish his poetry in some of Havana's leading magazines. His first book of poems, *Motivos de son,* which had first appeared in 1928 in *Diario de la*

Marina, came out in book form in 1930, and was followed by *Sóngoro Cosongo* (1931) and *West Indies Ltd.* (1934).

This earliest stage of his work is concerned with portraying blacks as an essential element in Cuban national identity. As such, his poetry often shocked those who associated black culture with criminality and superstition. Instead, Guillén sought to write his poetry *en negro de verdad;* that is, he based his poetic voice on the natural rhythms of Afro-Cuban speech, while rejecting the exoticism that often accompanied even sympathetic portrayals of Afro-Cuban culture by whites. Guillén also befriended other non-Cuban writers who were engaged in similar work in their countries, including Langston Hughes in the United States and Jacques Roumain in Haiti.

By the mid-1930s, Guillén had begun to collaborate in the cultural activities of the Cuban Communist Party. In 1937 he traveled to Mexico and Spain as a representative of the party, attending a number of progressive writers' congresses in the company of the leading leftist Cuban writers Juan Marinello and Alejo Carpentier. It was during this period that he began to publish work of a more overtly political nature, including *Cantos para soldados y sones para turistas* (*Songs for Soldiers and Sones for Tourists,* 1937) and *España, poema en cuatro angustias y una esperanza* (*Spain, Poem in Four Anguishes and One Hope,* 1937).

Increasingly persecuted as a communist in the late 1940s and early 1950s as the Cold War heated up, Guillén remained in exile after a 1953 trip to Chile, living between Latin America and Europe until 1959. After returning to Cuba, he was named president of the Cuban Union of Writers and Artists (UNEAC), and he set to work on the poetry that would seal his reputation as one of Cuba's most vital and versatile poets. This stage of his career saw the publication of *Tengo* (*I Have,* 1964), a work that proudly celebrates the new lease on life that the revolution had given to the formerly downtrodden, especially blacks, *El gran zoo* (*The Great Zoo,* 1967), and *El diario que a diario* (*The Daily Diary,* 1972).

The last great Cuban literary movement prior to the arrival of the Cuban Revolution was led by writer and intellectual José Lezama Lima (1910–1976) and took place in the pages of the literary magazine *Orígenes* (1944–1956). The most important and long-lasting of a series of seven literary reviews published in Cuba between 1937 and 1959, *Orígenes* was different from the politically progressive literary journals that had preceded it in that it largely eschewed sociopolitical commitments, placing aesthetics over politics. The journal was based on the ideal that art and poetry seek the origin of artistic being (thus its name) and that artists had a responsibility to disseminate this visionary ideal to other members of their society.

Like many educated Cuban men of his time, Lezama Lima earned a law degree and practiced his profession until the mid-1940s, but his true passion was literature, to which he dedicated most of the rest of his life. Unlike most other Cuban writers and intellectuals, he rarely traveled, never visited Europe or the United States, and left his beloved Havana only twice, once for a trip to Mexico in 1949 and again the following year to Jamaica. Prior to founding *Orígenes* in 1944, he was extremely active as an editor and literary critic, helping to found *Verbum* (1937) at the University of Havana Law School, *Espuela de Plata* (1939–1941), *Nadie Parecía* (1942–1943), and *Clavileño* (1943). The cofounder and principal funding source for *Orígenes* was José Rodríguez Feo, and the journal's principal collaborators included Virgilio Piñera, Eliseo Diego, Cintio Vitier, and Fina García Marruz, along with many of the leading painters of the *Vanguardista* movement, including Mario Carreño and René Portocarrero (Martínez 1994). *Orígenes* was forced to close in 1956 after Lezama Lima and Rodríguez Feo had fallen out over editorial policy.

Lezama Lima's style can be described as modern baroque in that it was sensuous, colorful, full of life, and playfully intellectual, while at the same time being highly ornate and seriously classical in its concerns. After 1959 he enjoyed brief, if obligatory, recognition, being appointed director of the Literature and Publications Department of the National Council of Culture. He was also named one of six vice presidents of the Cuban Writers and Artists Union. However, his work was generally marginalized, in part because of its non-political bent and homosexual undertones, and he lived and worked in virtual isolation for the last decade of his life. Apart from his most important novel, *Paradiso* (*Paradise*, 1966), other major works include the book of poetry, *Muerte de Narciso* (*Death of Narcissus*, 1937), the collections of essays *Analecta del reloj* (1953) and *La expresión americana* (1957), and the unfinished novel *Oppiano Licario,* published posthumously in 1977 (Luis 2001).

Literature under the Revolution

After 1959, the Cuban Revolution initially opened up the field of culture and inspired an effervescence among artists of all stripes to participate in building a new revolutionary society, allowing the avant-garde world of art briefly to come together with the world of the political vanguard (Franco 2002). However, unlike the case in the cinema, Cuban writers have been much less successful at preserving their aesthetic autonomy and creative subjectivity in the face of the constant demands of revolutionary discipline and dogmatic austerity. The revolutionary goal of encouraging writers to produce politically "committed" art came up against a series of dilemmas not the least of which was the traditional value of artistic subjectivity, as well as the very meaning of the words *revolution* and *liberation.* That is to say, the question over exactly what the revolution was to liberate Cubans from in the realm of culture was never completely clear, leaving writers on their own to interpret the parameters of what was permissible and producing a legacy of censorship and self-censorship in Cuban literature (Benítez-Rojo 1990; Dopico-Black 1989).

Also, during the 1960s questions lingered in the minds of many writers over exactly by whom, for whom, and to what end literature was to be written. It would seem that Fidel Castro's June 30, 1961, speech, "Words to the Intellectuals," which included the famous declaration, "Within the revolution, everything; against the revolution, nothing" (Castro 1961), established a cultural policy of inclusion, allowing autonomy and creative freedom to all writers and intellectuals as long as they were not *against* the revolutionary project; that is *counter*-revolutionaries. However, in practice the vagueness and paternalism of this decree allowed it to be applied in a manner equivalent to: "You're either with us or against us." In short, being critical of, ambivalent toward, or outside the revolution was often equated with being against it. In the tense context of the Cold War, the "necessity" for revolutionary unity always won out over the "luxury" of artistic subjectivity.

In the first few years of the revolution the government established numerous cultural institutions and literary magazines and journals, including the international center of literary promotion and research *Casa de las Américas,* the Union of Cuban Writers and Artists (UNEAC), the previously mentioned ICAIC, *Lunes de revolución* (a literary supplement to the newspaper *Revolución*), the cultural magazine *El caimán barbudo,* the youth-oriented newspaper *Juventud Rebelde,* and the political and philosophical journal *Pensamiento Crítico.* Also during this period the government successfully focused its attention on the expansion of literacy, access to basic education, and transforming "high" culture from the exclusive realm of a privileged few to the right of all. In line with these laudable goals, in 1961 the government mobilized the population in a yearlong effort to teach reading and writing skill to peasants in some of the most remote and neglected areas of the country in the legendary literacy campaign.

However, beginning around 1966 and culminating in the Padilla affair and First National Congress of Education and

Culture of 1971, it became increasingly clear that "the ideal-ized austerity of the guerrilla and the idealized simplicity of the peasant could not be reconciled with the exuberance and excess of the aesthetic, nor with the status of the writer as hero" (Franco 2002: 3). During these years many of the afore-mentioned journals and magazines were closed down or co-opted by the state. Many valuable but revolutionary ambivalent literary works were ignored by the powerful new cultural apparatus, officially denounced, or banned outright. Finally, many leading writers were either dismissed from their official posts, imprisoned, or escaped into exile.

Also during these years the heroic guerrilla as a macho man of action was praised over the supposedly effeminate intellectual. Indeed, the revolution inherited from Cuban his-tory a deep homophobia and a "masculinist bias" that saw armed revolution as the only means to achieve the end of social justice. With political militancy becoming the true test of the authentic intellectual, many of Cuba's ambivalent and irreverent writers and intellectuals (a significant portion of whom were homosexual) found themselves increasingly alienated from a revolution they had initially supported. Per-haps Che Guevara's judgment that the greatest sin of the Cuban intellectual was to have not joined the revolution best symbolizes this devaluation of the critical role of the Cuban intelligentsia in the revolutionary process. Instead of their being valued as the core of a civil society who could function as a corrective check on the growing power of the state, intel-lectuals were pressured to purge themselves of their original sin of their middle-class origins and values and fall in line as fellow soldiers in the class struggle (ibid.).

The work of two writers who had already emerged prior to the triumph of the revolution highlights the breakdown in the temporary alliance between the cultural avant-garde and the ideological vanguard. The poet and longtime editor of the lit-erary journal *Casa,* Roberto Fernández Retamar (b. 1930), is best-known as the author of "Calibán: Notes toward a Discussion of Culture in Our America" (1971), which declared Cuba's right to determine its own cultural and political destiny without outside interference. A longtime progressive intellectual, Fernández Retamar was instrumental in the formation of the cultural society Nuestro Tiempo in 1951, and he won the National Poetry Prize for his book *Patrias* in 1952. In the late 1950s, he was a frequent lecturer in major universities in Europe and the United States. After 1960, Fernández Retamar briefly served as Cuban cultural attaché in Paris and later took on the responsibility as editor of Cuba's two most important literary magazines, first of *Unión,* and after 1965, of *Casa.* After the revolution, his poetry began to reflect a deep commitment to the socialist ideals of the revolution. The most important of these include *Buena suerte viviendo* (1967), *Revolución nuestro, amor nuestro* (1976), and *Cincunstancia y Juana* (1980).

Like Fernández Retamar, Cuban writer Guillermo Cabrera Infante (1929–2005) first emerged in the 1950s as a leading writer and movie critic. In 1959, he became the editor of *Lunes de Revolución.* One of the most significant, original, and widely read publications of its kind in the history of Latin American literature, *Lunes* lasted only a little more than two and a half years before it was closed in the wake of the *P.M.* controversy and Castro's "Words to the Intellectuals." In 1966 after serving as a cultural attache in Europe, Cabrera Infante defected and moved to London, becoming a leading critic of the regime. He is most famous for his experimental novel *Tres tristes tigres* (*Three Trapped Tigers,* 1967), which paints an elaborate picture of the glories and decadence of Havana's 1950s nightlife. In this novel, as well as in many of his other works, he established himself as a consummate wordsmith, seeking to recreate Cuban popular speech on the written page. The book has since become part of the cannon of the Latin American literary "boom" of the 1960s (Padura Fuentes 2006: 263-266).

Easily the most infamous instance of repression against a Cuban writer was the Padilla affair, a series of events that took place in Cuba between 1968 and 1971, throwing into relief the limits to artistic expression in revolutionary Cuba. Between 1959 and 1961, Heberto Padilla (1932–2000) collaborated with Cabrera Infante as a writer and critic for *Lunes.* In the mid-1960s Padilla gave a positive review to Guillermo Cabrera Infante's novel *Three Trapped Tigers* (after Cabrera Infante had defected), while criticizing another novel written by Lisandro Otero, the secretary of the Cuban Writers' Union. The final episode of Padilla's troubles with the government began in 1968, when his book of poems *Fuera del juego* (*Out of the Game*) won the Writers' Union poetry prize. The book was eventually published, but the editors attached a denouncement of its content to the beginning, given the critical nature of many of its poems. As a result, in 1971 Padilla was arrested and made to read a public confession of his crimes against the revolution. These events provoked an international incident, with many erstwhile friends of Cuba signing an open letter of protest. After years of house arrest, Padilla was eventually allowed to go into exile in 1980 to the United States, where he continued to write, including an autobiography, *Self Portrait of the Other* (1989), which recounts these events in detail. Leading Cuban literary critic Ambrisio Fornet has since coined the term *quinquenio gris* to describe this repressive period, except that "it lasted more than just five years and its color was much darker" (Padura Fuentes 2007).

Another writer whose career has many parallels to that of Padilla is Reinaldo Arenas (1943–1990). In 1962, after earning a degree in agricultural accounting, Arenas moved to Havana and immediately launched into a prolific if often tragic literary career. While working in various cultural institutions in Havana, including the National Library, Casa de las Américas, and various literary magazines in the late 1960s, Arenas began to publish short stories that consistently won prizes in the UNEAC's literary competitions, earning him increasing notoriety. Although his first books, *Celestino antes del alba* (*Celestino before the Dawn*, 1967) and *El mundo alucinante* (*Hallucinations*, 1968), impressed the judges, their only slightly veiled criticisms of the government and open flaunting of the author's homosexuality landed Arenas on the government's blacklist. As a result, he spent some time in the infamous UMAP work camps in the late 1960s and was repeatedly sent to prison during the 1970s. Forced to smuggle his work out of the country to be published abroad, Arenas became well known internationally while remaining virtually a nonperson in Cuba. He was able to escape from Cuba as part of the Mariel boatlift in 1980 and died of AIDS in New York City in 1990 (Luis 2001).

The careers of two final writers help illustrate the fact that during the 1980s and especially the 1990s, new spaces opened up for Cuba's writers to express their criticisms more openly than in the past. Writer and editor Jesús Díaz (1941–2002) had worked in the middle to late 1960s as a writer and editor for *Juventud Rebelde* (1965–1966) and *El Caimán Barbudo* (1966–1967). At this time he openly identified with the revolution, becoming a party militant. Later, he discovered the limits to open debate within the revolution when the provocative Marxist philosophy journal *Pensamiento Crítico* (1967–1971) that he helped to edit was closed down by the government. In the late 1970s, Díaz actively began to cultivate ties with returning exiles who had favorable attitudes toward the revolution, an experience he chronicled in his book of interviews, *De la patria y el exilio,* and the film *55 Hermanos* (*55 Brothers and Sisters*). As a member of the Cuban Film Institute, he directed dozens of documentaries and feature films in Cuba, including his most successful, *Lejanía* (*Distance: The Parting of the Ways,* 1985).

In the late 1980s, after a long literary silence, he published *Las iniciales de la tierra* (*The Earth's Initials,* 1987), followed in 1991 by *Las palabras perdidas* (*The Lost Words*). Both books portrayed the ideological crisis of the artist within the revolution, a constant theme in almost all his work. In 1991, Díaz went into exile in Spain, where he spent the rest of his life. While his work in Cuba was of vital importance, he is likely best remembered for his final novels written in exile in Madrid, including *Dime algo sobre Cuba* (*Tell Me Something about Cuba,* 1998), and for founding *Encuentro de la cultura cubana* in 1996, the leading journal of Cuban culture and literary criticism published today (ibid.; Padura Fuentes 2006: 195–198).

Finally, Leonardo Padura Fuentes (b. 1955), contemporary Cuba's leading novelist, is most emblematic of the generation of writers who began to emerge in the 1980s and have been able to carefully carve out a space in which to create works that are often critical of the current condition of Cuban socialism and society (Cancio Isla 2002). His most ambitious work to date, what many consider his obra maestra, is *La Novela de Mi Vida* (*The Novel of My Life,* 2001), a fictionalized account of the life of the nineteenth-century Cuban poet José María Heredia. Also a leading essayist, journalist, and literary critic, Padura is most famous for creating the disillusioned crime detective Inspector Mario Conde in his four-part series of crime novels (known collectively as "The Havana Quartet"). These four novels are *Pasado perfecto,* 1991 (*Havana Blue,* 2007), *Vientos de cuaresma,* 1994 (*Havana Yellow,* 2008), *Mascaras,* 1997 (*Havana Red,* 2005), and *Paisaje de otoño,* 1998 (*Havana Black,* 2006). In these novels, as well as in the more recent follow-ups, *Adiós, Hemingway* (2004) and *La neblina de ayer* (*Yesterday's Fog* 2005), Padura is able to speak quite honestly and openly (through Conde and the situations in which he finds himself) of the many socioeconomic contradictions and political abuses that characterize contemporary Cuba.

Describing Conde, Padura indicates that tolerance of criticism has increased significantly over the last fifteen years.

Because Conde is "a man who is a bit disenchanted, skeptical, who defends himself with irony, and who has great loyalties and great phobias," he was initially inadmissible and considered politically incorrect for Cuba's cultural orthodoxy. As a result, the first novel in the "Quartet," *Pasado perfecto,* was passed over by Cuban juries and had to be published in Mexico. However, by 1994, when Padura was ready to publish the follow-up, *Vientos de cuaresma,* he claims that Cuban publishers jumped at the chance to praise and publish it, even though this time Conde "is revealed in all his sadness, his pessimism, his painful feelings about life and his merciless examination of the reality in which he lives." Padura continues:

> Readers will ask how is it possible that an author who lives, writes, and publishes in Cuba can talk so freely about the reality of life in Cuba and even criticize decisions of the authorities. But this is the truth. I live in Cuba, I write in Cuba, and my books have never been censored. On the contrary, they have all won important prizes and they are all read widely. What is certain is that, in the 1990s, the levels of tolerance increased. (Padura Fuentes 2005)

And it seems that Conde's pessimism and disillusionment increase with each subsequent novel, as does Padura's national and international acclaim.

CONCLUSION

As 2007 began, a new cultural controversy exploded into public view that illustrated once again how past cultural policies of the revolutionary government continue to define the terms of the ongoing and often heated debate over the proper balance between the artistic avant-garde and the political vanguard. However, this time around the indignant and vociferous public reaction of Cuba's leading intellectuals (both at home and abroad) seemed to indicate that some of the more repressive and arbitrary policies of the 1960s and 1970s would not be allowed to return. The crisis began on January 5 when the Cuban television programs *Impronta, Diálogo abierto,* and *La diferencia* each successively featured retrospective interviews with three figures responsible for designing and implementing the repressive cultural policies of the 1970s: Luis Pavón Tamayo, Armando Quesada, and Jorge Serguera, respectively. Because the interviews seemed to vindicate these figures and willfully ignore the deep scar their dogmatic, Stalinist policies left on Cuban culture, many of Cuba's leading intellectuals and writers protested publicly demanding an explanation and apology (Padura Fuentes 2007).

What began as a series of e-mails shared among those writers and intellectuals soon began to spread via the Internet beyond Cuba, finally being addressed in a meeting between the leadership of the Cuban Writers Union (UNEAC). Eventually, the UNEAC together with the Communist Party attempted to put an official end to the debate by publishing a partial explanation in the pages of *Granma* on January 18, under the confusing title, "The Cultural Policy of the Revolution Is Irreversible." While the declaration made clear that the UNEAC shared the writers' indignation, the statement seemed more preoccupied with disqualifying from the debate certain exiled writers as "annexationists [. . .] obviously working in the service of the enemy," that is, the United States government (Padura Fuentes 2007: 6).

Despite the official attempt to quell the growing debate, the crisis snowballed into a series of public debates in late January and February, 2007. Many participants in the debate sought to use this particular instance to make the point that the entire dark period of cultural repression that lasted between the late 1960s and 1976 (the *quinquenio gris*), had never been officially rectified, addressed, or even recognized as having taken place. Others contended that as bad as they were, the three officials in question had only implemented cultural policies conceived and approved by Castro. In an article chronicling the debate, Cuban journalist Dalia Acosta noted, "[M]any of those taking part in the e-mail exchange underscored the need to lift the veil of silence on that sad episode in history, and to study its causes and effects and recognize the mistakes made in order to prevent a repeat." Acosta also quoted Cuban writer Reynaldo González, 2002 National Literature Prize winner, who argued, "Errors are part of the past only if they are rectified" (Acosta 2007b).

Expanding the debate further into the public realm, Cuban poet César López challenged attendees at Havana's International Book Fair in February 2007, by dedicating the event to "all Cuban creators," specifically singling out four writers who died in exile still staunchly opposed to the policies of the Cuban government: Guillermo Cabrera Infante, Reinaldo Arenas, Jesús Díaz, and Heberto Padilla. Perhaps the best epitaph to this brief but significant episode was pronounced by Reynaldo González who told Acosta, "They have let the genie out of the bottle. And it will not go back in" (ibid.). Thus, the long fight by members of Cuba's avant-garde to open up and defend spaces of autonomous creation and critical debate during the toughest years of the 1980s and 1990s has made the outcome of this most recent controversy decidedly more positive for Cuban writers and artists, if still within the limits set by Castro long ago in his, "Words to the Intellectuals"— "Within the revolution, everything; against the revolution, nothing" (Castro 1961; Padura Fuentes 2007).

References

Acosta, Dalia. "Hip Hop Sidelined but Still Rapping," *Inter Press Service News*, March 19, 2007a. Available online at: http://www.ipsnews.net/news.asp?idnews=36988.

Acosta, Dalia. "Exorcising the Ghosts of the Past," *Inter Press Service News*, February 23, 2007b. Available online at: http://www.ipsnews.net/news.asp?idnews=36701.

Acosta, Leonardo. *Cubano Be, Cuban Bop: One Hundred Years of Jazz in Cuba.* Translated by Daniel S. Whitesell. Washington, D.C.: Smithsonian Books, 2003.

Alén Rodríguez, Olavo. *De lo Afrocubano a la Salsa: Géneros musicales de Cuba.* San Juan: Editorial Cubanacán, 1992.

Alfonso, Pablo. "Los vitrales rotos de Pinar del Río." *Cuba por dentro,* April 10, 2007. Available online at: http://www.cubapordentro.com/Archivo-2007-04/pab-2007-04-10-a.htm.

Bachelet, Pablo. "Fewer Support Sanctions on Cuba." *Miami Herald.* April 2, 2007. Available online at: http://www.miamiherald.com/884/story/60526.html.

Benítez-Rojo, Antonio. "Comments on Georgina Dopico-Black's 'The Limits of Expression: Intellectual Freedom in Postrevolutionary Cuba.'" *Cuban Studies* 20 (1990): 171–174.

Cancio Isla, Wilfredo. "Imparable el éxodo de cubanos." *El Nuevo Herald,* October 26, 2006.

Cancio Isla, Wilfredo. "Leonardo Padura Fuentes," in *Encyclopedia of Cuba: People, History, Culture.* Edited by Luis Martínez-Fernández, D. H. Figueredo, Louis A. Pérez, Jr., and Luis González. Westport, CT: Greenwood Press, 2002.

Carpentier, Alejo. *Music in Cuba.* Minneapolis: University of Minnesota Press, 2001.

Casal, Lourdes. "Race Relations in Contemporary Cuba," in *The Cuba Reader: The Making of a Revolutionary Society.* Edited by Philip Brenner, William M. LeoGrande, Donna Rich, and Daniel Siegel. New York: Grove Press, 1989.

Castro, Fidel. "Words to the Intellectuals: Castro's Speech to Intellectuals." FBIS report, June 30, 1961. Available online at: http://lanic.utexas.edu/la/cb/cuba/castro/1961/19610630.

Chanan, Michael. *Cuban Cinema.* Minneapolis: University of Minnesota Press, 2004.

Conde, Yvonne. *Operation Pedro Pan: The Untold Exodus of 14,048 Cuban Children.* New York: Routledge, 2000.

Crahan, Margaret E. "Whither Cuba? The Role of Religion." Woodrow Wilson Center Update on the Americas. No. 14, October 2003.

De Aragón, Uva. "Winds of Change: Cuban-Americans in the Post-Papal Era." *Hemisphere* 8, no. 3 (fall 1998), pp. 6–7.

De la Campa, Román. *Cuba on My Mind: Journeys to a Severed Nation.* New York: Verso, 2000.

De la Fuente, Alejandro. *A Nation for All: Race, Inequality, and Politics in Twentieth-Century Cuba.* Chapel Hill: University of North Carolina Press, 2001.

Didion, Joan. *Miami.* New York: Simon & Schuster, 1987.

Díaz-Briquets, Sergio. "Cuban Global Emigration at the Turn of the Century: Overall Estimate and Selected Characteristics of the Emigrant Population," in *Cuba in Transition—Volume 16.* Washington, DC: Association for the Study of the Cuban Economy, 2006.

Domínguez, Jorge I. "Cooperating with the Enemy?: US Immigration Policies toward Cuba," in *Western Hemisphere Immigration and US Foreign Policy.* Edited by Christopher Mitchell, pp. 31–88. University Park: Pennsylvania State University Press, 1992.

Dopico-Black, Georgina. "The Limits of Expression: Intellectual Freedom in Postrevolutionary Cuba." *Cuban Studies* 19 (1989), pp. 107–142.

Fernández, Ariel "Asho". Information, music, and videos provided the author in interviews, lectures, and personal communication with Cuba hip-hop promoter and impresario Ariel "Asho" Fernández, 2006.

Fernández, Damián. "Religion under Castro," in *Encyclopedia of Cuba: People, History, Culture*. Edited by Luis Martínez-Fernández, D. H. Figueredo, Louis A. Pérez, Jr., and Luis González. Westport, CT: Greenwood Press, 2002.

Fernández, Raúl A. "The Musicalia of Twentieth-Century Cuban Popular Musicians," in *Cuba, the Elusive Nation: Interpretations of National Identity*. Edited by Damián Fernández and Madeline Cámara-Betancourt. Gainesville: University Press of Florida, 2000.

Fernández, Raúl A. "The Course of U.S. Cuban Music: Margin and Mainstream." *Cuban Studies* 24 (1994): 105–122.

FIU. "2007 FIU Cuba Poll." Institute for Public Opinion Research and the Cuban Research Institute, Florida International University, 2007. Available online at: http://www.fiu.edu/~ipor/cuba8/.

Franco, Jean. *The Decline and Fall of the Lettered City: Latin America in the Cold War*. Cambridge, MA: Harvard University Press, 2002.

Goodnough, Abby. "Tensions Rise as More Flee Cuba for U.S." *New York Times*, December 18, 2005.

Grenier, Guillermo J., and Lisando Pérez. *The Legacy of Exile: Cubans in the United States*. Boston: Allyn and Bacon, 2003.

Guillermoprieto, Alma. *Dancing with Cuba: A Memoir of the Revolution*. Translated by Esther Allen. New York: Pantheon Books, 2004.

Holgado Fernández, Isabel. *Mujeres cubanas y la crisis revolucionaria*. Barcelona: Antrazyt, 2000.

Lacey, Marc. "Cuba's Rap Vanguard Reaches Beyond the Party Line," *New York Times*, December 15, 2006.

Loomis, John. *Revolution of Forms: Cuba's Forgotten Art Schools*. Princeton, NJ: Princeton Architectural Press, 1999.

López, Rigoberto, and Leonardo Padura. *Yo soy del son a la salsa*. New York: RMM Filmworks, 1997.

Luis, William. *Culture and Customs of Cuba*. Westport, CT: Greenwood Press, 2001.

Manuel, Peter, with Kenneth Bilby and Michael Alrgey. *Caribbean Currents: Caribbean Music from Rumba to Reggae* (revised and expanded edition). Philadelphia, PA: Temple University Press, 2006.

Martí, José. *Selected Writings*. Translated by Esther Allen. New York: Penguin, 2002.

Martínez, Juan A. *Cuban Art and National Identity: The Vanguardia Painters, 1927–1950*. Gainesville: University Press of Florida, 1994.

Martínez, Julio A. *Dictionary of Twentieth-Century Cuban Literature*. Westport, CT: Greenwood Press, 1990.

Martínez-Fernández, Luis. "Cuban Population in the United States," in *Encyclopedia of Cuba: People, History, Culture.* Edited by Luis Martínez-Fernández, D. H. Figueredo, Louis A. Pérez, Jr., and Luis González, pp. 601–602. Westport, CT: Greenwood Press, 2002.

Montoya, Roberto. "Nuestro sistema no lo impuso la URSS con sus tanques: Entrevista a Ricardo Alarcón, presidente de la Asembla Nacional de Poder Popular de Cuba." *El Mundo,* November 6, 2006. Available online at: www.defensahumanidad.cult.cu/artic.php?item=1223.

Moore, Kevin. "Artists: Charanga Habanera," 2001. Available online at: http://www.timba.com.

Moore, Robin D. *Music and Revolution: Cultural Change in Socialist Cuba.* Berkeley: University of California Press, 2006.

Moore, Robin D. *Nationalizing Blackness: Afrocubanismo and Artistic Revolution in Havana, 1920–1940.* Pittsburgh, PA: University of Pittsburgh Press, 1997.

Ojito, Mirta. *Finding Mañana: A Memoir of A Cuban Exodus.* New York: Penguin, 2005.

Ojito, Mirta. "Best of Friends, Worlds Apart," *New York Times,* June 5, 2000.

Orovio, Helio. *Cuban Music from A to Z.* Durham, NC: Duke University Press, 2004.

Ortiz, Fernando. *Cuban Counterpoint: Tobacco and Sugar.* Durham, NC: Duke University Press, 1995.

Padura Fuentes. "La memoria y el olvido," *Cultura y Sociedad* 13, no. 1, Havana: Inter Press Service, January, 2007.

Padura Fuentes, Leonardo. *Entre dos siglos.* Havana: Inter Press Service, 2006.

Padura Fuentes, Leonardo. "Cuba's Hammett: Interview with Leonardo Padura Fuentes." By Stephen Wilkinson. *PoliticalAffairs.net: Marxist Thought Online.* April 11–16, 2005. Available online at: http://www.politicalaffairs.net/article/view/941/1/88.

Padura Fuentes, Leonardo. *Faces of Salsa: A Spoken History of the Music.* Translated by Stephen J. Clark. Washington, D.C.: Smithsonian Books, 2003a.

Padura Fuentes, Leonardo. *José María Heredia: La patria y la vida.* Havana: Ediciones Unión, 2003b.

Padura Fuentes, Leonardo. *La novela de mi vida.* Havana: Ediciones Unión, 2001.

Pedraza, Silvia. "Cuban Migrations to the United States," in *Encyclopedia of Cuba: People, History, Culture.* Edited by Luis Martínez-Fernández, D. H. Figueredo, Louis A. Pérez, Jr., and Luis González. Westport, CT: Greenwood Press, 2002.

Pérez, Lisandro. "De Nueva York a Miami: El desarrollo demográfico de las comunidades cubanas en Estados Unidos." *Encuentro de la cultura cubana* 15 (2000), pp. 13–23.

Pérez, Louis A. *On Becoming Cuban: Identity, Nationality, and Culture.* Chapel Hill: University of North Carolina Press, 1999.

Pérez Firmat, Gustavo. "A Willingness of the Heart: Cubanidad, Cubaneo, Cubanía." *Cuban Studies Association Occasional Paper Series 2,* no. 7 (October 1997).

Pérez Sarduy, Pedro, and Jean Stubs, eds. *Afro-Cuban Voices: On Race and Identity in Contemporary Cuba.* Gainesville: University Press of Florida, 2000.

Pérez Sarduy, Pedro, and Jean Stubs, eds. *AfroCuba: An Anthology of Cuban Writing on Race, Politics, and Culture.* Melbourne: Ocean Press, 1993.

Perna, Vincenzo. *Timba: The Sound of the Cuban Crisis.* Hampshire, England: Ashgate, 2005.

Pew Hispanic Center. "Cubans in the United States: A Profile," August 25, 2006. Available online at: http://pwehispanic.org/files/factsheets/23.pdf.

Portes, Alejandro. "The Cuban-American Political Machine: Reflections on Its Origins and Perpetuation," in *Changes in Cuban Society since the Nineties.* Edited by Joseph S. Tulchin, Liliam Bobea, Mayra P. Espina Prieto, and Rafael Hernández, pp. 187–205. Washington, D.C.: Woodrow Wilson Center Report on the Americas no. 15, 2005.

Portes, Alejandro. "Morning in Miami: A New Era for Cuban Americans." *American Prospect* 9, no. 38 (May–June 1998), pp. 28–32.

Portes, Alejandro, and Alex Stepick. *City on the Edge: The Transformation of Miami.* Berkeley: University of California Press, 1993.

Roberts, John Storm. *The Latin Tinge: The Impact of Latin American Music on the United States* (second edition). New York: Oxford University Press, 1999.

Robinson, Eugene. *Last Dance in Havana: The Final Days of Fidel and the Start of the New Cuban Revolution.* New York: Free Press, 2004.

Ross, Alex. "Rock 101." *New Yorker,* July 14 and 21, 2003.

Roy, Maya. *Cuban Music: From Son and Rumba to the Buena Vista Social Club and Timba Cubana.* Princeton: Markus Wiener Publishers; London: Latin American Bureau, 2002.

Seitz, Matt Zoller. "Courage Through Rhymes: 'East of Havana,'" *New York Times,* February 1, 2007.

Sublette, Ned. *Cuba and Its Music: From the First Drum to the Mambo.* Chicago: Chicago Review Press, 2004.

Sweeney, Philip. *The Rough Guide to Cuban Music.* London: Rough Guides, 2001.

Thomas, Hugh. *Cuba or the Pursuit of Freedom.* New York: DaCapo Press, 1998.

Vitral. "Cuba: Hora de oportunidades." *Boletín Vitral* Year 6, no. 214, April 9, 2007.

Zamora, Antonio. "The Political Evolution of the Cuban-American Community of South Florida: 1959–2005." Paper prepared for the Wisconsin Symposium on Cuba, March 3–5, 2005.

PART TWO
REFERENCE SECTION

Key Events in Cuban History

Pre-Columbian History

1250   The Siboney (Ciboney), costal cave dwellers, populate the western extreme of the island; Siboney are gradually overrun by a subgroup of the Arawaks, called the Sub-Taínos, who occupy the eastern and northeastern parts of the island starting in 1250.

Spanish Conquest

1492   Columbus sights and briefly stops at the island, describing it as "the most beautiful land that human eyes have ever seen."

1508   Sebastián de Ocampo circumnavigates the island.

1511–1515 Diego de Velázquez leads an expedition and battles Taíno natives; Taíno leader Hatuey executed; Major cities Bayamo, Trinidad, Havana, Sancti Spíritus, Puerto Príncipe (Camagüey), and Santiago established; Encomienda system of land and labor grants begin; Hernán Cortés, mayor of Santiago, departs for Mexico; Havana relocated to present site (1519).

1522   First African slaves brought to Cuba.

Depopulation and Abandonment, 1519–1760

1519–1540 Depopulation of Cuba for Mexico and Peru; Last major Indian uprisings are put down; First recorded slave rebellions take place (1533).

1538   Santiago established as capital.

1555   French privateer Jacques de Sores sacks Havana.

1564   First treasure fleet (*La Flota*) departs from Havana headed for Spain.

1586	Sir Francis Drake attacks Santo Domingo and Cartagena, threatening Havana.
1607	Havana is made the capital; First settlements are established by English colonists in Jamestown, Virginia, in what will become the United States.
1628	Sailing for the Dutch West India Company, Admiral Piet Heyn routs Spanish silver fleet.
1674	Construction of Havana city walls begins.
1688	Sailing from Jamaica, Welsh buccaneer Captain Henry Morgan sacks Camagüey.
1700	Tobacco, native plant first cultivated by Taínos (called *cohiba*), becomes main export.
1717–1723	*Factoría* tobacco system established, leading to revolts by tobacco growers (*vegueros*).
1728	University of Havana established.

The British Occupation and Its Consequences, 1762–1800

1762–1763	British seize Havana, leading to major growth in world trade for Cuba; British trade Cuba for Florida in 1763.
1776	American Revolution leads to increased trade between Cuba and the United States.
1790	Mass importation of African slaves begins as sugar cultivation spreads across the island.
1791	Major slave rebellion in Saint-Domingue culminates in Haitian Revolution and destroys Haitian sugar industry, leading to French immigration and boost in sugar output in Cuba.

Sugar and Slavery, 1795–1850

| 1795–1824 | Attempts to establish independence fail, including the Aponte conspiracy (1812). |
| 1817 | Spain and England sign treaty ending slave trade by 1820; illegal Cuban trade continues. |

1820   Cuban trade with the United States grows to over half of all its international trade.

1823   Monroe Doctrine declared; John Quincy Adams likens Cuba to a ripe fruit that, "incapable of self-support, can gravitate only towards the North American Union" if ever free from Spain; Cuban abolitionist Father Félix Varela arrives in exile in New York City.

1837   First railway line in Spanish-speaking world is built in Cuba to transport sugarcane.

1844   Major slave revolt, "La Escalera conspiracy," discovered and harshly repressed.

1847   Beginning of importation of Chinese indentured labor in Cuba.

U.S. Interest in Cuba Increases, 1848–1867

1848–1851 Annexationist, proslavery rebel Narciso López leads three failed expeditions from New Orleans to free Cuba from Spain; López raises Cuban flag above Cárdenas in May 1850; United States offers to buy Cuba from Spain.

1853   José Martí born in Havana to Spanish immigrant parents; Arrested for disloyalty to Spain (1869); Condemned to hard labor but granted clemency and deported to Spain (1870).

1854   Ostend Manifesto: "U.S. justified in wresting [Cuba] from Spain" if Spain cannot hold it.

1865   Contraband importation of African slaves ends.

The Struggle for Independence, 1868–1902

1868–1878 Grito de Yara begins the Ten Years' War led by Carlos Manuel de Céspedes; Pact of Zanjón ends the war but is rejected by General Antonio Maceo (1878); Liberal Autonomist party founded; *Guerra Chiquita* (little war) ends in defeat (1879–1880).

1880–1886 *Patronato* set to gradually abolish slavery over eight years; Slavery abolished (1886).

1881–1895 Martí lives in New York City working as a journalist; Prepares Cuban insurrection.

1884 Martí breaks with Cuban generals Máximo Gómez and Maceo over issue of military government for independent Cuba; Martí later reconciles with them (1890s).

1892 Martí founds *Partido Revolucionario Cubano* (PRC, Cuban Revolutionary Party) in Key West, aimed at achieving full independence for Cuba through armed struggle.

1895 Grito de Baire marks beginning of final Cuban War for Independence (Feb.); United States seizes three shiploads of arms intended for Cuban rebels (Feb.); Martí killed in battle (May).

1896 Spanish General Valeriano Weyler begins brutal *reconcentración* policy; Maceo killed.

1897–1898 Weyler recalled and autonomy granted to Cuba, rebels vow to fight on.

1898 *Maine* explosion (Feb. 15); Joint Resolution and Teller Amendment (April); U.S. intervention at Santiago (July); Spain capitulates (Aug.); Spain and United States sign the Treaty of Paris (Dec.); United States begins three-year military occupation.

Cuban Independence, American Protectorate, 1902–1940

1902 Military occupation ends; Cubans forced to add Platt Amendment to new constitution.

1906–1909 Second U.S. military occupation.

1912 Afro-Cuban movement repressed, with United States threatening intervention.

1920	Dance of the Millions; sugar prices reach all-time high but bust by the end of the year; Communist student leader Julio Antonio Mella holds first National Student Congress; Mella is assassinated in exile in Mexico (1929).
1923	Crowder named first official U.S. ambassador; Movement for National Renovation begun by Fernando Ortiz; Two groups of young leftist, nationalist intellectuals (*Grupo Minorista* and *Protest of the 13*) form to protest corruption of Zayas government.
1925	Cuba's first "international" Communist Party founded.
1930	Hawley-Smoot Tariff Act reduces Cuban sugar quota; Great Depression and government repression cause extreme unrest and violence in Cuba.
1931	Former presidents Menocal and Mendieta launch unsuccessful uprising against Machado.
1933	U.S. envoy Sumner Welles arrives to mediate removal of Machado; Machado replaced by Carlos Manuel de Céspedes, who is then overthrown by Sergeant's Revolt; Ramón Grau San Martín, Antonio Guiteras, and Fulgencio Batista orchestrate an unstable governing coalition.
1934	Batista purges Grau and begins military rule; Partido Revolucionario Cubano—Auténtico (PRC-A) is organized in exile by Grau; The Platt amendment is abrogated; Guiteras organizes Joven Cuba, a radical underground organization, but he is killed in 1935.

The Cuban Democratic Experience, 1940–1952

1940	New liberal constitution passed and Batista is elected president in 1940.

1944   Grau elected president and Batista hands over
            power without incident; Both Grau (1944–1948)
            and Carlos Prío Socarrás (1948–1952) presiden-
            cies are extremely corrupt.

1947   Eduardo Chibás breaks with Auténticos and
            establishes Ortodoxo Party (Partido del Pueblo
            Cubano); Chibás commits suicide during his
            live weekly radio show (1951).

            U.S. mafia bosses Charles "Lucky" Luciano,
            Meyer Lansky, and Santo Trafficante, Jr., con-
            solidate casino control and drug trafficking in
            Havana.

The Struggle against the Batista Dictatorship, 1952–1958

1952   Batista carries out a bloodless military coup
            (Mar. 10).

1953   Castro attacks Moncada barracks (July 26);
            Gives "History Will Absolve Me" speech.

1955   General amnesty leads to release of Castro;
            Castro founds the 26th of July Movement;
            Departs for Mexico to plan revolution (meets
            Ernesto "Che" Guevara); Student organization
            Revolutionary Directorate founded by José
            Antonio Echeverría.

1956   Yacht *Granma* lands near Sierra Maestra with
            eighty-three revolutionaries onboard; Most are
            immediately killed or captured leaving just eigh-
            teen, including the Castro brothers and
            Guevara.

1957   *New York Times* reporter Herbert Matthews
            makes clandestine visit to Castro's hideout,
            embarrassing Batista government by publishing
            sympathetic report proving he is alive;
            Echeverría killed in attack on Presidential
            Palace.

1958   United States enacts arms embargo against Batista;
            General strike fails; Batista flees (Dec. 31).

Consolidation of the Revolution and Confrontation with the United States, 1959–1962

1959   Castro arrives in Havana (Jan. 8), Urrutia made
            president and Miró Cardona made prime minis-
            ter; Trials against accused war criminals draw
            U.S. criticism; Castro visits United States, refuses
            aid (April); Agrarian Reform Bill passed (May);
            Castro's moderate cabinet breaks apart (June);
            President Urrutia forced out (July); General
            Huber Matos resigns, jailed by Castro (Oct.).

1960   Cuba and USSR re-establish diplomatic rela-
            tions (May) after Mikoyan's visit (Feb.); French
            ship *La Coubre* explodes in Havana harbor;
            President Eisenhower secretly authorizes CIA to
            begin planning Castro's overthrow (Mar.); Cuba
            nationalizes U.S. petroleum refineries after their
            refusal to process Soviet crude (June); United
            States eliminates Cuban sugar quota and USSR
            immediately offers to purchase the rest (July);
            All U.S. businesses nationalized (Aug.–Oct.);
            U.S. trade embargo imposed on Cuba and
            Ambassador Bonsal recalled to Washington
            (Oct.); Cuba establishes its mass organizations.

1961   United States cuts diplomatic relations with
            Cuba (Jan.); Exile organization Cuban
            Revolutionary Council formed with U.S. govern-
            ment support (Mar. 22); Bay of Pigs invasion
            fails (April); Castro makes "Marxist-Leninist"
            speech declaring socialist nature of Cuban
            Revolution; Severe crackdown against internal
            opposition accompanies invasion; Massive emi-
            gration continues; Castro establishes cultural
            policy, "Within the Revolution, everything;
            against it, nothing."

1962   Cuban Missile Crisis (Oct.) leads to removal of
              missiles by the Soviets; United States promises
              not to invade Cuba; Castro is not consulted.

Socialist Experimentation, 1962–1970

1965   Last significant counter-revolutionary fighters
              are eliminated in Escambray mountains;
              Emigration through "freedom flights" begins,
              more than 250,000 leave by 1973.

1965–1968   UMAP camps established to "re-educate anti-
              social elements," including gays.

1967   Guevara killed in Bolivia; Cuba approves of
              Soviet invasion of Czechoslovakia (1968).

1968   All remaining small businesses nationalized in
              the Revolutionary Offensive.

1970   Failure to harvest 10 million tons of sugar leads
              to a Soviet-style "institutionalization" of the
              revolution, accompanied by a turn to new
              "market-socialist" economic policies.

Communist Institutionalization, 1970–1986

1971   Forced confession of prize-winning poet Heberto
              Padilla causes an international scandal; First
              National Conference of Education and Culture
              outlines policies for "true creative freedom,"
              beginning the *quinquenio gris*—a five-year gray
              period for art and culture.

1972   Cuba joins the Eastern Bloc trade organization
              COMECON.

1974   Grass-roots governance organization, *Poder
              Popular* (People's Power), is established.

1975   First Communist Party Congress; Provincial
              divisions reorganized; Cuba sends large force to
              Angola to help repel an invasion by South
              African forces.

1977   Brief reconciliation between the United States and Cuba, including the opening of "interest sections" and the release of Cuban political prisoners; First ever family visits to Cuba.

1979   Castro elected the president of the Non-Aligned Movement; Castro supports the Soviet invasion of Afghanistan.

1980   More than 10,000 Cubans take refuge in the Peruvian embassy; Castro declares, "Let the scum leave"; Massive boatlift out of port of Mariel sends 125,000 refugees to Miami.

The Rectification Campaign, 1986–1990

1986   Start of the Rectification Campaign, Cuba's answer to Soviet perestroika (opening).

1988   Cuban troops withdrawn from Angola.

1989   Decorated Cuban general Arnaldo Ochoa is executed for high treason.

The Special Period, 1990–2006

1990   USSR switches to hard-currency deals with Cuba; Special Period crisis declared (Aug.).

1991   Soviet Union collapses, ending its special political and economic relationship with Cuba.

1992   Cuban Democracy Act is passed, hardening the U.S. embargo.

1993   Cuban government authorizes limited self-employment in 117 trades.

1994   Cuban government legalizes use of the U.S. dollar and allows for private farmer's markets; First ever riot occurs in Havana; Massive rafter emigration from Cuba leads United States to change its policy of automatic acceptance; Rights group Concilio Cubano meets in Havana and Madrid.

1995   Direct foreign investment approved; Private family-run restaurants (*paladares*) legalized.

1996	Shoot-down of Brothers to the Rescue plane over international waters; Helms-Burton law passed by U.S. Congress; Clinton signs it, yet suspends its implementation.
1997	Cuban Dissidence Working Group issues the statement *La Patria es de Todos* ("The Homeland Belongs to Us All").
1998	Pope John Paul II makes an extended visit; Holds public mass in Revolutionary Plaza.
1999	Castro launches law-and-order crackdown carried out by new specialized police force.
1999–2000	Migration problems erupt when Elián González case creates international incident; Massive rallies in Havana demand Elián's return; Miami rallies demand that the child remain in the United States; After dramatic raid and legal battle, child returned to Cuba (summer 2000).

Cuba in the Twenty-first Century

2001	Castro faints during a speech, causing frenzy in Miami; First major purchases of U.S. foodstuffs by Cuban government follow destruction of Hurricane Michelle.
2002	Former U.S. president Jimmy Carter leads a delegation to Cuba; Reads a nationally televised speech (in Spanish) condemning the U.S. embargo, recognizing Proyecto Varela, and criticizing human rights abuses in Cuba; Full text of Carter's speech is published in *Granma*, the Communist Party newspaper.
2002–2003	Chief of U.S. Interest Sectio James Cason meets repeatedly with Cuban dissidents; Seventy-five dissidents are arrested and charged with sedition (spring 2003); After two successful air hijackings to the United States, the Cuban Coast Guard apprehends a group of boat hijackers;

The three ringleaders are executed after secret trials.

2004   The Bush administration sets a new hard-line policy under the Commission for Assistance to a Free Cuba, designed to deny funds to the Cuban government; The policy names a "transition coordinator," restricts educational exchange, and limits remittances and family visits.

2005   The Cuban government scales back economic reforms and recentralizes control over the economy, raises minimum and retirement wages, removes the U.S. dollar from circulation, and begins a new offensive against economic crime and corruption; Oil reserves are discovered off north coast and economic relations deepen with China and Hugo Chávez's oil-rich Venezuela; United States refuses Cuban offers of aid after Hurricane Katrina destroys parts of the Gulf Coast.

2006   The Commission for Assistance to a Free Cuba issues a second report on Cuba under the motto "Transition, not succession"; On July 26, the Cuban government celebrates its forty-seventh anniversary; On July 31, before undergoing a serious intestinal operation, President Fidel Castro issues a written statement temporarily transferring his presidential duties to his younger brother, Raúl, for the first time; After premature celebration in Miami, Castro is shown in the Cuban news media in his hospital room, recuperating but noticeably thinner; General calm prevails in Cuba; On Aug. 13, Castro turns eighty.

2007   In January, a controversy erupts in Cuba following a series of Cuban television programs that feature retrospective interviews praising three figures associated with the repressive cultural policies of 1968–1976; In April, the critical minded socio-religious magazine *Vitral,* published by the diocese of Pinar del Río, announces that it can no longer assure future publication because of "a lack of resources."

Significant People, Places, and Events

José Antonio Aponte (d. 1812) and the Aponte Conspiracy. José Antonio Aponte was a former first corporal in Havana's black militia, a skilled woodcutter, and the leader of his local Yoruba association, or cabildo de nación. These prominent positions allowed Aponte to plan the most significant conspiracy for independence of the early nineteenth century. The goals of the Aponte conspiracy were political independence and emancipation. However, the conspiracy was betrayed in 1812, and its leaders, including Aponte, were executed by the Spanish government.

Francisco de Arango (1765–1837). Trained as a lawyer, Francisco de Arango y Parreño was the Cuban Creole planter most responsible for convincing the Spanish Court to allow the open introduction of slaves into Cuba directly from the African coast starting in 1789. Arango was the guiding force behind the formation of the Sociedad Económica de Amigos del País (1792) and the subsequent Consulado Real de Agricultura, Industria y Comercio (1794), as well as the island's first newspaper, the *Papel Periódico*.

Fulgencio Batista (1901–1973). Born with the century in Banes, Oriente Province, the year before Cuba gained its nominal independence in 1902, Fulgencio Batista y Zaldívar's life closely paralleled the bloody struggles, democratic hopes, deep corruption, and ultimately frustrated hopes of the Cuban Republican period (1902–1959). Batista first came to prominence in September 1933 when a revolt of disgruntled sergeants he led coincided with an unstable transfer of presidential power from the deposed Gerardo Machado to the untested Carlos Manuel de Céspedes. Joining forces with a more radical group of university students, Batista and his fellow soldiers quickly found themselves holding military power alongside a new civilian professor, President Ramón Grau San Martín, whom the United States refused to recognize. After more than three months of political intrigue, Batista replaced Grau with U.S. backing and ruled Cuba through a series of puppet-presidents until he, himself, was elected president under a new constitution in 1940. Batista served this first four-year term ably, in an ironic coalition with organized labor and Cuba's Communist Party. He also increased the military's presence in Cuban life by expanding its educational and social services. Strongly supportive of the United States during World War II, Batista stepped down and went quietly into exile in Florida after his party lost out to his erstwhile presidential partner from 1933, Grau, who now became president as head of the Auténtico Party. However, after two administrations of Auténtico corruption and incompetence, Batista returned to Cuba in 1951 to run for president once again. Running a distant third in early polls, Batista decided not to wait for the election and instead carried out a bloodless military coup on March 10, 1952, a year after the leading candidate, Eduardo Chibás of the Ortodoxo Party, committed suicide. For the next six and a half years Batista ruled Cuba as an increasingly repressive and corrupt dictator. After his massive army slowly lost control over rapidly growing revolutionary forces in the mountains and in the urban underground, Batista finally lost U.S. backing and went into permanent exile on December 31, 1958. After living briefly in Portugal, Batista settled in southern Spain, where he wrote a series of apologia-like books about the "betrayal" of Cuba, until his death in 1973.

The *Balsero* ("Rafter") Crisis, 1994–1995. As Cuba's economic crisis began to deepen in the early 1990s, the number of Cuban *balseros* ("rafters") intercepted en route to the United States reached 4,731 in just the first seven months of

1994. Still, the United States maintained its policy of allowing virtual free entry to all Cuban rafters. A frustrated Castro decided to call Washington's bluff after embassy occupations and dramatic boat hijackings culminated in an antigovernment riot in Havana on August 4–5, 1994. Castro instructed the Cuban Coast Guard to cease interfering with "illegal" departures from the island, allowing thousands more rafters to flee. More than 20,000 were picked up at sea in the month of August alone. As a result, the Clinton administration reversed long-standing policy and announced that any rafter picked up in the future would *not* be allowed to enter the United States but would be indefinitely detained at a "safe-haven" at the U.S. Naval Base at Guantánamo Bay, Cuba. A September agreement between the Cuban government and the Clinton administration stipulated that Guantánamo detainees would be encouraged to return to Cuba and apply to immigrate through official channels, while the Cuban government would once again stop Cubans from leaving by raft. The terms of the agreement also indicated that the United States would henceforth grant a minimum of 20,000 immigrant visas to Cubans each year. While this agreement ended the outpouring of rafters from Cuba, it was not until May 1995, after a new round of secret meetings, that the United States announced that all Cuban rafters still held at Guantánamo would gradually be paroled into the United States. This new agreement also declared that any future Cuban rafters intercepted at sea would be returned to Cuba. The new policy inadvertently led to the now infamous "wet-foot, dry-foot" policy, since the 1966 Cuban Adjustment Act still gives legal status to any Cuban actually making it to dry land.

The Bay of Pigs (*Playa Girón*), April 1961. The Bay of Pigs is the name given to an unsuccessful invasion attempt by Cuban exiles in April 1961 secretly sponsored by the CIA. The invasion was led by Brigade 2506, a force made up of some of the tens of thousands of Cubans who had fled the island during the first two years of revolutionary rule. CIA deputy director Richard Bissell based the plan on the previously successful overthrow of Guatemala's president, Jacobo Arbenz, in 1954, also backed by the CIA. However, the planners miscalculated the revolutionary commitment of the Cuban people and the popularity and resourcefulness of Fidel Castro. Also, the overconfidence of almost everyone involved, coupled with the fact that the "secret" invasion was in fact a subject of much macho bragging on the streets of Miami, doomed it from the start. On April 15, U.S. planes tried to cripple the Cuban Air Force and allow for the unimpeded landing of the invasion force. However, Castro rallied the nation into a frenzy after this bombing raid alerted him to the impending invasion. Castro also used the opportunity to round up suspected dissidents and publicly declare for the first time that his revolution was socialist in ideology. Cubans responded with nationalist support for the defense of the homeland. The subsequent invasion that began in the early morning hours of April 17 at the Bay of Pigs (usually referred to in Spanish as *Girón,* the name of the beach on which the landing was to take place) was over almost before it began. As Che Guevara later explained to U.S. diplomats at a summit in Uruguay, the invasion had not only failed to dislodge Castro; it had actually worked to help him consolidate and radicalize his rule.

Guillermo Cabrera Infante (1929–2005). One of Cuba's most celebrated and original writers, Guillermo Cabrera Infante was born into a family of activists who helped found Cuba's first Communist Party. However, he was attracted more to art and cinema than politics and became active in Havana's literary circles in the early 1950s, writing numerous film reviews and developing a lifelong addiction to Hollywood movies. Legend has it that he attended his first movie with is mother at the impressionable age of just twenty-nine days. As a result, he liked to claim, "I was born with the silver screen in my mouth." Although he was an early supporter of the revolution, he went into exile in London in 1965. He is most famous for his masterwork, *Tres tristes tigres* (*Three Trapped Tigers,* 1967), an experimental novel full of wordplay that describes the beauty and decadence of 1950s Havana. Just before his death in 2005, he wrote the screenplay to Andy García's film *The Lost City* (2006).

Alejo Carpentier (1904–1980). Born in Lausanne, Switzerland, before moving with his French father and Russian mother to Havana as an infant, Alejo Carpentier is among Cuba's leading twentieth-century novelists. At a young age Carpentier moved to Paris, where he studied music. He returned to Cuba and began studying architecture in 1921. However, he soon abandoned his studies and turned to journalism, working at a number of leading magazines of the era, including *Social, Hispania,* and most notably *Carteles,* where he would remain a fixture until 1948. During this time, Carpentier also became involved in radical nationalist politics as a member of both the famous Protesta de los trece and the Grupo Minorista (1923). In 1927, he was one of the founders of the leading political and literary magazine of the period, *Revista de Avance* (1927–1930). Carpentier coined the term *lo real maravilloso,* later popularized as "magical realism." His most important works include *Music in Cuba* (1946), *The Kingdom of This World* (1949), *The Lost Steps* (1953), *Explosion in the Cathedral* (1962), and *Baroque Concert* (1974).

Fidel Castro (b. 1926). Born on August 13, 1926, Fidel Alejandro Castro Ruz has become a political and historical figure of truly mythic proportions, not only in the daily lives of Cubans everywhere but also across the Third World as a leading inspiration for the anticolonial and anti-imperialist struggles of the twentieth century. Consistently underestimated by his Cuban and North American enemies, Castro has now managed to retain power in Cuba for almost fifty years and has successfully defend his vision of a revolutionary society against constant external threat and periodic internal dissention. Unlike other Latin American caudillo dictators, Castro's iron hand is often covered by a velvet glove, permitting him to rule more often through his extraordinary rhetoric, often convincing ideology, and spellbinding charisma than with brute force and coercion (though he has not hesitated to resort to those when deemed necessary). Castro has also benefited from the convergence of three key sociopolitical and historical facts: the powerful, if often frustrated, nationalism of the Cuban people; the consistent and often arrogant attack on Cuban sovereignty by the United States; and the enactment of a successful program of social justice in Cuba since 1959.

Originally from the town of Birán in the eastern province of Oriente, Castro came of age as the son of the self-made sugar planter and Spanish immigrant, Ángel Castro. The economy of the area was dominated by U.S. mining and agricultural concerns, and early on Castro exhibited solidarity with the impoverished sugar workers in defiance of his powerful father. As a young man, Castro was sent to be educated first in Santiago and later in Havana, where he studied in private Catholic/Jesuit schools and excelled both in the classroom and at a wide array of sports, exhibiting a sense of discipline, dedication, and assertiveness, as well as a tireless work ethic, a fierce competitive streak, and an almost egomaniacal self-confidence that would serve him well in the years to come. Later, after entering the University of Havana to study law, he became involved in the often violent student-led political activities of the time, which frequently degenerated into gangsterism. Castro also showed an interest in international politics at this time, becoming involved in an ill-fated attempt to overthrow Dominican dictator Rafael Trujillo in 1947 and in the riots, known as the *Bogotazo,* that followed the assassination of populist leader Jorge Eliecer

Gaitán in Bogotá, Colombia, in 1948. One of his earliest and deepest intellectual influences was the Cuban nineteenth-century independence leader José Martí, whose speeches he memorized. While not a member of Cuba's Communist Party at this time, Castro was a radical nationalist influenced by anti-imperialism and European socialism.

In 1948, Castro married Mirta Díaz Balart, whose father and brother were both governmental officials under President Carlos Prío and later under the Batista dictatorship. This contentious relationship eventually led to the couple's divorce, though the marriage produced one son, Fidel Castro Díaz Balart (known in Cuba as Fidelito). Castro later quietly remarried, to Dalia Soto del Valle, a schoolteacher he met in the mid-1960s with whom he has fathered five children. By 1951, Castro had become a leader in the growing populist political movement led by the Partido del Pueblo Cuban (known as the Ortodoxo Party), an anti-Communist nationalist group aimed at combating corruption and implementing major social, economic, and political reforms. However, in 1951, Ortodoxo leader Eduardo Chibás commited suicide leaving his movement leaderless. Unable to run for congressional office in the canceled elections of 1952 because of Batista's coup, Castro organized an unsuccessful raid on the Moncada Army barracks on July 26, 1953. After famously declaring in his defense speech that "History will absolve me" for the uprising, he was eventually amnestied from prison two years later, regrouping his guerrilla forces in Mexico. He clandestinely invaded Cuba at the end of 1956 and two years later marched triumphantly into Havana as the wildly popular leader of a wide and ideologically diverse revolutionary coalition.

Upon the triumph of the revolution in 1959, Castro could count on the goodwill of the vast majority of Cubans who had supported his movement as a means of overthrowing Batista. However, as he began to consolidate his power and push through a number of increasingly radical socio-economic reforms the Cuban bourgeoisie began to criticize his rule, demanding elections, a return to constitutional rule, and the reinstitution of civil and political rights. On the other hand, the majority of Cubans saw social justice as the primary goal and supported a more throughgoing revolution that would include a major restructuring of society. Initially taking on the post of commander in chief of the armed forces in January 1959, Castro soon took over as Cuba's prime minister, serving in that capacity from 1959 until 1976, when he officially became president. Throughout his rule but especially during the 1960s, Castro's authority has been based on his formidable gifts of personal charisma and courage, powerful and contagious self-confidence, talents as an orator and political strategist, and his unique ability to inspire unwavering loyalty in his followers. He has been especially talented at rising to seemingly insurmountable challenges and thrives under pressure, repreatedly transforming almost certain defeats into victories. At the same time, he has tended to reject alternative views out of hand. He associates dissent with sedition, represses all alternative political groups and movements, and refuses to allow any political debate or competition outside of the narrow confines of the revolution. His almost absolute confidence in his own vision and decisions has led to numerous disastrous mistakes, especially in economic planning. Finally, given his omnipresence in all areas of Cuban governance and planning, one wonders wheather he has been able to build institutions that will continue to function after his death.

From 1976 until July 2006, Castro concurrently held the powerful governmental posts of president of the Council of State and the Council of Ministers, and was first secretary of the Cuban Communist Party. While his rule has been dogged by accusations of tyranny, abuse of human rights, and economic incompetence, Castro has also distinguished himself as a consummate political operator on the world stage, leading successful interventions in Africa and offering aid and inspiration to leftist regimes across the world. Perhaps his greatest geopolitical achievement, however, is his sheer survival decade-after-decade just 90 miles from the most powerful country in the world—a country whose expressed policy objective has long been his ouster or assassination. Many also laud the social, health, and educational programs that have flourished under Castro's leadership. His long and often tense relationship with the Soviet Union guaranteed Cuba an economic and ideological lifeline when most of the rest of the Western Hemisphere had cut communist Cuba off. More recently, Castro's Cuba has managed to survive the collapse of most of the rest of the communist bloc. He has also successfully cultivated new, strategically important allies in a rising China and Chávez's oil-rich Venezuela. Although long seen as impervious to the frailty of old age, a recent grave illness has caused him to temporarily cede power to his younger brother, Raúl, indicating that his rule may soon be over. His controversial legacy, however, is sure to loom large in Cuba's future.

Raúl Castro (b. 1931). At Fidel Castro's side since the very beginnings of his political career, Raúl Castro Ruz was born on June 3, 1931, also in Birán, to Angel Castro and his second wife and former cook, Lina Ruz. Active as an ideologically committed communist much earlier than his older brother, Raúl accompanied Fidel in his attack on Moncada, in prison on the Isle of Pines, and in exile in Mexico in the mid-1950s. It was Raúl who introduced Fidel to the Argentine doctor and revolutionary Ernesto "Che" Guevara in Mexico. During the guerrilla war, Raúl was given the title of "comandante" and led a guerrilla column in northeast Oriente province, where he united the many disparate anti-Batista forces and established a public works corps, health unit, functioning air base, and munitions productions facility. Just after the triumph of the revolution, Raúl was appointed minister of the revolutionary armed forces by his older brother, a post he has held for the past forty-seven years. In addition to being armed forces minister, Raúl holds the second most powerful position in virtually every major governmental organization, including the Cuban Council of State and the Council of Ministers; he is the vice secretary of the Politburo and the Central Committee of the Communist Party of Cuba. In August 2006, Raúl took over as acting president and commander in chief, while Fidel underwent emergency surgery. As of this writing in July 2007, he has managed the country's affairs with efficiency and diligence, but without any of the charisma or public persona of his older brother.

Carlos Manuel de Céspedes (1819–1874) and the "Grito de Yara." Born in Bayamo, Oriente, on April 18, 1819, Carlos Manuel de Céspedes traveled to Spain to study law in 1840. After extensive travels in Europe and the Middle East, he returned to Cuba in 1844 and opened a law practice in his hometown. He soon became caught up in politics as Spain refused to grant Cuba even limited reforms. His political activity landed him in prison on numerous occasions between 1852 and 1855. Inspired by Narciso López's failed filibustering attempts in the early 1850s, Céspedes began to organize a war for independence under the cover of his membership in a Masonic lodge. When Spain was thrown into chaos during its own "glorious revolution" of 1868, Céspedes hastily declared Cuban independence on October 10, 1868. On that date, Céspedes assembled his supporters as well as his slaves at his own sugar plantation, La Demajagua, near the town of Yara, and proclaimed Cuba's sovereignty in his historic address, the "Grito de Yara." Soon thereafter he freed his slaves, adding them as foot soldiers in his growing rebel army, and took the town of Bayamo from the Spanish. Calling for universal suffrage, complete independence from Spain, and the liberation of all of Cuba's slaves (with indemnification for slave owners), Céspedes immediately met resistance from his more conservative supporters who favored annexation to the United States. Céspedes also antagonized the more liberal members of his coalition, led by Ignacio Agramonte, by hedging on the immediate freedom for all of Cuba's slaves and assuming near absolute civil and military control of the independence movement. He managed to quell this rising dissension temporarily and was elected president of the Cuban Republic in Arms in April 1869 at the Guáimaro Convention. However, he was deposed in 1873 and killed a year later by Spanish troops. Céspedes is honored today as a "father of the Cuban nation." His grandson of the same name served briefly as an appointed, compromise president after Gerardo Machado was overthrown in 1933. Another descendant, also sharing the same name, is currently the vicar-general of Cuba's Catholic Church.

Eduardo Chibás (1907–1951). A longtime Auténtico Party member during the late 1930s and early 1940s, Eduardo "Eddie" A. Chibás became its most vociferous critic during the final years of that decade, making it his vocation to expose the party's extensive corruption each week in his national radio broadcasts. After breaking with the Auténtico Party, Chibás started the Orthodox Party (Partido del Pueblo Cubano—Ortodoxo), of which a young Fidel Castro was an early member. As head of the Ortodoxos, Chibás was set to run for president in 1952. However, unable to prove his accusations of corruption against Auténtico politician Aurelio Arango, Chibás killed himself at the end of his last live radio broadcast on August 5, 1951, making a "last call" to the Cuban people to rise up and root out governmental corruption.

Ciénaga de Zapata (Zapata Swamp). Bordering the southern coast of Cuba in the province of Matanzas, the Ciénaga de Zapata is the Caribbean's largest wetland. Similar to the Florida Everglades, it is an extremely important reserve for a variety of flora and fauna unique to Cuba, including the

Cuban crocodile, many species of bird, and countless plants and flowers. Because it borders on the Bay of Pigs to the east/southeast, its impassable terrain became a crucial factor in the defeat of the exile invasion of Cuba in April 1961.

The Conquest of Cuba: Diego Velásquez (1465–1524), Hernán Cortés (1485–1547), Bartolomé de Las Casas (1484–1566), and Hatuey (d. 1512). The conquest of Cuba, led by Diego Velásquez de Cuéllar, and the subsequent epic conquest of Mexico, led by Velásquez's one-time secretary and longtime protege, Hernán Cortés, are often understood as expeditions carried out at the direct instruction of the Spanish Crown. In fact, it was the restless, ambitious conquistadors themselves who often paid for and instigated such costly and potentially lucrative adventures of conquest, occasionally in direct violation of royal orders—or at least without expressed royal permission. That fact led to heated rivalries between competing conquistadors, as was the case between the one-time friends and near relatives, Velásquez and Cortés. Velásquez went so far as to order the arrest and deportation of Cortés back to Santo Domingo after discovering that Cortés had been lobbying for an increase in the permitted number of Indians allowed to each landowner (*encomendero*). Later, Velásquez placed Cortés in jail for breaching his promise to marry Catalina, a fellow Spanish colonist who indeed would later become Cortés's first wife. Thus, it is quite surprising that when it came time for Velásquez to select a captain to lead a reconnaissance mission to Mexico, following two previous exploratory missions in 1517 and 1518, he turned to the wealthy and able, but scheming and unpredictable, Cortés. Velásquez quickly came to regret his decision, however, and even tried to prevent Cortés from departing from Santiago on November 18, 1518. However, a letter Velásquez sent to Luis de Medina, stripping Cortés of his commission and transferring it to Medina, was intercepted by Cortés's brother-in-law, Juan Suárez. Getting wind of his reversal of fortune, Cortés made hasty preparations to depart. Despite all this political intrigue, it seems that Cortés did in the end leave Cuba with Velásquez's tacit, if grudging, approval. Nevertheless, Cortés went on to violate nearly every prohibition outlined in his commission (committing blasphemy, sleeping with native women, playing cards, taking Cuban Indians along with him, treating the Mexican Indians harshly, and even sleeping ashore in these new lands). As a result of what he judged as wanton insubordination, Velásquez sent another conquistador, Narváez, after Cortés to arrest him and bring him back to Cuba in chains. That strategy backfired when Cortés convinced Narváez to join him in his conquest of the Aztecs in Mexico.

Upon assuming the role of first governor of Cuba in 1512, Diego Velásquez sought to pacify the country's natives while simultaneously ending wanton massacres, since natives were desperately needed as laborers. Velásquez's most important, if unwitting, ally in achieving this goal was a former *encomendero* from the island of Hispaniola who had since become a priest in 1510. His name was Bartolomé de Las Casas. Knowing from bloody experience the cost the Taínos would pay for resistance, Las Casas would often try to convince them to cooperate with the conquistadors. This marriage of convenience between Velásquez and Las Casas was short-lived, however, and as time went by, the friar became more vociferous in his condemnation of Spanish abuses. In his lifetime Las Casas wrote many volumes and fought many legal battles in Spain in defense of the essential humanity of the natives. He succeeded in finally having the *encomienda* system abolished in Cuba in 1542; it was replaced in that year with a set of New Laws intended to govern the Indies. Las Casas was later named bishop of Chiapas, Mexico, and official protector of the Indians. Of all the pages Las Casas wrote and the many sometimes wildly exaggerated claims of abuse he recounted, perhaps the most legendary is his dramatic retelling of the resistance and eventual capture and execution

of the Taíno cacique Hatuey. Even though Hatuey is still celebrated today in Cuba as a symbol of native resistance, he was
in fact an immigrant to Cuba himself, coming to the island, in
Las Casas's words, "to flee the calamities and inhuman acts of
the Christians" in his homeland of Hispaniola to the east.
Upon arrival in Cuba, Hatuey decided that the Spaniards persecuted them because they wanted them to worship their
God. Hoping to protect themselves, Hatuey and his followers
proceeded to give honor to the Spanish God by dancing
around a basket of gold, thinking that it must be their God.
Later, realizing that the Spanish would eventually kill them if
they discovered that they possessed such riches, the Taíno
threw their gold into a nearby river. Nevertheless, the Spanish eventually captured Hatuey; before burning him alive on
February 2, 1512, they offered him a Christian baptism.
When the Spanish told him that the flames of the stake were
nothing compared with the flames of everlasting damnation,
Hatuey asked the Franciscan priest Juan de Testín, "Do all
Christians go to Heaven?" When the priest replied that they
did, Hatuey refused baptism, declaring that he preferred Hell
to having ever again to endure the cruelty and wickedness of
such Christians. Inadvertently, the Spaniards had given Cuba
its first martyr for independence.

The Cuban Missile Crisis, October 1962. Known in Cuba
as *La crisis de octubre* ("The October Crisis"), what became
known in the United States as the Cuban Missile Crisis began
as a result of the continued threat of U.S. invasion after the
failure of the Bay of Pigs a year and a half earlier. Castro suggested signing a military pact with the Soviet Union as a way
to keep the Americans at bay. However, when the Soviets proposed to back up this public pact with the secret plan of placing Soviet nuclear missiles on the island, Castro agreed. His
only misgiving, however, was what would happen if the missiles were discovered prior to their being fully operational.
As it turned out, Castro feared exactly what eventually

happened: The missiles were discovered prematurely by the United States, and their fate (and that of Cuba) was completely out of his hands since control over the missiles and negotiations with the United States took place through Moscow, not Havana. Discovering the existence of the bases on October 21, Kennedy made a national address the next day, demanding that the Soviets remove the missiles and declaring that the United States would "quarantine" the island of Cuba (since a "blockade" was against international law). After a long wait and a confusing exchange of secret, contradictory diplomatic notes, Khrushchev took Kennedy's offer and decided to remove the missiles. However, because he did not first consult Castro, Soviet-Cuban relations suffered. Off the record, the United States promised not to invade Cuba and to deactivate its obsolete missiles in Turkey.

The Dance of the Millions, 1920–1921. Following World War I, during which the United States had kept the price of sugar artificially low at 4.6 cents per pound, the Anglo-American committee removed all price controls on Cuba's principal export in 1919. As a result, in the first half of 1920 literally millions of dollars were made as the price of sugar rose to 10 cents a pound by March, reaching 23 cents per pound in May. However, the sugar "boom" soon became a sugar "bust" with the proverbial *vacas gordas* (fat cows) of May becoming the *vacas flacas* (skinny cows) of December, with prices back below 4 cents per pound. The resulting wave of bankruptcies led to an increase in the number and size of large sugar estates, forcing many small planters of Cuba's rural middle class to sell their land to foreigners. Surviving mill owners began to look abroad for foreign labor from Jamaica and Haiti to ensure their dwindling profit margin.

José Antonio Echeverría (1933–1957). Only twenty-four years old when he was killed in 1957 in the aftermath of a failed student-led assassination attempt on Fulgencio Batista, José

Antonio Echeverría was the leader of the Directorio Revolucionario Estudiantil (DRE). One of the main urban underground groups of the 1950s, the DRE was essentially a terrorist organization dedicated to assassination and sabotage in the mold of the student-let underground groups of the early 1930s. Emerging out of the Federation of University Students (FEU), the DRE and its talented organizational leader Echeverría had had their differences with Castro and his 26th of July Movement and counted on clandestine support from the underground Auténtico organization to carry out their doomed attack on the presidential palace on March 13. While 150 armed young men fought their way inside the palace, Echeverría led a takeover of a radio station from where they planned to broadcast news of Batista's death. In fact, Echeverría did just that (though the station had already gone off the air), before fleeing into a barrage of police gunfire that ended his life.

La Escalera Conspiracy and Massacre. What is known as the Escalera conspiracy took place in 1843–1844 and constituted the most important uprising of the nineteenth century between the 1812 Aponte rebellion and the first war for independence in 1868. Although it is known historically as a "conspiracy," it is unclear whether the various slave uprisings that struck Cárdenas and Matanzas in 1843 were in fact part of a larger, coordinated movement. What is clear is that the various slave rebellions exacerbated the almost hysterical fear among Cuban whites that they were being overwhelmed in number by African slaves. Guarding against a slave uprising that would turn Cuba into another Haiti, Spanish captain-general Leopoldo O'Donnell granted his Comisión Militar Ejecutiva unchecked powers to unleash a reign of terror not only against the rebellious slaves themselves but also on the free black and mulatto population. In the carnage that followed, more than 300 blacks and mulattoes (slave and free alike) were killed, with many others fleeing into exile.

Tomás Estrada Palma (1835–1908). Involved in efforts for Cuban independence from as early as 1873 and later recruited by José Martí to serve as an agent for Cuban independence in New York, Tomás Estrada Palma was the first president of an independent Cuba, serving from 1902 until the second American intervention in 1906. Although born in Cuba, Estrada Palma spent the majority of his adult life living in exile in the United States. He was a U.S. citizen when he returned to Cuba to run for president and therefore had a great appreciation of that country and its role in securing Cuban independence. He also had many enemies in Cuba during his term as president and is vilified today by Cuba's Communist government as a pawn of the United States.

Máximo Gómez (1836–1905). Born in the Dominican Republic and originally trained as a soldier to defend Spanish rule in that country against neighboring Haiti and later in Cuba, Máximo Gómez y Báez changed sides to support the Cuban rebels after arriving there in the 1860s. Along with Antonio Maceo, he became the chief Cuban general opposing Spanish forces during both the Ten Years' War (1868–1878) and the later Cuban War for Independence (1895–1898). He is the only general to have served in and survived both conflicts. Many suggested him as the ideal candidate for president in 1901, but he declined to be nominated, partly because he felt that his Dominican birth should disqualify him. However, he was granted Cuban citizenship before he died in his villa outside Havana in 1905.

The Elián González Affair, 1999–2000. Elián González is the only child of Elizabet Brotóns and Juan Miguel González. After his parents' divorce, Elián lived with his mother but maintained a close relationship with Juan Miguel. Brotóns soon developed a romantic relationship with a man named Rafa who was a resident of Miami and had become a migrant

Built during the international custody battle over the child Elián González, this statue depicts José Martí holding his young son and pointing accusingly at the U.S. Interest Section in the distance. It was meant to represent the right of Cuban fathers, and the Cuban nation, to raise their children as they saw fit. However, with their characteristic mockery, Cubans often joke that Martí is actually whispering to the child, "Go that way toward freedom!" (Ted Henken)

smuggler illegally ferrying passengers from Cuba to the United States for a fee. In November 1999, he loaded a group of four-teen other passengers onto a motorboat and set off for Florida. En route the boat capsized, killing Brotóns, Rafa, and all but three other passengers. The following day five-year-old Elián was discovered floating on a piece of wreckage and was brought to Miami to recover. His father's Miami relatives were notified of his arrival, and he was placed in their custody. Over the next six months, an international custody dispute raged between the boy's Miami relatives, who wanted him to stay with them after his mother's death, the father in Cuba, who wanted him returned to the island, and the U.S. and Cuban governments. The immigration and child custody bat-tle came to a dramatic climax on April 22, 2000, when U.S. federal agents raided the home where Elián was staying after his Miami relatives repeatedly refused to heed rulings that he be released to federal officials. After extensive legal efforts on the part of Elián's Miami relatives failed, Juan Miguel was eventually allowed to come to the United States in the sum-mer of 2000 to retrieve his son. They returned together to Cuba on June 28, 2000. As a result of the whole affair, many members of the Cuban-American community in Miami felt betrayed by the U.S. government, while their often emotional struggle to keep the child in the United States tainted their image for most other Americans.

Ramón Grau San Martín (1887–1969). One of the most tragic figures of the Cuban republic, Ramón Grau San Martín was trained as a medical doctor and eventually came to serve as dean of the Medical School of the University of Havana in the early 1930s. From that post, he was nominated by a group of radical students to join the five-man revolutionary junta (*pentarquía*) in September 1933. After the junta dissolved, Grau served as president of Cuba for the next 100 days until he was ousted by Army chief of staff Fulgencio Batista. In early

Looking westward from the statue of Jose Martí, one can see the faux palm trees and arches of the Tribuna Abierta Anti-Imperialista José Martí, *with the U.S. Interest Section in the distance. Tired of constant political mobilizations and propaganda, however, Cubans have privately rechristened this area* el protestódromo *(the protest-o-drome). (Ted Henken)*

1934, Grau went into exile, where he formed the Auténtico Party. He returned to Cuba in 1940 to participate in the drafting of the new constitution and to run against Batista for president. Although he lost that contest, he ran again in 1944 and won, serving as president until 1948. Many Cubans hoped that his return would mean a realization of the ideals of the frustrated nationalist revolution of 1933. However, Grau's administration was tainted by cynicism, nepotism, and corruption.

Guantánamo Bay Naval Base. Affectionately referred to by U.S. military personnel as "Gitmo," the U.S. Naval Base at Guantánamo Bay has straddled the entryway to the much larger Inner Bay of Guantánamo, 21 miles south of the city of Guantánamo itself, since February 19, 1903. On that date the original Platt Amendment that established the base was transformed into a permanent treaty and signed by presidents Tomás Estrada Palma and Theodore Roosevelt. The formal handover of the base took place ten months later aboard the USS *Kearsarge,* then anchored in the bay, on the symbolic date of December 10, 1903, exactly five years after the signing of the Treaty of Paris between the United States and Spain. The original purpose of the base was to serve as a strategic bulwark protecting the eastern approach to the Panama Canal, the construction of which began in 1904. Following the repeal of the Platt Amendment in 1934, a new agreement stipulated that the United States would hold the base for another ninety-nine years, the lease expiring only with mutual consent. Since 1960, Castro has refused to cash the annual lease checks, as a protest against U.S. control of sovereign Cuban territory. In the 1990s, the base has become perhaps more geographically and strategically important than ever, although U.S. military officials have concluded that it serves no clear military purpose. Between 1993 and 1996, the base held upward of 40,000 Cuban and Haitian refugees in a "safe haven." Later, the base temporarily housed various refugees from Kosovo and Cuba itself, and indefinitely detained enemy combatants from Al-Queda and the Taliban.

Ernesto "Che" Guevara (1928–1967). Born in Rosario, Argentina, Ernesto Guevara de la Serna, better known the world over as Che Guevara, suffered from asthma as a child and took refuge in his books. He also developed an iron willpower in his efforts to overcome his physical limitations. While studying medicine as a young man, Guevara made two trips across the continent of Latin America. After returning home to Buenos Aires from his first junket (later made famous in his *Motorcycle Diaries*) and graduating from medical school in 1953, he surprised his family by embarking on what would become a life of travel and revolutionary adventure. In search of meaning and undergoing a process of political formation and eventual radicalization, Guevara traveled to Bolivia, where he was disappointed to find that the country's so-called revolution had been compromised. After meeting the woman who would become his first wife, the Peruvian Marxist intellectual Hilda Gadea, Guevara moved on to

This triptych features three renderings of Ernesto "Che" Guevara. At the top is a three-peso bill with Che wielding a machete as he performs voluntary labor in Cuba's sugarcane fields. To the left is a commemorative 13-cent stamp issued in 1968 upon the first anniversary of Guevara's death in Bolivia. To the right is the massive visage of Guevara that acts as the façade of the Ministry of the Interior building on the Plaza of the Revolution. Like the stamp, the building intones Guevara's signature call to arms, Hasta la victoria siempre *(Onward ever toward victory). (Ted Henken)*

Guatemala in 1953 just in time to witness the overthrow of the reformist Jacobo Arbenz government by CIA-backed exile forces in 1954. After attempting to aid the falling government, Guevara fled frustrated to Mexico, where he would encounter his destiny.

In 1955 in Mexico City, Guevara was introduced to a group of Cuban exile revolutionaries. One fateful night at a party, he was presented to the group's leader, Fidel Castro, with whom he spent the rest of the evening engaged in a marathon one-on-one political discussion. By morning, Guevara had agreed to join the group as its medic and commenced an intense period of training in the mountains on the outskirts of the capital. In late November 1956, Guevara departed Mexico on board the U.S. yacht *Granma* in the company of more than eighty fellow rebels en route to Cuba. He was the only non-Cuban. After a disastrous landing in the swampy foothills of the Sierra Maestra, Guevara managed to regroup with the small band of remaining guerrillas, which included both Fidel and Raúl Castro. Over the next two years, Guevara distinguished himself as a brave and loyal member of the rebel force, exchanging his role as medic for one of military leadership as a *comandante*.

After the triumph of the revolution in January 1959, Guevara took on many unpleasant and sometimes hidden tasks deemed necessary to consolidate revolutionary rule, including the execution of those considered war criminals and the planning for an eventual more institutional role of communism in the country. Guevara was named the director of Cuba's National Bank and later head of the industrial department of the National Institute of Agrarian Reform (INRA). After 1964, however, Guevara became increasingly frustrated with these bureaucratic tasks.

Eager to spread the success of the Cuban Revolution to other lands and possibly at odds with Castro over the proper political orientation and strategy that the revolution should take, Guevara began to focus his efforts on bringing revolutionary change to Africa and Latin America. After a frustrating guerrilla experience in the Congo in 1965, Guevara secretly returned to Cuba and soon departed for Bolivia in disguise, in order to lead a guerrilla force there. Receiving little support from either the Bolivian peasantry or the country's Communist Party, Guevara's small guerrilla *foco* became disoriented and divided by mid-1967. Guevara himself was captured on October 8, 1967, and executed by the Bolivian military the next morning. He has since become a potent symbol of social justice and radical social change to many progressive groups around the world.

Nicolás Guillén (1902–1989). Born in Camagüey, Nicolás Guillén was a mulatto writer who is considered the national poet of twentieth-century Cuba. His extensive body of work spanned the republican and revolutionary eras and encompassed elements of Modernismo, folklorism, social protest, and, most important, *poesía negrista*. A committed and active member of the Communist Party long before the revolution, in his poetry Guillén frequently addressed the topics of racism and U.S. cultural and economic imperialism in Cuba. He is best-known for his two early books of poetry, *Motivos de son* (1930) and *Songoro Cosongo* (1931), and the more mature work done after the triumph of the revolution, *El gran zoo* (*The Great Zoo,* 1967) and *El diario que a diario* (*The Daily Diary,* 1972).

Antonio Guiteras (1906–1935). The revolutionary government set up in September 1933 as a result of the sergeants' revolt was not only divided between civilian Ramón Grau and military Fulgencio Batista. It was also internally divided between moderates from the Student's Directorate and the more radical members of the Unión Revolucionaria led by Antonio Guiteras Holmes. In many ways, it was Guiteras's revolutionary program that was enacted during the short-lived 100 days of Grau's incumbency. Guiteras was essentially the motor that gave direction to the administration, serving as its minister of the interior, war, and navy, positions that allowed him nominal civilian control over the country's armed forces (military and police). Guiteras was especially enamored of using direct, violent action in a context in which electoral politics itself was thinly veiled gangsterism. Although not a communist, Guiteras was perhaps Cuba's most radical and resourceful political leader between Julio Antonio Mella of the 1920s and Fidel Castro after the 1950s. After fleeing into exile when the revolutionary government of 1933 was overthrown by Batista, Guiteras returned clandestinely and founded a new nationalist/socialist–oriented political movement that he named Joven Cuba. He was killed in 1935 while trying to escape into exile once again.

José Lezama Lima (1910–1976). Often referred to as the Marcel Proust of the Caribbean, José Lezama Lima was the intellectual leader of his generation. He is best-known as the founding editor of the leading literary magazine of the republican period, *Orígenes* (1944–1956), and as the author of the novel *Paradiso* (*Paradise,* 1966). Although he was given a number of symbolic posts in the revolutionary government's cultural institutions, his works were largely ignored in Cuba after 1959 because of his apolitical aesthetic approach and his thinly veiled homosexuality.

Antonio Maceo (1845–1896). Known to Cubans as the Bronze Titan, mulatto General Antonio Maceo played a major role in both of Cuba's major nineteenth-century wars of independence, the Ten Years' War (1868–1878) and the Independence War (1895–1898). One of the most popular figures in Cuban history, Maceo is revered for his intelligence, bravery (he is known to have suffered twenty-four battle wounds), and his unbending defense of the principles of complete independence, the abolition of slavery, and equal treatment for all

Cuban rebel fighters. Born in Santiago in 1845, Maceo and his brothers joined Céspedes's first war for independence in October, just weeks after the start of hostilities. Although just twenty-four years old, Maceo became a field commander after only five months, and was soon promoted to lieutenant colonel. Because of his growing popularity and intelligence, some of the more conservative members of the liberation army accused him of seeking to establish a "black republic" after the model of Haiti. Though he vociferously denied any such aims, this dissension contributed to the failure of the war in 1878. Maceo is remembered today for his protest of the peace of Zanjón that ended the first war and for the effective struggle he waged in western Cuba during the second independence war. Following his father and many of his brothers, Maceo died in battle on December 7, 1896.

Gerardo Machado (1871–1939). A former general in the Cuban War for Independence, Gerardo Machado y Morales was elected the fifth president of Cuba in 1924 as a populist reform candidate on the platform "Water, roads, and schools." Intent on modernizing Cuba, he set to work constructing the central highway, but his election coincided with a fall in world sugar prices; he quickly began to resort to autocratic methods to impose his vision of progress on the country. As opposition to his tactics increased, so did his brutality. In fact, his administration holds the distinction of coining the phrase *la ley de fuga* ("shot while trying to escape"), which was the explanation given when a political prisoner was found dead. As he became increasingly unpopular, he forced Congress to modify the constitution, granting him a second term and postponing new elections until 1935. However, he was not to make it that far. As economic conditions worsened in the early 1930s, protest against his corrupt rule exploded. The United States felt obliged to convince Machado to leave quietly and sent Sumner Welles to negotiate his resignation in the summer of

Standing astride Havana's Malecón is the monument to the 266 American sailors who perished aboard the USS Maine in 1898. The monument, constructed in 1926, features two of the original cannons rescued from the sunken ship but is missing the busts of the three American politicians most responsible for American involvement in Cuba at the turn of the century: President William McKinley, Leonard Wood, the first administrator of the island, and famed "Rough Rider" President Theodore Roosevelt. The monument is also missing the imperial eagle that once crowned its twin pillars. The busts and eagle were removed in protest in 1961. The eagle's mangled remains can be found in a downtown museum. A replica of the eagle stands guard in the backyard of the home of the Chief of the U.S. Interest Section in western Havana. (Ted Henken)

1933. However, a national strike forced him out before Welles could negotiate a smooth transition.

The Explosion of the USS *Maine*, 1898. The USS *Maine* was a U.S. battleship sent to Havana harbor in the winter of 1898 after sympathizers with the Spanish cause began a series of riots in the city. On the evening of February 15 the battleship exploded, killing 266 U.S. sailors, nearly all those aboard at the time. It was clear from the start that the ship's own five tons of powder charges had exploded. However, what was unclear for many years (and is still a mystery to some) is what ignited the charges. The basic debate was whether the explosion was caused by heat from coal on the inside of the vessel or from an external source, such as a Spanish mine. Soon after the explosion, a U.S. Naval inquiry determined that a mine had caused the explosion. That, of course, made the explosion an act of war and propelled the United States directly into war with Spain, with the rallying cry "Remember the Maine, to Hell with Spain!" However, later studies, especially one concluded in 1976 by U.S. Admiral Hyman Rickover, concluded that the tragedy was more likely caused by a fire in the coal bunker.

The Mariel Boatlift, 1980. Taking place over a period of a little more than six months in the summer of 1980, the Mariel boatlift was the most massive and dramatic exodus of emigrants from Cuba in the island's history. In the late 1970s, Cuba had begun to allow family visits for the first time since 1959; that, combined with the lack of a practical means for potential emigrants to leave the island, helped to increase the pressure on many to leave the country. The trigger that unleashed this wave of 125,000 refugees, however, was the spontaneous crashing of the gates of the Peruvian embassy in mid-April by a number of desperate Cubans who had hijacked a bus. After the Peruvian ambassador refused to turn over the gatecrashers, Castro removed the Cuban guard from the embassy. In a matter of hours, the grounds of the embassy were filled with more than 10,000 expectant Cubans hoping to leave the island. This trickle became a flood, however, when Castro declared that anyone wanting to leave for the United States could join the "parasites, lumpen, criminals, and scum" at the embassy. U.S. president Jimmy Carter responded by giving an "opened armed welcome" to all potential Cuban refugees. For their part, Cubans in Miami responded by setting out for Cuba en masse to collect their relatives. The Cuban government directed all potential emigrants to the Port of Mariel, west of Havana, where they could wait for their relatives. Unbeknownst to the relatives, however, the government also allowed many convicted criminals out of prison with the understanding that they, too, would emigrate. Although they made up a very small proportion of the overall number of *Marielitos,* this criminal element tainted the overall image of the arrivals in the United States. Moreover, the Cuban government often forced the boat captains to take on these unknown passengers before they were permitted to board the people they had come to collect. This massive, spontaneous exodus ended on October 31, 1980.

José Martí (1853–1895). Born José Julián Martí y Pérez on January 28, 1853, in Havana, Martí was the son of Spanish immigrants with his father a first sergeant in the Spanish army. In the more than 150 years since his birth, he has come to embody all that is pure, just, and right in Cuba's long-frustrated nationalist cause. If George Washington, Thomas Paine, Abraham Lincoln, Ralph Waldo Emerson, and Walt Whitman were rolled into a single individual, then we might have some idea of the importance that this man, reverently referred to by Cubans on both sides of the Straits of Florida as *el apóstol,* has for the divided and long-suffering Cuban nation.

Ironically for a man who would come to embody the fight for Cuban nationhood, Martí was arrested at the age of sixteen and sentenced to six years' hard labor but was deported from Cuba by the Spanish government for his separatist views within a year. He lived most of the rest of his life in itinerant exile between Spain, Central America, and the United States, and would return briefly to his native home only three times in his forty-three years of life—once under a false name in 1877, another time in 1878 only to be deported again to

Inside a massive mausoleum at the Santa Ifigenia Cemetery on the outskirts of Santiago de Cuba is the tomb of José Martí, draped with the Cuban flag. (Ted Henken)

Spain, and the final time in 1895 to lead the final War of Independence, in which he would meet his death.

Martí's significance as a writer, thinker, and political activist for the Cuban cause of independence and for the wider hemispheric Latin American cause of unity can scarcely be overestimated. While he distinguished himself during his lifetime as a teacher, journalist, editor and publisher, orator, political organizer, diplomat, translator, children's writer, and sometime novelist, Martí is perhaps best remembered today for a group of interrelated causes that sprang from the single unifying goal of his life: to see his beloved *patria* free from Spanish colonialism, U.S. imperialism, and Cuban despotism—in short, the achievement of *Cuba libre.*

Martí stood out from his Cuban contemporaries for his uncompromising yet inclusive and convincing stand for Cuba's absolute independence from Spain (as opposed to those who favored some kind of autonomy or self-rule under Spain). He also vehemently rejected the idea that Cuba's future lie in annexation to the United States. In fact, he spent the most extended period of his life (fifteen years) living, working, and planning revolution in New York City and in the process developed an intimate knowledge of American society, respect for its principles and progress, and healthy fear of its growing materialism and expansionism.

In his essay, "The Truth about the United States," Martí wisely wrote, "It is urgent that our America learn the truth about the United States. Its faults should not be deliberately exaggerated out of an urge to deny that it has any virtues, nor should they be concealed, or praised as virtues." In short, in his fight for Cuban independence, Martí aimed to avoid the enmity of his Spanish enemies and the greed of his American friends.

As critical Martí was of the United States' imperialist designs on the Cuban nation, he reserved his harshest condemnation for those among his fellow Cubans who would "bring a regime of personal despotism to my land, [and] take advantage of a great idea to serve [their] own personal hopes for glory or power." While Martí was a admirer and sometimes follower of the great South American independence fighters such as Simón Bolívar, he was also critical of their inability to combine their achievement of political independence with a project of social justice that would recognize and repair the great many social inequalities that plagued the continent. Thus, while he aimed at political independence for Cuba, he also sought to simultaneously create a nation "for all and for the good of all." In doing this, Martí is frustratingly difficult to pin down as a follower of any single, unified political ideology such as capitalist democracy, democratic socialism, or Marxist communism. He was a Freemason and subscribed to a philosophy of harmonious idealism.

It is also clear that while Martí admired Marx as an honorable fighter who "placed himself on the side of the weak," he thought the solution of violent revolution was more suited to Europe than Latin America. Due to such a tenuous and tentative political ideology, and since his untimely death denied him the opportunity to implement any specific political program in Cuba, different Cuban factions have repeatedly donned his mantle and claimed to represent the embodiment of his vision, especially since the Cuban Revolution of 1959 divided the Cuban nation into a fractured collection of hostile camps.

The final reason for Martí's transcendent importance has to do with his ability to articulate a proud, inclusive vision of hemispheric solidarity that rejected both the suspect Pan-Americanism that issued from the United States and the fawning imitation of European culture and institutions that were like twin cancers gnawing away at Latin America's own originality and potential greatness. Martí best expressed these convictions in "Nuestra América" ("Our America"), perhaps his most well-known essay in which he takes Latin America's political and military leaders to task for ignoring native traditions and instead "try to rule unique nations [. . .], with laws inherited from four centuries of free practice in the United States and nineteen centuries of monarchy in France." Instead, Martí insisted that:

> The history of America from the Incas to the present must be taught in its smallest detail, even if the Greek Archons go untaught. Our own Greece is preferable to the Greece that is not ours. We need it more. Statesmen who arise from the nation must replace statesmen who are alien to it. Let the world be grafted onto our republics, but we must be the trunk.

Related to this vision of "Latin" solidarity is Martí's role as one of the leading literary figures of his day, and as a poet in what was perhaps Latin America's first wholly unique literary movement, Modernismo. In all these ways, Martí strove to distinguish what he celebrated as the romantic, idealistic "our America," from what he considered the efficient and productive but overly practical, crass, and materialistic "other America" (the United States). Like the great Cemi, a deity worshiped by Cuba's native inhabitants and celebrated in the last line of his essay, "Nuestra América," Martí sought to plant the seeds of a new America with his writings and his revolutionary example; seeds that could blossom into a continent that would inspire pride in its throng of diverse inhabitants and demand respect both from the "other America" and from its former European colonial masters.

Julio Antonio Mella (1903–1929). Born Nicanor McPartland in Havana in 1903, Julio Antonio Mella was a charismatic student leader and orator and one of the founders of the first, international Cuban Communist Party in 1925. Because of his out-of-wedlock birth, Mella changed his name as a young man and eventually became the secretary of the Federation of University Students (FEU) at the University of Havana. He soon became involved in progressive, anti-imperialist activities in

Cuba and abroad. In 1924 he created the Anticlerical League, and the following year he founded the Cuban chapter of the Anti-imperialist League of the Americas. That same year he joined Carlos Baliño, Fabio Grobart, and others in the formation of Cuba's first Marxist-Leninist party with direct ties to Moscow. After being expelled from the university for his political activities and fearing for his life under the new Gerardo Machado presidency, Mella went into exile in Mexico in 1927. In 1929, Mella was assassinated (it is believed by Machado agents) in Mexico City while in the company of the Italian photographer Tina Modotti. He died later in the house of the Mexican painter Diego Rivera.

Moncada, July 26, 1953, and "History will absolve me." Planned to coincide with the final day of Santiago de Cuba's carnival celebration and 100 years after the birth of Cuban patriot José Martí, Fidel Castro's attack on the Moncada military barracks was as audacious as it was disastrous. The eighty-three-man attack force was immediately divided, with the majority being hunted down and brutally killed over the next few days. However, Batista's brutality came to Castro's aid when it came out that only eight rebels were killed in combat, while another sixty-one were in fact murdered in captivity. With that public relations victory in hand, Castro wisely turned his own trial a few months later into a surreal public indictment of the Batista regime. In his famous address, Castro listed the many needed reforms that his group would have enacted had they been successful. Then he meticulously outlined the crimes of the Batista regime, ending his defense with the ringing declaration, "Condemn me. It does not matter. History will absolve me." Given his seemingly democratic aims and his skills as an orator, Castro's words quickly spread across the country, catapulting him into the limelight.

Fernando Ortiz (1881–1969). Sometimes referred to as Cuba's "third discoverer" after Christopher Columbus and

Alexander von Humboldt, Fernando Ortiz Fernández was the leading anthropologist of twentieth-century Cuba and easily one of the most influential scholars of his generation. Trained as a lawyer, Ortiz both practiced and taught law in Cuba and was elected to the Cuban House of Representatives in 1917, serving until 1927. Later, his nationalist political activities against the Machado dictatorship forced him into exile in the United States in the early 1930s. Nevertheless, Ortiz is most famous for his reconceptualization of Cuban national identity as a rich mixture of African and European elements. Ortiz also coined the related anthropological concept of "transculturation" to describe the complex process that takes place when various cultures come together to form something distinct. Apart from his revalorization of Afro-Cuban culture, Ortiz's other major accomplishment was his 1940 book on the impact of sugar and tobacco in the socioeconomic life of the Cuban nation, *Cuban Counterpoint: Tobacco and Sugar.* He also wrote many ethnographic studies of Afro-Cuban language, religion, and music.

The Platt Amendment, 1902–1934. As the Cuban Constitution neared completion between 1900 and 1902, the United States required the Cuban constituent assembly to include in it the infamous Platt Amendment, giving the United States the right to intervene in Cuba's internal affairs in order to protect the island's security and sovereignty. While many Cubans objected to such mitigated sovereignty, others understood that the Platt Amendment was the price they had to pay in order to bring the four-year U.S. military occupation to an end. Originally conceived by U.S. Secretary of War Elihu Root, the amendment was proposed to the U.S. Congress by Senator Orville H. Platt and enacted in 1901. Its major provision was, "That the government of Cuba consents that the United States may exercise the right to intervene for the preservation of Cuban independence, the maintenance of a government adequate for the protection of life, property, and individual liberty." In the end, the amendment did exactly what it was presumably designed to protect against: It denied Cuba effective independence and made it a formal protectorate of a foreign power—the United States. That fact would hang like a dark cloud over the birth of the Cuban nation for the next thirty-two years, until the amendment was finally abrogated in 1934.

Pope John Paul II's visit to Cuba, February 1998. Given the fact that the Catholic Church is the only truly national institution in Cuba that is independent from the state, the visit of Pope John Paul II to Cuba in February 1998 was charged with more than spiritual meaning. For the Church, the visit represented an opportunity for the pope to address a number of pastoral, political, and practical issues. He reiterated his rejection of the U.S. embargo as a form of violence against the poor and vulnerable. However, he also spoke out against overzealous political control and enunciated a number of Catholic values at odds with communist dogma. He also attempted to open up a wider space on the island within which the Church could operate. He endorsed the primacy of family ties over political concerns, advocating for family reunification and reconciliation. Finally, John Paul II called on "Cuba to open itself to the world, and the world to open itself up to Cuba," indicating his belief that dialogue and flexibility were preferable to continued isolation and rigidity.

The Revolution of 1933. After years of increasingly corrupt and brutal dictatorship, President Gerardo Machado was forced out of office in the summer of 1933 by a general strike. In the political chaos that followed, a group of army sergeants joined forces with a group of radicalized university students and ousted the U.S.-sanctioned provisional president, Carlos Manuel de Céspedes. Over the next 100 days, a new, more radical administration came to power, led by Ramón Grau San Martín and Antonio Guiteras on one side, and Fulgencio

Batista on the other. The Grau/Guiteras "revolutionary" government of 1933 enacted many progressive reforms before being ousted by Batista with the implicit backing of the United States in January 1934.

José Antonio Saco (1797–1879). An early student of Father Félix Varela and a constant critic of Spanish rule in Cuba, José Antonio Saco worked tirelessly over the course of the nineteenth century to "whiten" Cuba. Unlike many of his intellectual contemporaries, however, Saco initially saw the solution to Cuba's racial and economic "problems" in eventual annexation to the United States. In 1928, together with Varela, Saco founded the publication *El Mensajero Semanal* (*The Weekly Messenger,* 1828–1831) in the United States, and later became the director of Cuba's influential *Revista Bimestre Cubana* (1932). However, his intellectual and political activities led to his deportation from Cuba by the Spanish government in 1834. Later in life he changed his stance on annexation and became the leader of the antiannexationist Reformist Movement. However, Saco never believed that Africans could be a part of his new "reformed" Cuba. He favored returning them to their homelands in Africa and shifting Cuba's economic and labor base away from plantation agriculture toward small, rural family farms owned and operated by a white peasantry.

The Sierra Maestra. Most famous as the strategic hideout and occasional battleground for Castro's guerrilla fighters during late 1956 and 1957, the Sierra Maestra begins at Cabo Cruz in Granma Province, east for 155 miles, dipping briefly at Santiago Bay, extending into Guantánamo Bay. The mountain range is home to Pico Turquino, Cuba's highest point at 6,474 feet above sea level. Throughout its history the Sierra Maestra suffered extensive deforestation from timbering, cattle ranching, and subsistence agriculture, before becoming a national park in 1980. The high altitude, cool climate, and rich soils make it ideal for coffee growing, and fully half of Cuban coffee is grown on its slopes.

The Special Period, 1990–present. Mainly as a result of the collapse of the Soviet Union, the Cuban economy entered a freefall in 1989 and did not reach bottom until 1993. During that time, foreign trade fell by 75 percent because as much as 70 percent had been concentrated with the USSR. Furthermore, Cuba's gross social product (a measure similar to GDP) fell perhaps 35 to 50 percent between 1990 and 1993. Twenty percent of the island's labor force was thrown out of work, and Cubans from all walks of life were forced to make major sacrifices in their standard of living. President Fidel Castro reacted by declaring a "special period" (*período especial*) to begin on August 30, 1990. Essentially a Faustian bargain, the economic reforms enacted during the early years (1990–1995) amounted to using elements of capitalism to save socialism. Some of the most important reforms included the expansion of foreign investment and international tourism, the reopening of private farmer's markets, a reorganization of agricultural cooperatives, an allowance of foreign remittances, the legalization of the use of the U.S. dollar, and the licensing of self-employment.

The 10-Million-Ton Sugar Harvest, 1970. In an all-out effort to free itself from economic dependency on the Soviet Union during the ideologically polarized Cold War, the Cuban government named 1969 the Year of the Decisive Struggle (*El año del esfuerzo decisivo*), while christening 1970, the Year of the Ten Million (*El año de los diez milliones*). This was an ultimately unsuccessful attempt to harvest the somewhat arbitrary goal of 10 million tons of sugarcane, harnessing Cuba's age-old agricultural resource. For an entire eighteen months, every available resource was recklessly diverted toward the singular goal of achieving the 10-million-ton goal. The failure of this massive undertaking led to the institutionalization of Cuban socialism under a more bureaucratic and pragmatic Soviet model.

The Ten Years' War (1868–1878). Launched by Carlos Manuel de Céspedes at his sugar plantation La Demajagua near the town of Bayamo in Oriente, Cuba's Ten Years' War for independence from Spain is most closely associated with the generals Máximo Gómez and Antonio Maceo. Although fought long and hard on both sides from 1868 to the culminating "bad peace" of 1878, the potential success of the war was compromised by strategic and socioeconomic differences among the rebels. The civil and military rebel leadership seemed constantly divided over exactly what their ultimate goal was (independence, annexation, or autonomy). Also, the issue of Cuba's sugar economy, based as it was on slave labor, prevented the rebels from gaining the necessary Cuban Creole support needed to defeat the Spanish troops. Finally, the Pact of Zanjón that ended the war was rejected by the war's rebel generals, with mulatto general Maceo making a formal protest at Baraguá that there could be no peace without independence and the complete abolition of slavery.

Father Félix Varela (1787–1853). Born in the Spanish city St. Augustine, Florida, to a Cuban-Spanish military family, Father Félix Varela y Morales did not arrive in Cuba until age fourteen. Against his father's wishes, he was ordained a priest in 1811 in Havana. Thereafter he quickly became Cuba's leading educator, teaching philosophy, chemistry, physics, theology, and music at the University of Havana. Although his tenure in Cuba was short, his influence on later nationalist political and cultural leaders was unquestionable, as his students included José Antonio Saco, Domingo del Monte, and José de la Luz y Caballero. Varela was elected to the Spanish legislature as a Cuban representative in 1821, where he took the unprecedented step of advocating for the independence of Spain's Latin American colonies. He also advocated Cuban self-rule and an end to slavery. While attending government consultations in Spain in 1823, these positions were interpreted as tantamount to sedition, and he was sentenced to death by the Spanish government. Varela escaped to Gibraltar, and from there he managed to flee aboard the cargo ship *Draper,* arriving in New York harbor on December 17, 1823. He spent the last decades of his life as the first prominent Cuban exile in the United States, ministering to and defending New York City's Irish Catholic immigrants for the next twenty-five years. While in exile, Varela worked as a journalist and published the nationalist newspaper *El Habanero,* which he sent into Cuba clandestinely. He also became vicar-general of the Catholic Church of New York in 1837, a position he used to condemn the anti-Catholic sentiment and denounce superstition and fanaticism within the Church itself. Varela died in his hometown, St. Augustine, Florida, on February 25, 1853, the same year in which Cuban patriot José Martí was born. Although originally buried in St. Augustine, his body was exhumed in 1912 and transferred to Havana, where it continues to lie in state in the Aula Magna of the University of Havana.

The Varela Project and Osvaldo Payá. Engineered by leading Cuban dissident Osvaldo Payá Sardiñas and his Christian Liberation Movement, the Varela Project took advantage of an obscure provision of the 1976 constitution that allowed citizens to propose new legislation provided they could come up with a minimum of 10,000 signatures. Apart from the main goal of the petition, which was to call for a referendum on the country's one-party system, the Varela Project reiterated many of the demands of previous dissident and human rights movements, including amnesty for political prisoners, freedom of speech and association, a private business sector, and an electoral law that would permit new elections. Payá delivered his petition, supported by 11,000 signatures, to Cuba's National Assembly in May 2002, just before former president

Jimmy Carter's plane touched down in Havana for his historic visit. Despite Carter's laudatory remarks about the Project (delivered in Spanish on Cuban national television and reprinted in the Communist Party newspaper the next day), Castro mobilized his considerable state security apparatus and much of the population in an effort to crush the petition by amending the constitution to make socialism officially "irrevocable."

The War of Cuban Independence (1895–1898) and the Spanish-American War (1898). The War of Cuban Independence was the second major struggle by Cuban rebels to win independence from Spain. Unlike the case with the previous Ten Years' War, the rebels were now no longer divided over the issue of slavery, which had ended in 1886. The war was waged brutally, with the rebels burning thousands of sugar-cane fields and Spanish general Valeriano Weyler enacting a murderous policy of reconcentration on the Cuban civilian population. The rebel side was dealt a terrible blow when both José Martí and General Antonio Maceo were killed in battle (in 1895 and 1896, respectively). Still the war raged on for more than a year longer, until the United States intervened in 1898, ostensibly against the Spanish, in what has come to be known as the Spanish-American War. The Spanish were soon defeated, losing nearly all their ships in the decisive Battle of Santiago Bay, and the U.S. (not Cuban) flag was raised over the Morro Castle in Havana after the Treaty of Paris on December 10, 1898.

Cuban Language, Food, Etiquette, and Holidays

LANGUAGE, NAMES, AND GREETINGS

Cubans speak Spanish, which, as a phonetic language, is written as it is spoken. However, there is great variation across the Spanish-speaking world. For example, you can happily (though not very easily!) *coger una guagua* ("catch a bus") in Cuba, but don't try to take a *guagua* in Bolivia or *coger* a bus in Mexico. In the first case, you might be arrested for kidnapping and in the second for indecent exposure! Despite this variation, native speakers of Spanish can be mutually understood almost anywhere in the Spanish-speaking world. Written Spanish is highly regular in its grammatical rules, syntax, and spelling. If you know even a little Spanish, you can make yourself understood in Cuba.

Alphabet, Pronunciation, and Basic Rules of Stress and Accent

Luckily, Spanish vowels each have only one sound. Use the following as a general guide to the sound of Spanish letters:

a is like the "a" in "father," but a bit shorter.

e is like the "e" in "bed," but never like the "e" in "behavior."

i is like the "ee" in "feet" or the "i" in machine, but never like "I" in "I love you."

o is like the "o" in "vote" or "phone," but never like the "o" in "operator."

u is like the "oo" in "food" or the "u" in "rule." However, when it carries the umlaut, as in "güiro" or "Camagüey," it is pronounced as a "w." This rule also applies to the "u" after an "h" or "g" as in "huevo" or "guajiro." (Incidentally, the "gua-" prefix is very common in Cuban Spanish, originating from the Taíno Arawak language.) If the "u" follows a "q" it is silent as in "quitar." It is also silent when it comes between a "g" and "e" or "i" as in "Guevara" or "guión."

y is considered a consonant except when standing alone (meaning "and") or ending a word. In those cases it is pronounced identically to the Spanish "i." If coming at the beginning of a word, it is similar to the English "y" but with a slight "j" sound as in "Yo" or "Yolanda."

Most Spanish consonants sound the same as their English equivalents. The **f, k, l, m, n, p, q, s, t, w,** and **x** generally follow this rule. Important exceptions include:

b and **v**—the sounds of these letters generally run together in Spanish to make a sound somewhere in between. To distinguish, Cubans might ask "*v de vaca*" or "*b de burro,*" or simply "*v corta*" or "*b larga.*"

c—is like the "c" in "cat" before "a," "o," or "u," as in "cuánto" or "comida," but like an "s" before "e" or "i," as in "cena" or "cita."

ch—carries the same sound as in English but until recently was considered a separate letter.

d—sounds the same as in English when coming at the start of a word as in "dolores" (pains) or "dólares" (dollars), otherwise the Spanish "d" often takes on a soft "th" sound as in "feather." This is especially pronounced when coming between vowels, as in "Teodoro."

h—is always silent—especially hard for English speakers to remember when coming at the start of words like "hay" (pronounced "ay") and "La Habana" (pronounced "Labana").

j—is much like the English "h," but stronger and more guttural. For example, a common expression of exasperation in Cuba is "¡no me *jodas!*" ("don't screw with me!"), pronounced HO-das.

k—does not exist in Spanish and is used only in foreign words.

ll—is like the "y" in "yellow" or "yes."

ñ—is like the "ny" in "canyon" or the "ni" in "onion."

r—is the same as in English except when beginning a word, as in "rápido" when it is trilled.

rr—is very strongly trilled, as in "guerra." Be careful, because these differences can change the meaning of a word in Spanish, as in "carro" (car) vs. "caro" (expensive). To practice the difference, try saying that you own an expensive car—*"un carro caro"* (remember adjectives normally come *after* the noun they modify, not before as in English). Better yet, practice the famous children's tongue-twister, *Erre con erre cigarro, erre con erre bárril, rápido corren los carros por la línea del ferrocarril.*

x—is almost always the same as "taxi" in English or "conexión" in Spanish, apart from the very rare exception when it takes on the sound of the English "h" as in "México" (ME-hi-co).

z—loses the buzzing sound it has in English and closely resembles the "s" in "soft" or "sun." Take for example the word "Zorro," which English-speakers pronounce with a "zzz" vibration at the start. In Spanish, the same word (which incidentally means "fox") loses the buzz and begins with the sound of "s" as in "snake."

Most non-Spanish speakers are scared away from the language by having to learn the proper placement of stress and the use of written accents. However, the rules for stress in Spanish are actually quite simple and consistent. Learning the rules is important, since words can change meaning based on stress and accent. For example, "jugo" means "juice," while "jugó" means "(he/she) played." Similarly, "si" means "if," while "sí" means "yes." If a word ends in a vowel, "n," or "s," the (natural) stress falls on the second-to-last syllable. Words with other endings (all consonants except "n" or "s"), carry a (natural) stress on the final syllable. Any word that departs from this rule must carry a written accent. For example, common words with natural stress include "comida" (co-MI-da), "hombre" (OM-bre), "vasos" (VAS-os), "mujer" (mu-HAIR), "vivir" (vi-VIR), and "actual" (ac-tu-AL)—and thus none of these words carry a written accent, though all have a (natural) stress.

Common words that must carry a written accent mark (often referred to as a *tilde*) include "lámpara" (LAM-pa-ra), "árbol" (AR-bol), and "unión" (un-i-ON). Incidentally, nearly all words ending in "-ión" in Spanish will carry an accent over the "o." Only vowels are given written accents, since they separate Spanish words into different stressed and unstressed syllables. For example, "co-MI-da," caries no accent mark but has a natural stress on the second-to-last syllable. In contrast, "lám-pa-ra," breaks the rule and so must carry a written accent on the third-to-last syllable. Finally, single syllable words, such as "si" and "sí," mentioned above use accents to distinguish between different meanings, not different sounds, since single-syllable words cannot carry stress. Likewise, certain words used in interrogatory sentences, such as "¿cuándo?," "¿cómo?," or "¿qué?," are distinguished by a written accent mark from the same-sounding words when they are used in declarative sentences: "cuando," "como," or "que."

Characteristics of Cuban Spanish

Despite such simple rules, understanding what Cubans are saying (especially when they are speaking with each other) can be a challenge. In Cuba, Spanish becomes a kind of fast-paced contact sport where informality, invention, word-play, coquettishness, satire, mockery, and speed are all highly regarded qualities. Moreover, Cuban Spanish vividly reflects the many transculturized ethnic and geographical influences absorbed by the island over its more than 500-year history. In Cuba, the Spanish of European conquistadores, colonists, and immigrants has been modified, enriched, and "Cubanified"—

if you will—by Taínos, Africans, North Americans, and many others over such a long time and to such a degree that Cubans no longer speak standard Spanish, but (as a Dominican friend of mine likes to joke) *Cubonix*. For this reason, I have always been fascinated, and sometimes baffled, by Cuban Spanish.

Two examples will suffice. Cubans love nicknames and use them lavishly. Any pronounced personal characteristic, it seems, will lead to an affectionate but often mocking *apodo* ("nickname"). These diminutive nicknames are tenacious, and before long you will have close friends whose real names you may not even know. There is even one infamous Cuban president, José Miguel Gómez (1908–1912), who is universally known to Cubans simply as *El Tiburón* ("The Shark") for his less-than-conscientious handling of the country's finances. Castro himself, often called simply "Fidel" by Cubans, is just as often referred to by one of his many nicknames: *El Comandante* ("The Commander"), *El Viejo* ("The Old Man"), or *El Caballo* ("The Horse"). Cubans are especially fond of nicknames that highlight a certain distinctive physical characteristic, and it is not uncommon to hear someone referred to in a way that might be cause for offense elsewhere: *Negrita* ("Blacky"), *Gordita* ("Fatty"), *Loqui* ("Crazy"), *El Chino* ("The Chinaman"), *El Gago* ("The Stutterer"), *Flaco* ("Skinny"), or *El Cojo* ("Limp"). My own Cuban wife has transformed the Cuban term for North American, *yuma* (Cubans don't use the term *gringo*), and taken to calling me *Yumi*.

For many years I had a taxi driver in Havana who was universally referred to (even by his own wife) as *Mechán*. He became a good friend and confidant as we often argued politics or counseled one another in matters of love. One day I thought to ask him his last name. He looked at me incredulously and said, "You know my last name. It's an American name, *Mechán!*" Not recognizing the name as American, I asked him to spell it out slowly, letter by letter. "Ernesto M-E-R-C-H-A-N-T," he said. When I responded, "Oh, MER-chant," pronouncing the name as it would be in English, he shot back,

"You Americans are always making fun of our English. Try to say this correctly in Spanish: *Éteque tacatrá.* I retorted that even I knew that was not Spanish. But Mechán insisted that it was. Gesturing over the driver's seat into the back of the cab and pointing to me, he repeated himself more slowly this time, *Éste que está acá atrás* ("This guy that is here in the back"). Now laughing, he said, "You see, that's perfect Spanish—at least here in Cuba!"

Having learned to speak a more formal Spanish while living and traveling in Ecuador and Mexico, I was ill prepared initially for the casual, even flirtatious attitude of Cubans and their signature rapid-fire Caribbean Spanish. In fact, Cubans are renowned among Latin Americans for their particular mode of dropping their voice at the end of phrases and even clipping words in half in order to communicate more quickly and with more personality and emotion. As the above phrase indicates, Cubans are especially notorious for swallowing their "Ss." Ironically, while Cubans often take great pride in the way they speak the language, other native speakers of Spanish often find Cuban Spanish strange, difficult to understand, overly informal, and even outright rude. I remember once standing obediently in line at a little cafeteria in Havana, going over my order word-by-word in my mind: *Discúlpame Señora, pero me gustaría pedirle un bocadito de croqueta y un batido de mamey por favor.* While I was lost in my thoughts, an old Cuban woman pushed past me to the front of the line and shouted, *Oye chica, dame un pan con croquetica con jugo de mamey!* She was gone with her order before I could get a word out of my mouth.

There is even a joke about a Cuban who has been given a small part in a play. He spends weeks repeating his single line over and over to himself: *Dios mío, hay un cadáver en el umbral del alcoba* ("My God, there is a cadaver in the entryway to the bedroom"). However, once on stage under the bright lights, with all eyes on him, the Cuban reverts to his tried and true Cuban Spanish, uttering, *¡Ñó, un mueto nla* *pueta de cuato!* ("S***, there's a dead guy in the doorway"). There is also a generational and geographical cleavage in the way Cubans speak the language, both within Cuba and between the island and its diaspora. Slang terms that have been popularized on the island over the past forty years, such as *asere* ("buddy"), are rejected as vulgar by the older generation both on the island and in exile.

Furthermore, there are innumerable *cubanismos* (words and idioms particular to Cuba) that distinguish Cuban slang and reflect the island's history, diverse cultural influences, and current reality. Common *cubanismos* today include *no es fácil* ("it ain't easy"), *ya tu sabe(s)* ("right on"), and *no cogas lucha* ("don't fight it"). There is also the infamous, universal, and multipurpose Cuban expression, *coño,* which though just four letters has innumerable variations, among which are the abbreviated *¡ñó!,* mentioned above, as well as the elongated *¡ñooooooo!* In fact, Cuban-American comic, businessman, and anti-Castro activist Guillermo Álvarez Guedes has an entire skit famously dedicated to the many nuances of *¡ñó!* These *cubanismos* can be described as "short sentences drawn from long experience," and in Cuba they have become almost an art form, known alternately as *refranes, adagios,* or, when used for the purpose of catching a woman's eye, *piropos* (one-liners/come-ons).

One common example of this last form is: *Oye linda, si cocinas como caminas, me como hásta la raspita* ("Hey beautiful, if you cook like you walk, I'll even eat the leftovers"). I remember once when I made the mistake of calling a Cuban *paladar* ("private restaurant") by phone and beginning the conversation by saying, *Hola, estoy buscando La mulata de sabor* ("The tasty mulata"), since that was the actual name of the place. The immediate response to my query was, *Ay mi niño lindo, es ella que habla* ("Oh my lovely child, that's who is speaking"). I spent the next half-hour engaged in coquettish banter with a woman twice my age and ended up with an invitation to dinner from a complete stranger. Cubans are notoriously forward (*atrevidos*), even when not trying to come on to you. Once, as I strolled leisurely down a street in Santiago de Cuba, I noticed an old man busily sweeping out his front room. Catching my eye and probably imagining what I was thinking, the man smiled and proudly declared, *Sé cocinar también, no ronco por la noche y chiflo una cuadra antes de llegar a la casa* ("I can cook too, don't snore at night, and whistle a block before arriving home")! Perhaps Cuban poet, patriot, and independence leader José Martí was the most prolific inventor of these powerful phrases. His, of course, are much less *atrevido* but no less powerful or witty. Some of his more memorable *refranes* include: *La patria necesita sacrificios; Es ara y no pedestal* ("The fatherland needs our sacrifice; It is an altar not a pedestal"); *Preferible es no ser, a no ser sincero* ("It is preferable not to be, than not to be sincere"); and *El dogma que vive de autoridad, muere de crítica* ("The dogma that lives from authority, dies from criticism").

Despite the great variation across Latin America and the Caribbean in Spanish phonology (sound), morphology (word structure), syntax (word order), and style (cadence and rhythm), there are two great language families in the region. One is "dynamic," an Andalusia-influenced "traderoute Spanish" that includes the Caribbean and other lowland, costal areas. The other is "static," the "viceregal Spanish" of Mexico, Peru, and other interior highlands. This explains why the linguistic characteristics of Cuban Spanish are very similar to those of other areas connected to the slave trade and the mercantilist commodity trade route of the colonial period, such as Andalucía, the Canary Islands, the Dominican Republic, Puerto Rico, and those costal or sugar regions of Mexico (Vera Cruz), Colombia (Cali, Cartagena, and Barranquilla), and Ecuador (Esmeraldas), which share similar histories.

Like the Spanish spoken in these other regions, Cuban Spanish is the result of a true transculturation of a variety of ethnolinguistic influences, the strongest of which are Southern Spain (Andalucía) and the Canary Islands, West Africa (Yoruba, Kikongo, Bantu, and as many as twenty other African ethnolinguistic groups), and the Arawak/Taíno. To these major constituent elements can be added two other less significant linguistic infusions: the more than 125,000 Chinese laborers who came to the island between the 1860s and the 1890s, and perhaps an equal number of black migrant workers who came to labor in Cuba's cane fields during the first half of the twentieth century, primarily from Jamaica and Haiti. I once met an elderly man sitting on a park bench in Santiago de Cuba who, after discovering that I spoke English, began reciting Marc Antony's speech from Shakespeare's *Julius Caesar,* "Friends, Romans, countrymen, lend me your ears . . . ." He explained that he had memorized the speech as a child in Jamaica where he was able to attend a private school for free, because his mother worked as the school's cook. Only later did he immigrate to Cuba when his father came looking for work in the 1930s. A final addition to this already polyglot mixture arrived with the U.S. soldiers in 1898, American English. Surprisingly, there seems to have been little if any influence of the Russian language on Cuban Spanish, though an entire generation of Cuban students were taught the language and raised on *muñequitos rusos* ("Russian cartoons"). One exception to this rule is the use of the Russian term *nomenklatura* to refer to privileged members of the Communist Party hierarchy.

Examples of Africanisms common in everyday Cuban speech include, *asere* ("buddy"), *ecobio* ("friend"), *monina* ("friend"), *chévere* ("cool"), *¿Qué bolá?* ("What's up?"), *nagüe* ("buddy"), *fula* ("bad" or "money"), *iria* or *iriampo* ("food"), and *aché* ("spirit" or "soul force"), as well as the many African words used in Cuban sacred rituals (such as *orisha,* meaning deity) and popular music. Perhaps the most commonly heard Africanism in Cuban Spanish is the expression *¿Qué bolá, asere?* ("What's up, buddy?"), which

originates in the sacred language of the Afro-Cuban secret
society, alternately called Abakuá or Ñáñigo, which came from
the Calabar region of Africa, thus the other common name for
the ethnic group in Cuba, Carabalí. While the majority of these
Africanisms originate in Nigeria with the language of the
Yoruba, the Bantu-speaking people of the Congo have also contributed a number of words to the Cuban lexicon, including
two words intimately connected with dance music: *sandunga*
(flirtatiousness or mischievousness) and *bemba* (lips, forever
associated with Cuban singer Celia Cruz's version of the song
"Bemba Colorá", "Red Lips"). This popular Bantu word is also
commonly used in Cuban Spanish when referring to the
"rumor mill" (*radio bemba*) and in the popular expression, *No
te pongas esta bemba* ("Don't put on that sad/angry face").
Other terms associated with specific musical genres include
rumba, conga, and mambo, while some of the many African-
termed percussion instruments include the tambor, chéqere,
bongo, conga, tumbadora, and maraca (though this last one
more likely comes from the Taíno). Many African words are
recongizible in Spanish as they preserve the letter combina-
tions "mb" (as in bemba, rumba, mambo, and timba) or "ng"
(as in conga, bongo, sandunga, and songo).

The Africans also inadvertently contributed a number of
Anglicisms to Cuban Spanish that they learned from English
slave traders. Some of these include, *fufú* ("food—plantain
mash"), *tifi-tifi* ("thief"), *yari-yari* ("yearn"), and *luku-luku*
("look"). Aside from actual African-derived words, perhaps a
deeper impact from the Yoruba and Bantu languages is evident in the informal, playful nature of Cuban speech. While
native influences on Cuban Spanish are less significant, the
Taíno did contribute many place names to Cuba, including
Guamá, Guanabacoa, Baracoa, Guanabo, Guantánamo,
Yumurí, and Guanahacabibes, as well as enriching Latin
American Spanish (and American English) with the following
words: *tabaco* ("tobacco"), *barbacoa* ("barbecue"), *cacique*

("chieftain"), *canoa* ("canoe"), *yuca* ("cassava"), *hamaca* ("hammock"), *huracán* ("hurricane"), and *iguana*.

A final, if somewhat surprising influence on Cuban Spanish comes from the almost sixty-year U.S. presence on the island. There are a host of common Cuban words and even some expressions that have clear origins in standard American English of the first part of the twentieth century. Examples include, *claxon* ("horn"), *blúmer* ("bloomers/panties"), *bróder* ("brother/buddy"), *restaurán* ("restaurant"), *vivaporú* ("Vic's Vapor Rub," more commonly heard in Miami), *pulóver* ("T-shirt"), *fílin* ("feeling, an emotive genre of music"), *doile* ("doily or placemat"), *plo* ("plug"), *breiker* ("breaker"), *fei* ("face"), *cake* (with the same meaning as in English, but pronounced like the letter "k"), *noháu* ("know-how"), and *sidecar* ("motorcycle sidecar") (ibid.), as well as many drinking, boxing, and baseball terms incorporated along with American leisure culture, such as *strike* ("straight up/neat"), *a la roca* ("on the rocks"), *jaibol* ("highball glass"), *lager* ("beer"), *shor* ("shorts"), *estrai* ("strike" as in baseball), *nocaut* ("knock out"), *ring* ("boxing ring"), and *jonrón* ("homerun").

Like Andalusians, Canarians, Dominicans, and Puerto Ricans, Cubans are notoriously hungry for "Ss." Thus, perhaps the most distinctive characteristic of the sound of Cuban Spanish is the tendency to aspirate the "s" at the end of words. For example, *los amigos* suddenly becomes *loh amigo*. Cubans also commonly clip off the final consonants of words, as in saying *comé* for the infinitive *comer*. The letter "d" also often falls victim to this tendency, especially in the ending *-dad*. That can be heard, for example, in the common use of the word *cantidad* at the end of a sentence to mean "very," "much," or "a lot," as in *Me gustó cantidá* ("I liked it a lot") or *Soy malo cantidá* ("I'm very bad"). The "d" is also often aspirated when Cubans use past participle constructions like *-ado*. Perhaps the most famous example of this characteristic is found in Ernest Hemingway's *The Old Man and the Sea,* in which the old Cuban fisherman Santiago, who has gone for so long without catching anything, is described as being *salao* (instead of the proper, *salado*), which literally means salty, but in Cuban and southern Spanish slang indicates "the worst kind of bad luck." This trait grows directly out of Andalusian Spanish where the vocabulary associated with traditional flamenco dancing features terms like *tablao* (from *tablado* or "stage"), *cantaor* (from *cantador* or "singer"), and *bailaor* (from *bailador* or "dancer").

A final pair of phonological tendencies in Cuban Spanish have to do with words that end with an "r." Often a final "r" is replaced by an "l" sound, as in the word *actuar* ("to act") becoming *actual* ("current"). Another modification some-times made to words ending in "r" is most common among the rural, working class who generally shift the "r" to a "y" as when *comer* becomes *comey* or *compadre* becomes *compay.* Thus, the stage name of the late son musician Francisco Repi-lado was Compay Segundo.

In terms of word structure, Cuba is *tú* territory ("you" familiar), eschewing the familiar *vos* (also meaning "you") that is used in parts of Central and South America. Moreover, Cubans rarely use the more formal pronoun *usted* ("you") even when addressing an elder or figure of authority. When employing a diminutive, Cubans frequently replace the more common *-ito* with *-ico.* They say *chiquitico* (not *chiquito*), *ratico* (not *ratito*) and *puntica* (not *puntita*). Cubans also invert the word order (syntax) in many common phrases. For example, they often fail to reverse the verb-pronoun in inter-rogative sentences, saying, *¿Qué tú quieres?* instead of *¿Qué quieres (tú)?,* a habit that may have originated through influence from English. Another common Cuban word inver-sion occurs in expressions using an initial *más* as a negative combination. Instead of the more standard *nada más* ("noth-ing more") or *nunca más* ("never again"), Cubans are more likely to say *más nada* and *más nunca.* Cubans are also more likely to use the word *cantidad* as an adjective, as in *Está bueno cantidad,* instead of the standard, *Está muy bueno* ("It's very good").

Socio-lismo and el Choteo

In Cuban Spanish, the term *socio* (literally meaning "associate") is used to refer to a close friend. In practice, *socio* is often used to refer to a connection in Cuba's ubiquitous underground economy. The term *socio-lismo,* then, is a playful combination of *socio* with *socialismo,* and can be defined as, "the system of access to goods and social standing based on who you know and who you love." As never before, the 1990s were years when Cubans had to *inventar* ("invent") and *resolver* ("resolve") creative, often illegal solutions to everyday problems. Cuban speech came to directly reflect this reality. A typical exchange might be: *Oye, mi socio, como e' que tiene langosta?* ("Hey buddy, how'd you get lobster?") To which the resourceful *socio* would respond: *Me la resolví, Me la inventé,* or *Me la luché.* Purposely elusive, each of these responses loosely translates as: "I took care of it. Don't worry about the details." Thus, in practice the use of the term *socio-lismo* in Cuban speech simultaneously mocks the tattered ideal of state socialism and points to what has come to replace it on a daily basis for most Cubans: friends, family, and *socios.*

In the 1940s, leading Cuban intellectual Jorge Mañach published a slim volume entitled *Indagación al choteo.* This book was the first serious effort to describe what was already by then a deeply rooted Cuban characteristic, *el choteo.* Best described as Cuba's unique brand of irreverent mockery or satire, intended to undercut and question authority, *choteo* is deeply ingrained in Cuban culture and has only been nurtured by what many see as illegitimate revolutionary authority. *Socio-lismo* and many other facetious terms like it constitute a "hidden transcript" employed by everyday Cubans to deflate the government's ubiquitous "officialese," making light of their daily struggle for survival. Derived from the Spanish verb *chotearse,* which means to poke fun at someone or something, in practice today, the *choteo* constitutes a peculiar Cuban brand of humor that aims to desanctify the near-sacred revolutionary discourse of the state (known as *el teque*). Whereas the state may declare: *La lucha sigue. Socialismo o muerte, venceremos* ("The struggle continues. Socialism or death, we shall overcome"), in private, everyday Cubans might modify this slogan among themselves with the mocking, tongue-in-cheek declaration: *No cogas lucha, aquí lo que no hay es que morirse* ("Don't fight it so much, here what we must do is not die").

Common Cuban proverbs

A río revuelto ganancia de pescadores—It's good fishing in troubled waters.

El ojo del amo engorda el caballo—If you want something done right, you have to do it yourself.

No te dicen perro, pero te enseñan el collar—Actions speak louder than words.

El mismo perro con otro collar—You can't teach an old dog new tricks.

Pueblo pequeño, infierno grande—There are no secrets in a small town.

Specialized Cuban words

Una barbacoa—Loft or split level housing arrangement (usually for lack of space).

Un/una puro/a—Old man/old woman (also slang for cigar).

La jeta—Face.

Una jeva—Woman.

Una jaba—Bag.

Un nylon—Plastic bag.

Un carro—Automobile, car.

Un coche—Coach, carriage (yes, the horse-drawn kind—they're still used in Cuba).

Una máquina—Old American car.

Un almendrón—Old American car.

Hacer botella—Hitchhike.

Una guagua—Bus.

Common Cubanismos (slang expressions)

Pa'que te intere(s)—For your information.

Pa'que lo sepa(s)—For your information.

Pa' lo que sea—For whatever it's worth.

¡¿Qué va?!—fig. What's going on?; Are you crazy? (more an exclamation than a question).

¡Caballero!—Used to greet an old friend or to express surprise (lit. gentleman or horseman).

¡Está en candela!—S/he's hot! (lit. That wo/man is on fire!).

Voy p'al gao .—I'm going home (in this case *gao* is thought to come from gypsy Spanish).

Mi (hi)jito/a—Used to express affection (lit. my child).

Ya tu sabe(s).—You're right; I agree (lit. You already know).

¡Alaba(d)o (sea santo)!—Oh, my God! (lit. blessed be the lord!).

¿Te da(s) cuenta?—Don't you realize?

No te pierda(s)—fig. Stay in touch; Don't be a stranger.

Estoy complicado.—I'm busy (lit. I am complicated).

Estoy embarca(d)o.—I'm out of luck, stranded.

¡Ay, mi madre!—An expression of frustration or surprise (lit. Oh, my mother!).

¡Ay, por tu madre!—An expression of frustration or surprise (lit. Oh, by your mother!)

¡Que manera de ... !—An expression used when impressed or shocked by an action or feeling, as in *¡Qué manera de quererte!* ("Oh, how much I love you!").

¡Qué clase de ... !—Another expression used when impressed, but in this case by a more specific thing or event, as a sign I saw during a recent trip to Cuba declared, *¡Qué clase de Comandante!* ("What a great Commander we have!"), complete with a large adoring photo of Fidel Castro.

Dígole . . . .—Technically improper Spanish grammatical usage of the verb *decir* (*digo,* "I say"). In this case, *dígole* is most often used by Cubans when recounting an event to a third party. The English equivalent would be something like, "So then I **say** to this guy . . . ."

Pero, ven acá . . . .—A figurative expression used when hearing something unexpected (lit. "But, come here").

Me da tremenda pena!—That's too bad! (I'm extremely regretful/embarrassed).

Se corre la bola.—The news is spreading.

No me fríe huevo, porque no soy manteca.—Don't smack your lips (lit. Don't fry me an egg, because I'm not fat grease).

¡Ponte pa' tu número!—Behave! (Make sure you take care of your responsibilities!).

Hacerse de la vista gorda.—Look the other way; Act as if you don't notice something.

Echarla pa'lante—To inform on someone; To tattle.

Chivatear—To inform on someone; To tattle.

Chiva (or chivato)—Informer; Bigmouth; Tattletale.

Vamos a marcar—A common expression used in Cuba when having to reserve a place in line.

¿Quién es el último?—Who is the last one in line? (Used upon arriving at a bus stop or other place where one must want in line, a very common occurrence in Cuba).

Colarse—To sneak into a place without paying or butt in line (lit. to line up). Also a very common practice in Cuba.

Eso le paga Roberto/Liborio—Used to indicate that the goods in question have been pilfered (from the state). Cubans will often use *Roberto* in place of *robo* (robbery), and Liborio is the name given to a famous caricature who is the epitome of Cubanness (lit. Roberto/Liborio is paying for this).

Names

Under socialism, there has been a marked tendency to "revolutionize" the practice of naming children. Although traditional names like Juan, José, Miguel, Julio, Pedro, and Rafael (for males) and Juana, Silvia, Mayra, Gloria, Alejandra, and Celia (for females) are still used, they have lost ground over the past forty-five years. Cubans under forty are more likely to have names derived from Russian, French, Italian, and American culture, or even more commonly invented names with no clear national origin. For example, the pitching staff of the powerful Cuban National Baseball Team includes players with the following first names: Maikel, Yulieski, Yadel, Jonder, Yunieski, Vicyohandry, Adiel, Yadiel, Yosvany, and Ormari. Not to be outdone, the starting roster for Cuba's dominant women's National Volleyball Team includes the following names: Yanelis, Nancy, Yaima, Rosir, Liana, Marta, Zoila, Daima, Ana Ibis, Maisbelis, Anniara, and Dulce! Two other prominent examples are the five-year-old subject of the international child custody dispute in 2000, *Elián* González, and the lead singer of the Cuban-French Hip-Hop group Orishas, *Yotuel* Romero. Elián's name derives from the combination of his parents' names, *Elizabet* and Ju*an,* while Yotuel got his name when his parents could not agree and so decided to combine the three Spanish pronouns *yo, tú* and *él* (I, you, and him) to come up with Yotuel.

In Cuba, women do not generally change their family name upon marriage. Nor do they add the "de + . . ." construction that is used elsewhere in Latin America. Instead, Cuban women retain their maiden names. On the other hand, while Cubans only occasionally have second or middle names, they do use a double last/family name. Cuban last names are formed by placing one's father's first last name in front of one's mother's first last name. For example, Cuba's vice president and minister of defense, Raúl Castro (who is now the acting president) is more properly known as Raúl **Castro Ruz** (his better-known older brother is President Fidel Castro Ruz). The double last name Castro Ruz originates from the fact that their father was named Ángel **Castro** y Argiz (the use of *y* is an antiquated form of conjoining surnames) and their mother Lina **Ruz** González. Raúl **Castro** Ruz married fellow rebel Vilma **Espín** Guillois (recently deceased) just after the revolution. Thus, one of their children, the director of the Center of Sex Education and Research in Havana (Cenesex), is named Mariela **Castro Espín**. While the mother's family name does eventually drop out, as in the United States, the tradition of using double family names preserves it for at least two generations. Cubans in the United States often dispense with the use of double last names, simply adopting the American practice of using only the father's surname (as do musician Gloria Estefan and actor/filmmaker Andy García). Others may attempt to preserve the Cuban-Spanish tradition of using both last names but are often forced to place a hyphen between them (as did the late writer and literary critic Antonio Benítez-Rojo), since Americans are easily confused by two family names.

Greetings (Words and Gestures)

Cubans are very informal and can be quite affectionate in their greetings, even with a complete stranger. When two women or a man and a woman greet one another (even for the first time) it is quite common for each to do so by shaking hands and pulling one another close for a polite kiss on the "cheek" (without one's lips actually touching skin). Two men almost never do this, though they will often vigorously shake hands or pat one another on the back. Following from this familiarity, Cubans often dispense with the Spanish formal *usted* and prefer to use the familiar *tú* in their daily interactions when addressing others. This tendency toward informality has been exacerbated by a revolution that sought to do away with hierarchical greetings of respect or deference such as *Don* and *Doña* or *Señor* and *Señora,* replacing them with the standard socialist *compañero* and *compañera*. Newly arrived Cuban immigrants in Miami have to quickly relearn the "bourgeois" greetings of old, since addressing someone as *compañero* in Miami will not be well received.

Common greetings (Latin America in general)
Sí—Yes.
No—No.
Gracias—Thank you.
De nada—You're welcome.
Hola—Hello.
Hasta luego—Good-bye (short-term).
Adios—Good-bye (longer term).
Buenos días—Good morning.
Buenas tardes—Good afternoon.
Buenas noches—Good evening/night.
¿Cómo está usted?—How are you? (formal—rarely used).
¿Cómo estás?—How are you? (familiar—more common).

Other common greetings more specific to Cuba (slang)
¿Qué me cuentas?—What do you say?
¿Qué tal?—How's it going?
¿Cómo andas?—How goes it?
Chau—See ya later.
¿Qué bolá, asere?—What's up, dude?
¡Dime!—Yo!
Dime—Hello (on a telephone).
Oigo—Hello (on a telephone).
¿Oiste?—Did you hear (me)? Did you understand (me)?

CUBAN CUISINE AND BEVERAGES

While Cuban cuisine has much in common with that of other Caribbean islands, it is unique in many ways. Foreigners are often surprised that despite the fact that the *habanero* pepper takes its name from Cuba's capital, chili peppers and most other kinds of hot spice are notably absent from Cuban kitchens. For most Cubans, even black pepper is considered too spicy! (That is less true in Oriente, where centuries of influence from French and Haitian Creole cuisine has given the *orientales* a broader palate.) In place of hot spice, Cubans make constant and creative use of garlic, onions, cumin, oregano, and a concoction called *sofrito* (described below). As with language, Cuban cuisine has absorbed influences from Spain, Africa, its indigenous inhabitants, Haiti, and the United States. Paradoxically, despite being an island with many kinds of fish, lobster, and other seafood in abundant supply, Cubans tend to prefer meat, especially beef (when they can get it, which is rarely) and pork (which is more readily available), though chicken is also popular.

The Spanish and later the Chinese made rice a mainstay of the Cuban diet, along with beans (red and especially black) and the abundant variety of rooted vegetables indigenous to the island. Cubans also love sweets and tend to consume them in copious quantities. Ironically, whereas many foods are in short supply in today's Cuba, one visit to the legendary ice cream mecca *La Coppelia* (known popularly as *la catedral del helado,* the "ice cream cathedral," with branches in Havana and Santiago) will teach you that when Cubans finally sit down to eat their *helado* after a lengthy wait in line, they do so with decadent abandon and unapologetic gluttony! I remember once being embarrassed by a woman in Santiago who, though only half my size, easily ate three times as much ice cream as I could. I watched astonished as she gingerly consumed each portion of her *ensalada de helados* (ice cream salad platter), moving greedily from flavor to flavor and plate to plate. Other Cuban desserts are made with either milk or fruit and contain lots of sugar, as does Cuban coffee (*café criollo*), which is usually brewed syrupy thick and drunk in tiny demitasse cups in the late afternoon as a pick-me-up with a kick.

There are perhaps seven dishes that have become symbolic of Cuban cuisine. They are the main meat dishes:

A very happy Cuban woman eating her ensalada de helados *at the famed Coppelia ice cream parlor in Santiago de Cuba. (Ted Henken)*

ajiaco (Cuban stew), *lechón asado* (roasted pork/roast suckling pig), *ropa vieja* (shredded beef, or literally, "old clothes," surely one of the best names for a dish ever invented), and *picadillo* (ground beef/mincemeat). Three popular side dishes that normally accompany the above meat dishes are *frijoles negros* (black beans, always served with white rice), *moros y cristianos* (black beans mixed with rice, often referred to simply as *moros*, literally meaning "Moors and Christians," runner-up for best name of a Cuban dish), and *yuca con mojo* (cassava with garlic sauce). Black beans prepared alone and served with white rice is distinct from the equally common *moros*. A popular variant of *moros* is *congrí oriental* ("dirty rice," sometimes written *congrís*). Typically, *moros* is eaten in western Cuba and features black beans, while *congrí* is more common in the east and contains red beans (*frijoles colorados*) and rice (though the terms are often used interchangeably). The gourmet chef of Cuban television, Nitza Villapol, suggests that the strange term *congrí* originated from the popular Haitian Creole term for "beans and rice," *congó et riz*. Other popular Cuban dishes include *arroz con pollo* (yellow rice with chicken), *tamales* (just like their Mexican cousin but without chile), and *croquetas* (croquets).

A final addition to the Cuban palate, in scarce supply on the island today, arrived with the North Americans at the turn of the nineteenth century. These are the famed sandwiches, the *media noche* ("midnight") and the *cubano* ("Cuban sandwich"). Now ubiquitous in the delis of South Florida and New York City, these sandwiches became popular in Republican Cuba (1902–1958), along with the *frita*—Cuba's version of the American hamburger—as a quick way to fill up during a busy day or, better yet, late at night. In fact, the name "midnight" originated from the practice of wolfing down one of these succulent sandwiches after going out dancing or to one of Cuba's ubiquitous movie theaters. Filled with roast pork, boiled ham, Swiss cheese, pickles, and mustard, the *media noche* is served hot and slightly toasted on soft, sweet bread. The very similar *cubano* is not normally toasted and comes on Cuban bread or a French baguette.

Additionally, Cubans have come up with innumerable ways to prepare *plátanos* (plantains, both ripe and green). There are *plátanos maduros fritos* (fried sweet plantains), *tostones* (cut into thick wedges, fried, mashed, and fried again, known as *patacones* elsewhere in the hemisphere), *mariquitas* (thinly sliced and fried into crunchy chips), and *plátano en tentación* (long-cut roasted sweet plantains coated with sugar and cinnamon). Another important food group is the rooted vegetable (tuber), also prepared in a variety of ways. Usually boiled or fried, Cuba's many tuber varieties can all be smothered in the rich garlic sauce known as *mojo* mentioned above. The three most common roots are the *yuca* (cassava or manioc), *malanga* (taro root), and *boniato* (white sweet potato). Popular desserts include *flan* (caramel custard), *natilla de chocolate* (custard pudding with chocolate), *arroz con leche* (rice pudding), *pasta de guayaba con queso* (guava paste with cheese, sometimes called *timbita*), and cake (often extravagantly decorated with lots of icing).

Fruits, such as mango and papaya (known as *fruta bomba* in western Cuba), and vegetables, such as avocado and tomato, are abundant. Cuba's famed espresso coffee comes in three varieties: *café criollo* (described above), *café con leche* (similar to French *café au lait* or Italian *caffelatte* and drunk in the mornings in a large coffee cup), and *café cortado* (a fifty-fifty mixture of *café criollo* and milk, drunk from a demitasse cup and usually referred to in Cuba simply as a *cortadito*). Finally, Cuba boasts a number of cocktails (nearly all of them rum-based), at least three of which are well-known abroad, including the *daiquirí,* the *Cuba libre* (Cuban rum, cola, lime, and ice), and the *mojito* (described below). Less well-known off the island are the *añjeo* (aged rum taken straight or on the rocks), the *ron collins,* the *Mary Pickford,* and the *Cubanito* (Cuba's rum-based version of the Bloody Mary). The following four recipes and one cocktail are the most representative Cuban cuisine, both on the island and among Cubans abroad.

Lechón Asado/Lechón a la Criolla (Roasted Pork/Roast Suckling Pig)

The preparation of roast suckling pig is a day-long event, usually engaged in by the whole family on special occasions. It is

Turning the name of the famed Cuban cocktail, Cuba Libre (Cuban rum and American Coca-Cola), into a political double entendre, the artist of this broadside describes the "ingredients" of a "Free Cuba" as: "a true revolution, a people who defend it, a single party, and an historic leader." Uncle Sam is depicted as a frightened cretin running away screaming, "I don't drink." Ironically, when this picture was taken, the artist asked that his name be withheld explaining that he wanted to be able to come to the United States to visit his brother. (Ted Henken)

the Cuban equivalent of the American Thanksgiving turkey, only a lot bigger, juicier, and tastier (though perhaps not as healthful, given the amount of pig fat involved). For Cubans in South Florida *lechón asado* is most typically prepared as the family meal (that means extended family, including aunts,

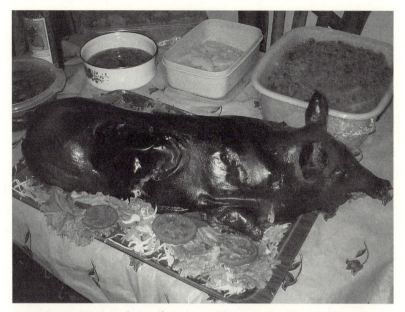

A traditional Cuban feast of roast suckling pig (lechón asado)*, complete with signature Cuban rice and beans* (congrí)*, yuca con mojo,
malanga, and all the fixin's. (Ted Henken)*

uncles, grandparents, nephews, children, grandchildren, and a
few brave or curious friends) on *Noche Buena* (Christmas Eve).
In Cuba, this tradition has waned because of the de-emphasis
of Christmas and the lack of access to entire piglets. Still, the
cooking of a roast suckling pig is often at the center of all traditional country fiestas in Cuba. In fact, despite the scarcity of
meat, Cubans continue to celebrate New Year's Eve in Cuba
today by getting ahold of at least a small piece of *lechón* with
which to ring in the new year. Also, given the Cuban penchant
for hospitality, the preparation of *lechón asado* frequently
accompanies the Cuban tradition of throwing extravagant welcome (*bienvenida*) or going-away (*despedida*) parties.

Typically, the pig (the recipe calls for a small pig, thus the
name *lechón*) is roasted over a long period (5 to 11 hours) on a
grill over a hole in the ground in which are placed leaves and

branches from a guava tree. While being roasted, the pig itself is covered with plantain leaves to retain the flavor and juices. Of course, this tradition was well-established long before Cubans on the island had access to the modern conveniences of indoor ovens or stoves. However, given the communal, family nature of the entire process, the tradition of preparing the *lechón* outside, over many hours, with every able-bodied Cuban male pitching in, continues (both on the island and in exile). The men typically spend all day with the pig, doing the killing and roasting/grilling, while the women prepare other side dishes, including *yuca con mojo,* black beans and rice, or desserts such as *flan* or *tres leches.* In short, cooking *lechón* is much like the American tradition of barbecuing, with the same combination of family lore, secret recipes, macho posturing, and grill pride and envy. There is a variant of this tradition in certain regions of Cuba that calls for a smaller piglet, which is not roasted but fried in a vat of lard. Thus, instead of a *lechón asado,* now we have a *lechón ahogado* ("drowned" or deep-fried suckling pig).

Ingredients:

1 suckling pig (10–15 pounds, calculate 1 pound per person) The pig can be purchased already gutted by a butcher or done at home for full effect

8–10 cloves garlic, or to taste

2 teaspoons dried oregano

3–4 teaspoons salt

Freshly ground black pepper to taste

2 cups bitter orange juice (or 1 cup sweet orange juice) mixed with ½ cup each fresh lime juice and lemon juice

2 bay leaves, crumbled

Olive oil for basting

1 apple, 1 orange, 1 lemon or lime for garnish

Directions: Since the recipe uses a whole pig, make sure you have a pan large enough to hold the pig sturdily, without the fat splattering. Also, check to see if the pan will fit in your oven and in your refrigerator for overnight marinating. A day or two before cooking, wash the pig inside and out and pat dry with paper towels. In a mortar, combine the garlic, oregano, and salt, and mash to a paste. Place the pig in a large pan, rub it inside and out with the garlic paste, season it liberally with salt and pepper and pour the soured juices over it. Sprinkle with the crumbled bay leaves. Cover the pig with aluminum foil and refrigerate for 24 hours.

If you plan to go all-out, follow these directions next: At 10:00 A.M. on the day of the party, lay the pig on its back on a grill over a pit (you can also use what's called a China Box, since it's much faster than a pit grill). The roasting process takes anywhere from 5 to 11 hours. Save the leftover juices from the marinade and continue basting the pig while it cooks. When the festivities begin, the pork should be kept on the grill for full effect. To eat, partygoers simply get a plate and a fork and begin to dig in, eating the meat directly from the body. For the faint of heart, the pig can be carved up and served as with a Thanksgiving turkey.

If you prefer to do this the "civilized" way, 5 to 7 hours before serving preheat the oven to 375° F, remove the pig from the marinade, and preserve the marinade. Put the pig in a shallow aluminum foil-lined roasting pan, insert a wad of foil in the pig's mouth to keep it open, cover the ears with foil, and brush the skin with oil. Insert a meat thermometer in the hind leg, making sure it does not touch bone. Roast the pig for one hour. Lower the oven to 350° F and roast for another 2 to 5 hours (depending upon the size of the pig). Be sure to baste the pig frequently with oil, juices, and the marinade. Finally, when the pig is done to an internal temperature of between 185° F and 190° F, the skin is a cordovan brown, and the juices run out when pierced with a fork, transfer the pig to a large platter and allow to cool for 20 minutes. Garnish as you like with fruit and serve. Serves: 15. Preparation: 1–2 days. Cooking time: 5–11 hours.

Picadillo (Cuban-style Ground Beef/Mincemeat)

If you're thinking, "Oh, ground beef, big deal," think again. Cuban-style ground beef is one of the true pleasures of the Cuban kitchen. It is easy to prepare and can be made quickly. It is best served over rice with a side vegetable or tuber such as *boniato* (Cuban white sweet potato) or potatoes (if you do not add them to the meat as is done in some recipes). The three ingredients that make this dish unique and give it a "Cuban" taste are the addition of tomato sauce (I use marinara), and just before the cooking is done, sliced green olives (stuffed with pimiento) and raisins.

Ingredients:

1¹/₂ pounds of top choice ground beef

1 teaspoon dried oregano

1 teaspoon ground cumin

A dash of salt

1 cup olive oil

1 orange

4 tablespoons of dry white wine or ¹/₂ teaspoon of white vinegar (optional)

2 garlic cloves, chopped fine

1 medium white onion, chopped fine

1 small red or yellow pepper (or a mixture of both), chopped fine

1 cup tomato sauce (marinara is best)

1 medium baking potato, peeled and cut into small cubes (optional)

1 dozen green olives stuffed with pimiento, sliced

¹/₄ cup of raisins

Cooked white rice (prepared separately)

Directions: Begin by mixing the ground beef together with a half-cup of olive oil, the juice of one orange, and the white wine (or vinegar). Season the mixture with the oregano, cumin, and salt. Place in a container and let it marinate in the refrigerator. Pour a half-cup of olive oil into a cooking pan and set the stove at a medium-low heat. Once the oil is hot, add the ground beef mixture and immediately begin to turn and mix the beef to avoid the formation of large chunks. Once this mixture has begun to soften, add the chopped garlic, onions, and peppers. When the meat begins to lose its redness, pour in the marinara sauce and keep stirring. If you decide to use a potato, now add in the potato cubes and cover, cooking for 10–15 minutes on a low flame. Uncover and add the olives and raisins and cook uncovered for another 5–10 minutes. Serve over white rice. Serves: 4. Preparation: 30 minutes. Cooking time: 20 minutes.

Frijoles Negros (Black Beans)

Any Cuban will tell you that there are three essential elements to making classic Cuban black beans: quality beans, *un buen sofrito* (a Cuban sauce composed of oil, onions, bell peppers, garlic, sautéed annatto seeds, and a bit of pork meat and fat), and of course what any self-respecting Cuban kitchen can hardly do without, a pressure cooker.

Ingredients:
1 pound of dry black beans
6 cups of water
1 large onion, finely chopped
3$^1/_2$ green peppers, chopped (set apart an entire half)
1 clove of garlic, finely chopped
$^1/_2$ cup of olive oil
$^1/_4$ pound ham bone (optional)
3 bay leaves, crumbled
1 tablespoon salt
1 teaspoon sugar
1 ounce white bacon (optional)
$^1/_2$ cup of white vinegar
Raw chopped onion

Directions: Soak the beans in four cups of water for a few hours (or if possible overnight) along with half of one bell pepper (remove the seeds). Add two more cups of water and place the lid on the pressure cooker, making sure it is sealed, and cook on medium high for 25 to 30 minutes. Meanwhile, prepare the *sofrito.* Slightly fry the onions, green peppers, garlic, and bay leaves in olive oil until they become soft and pasty. Add salt, vinegar, and sugar as necessary for taste. Turn off the flame on the pressure cooker and let it cool. Open the pressure cooker and mash the beans with a ladle, breaking their skin. Now add the *sofrito* to the beans and seal the pressure cooker again with the lid. Cook on the stove again for 20 minutes until the beans are tender and the liquid has thickened. Serve over rice. Serves: 3–4. Preparation: 15 minutes. Cooking time: 45 minutes to one hour.

Yuca con Mojo (Cassava with Garlic Sauce)

Ten years ago in the summer of 1997 on my first visit to Cuba, I stayed with Magda de la Uz and her family in an apartment near the University of Havana. While the nominal charge for using one of her extra rooms included meals, I really didn't expect to be eating at home much. Only later did I discover that the food "on the street" in Cuba is no comparison to the home cooking of a veteran Cuban mother working out of what is for many women their very own sanctuary, the kitchen. Since I was supplying her with dollars, she was able to get the proper ingredients to prepare the food the way her mother (and grandmother) had taught her. Over the next three weeks, Magda introduced me to most of Cuba's classic dishes. The two things that she consistently served me, both of which I still crave a decade later and 1,000 miles away, and neither of which have been yet surpassed in my many culinary adventures across the island since, are *batidos de mamey* (mamey milkshakes) and *yuca con mojo.* It was not until later that I discovered the difficulty of properly preparing the second dish, since most subsequent times I've had it (especially in New York City restaurants), it has been hard, undercooked, and all but inedible. However, Magda's yuca was as soft as ice cream and came bathed in a succulent *mojo* garlic sauce that was truly to die for.

Ingredients:

4 medium yucas (about 2 pounds), cut into steak fry size or into *trozos* (that is, cylinders of 1½-inch thickness)

4 large Spanish onions, sliced fine

½ cup bitter orange juice, or 1/8 cup fresh orange juice and 1/8 cup fresh lime juice combined

1 tablespoon fresh cilantro

6 garlic cloves, crushed

¼ cup extra virgin olive oil

Orange wedges, to garnish

Directions: Place the yuca in a saucepan and cover it with water. Boil it until tender for about half an hour. When the yuca starts to become soft while boiling (you can check by poking it with a fork), you must then *asustar la yuca* ("scare the yuca"). That is done by pouring very cold water into the boiling pot. This special technique causes the yuca to open up and further soften (if it is high-quality yuca). Drain the pot, place the yuca in a bowl, and remove any white, "woody" parts from the center. Set it aside. Combine the onions, cilantro, garlic, orange/lime juice, and extra virgin olive oil in a small bowl and mash them into a fine pulp. This is your mojo sauce. (Remember, don't make a fool of yourself by pronouncing it MO-jo. It is properly pronounced MO-ho). Pour the sauce over the yuca. (Some recipes call for heating it in a skillet first.) Now, heat the olive oil in a skillet until it is very hot and runs like water, but not so hot that it smokes. Pour the hot oil over the yuca. Serve the yuca with the mojo on top. Serves: 4. Preparation: 15 minutes. Cooking time: 30 minutes.

Mojito

One of three signature Cuban cocktails, the mojito is a sweet, minty, citrus drink perfect for those hot summer nights. It combines many ingredients native to Cuba and has become popular across the world.

Ingredients:

1 fluid ounce of fresh lime juice

6 to 8 leaves of fresh yerba buena

2 ounces of medium brown cane sugar

2 fluid ounces of white Havana Club, or other high-quality white rum

1 cup of ice cubes

1 fluid ounce of club soda or lemonade

Dark Havana Club, or other high-quality dark rum

1 sprig of yerba buena, to garnish

Directions: Wash and stem the mint leaves, reserving a few whole sprigs as a garnish. Combine the lime juice, yerba buena, and sugar in a glass. Crush the mixture well with a pestle—this extracts the tasty mint oils. Add the white rum and fill the glass with ice. Add the lime juice and stir until the sugar begins to dissolve. Just before serving, add the club soda (or lemonade) and top off the glass with a splash of dark rum. Stir gently. Garnish the glass with a sprig of yerba buena and serve with a straw. Serves: 1. Preparation: 10 minutes.

ETIQUETTE

Cuban social etiquette revolves around the national characteristics of boisterousness and loquaciousness, sensuality and secularism, jocularity and mockery, ambition and duplicity (known in Cuba as the *doble moral*), and modernity. The most distinctive social characteristic shared by Cubans is a deep sense of hospitality. This trait is exhibited in the universal practice of offering a visitor to one's home a cup of strong

Cuban coffee. If there is no coffee made, which is rare, your Cuban hosts will likely spring to their feet, run to the kitchen, and start brewing. Cuban hospitality is also on display whenever Cubans greet one another, or, more pointedly, when they take their leave. Unlike Americans, who might wave a general good-bye and be gone, Cubans insist on greeting each person individually with a handshake or a kiss. Upon departure, they repeat this ritual, often even more elaborately. However, this habit has the consequence of making a departure a long and endlessly drawn out process as new conversations are started and final words are shared. Cubans also tend to hold conversations at an unusually high volume and are masters at the art of conversation, often holding forth for hours. Non-Cubans can also be taken aback at the Cuban traits of forwardness and flirtatiousness. While these traits make Cubans some of the easiest people in the world to befriend, cultural outsiders may feel that their space is being invaded or that Cubans may harbor ulterior motives. In fact, the economic crisis that has ravaged Cuba since 1990 has caused many Cubans to use their natural friendliness, flirtatiousness, curiosity, and gift for gab as a way to make a living by constantly hustling foreign tourists. Luckily, few of these hustlers are truly dangerous.

Finally, a word should be said about what is known in Cuba as the *doble moral*. Much has been made of this Cuban trait of duplicity, exercised most commonly in regard to political matters. The *doble moral* is the practice of dissimulation in which one espouses one set of beliefs in public and another in private. The renowned Cuban historian Manuel Moreno Fraginals has argued that this penchant for Cubans to display a split personality is the result of an "utter ambivalence" they have about their own lives and futures. He insists, "Many times what people are faced with is not only a moral question, but a question of survival that leads them to maintain two separate attitudes, one official and the other personal" (Centeno and Font 1997: 214). Just as there exists a *doble moral* in terms of one's professed political beliefs, there is also a *doble discurso* ("dual discourse") in terms of the words one uses and the different, sometimes contradictory meanings invested in them. Faced with a constant barrage of doublespeak from the state, the Cuban people have invented their own *doble discurso*—their own hidden transcript of words and meanings. An example of this is given above with the use of the word *luchar* ("to struggle"). Another example is the invented word *insilio* ("insile"). For those not able or willing to emigrate (go into exile, *exilio*), often their only choice is to unplug as much as possible from the system—to live in *insilio*. While this double discourse is not often aimed at foreigners, Cubans can use it to tell outsiders what they think they want to hear or to get what they need from them.

HOLIDAYS

Holidays celebrated in today's Cuba reflect a combination of Catholic, African, nationalistic, and revolutionary influences. For example, while Christmas celebrations have recently reappeared after a long ban by the government, traditional New Year's celebrations have been combined with political pageantry recognizing the triumph of the revolution on **January 1**, 1959. Furthermore, the country's most important national holiday is celebrated on **July 26**, commemorating Castro's failed attempt to overtake the Moncada army barracks in Santiago on that date in 1953. Each year, Cuban cities compete to be the site of this national celebration, which includes marches, revolutionary pageantry, and a three- to four-hour speech by Castro. This holiday coincides with the end of the traditional, week-long Santiago Carnival celebration, which predates the revolution and has its origins in a syncretic mixture of Catholic saint day processions, African *orisha* ceremonies, and French-Haitian traditions brought from Haiti at the turn of the eighteenth century. Other parts of Cuba also celebrate pre-Lenten Carnival in February.

In exile, of course, January 1 is not celebrated as a patriotic holiday, and July 26 is not celebrated at all. Instead, some exiles celebrate **May 20**, commemorating the day in 1902 when Cuba became independent. Given that U.S. tutelage over Cuba lasted until 1934, others have mocked May 20 as amounting to a disgraceful "dependence" day. The U.S. government has developed the habit of announcing new policy measures against Cuba on May 20, in order to win favor with the exile community. Also popular among Cuban-Americans is the traditional family gathering and celebration on Christmas Eve, known as Noche Buena. Despite this ongoing split, nearly all Cubans can agree to celebrate October 10, commemorating the day in 1868 when Carlos Manuel de Céspedes let forth the "Grito de Yara," beginning the first war for independence.

Other important national or religious holidays or feast days celebrated in Cuba include:

El Día de los Reyes (Three Kings Day), January 6: This is traditionally the date when Afro-Cuban organizations were given permission to parade through the streets in *comparsas* and sing their songs.

May Day, May 1: This is the international day dedicated to recognizing the contribution laborers make to society. In communist countries like Cuba, May Day is celebrated with parades, speeches, and rallies. Although most people are off work, many are required (or at least encouraged) to attend political rallies.

Feast of Caridad del Cobre (The Virgin of Charity, or Oshún), September 8: On this day, many Cubans make a special pilgrimage to the town of Cobre, outside Santiago de Cuba. Caridad del Cobre, Cuba's patron saint, is also honored as Oshún (a Yoruba deity) by adherents of santería on this day.

Feast of San Lázaro (Babalú-Ayé), December 17: This date is the occasion of a massive annual pilgrimage by those who have made promises to San Lázaro (Babalú-Ayé). Taking place on the outskirts of Havana in the small chapel known as El Rincón, this pilgrimage is a true feast for the eyes as thousands of people walk, crawl, or drag themselves to this spot over the course of a three-day period. In fact, while the final point on the pilgrimage is a Catholic church, few of the pilgrims are in fact practicing Catholics. As such, El Rincón is an ideal place in which to witness the convergence of Cuba's many syncretic belief systems, including Catholicism, spiritism, santería, and communism, as well as the consumerism and commercialism evidenced by the throng of street vendors administering to the spiritual and physical needs of the many pilgrims.

Directory of Cuba-Related Organizations, On-Line Publications, and Websites

The primary purpose of this directory is to help build bridges between Cuba, its people, and the outside world—especially the United States. Having traveled to the island more than a dozen times over the past decade (1997–2007), I have had the privilege of meeting people and working with institutions on the island (both within the government and, more commonly, independent of it) who have much to teach (and are always hungry to learn from) the world outside. These individuals and institutions have normally received this curious and pesky *yuma* (North American) with graciousness and generosity, sharing their wealth of ideas, experiences, and information on a basis of mutual respect and reciprocity. It is hoped that this directory can facilitate this kind of fruitful dialogue and collaboration between Cuba and the world beyond its shores in the future.

This directory is organized into the following ten thematic sections: Education/Academic; Government, Nongovernmental Organizations (NGOs), and Think Tanks; Business and Economics; Art and Culture; Democracy and Human Rights; Diaspora and Exile Organizations; Travel and Tourism; Religion; News Media; and Miscellaneous. Within each section, I have listed organizations and websites in order of importance (based on my personal, somewhat arbitrary criteria), not alphabetically. Thus, inclusion on this list (or exclusion from it) should not be taken as an endorsement (or repudiation) of any particular organization or viewpoint. Each entry includes a title, web address, brief description, contact name and e-mail, and address and phone/fax number (if available). I have tried as much as possible to list well-established organizations that represent a wide variety of political and ideological perspectives.

Apart from years of traveling to Cuba, searching the web for information on Cuba, and subscribing to a number of Cuban-related list serves, two publications were most helpful in preparing the list of Cuba-related organizations and websites below. They are *Cuba and U.S. Nonprofits: Resource Guide and Directory* (Cuban Research Institute, Florida International University, 2002), compiled by Grisel Sangroniz and edited by Lisandro Pérez, and the final section of Louis A. Pérez's extensive bibliographic essay at the back of his *Cuba: Between Reform and Revolution* (Oxford University Press, 2006).

EDUCATIONAL/ACADEMIC

Latin American Network Information Center (LANIC)
http://lanic.utexas.edu/la/cb/cuba/
Description: Likely the best maintained, most extensive, and up-to-date list of links on Cuba, this site includes a useful collection of Castro's speeches from 1959 through 1996 compiled and translated into English by the Foreign Broadcast Information Service (FBIS).

Latin American and Latino Studies Program at the University of Indiana
http://www.latinamericanstudies.org/cuba.htm
Description: A site with well-organized and up-to-date information on Cuba and extensive Cuba-related links.

Cuban Research Institute (CRI), Florida International University
http://lacc.fiu.edu/centers_institutes/?body=centers_cri&rightbody=centers_cri
Description: The CRI's mission is to disseminate knowledge on Cuba and Cuban-Americans. The institute builds on

the university's wealth of Cuba experts and has developed strong relationships with scholars in Cuba through a variety of academic exchange programs. The CRI also holds a major multidisciplinary conference on Cuban Studies every eighteen months.

Contact: Damián Fernández, Director; Uva de Aragon, Associate Director

E-mail: crinst@fiu.edu

Address: University Park, DM 363, Miami, FL 33199

Telephone: (305) 348-1991; Fax: (305) 348-3593

Institute for Cuban and Cuban American Studies, University of Miami

http://www.miami.edu/iccas/

Description: ICCAS is a center for research and study of a wide range of Cuban and Cuban-American topics. Its website contains many useful research reports and links on Cuba and its diaspora.

Contact: Jaime Suchlicki

E-mail: iccas@miami.edu

Address: P.O. Box 248174, 1531 Brescia Ave., Coral Gables, FL 33124-3010

Telephone: (305) 284-CUBA (2822); Fax: (305) 284-4406, (305) 284-4875

Bildner Center for Western Hemisphere Studies, Cuba Program

http://web.gc.cuny.edu/bildnercenter/cuba/index.shtml

Description: The Bildner Center's Cuba Project is a collaborative effort to study changes in Cuban politics, economics, culture, and society. The Cuba Project works with other academic and policy-oriented institutions to promote dialogue between academics, policy makers, business and news media figures, as well as students from various countries and disciplines. The project holds monthly seminars and a major international conference every two years.

Contact: Mauricio Font, Director; Scott Larson, Administrative Assistant

E-mail: bildner@gc.cuny.edu; cubaproject@gc.cuny.edu

Address: Cuba Project, Bildner Center for Western Hemisphere Studies, The Graduate Center, CUNY, 365 Fifth Avenue, Suite 5209, New York, NY 10016

Telephone: (212) 817-2096; Fax: (212) 817-1540

Cuban and Caribbean Studies Institute, Tulane University

http://cuba.tulane.edu/

Description: The Cuban and Caribbean Studies Institute evolved out of several years of sustained effort in developing relations with Cuban counterpart organizations for the purposes of academic collaboration and exchange, curricular development, cultural enrichment, and international development and dialogue. The institute organizes lectures, performances, and courses aimed at promoting academic and cultural exchange between Cuba and the United States.

Contact: Ana M. López

E-mail: cuba@tulane.edu

Address: Caroline Richardson Building, New Orleans, LA 70118-5698

Telephone: (504) 862-8629; Fax: (504) 862-8678

Cuba Briefing Paper Series, Trinity University, Washington, D.C.

http://www.trinitydc.edu/academics/depts/Interdisc/International/Caribbean%20Briefing%20Papers.htm

Description: Originally published out of Georgetown University, the Cuban Briefing Paper Series is no longer in publication. However, the papers themselves are still available on-line via the above link. They were some of the best publications chronicling the changes in Cuban society during the 1990s.

Contact: Gillian Gunn Clissold; Robert Maguire
Address: Programs in International Affairs, Alumnae Hall,
Room 202, 125 Michigan, Avenue, NE, Washington, DC 20017
Telephone: (202) 884-9585; Fax: (202) 884-9597

**The David Rockefeller Center for Latin American Studies,
Harvard University**
http://drclas.fas.harvard.edu
Description: The David Rockefeller Center for Latin American Studies (DRCLAS) seeks to continue, consolidate, and extend its program of scientific and scholarly exchanges with Cuba. The Cuban Studies Program departs from two basic premises. First, restoring and enhancing cooperation between the U.S. and Cuban academic communities can play a significant role in promoting peaceful changes within and between our two countries. Second, strengthening and establishing institutional ties promotes interaction and collaboration among current and future intellectual and opinion leaders and thus catalyzes positive changes in Cuban and U.S. perspectives and government policies. Since its inception in 1999, the Center's Cuban Studies Program has evolved into one of the most extensive and diverse ventures of its kind. The program caters to scholars from areas across the wide spectrum of academic fields, namely the social sciences, environment, education, public health/medical sciences, humanities, library exchange and urban planning.
Contact: Lorena Barberia, Program Associate; Yadira Rivera, Program Coordinator
Email: drc_cuba@fas.harvard.edu; barberia@fas.harvard.edu
Address: David Rockefeller Center for Latin American Studies, Harvard University, 61 Kirkland Street, Cambridge, MA 02138
Telephone: (617) 495-9749; Fax: (617) 496-2802

EDUCATIONAL AND ACADEMIC INSTITUTIONS IN CUBA

The José Martí National Library

http://www.lib.cult.cu/

Description: The National Library hosts researchers from the United States as well as school librarians who have participated in professional exchanges and have attended conferences on topics related to the Cuban library system.

Contact: Siomara Carrillo

E-mail: bnjm@jm.lib.cult.cu

Address: Avenue Independencia and 20 de Mayo, Plaza de la Revolución, A.P. 6881, Havana, Cuba

Telephone: (537) 855-5442 through 5449; Fax: (537) 881-6224, 833-5938

José Martí Studies Center

http://www.cult.cu/marti/centro.html

Description: This research center is dedicated to carrying out studies and publishing work related to the life and writings of Cuban patriot José Martí. Center researchers have frequently participated in academic exchanges and often organize international conferences and lectures.

Contact: Reinio Díaz Triana

E-mail: jmarti@cubarte.cult.cu

Address: 807 Calzada at 4th Street, Vedado, C.P. 10400, Havana, Cuba

Telephone: (537) 855-2298; Fax: (537) 833-3721

Center for the Study of the United States (CESEU)

Contact: Soraya Castro Mariño, Esteban Morales

E-mail: seseu@comuh.uh.cu

Address: 1421 33d Street, between 14th and 18th Avenues, Miramar, C.P. 11600, Havana, Cuba

Telephone: (537) 203-8541, 203-5807; Fax: (537) 302-2350

Center for Psychological and Sociological Research (CIPS)

Description: CIPS is Cuba's foremost sociological and psychological research center focusing on changes in Cuban society.

E-mail: cips@ceniai.inf.cu

Address: 15th Street at Avenue B, Vedado, Plaza, Havana, Cuba

Telephone: (537) 833-5366, (537) 830-1451; Fax: (537) 830-6554

The University of Havana

http://www.uh.cu/

Description: The University of Havana offers various Spanish language and Cuban culture courses to foreigners throughout the year. Courses are often combined with recreational activities and taught at various levels, from one to three weeks.

Contact: Ileana Dopico

E-mail: dpg@comuh.uh.cu

Address: Edificio del Rectorado, San Lázaro and L Streets, Vedado, Havana, Cuba

Telephone: (537) 832-4245, 870-8490, 878-6200; Fax: (537) 833-5737

GOVERNMENT, NGOS, AND THINK TANKS

Cuban Government Organizations and Sites

Official site of the Cuban Government

http://www.cubagob.cu/ (in English: http://www.cubagob.cu/ingles/default.htm)

Castro Speech Database

http://www.cuba.cu/gobierno/discursos/index.html

Description: Many of Castro's public statements from 1959

to the present, as compiled by the Cuban government. Available in Spanish, with translations into English, French, and many other languages.

National Center for Sex Education (CENESEX)
http://www.cenesex.sld.cu/
Description: The Cuban Center of Sex Education is dedicated to research and understanding of sexual diversity. CENESEX is a teaching, research, and welfare institution in the area of human sexuality.
Contact: Mariela Castro Espín, Director
E-mail: cenesex@infomed.sld.cu
Address: 460 10th Street, between 21st and 19th Avenues, Vedado, Plaza, C.P. 10400, Havana, Cuba
Telephone: (537) 855-2528, 832-5464; Fax 830-2295

Cuban Interests Section, Washington, D.C.
http://embacu.cubaminrex.cu/Default.aspx?tabid=822
Description: Official site of the Cuban Interests Section in Washington, D.C.
Contact: Bernardo Guanche Hernández, Consul General
E-mail: secconscuba@worldnet.att.net; Información1@ sicuw.org
Address: Embassy of Switzerland, Cuban Interests Section, 2630 16th Street, NW, Washington, DC 20009
Telephone: (202) 797-8518, 797-8507, 797-8609, 797-8610

Cuban Mission to the United Nations, New York
http://www.un.int/cuba/Pages/main1ingles.htm
Description: The official website of the Cuban Mission to the United Nations.
E-mail: publicrelations@cubanmission.com
Address: 315 Lexington Avenue, New York, NY 10016
Telephone: (212) 689-7215; Fax: (212) 689-9073

U.S. Government Organizations and Sites

Office of Foreign Assets Control (OFAC)
http://www.ustreas.gov/offices/enforcement/ofac/programs/cuba/cuba.shtml
Description: Part of the U.S. Treasury Department, OFAC is responsible for obstructing economic relations with countries deemed to be enemies of the United States, Cuba among them.
Address: OFAC, U.S. Treasury Department, 909 Southeast First Avenue #736, Miami, FL 33131
Telephone: (305) 810-5140, (202) 747-5225

U.S. Department of State, Cuba Page
http://www.state.gov/p/wha/ci/c2461.htm
Description: Cuba page of the U.S. State Department website. It contains links to fact sheets, press releases, reports, and more. The U.S. policy as presented here can be summarized as "Hastening change in Cuba: Transition, not succession."

U.S. Interests Section
http://havana.usinterestsection.gov/
Description: The U.S. Interests Section's functions are similar to those of any U.S. government mission abroad: consular services, a political and economic section, a public diplomacy program, and refugee processing unique to Cuba. The objectives of the Interests Section in Cuba is to promote a peaceful transition to a democratic system based on the rule of law, individual human rights, and open economic and communication systems.
Current Chief of Mission: Michael E. Parmly (began service in summer 2005)
Address: Calzada between L and M Streets, Vedado, Havana, Cuba

Phone: (537) 833-3551; Emergency: (537) 833-3026; Fax: (537) 833-3700

CIA Fact Book, Cuba
http://www.cia.gov/cia/publications/factbook/geos/cu.html
Description: U.S. Central Intelligence Agency "Fact Book" on Cuba.

Independent Research and Public Policy Institutions

Lexington Institute—Cuban Politics and Economy
http://www.lexingtoninstitute.org/cuba/
Description: The Lexington Institute is a nonprofit, nonpartisan public policy research organization based in Arlington, Virginia. Its Cuba program aims to provide readable, original research on Cuba's economy and analysis of developments in Cuba, U.S.-Cuba relations, and U.S. policy toward Cuba.
Contact: Phil Peters
E-mail: peters@lexingtoninstitute.org
Address: Lexington Institute, 1600 Wilson Boulevard, Suite 900, Arlington, VA 22209
Phone: (703) 522-5828; Fax: (703) 522-5837

Cubasource (FOCAL)
http://www.cubasource.org/index_e.asp
Description: Cubasource is a web information system on Cuba produced by the Canadian Foundation for the Americas (FOCAL). It was created to facilitate the exchange of information related to Cuba's international relations and the political, social, and economic trends and challenges facing the island, and to stimulate and facilitate constructive and informed research and discussion of these issues within Canada and internationally.

Contact: Cristina Warren, Program Director
E-mail: cwarren@focal.ca
Address: One Nicholas Street, Suite 720, Ottawa, Ontario,
K1N 7B7, Canada
Telephone: (613) 562-0005, Ext. 226

The Cuba Study Group
http://www.cubastudygroup.org/
Description: The Cuba Study Group is a nonprofit, non-partisan organization, comprised of Cuban business and community leaders who share a common vision of a democratic Cuba. The group makes policy recommendations that promote a peaceful regime change in Cuba and lead to democracy, an open society, a market-based system, respect for human rights, and national reunification. The group's website features a wealth of useful information and links.
Contact: Tomás Bilbao, Executive Director; Carlos Saladrigas, Cochair
E-mail: tomas.bilbao@CubaStudyGroup.org
Address: Washington: 611 Pennsylvania Avenue SE #208, Washington, DC 20003
Miami: 5900 Bird Road, Miami, FL 33155
Telephone: (202) 544-5088; Fax: (202) 315-3271
Miami: (305) 668-5437; Fax: (305) 668-5410

National Security Archive, Cuba Archive
http://www.gwu.edu/~nsarchiv/index.html
Description: An independent, nongovernmental research institute and library located at George Washington University, the archive collects and publishes declassified documents obtained through the Freedom of Information Act (FOIA). The archive also serves as a repository of government records on a wide range of topics pertaining to the national security, foreign intelligence, and economic policies of the United States.
Contact: Peter Kornbluh

E-mail: nsarchiv@gwu.edu
Address: National Security Archive, Suite 701, Gelman Library, George Washington University, 2130 H Street NW, Washington, DC 20037
Telephone: (202) 994-7000; Fax: (202) 994-7005

Inter-American Dialogue, Cuba Program
http://www.thedialogue.org/programs/country/cuba.asp
Description: The Inter-American Dialogue seeks to facilitate Cuba's political and economic engagement with the international community, with the objective of enabling Cuba's participation in international institutions. Working group members frequently attend international economic conferences in Cuba, conduct primary research on the Cuban economy, and work with economists and policy makers from Cuba.
Contact: Dan Erikson
E-mail: derikson@thedialogue.org
Address: 1211 Connecticut Avenue NW, Suite 510, Washington, DC 20036-2706
Telephone: (202) 822-9002, Ext. 578; Fax: (202) 822-9553

Council on Foreign Relations
http://www.cfr.org
Description: The CFR hosts a Cuba and U.S.-Cuba Relations Roundtable in Washington, D.C., that addresses such issues as the status of the U.S. military base at Guantánamo Bay and the implications of Cuba's resuming normal trade relations with the United States. The CFR has also assembled an independent, bipartisan task force that produced the 2001 report "US-Cuban Relations in the 21st Century: A Follow-On Chairman's Report."
Contact: Julia E. Sweig
E-mail: jsweig@cfr.org
Address: 1779 Massachusetts Avenue NW, Washington, DC 20036
Telephone: (202) 518-3410; Fax: (202) 986-2984

Latin America Working Group

http://www.lawg.org/countries/cuba/intro.htm

Description: The Latin America Working Group's goal is to end the U.S. embargo against Cuba in order to benefit the people of both countries.

Contact: Mavis Anderson and Claire Rodríguez

E-mail: manderson@lawg.org; lawg@lawg.org

Address: 424 C Street, NE, Washington, DC 20002

Telephone: (202) 546-7010; Fax: (202) 543-7647

Washington Office on Latin America (WOLA), Cuba Project

http://www.wola.org/cuba/cuba.htm

Description: WOLA's Cuba program encourages U.S. policy-makers to normalize relations with Cuba. WOLA is committed to advancing human rights, democratic institutions, citizen participation, and equitable economic development in Latin America. WOLA's views are nicely summarized in its recent on-line publication "A Time for Change: Rethinking US-Cuba Policy."

Contact: Geoff Thale, Program Director

E-mail: gthale@wola.org, wola@wola.org

Address: 1630 Connecticut Ave NW, Suite 200, Washington, DC 20009-1053

Telephone: (202) 797-2171; Fax: (202) 797-2172

World Policy Institute, Cuba Project

http://www.worldpolicy.org/projects/uscuba/center.html

Description: Located at the New School for Social Research in New York City, the WPI's Cuba Project hosts an annual National Summit on Cuba in various locations across the United States.

Contact: Lissa Weinmann

Address: 66 Fifth Avenue, Suite 900, New York, NY 10011

Telephone: (212) 229-5808, Ext. 4268; Fax: (212) 229-5579

Center for International Policy, Cuba Program

http://www.ciponline.org/cuba/index.htm

Description: The CIP Cuba program opposes the current containment policy toward Cuba and seeks a policy that will be productive in terms of real interests and objectives. Areas of policy focus of CIP's Cuba Program include terrorism, travel, and trade. The CIP website also contains an extensive and up-to-date list of useful Cuba links.

Contact: Wayne Smith

E-mail: cip@ciponline.org

Address: 1717 Massachusetts Avenue NW, Suite 801, Washington, DC 20036

Telephone: (202) 232-3317; Fax: (202) 232-3440

Cuba Central

http://www.cubacentral.com/

Description: Cubacentral.com is dedicated to changing U.S. policy toward Cuba by ending the ban on travel by Americans to the island and lifting the U.S. embargo against Cuba.

Address: P.O. Box 53106, Washington, DC 20009

IFCO/Pastors for Peace

http://www.pastorsforpeace.org

Description: Pastors for Peace is a ministry of the Interreligious Foundation for Community Organization (IFCO) aimed at providing humanitarian aid to Latin America and the Caribbean. IFCO seeks to advance the struggles of oppressed people for justice and self-determination. In Cuba, IFCO has worked to end the U.S. blockade and has provided humanitarian aid to the Cuban people through "Friendshipment Caravans," construction brigades, and educational delegations.

E-mail: p4p@igc.org

Address: 418 W. 145th Street, New York, NY 10031

Telephone: (212) 926-5757; Fax: (212) 926-5842

BUSINESS AND ECONOMIC

Association for the Study of the Cuban Economy (ASCE)
http://lanic.utexas.edu/project/asce/
Description: ASCE is a nonpartisan, nonpolitical organization inaugurated in 1990 to analyze the transformations taking place in the Cuban economy. ASCE publishes a compendium of papers, *Cuba in Transition,* from its annual conference, available in PDF format on its website.
Contact: Stuart Lippe
E-mail: stuartlippe@hotmail.com
Address: 7010 Barkwater Court, Bethesda, MD 20817

The Center for Cuban Business Studies, Ohio Northern University
http://www.onu.edu/cuba/
Description: The Center for Cuban Business Studies conducts Cuban business and policy research, executes educational and advisory projects, and serves as a network of Cuba policy experts. Its various projects aim to facilitate interdisciplinary collaboration focused on Cuba.
Contact: Terry L. Maris, Executive Director
E-mail: t-maris@onu.edu
Address: Center for Cuban Business Studies, 525 South Main Street, Ada, OH 45810
Telephone: (877) 772-3272; Fax: (419) 772-1498

Cuban Agricultural Research Program, University of Florida Institute of Food and Agricultural Sciences
http://www.cubanag.ifas.ufl.edu/
Description: This research program produces economic analyses of Cuba's agricultural sector and assessments of the potential challenges and opportunities for the state of Florida and U.S. agriculture in the event of a normalization of relations with Cuba.

Contact: William A. Messina, Jr., James E. Ross
E-Mail: wamess@ufl.edu; jeross@ufl.edu
Address: Food and Resource Economics Department, P.O. Box 110240, Gainesville, FL 32611
Phone: (352) 392-1826, Ext. 308; Fax: (352) 846-0988

U.S.-Cuba Trade and Economic Council

http://www.cubatrade.org/

Description: Established in 1994, the U.S.-Cuba Trade and Economic Council provides an efficient and sustainable educational structure in which the U.S. business community may access accurate, consistent, and timely information and analysis on matters and issues of interest regarding U.S.-Cuba commercial, economic, and political relations.

E-mail: council@cubatrade.org
Address: 30 Rockefeller Plaza, New York, NY 10112-0002
Telephone: (212) 246-1444; Fax: (212) 246-2345

USA*Engage

http://www.usaengage.org/MBR0088-USAEngage/default.asp?id=1

Description: This organization lobbies against unilateral economic sanctions and seeks to open up opportunities for free trade with Cuba.

Contact: Jake Colvin, Director
E-mail: jcolvin@nftc.org
Address: 1625 K Street NW, Suite 200, Washington, DC 20006
Telephone: (202) 464-2025

U.S.-Cuba Trade Association

http://www.uscuba.org/

Description: The US-Cuba Trade Association is a membership-based, nonprofit organization based in Washington, D.C., that works on behalf of its U.S. business members to protect, expand, and increase the current trade and potential for future business between the United States and Cuba.

Contact: Kirby Jones, President

E-mail: kjones@uscuba.org

Address: 2300 M Street NW, Suite 800, Washington, DC 20037

Telephone: (202) 530-5236; Fax: (202) 530-5235

Cuba News

http://www.cubanews.com/

Description: Founded in 1993, CubaNews is a leading source of business information on Cuba. CubaNews publishes a monthly newsletter with business-related reports from the island and assessments of changes in U.S. policy affecting U.S.-Cuba trade and business opportunities.

Contact: Larry Luxner, Editor and Publisher

E-mail: larry@luxner.com

Addresses: Luxner News, 3005 Portofino Isle, Coconut Creek, FL 33066; Luxner News, 10454 Parthenon Court, Bethesda, MD 20817

Telephone: (954) 970-4518, (301) 365-1745; Fax: (954) 977-2923, (301) 365-1829

ART AND CULTURE

Cuban Ministry of Culture

http://www.min.cult.cu/main.html

Description: An institution of the central administration of the Cuban government created in 1976, the Ministry of Culture is charged with directing, orienting, controlling, and carrying out the cultural policies of the government. Its aim is to guarantee the defense, preservation, and enrichment of the cultural patrimony of Cuba.

Contact: Abel Prieto, Minister of Culture

Address: 2nd Street, between 11th and 13th Avenues, Vedado, C.P. 10400, Plaza, Havana, Cuba

Cubarte, The Ministry of Culture's Portal to Cuban Culture
http://www.cubarte.cult.cu/eng/
Description: This is the official portal for Cuban culture. It has extensive information and links to most of Cuba's cultural institutions.

UNEAC, Association of Cuban Writers and Artists
http://www.uneac.com/
Description: The UNEAC is the official administrative and cultural center for all Cuban writers and artists. It publishes the magazine *Unión* and holds literary competitions, among many other cultural activities. UNEAC describes itself as "a social, cultural, professional, and non-governmental organization."
Contact: Carlos Martí Brenes
E-mail: uneac@cubarte.cult.cu
Address: 354 17th Street, between G and H, Vedado, C.P. 10400, Havana, Cuba
Telephone: (537) 832-4551; Fax: (537) 833-3158

ICAIC, Cuban Film Institute
http://www.cubacine.cu/
Description: ICAIC (El Instituto Cubano de Arte e Industria Cinematográficos), founded on March 24, 1959, has the mission of producing, distributing, exhibiting, promoting, and conserving audiovisual materials produced in Cuba, principally films and documentaries.
Contact: Omar González
E-mail: presidenciaicaic@icaic.cu
Address: 1155 23rd Street, between 10th and 12th Avenues, C.P. 10400, Plaza, Havana, Cuba
Telephone: (537) 855-2859

International Festival of New Latin American Cinema

http://www.habanafilmfestival.com/

Description: Starting in December 1979, Cuba began hosting a Latin American Film Festival, bringing together the best of new cinema from around the hemisphere. Each December, Havana comes alive with the activities of this festival, which takes place in the city's many theaters.

Contact: Alfredo Guevara, President; Iván Giroud, Director

E-mail: festival@festival.icaic.cu

Casa de las Américas

http://www.casa.cult.cu/

Description: Dedicated to the promotion and study of culture and the arts since its founding in the early 1960s, the Casa provides a space for various forms of art and holds international literary competitions for writers of many different genres. Casa also works to disseminate the work of artists, writers, and musicians from Cuba, Latin America, and the Caribbean. The Casa also houses a literary research center and a center dedicated to the study of the Caribbean.

Contact: Roberto Fernández Retamar

E-mail: casa@cubarte.cult.cu; casa@casa.cult.cu

Address: 3rd Street at #52 G, Vedado, C.P. 10400, Havana, Cuba

Telephone: (537) 855-2706; Fax: (537) 833-4554

Casa del Caribe

http://www.cult.cu/ccaribe/

Description: The Casa del Caribe is a meeting place for those dedicated to the study of the Caribbean. It is also the host for the annual international convention, Festival del Caribe.

Contact: Julián Mateo Tornés, Rafael Duharte, Joel James

Address: 154 13th Street at 8th Avenue, C.P. 90400, Reparto Vista Alegre, Santiago, Cuba

Telephone: (53-266) 4-2285; Fax: (53-266) 4-2387

Advanced Institute of Art (ISA)

Description: The ISA is Cuba's highest school for the plastic arts.

Contact: Raquel Mendieta

Address: 778th Street between 9th and 11th Avenues, Casa 910, Miramar, Playa, Havana, Cuba

Telephone: (537) 303-3652; Fax: (537) 303-3659

Juan Marinello Center for Research on Cuban Culture

http://www.cubarte.cult.cu

Description: The Juan Marinello Research Center is dedicated to promoting Cuban culture both on the island and abroad. It works extensively with a wide array of researchers in Cuba and from abroad and periodically holds seminars on cultural and intellectual themes.

Contact: María Victoria Prado Ramírez

E-mail: cidcc@cubarte.cult.cu

Address: 63 Boyeros between Bruzón and Lugareño, C.P. 10600, Plaza, Havana, Cuba

Telephone: (537) 857-5770; Fax: (537) 877-5196

Wilfredo Lam Contemporary Art Center

Description: The Lam center is devoted to the study and dissemination of the work of Wilfredo Lam and other Cuban modernists of the Vanguardia movement. It also promotes the art of other contemporary painters and compiles information on developments in the field of the visual arts in Cuba. It is also the main body responsible for organizing the Havana Biennial, a major art exhibition that takes place periodically in Havana, attracting artists from around the world.

Contact: Dominica Ojeda Diez

E-mail: wlam@cubarte.cult.cu

Address: 22 San Ignacio Street at Empedrado, C.P. 10100, Habana Vieja, Havana, Cuba

Telephone: (537) 861-3419; Fax: (537) 833-8477

Fundación Fernando Ortiz

Description: One of the leading historical and anthropological institutions in Cuba, the Fundación is a repository of information and experts on research into Cuban history, music, and Afro-Cuban culture. It strives to disseminate the thought and work of Fernando Ortiz and sponsors various conferences, seminars, and publications.

Contact: Miguel Barnet Lanza
E-mail: uhlha@unesco.org
Address: 160 L Street at 27A, Plaza, Vedado, Havana, Cuba
Telephone: (537) 832-4334; Fax: (537) 830-0623

Art-Havana

http://www.art-havana.com/
Description: Art-Havana has been promoting Cuban contemporary art since 1999. Groups from museums, art centers, as well as individual collectors have visited Havana through Art-Havana. Art-Havana offers historian-guided city tours, museum and gallery visits, as well as visits to the studios of the most important contemporary Cuban artists.

Contact: Rolando Milián, Director (in the United States)
E-mail: rgmilian@art-havana.com; rgmilian@hotmail.com
Telephone: (203) 980-7564; (203) 415-1506
Contact: Susset Martinez, Art Curator (in Cuba)
E-mail: susyed@giron.sld.cu
Telephone: (537) 267-7989; Cell: (535) 889-4153

Galeria Servando

Description: One of Havana's leading contemporary art galleries with a very professional and friendly staff. They have rotating exhibitions and good contacts with the artists themselves.

Contact: Sachie Hernández Machín
E-mail: galeriaservando@icaic.cu; servando@galerias-cubanas.com

Address: 23rd Street between 10th and 12th Avenues, ICAIC Building, Vedado, Havana, Cuba
Telephone: (537) 833-9599

Temas Magazine
http://www.temas.cult.cu/
Description: Published since 1995 and on-line since 2002, *Temas* is the leading contemporary sociocultural journal published in Cuba today. It publishes articles on art, music, literature, the social sciences, political theory, and ideology. The editorial board is composed of Rafael Hernández, Alfredo Prieto, Natalia Bolívar, Rufo Caballero, Mario Coyula, Mayra Espina, Jorge Ibarra, Nelson P. Valdés, Oscar Zanetti, and Piero Gleijeses, among others.
Contact: Rafael Hernández, Alfredo Prieto
Email: temas@icaic.cu
Address: 1155 23rd Street, 5th floor, between 10th and 12th Avenues, C.P. 10400, Vedado, Havana, Cuba
Telefax: (537) 855-3010, 830-4759, 855-3650, Ext. 233

Center for Cuban Studies, New York
http://www.cubaupdate.org/
Description: The Center for Cuban Studies is a nonprofit educational institution located in New York City that promotes knowledge of Cuban culture and society with an emphasis on the achievements of the Cuban Revolution. Open since 1972, one of its aims is to end the U.S. embargo and achieve a normalization in relations between Cuba and the United States. It sponsors various trips to Cuba for licensable professionals.
Contact: Sandra Levinson
E-mail: cubanctr@igc.org
Address: 124 West 23rd Street, New York, NY 10011
Telephone: (212) 242-0559; Fax: (212) 242-1937

Cuban Cinema Classics, University of William and Mary

http://cubancinemaclassics.org/cubahome.htm

Description: Cuban Cinema Classics presents a showcase of Cuba's award-winning revolutionary documentaries. The initiative was established to address the difficulty of obtaining Cuban documentaries with English subtitles for educational and cultural purposes in the United States. CCC distributes the documentaries to colleges and universities, media arts centers, museums, and other agencies.

Contact: Ann Marie Stock

E-mail: cubancinemaclassics@wm.edu; amstoc@wm.edu

Address: Cuban Cinema Classics, c/o Ann Marie Stock, 104 Wakerobin Road, Williamsburg, VA 23185

Telephone: (757) 221-3590, 221-3591; Fax: (757) 221-3597

Cuban Poster Art Project of Docs Populi (Documents for the Public)

http://www.docspopuli.org/CubaPosters.html

Description: Docs Populi documents and disseminates late twetieth-century political poster art, including that of post-revolutionary Cuba.

Contact: Lincoln Cushing

E-mail: lcushing@igc.org; lcushing@docspopuli.org

Address: 822 Santa Barbara Road, Berkeley, CA 94707

Telephone: (510) 528-7161

Related Sites: http://www.lib.berkeley.edu/~lcushing/Home.html; http://libr.org/pl/15_Cushing.html

Stage of the Arts (SOTA), "Cubans in Hollywood" program

http://www.CubansInHollywood.com or http://www.stage-ofthearts.info

Description: SOTA is a nonprofit organization aimed at promoting the Cuban Music Festival of Echo Park, Los Angeles, since 1995. It has also produced "The Old Man and the Sea" multimedia concert featuring Aurelio De la Vega and Francisco Aguabella, Celia Cruz Square, and the "Cubans in Hollywood Song and Poetry contest" among other events.

Contact: Jorge Luis Rodríguez
E-mail: JorgeLuis@CubansInHollywood.com
Address: P.O. Box 26688, Los Angeles, CA 90026
Telephone: (323) 662-3750

Afrocuba Research Institute
http://www.afrocuba.org
Description: The Afro Cuba Research Institute is a research group that studies and promotes Afro-Cuban traditions. It also publishes the *Afrocuba Journal* and conducts the Palo Monte program of cultural academic exchange between Cuba and the United States, founded in Matanzas, Cuba, in 1976.

Contact: Jorge Luis Rodríguez, Director; María Esther Ortiz, Editor
E-mail: Director@afrocuba.org; Ortiz@Afrocuba.org
Membership: Afrocuba@Yahoogroups.com
Address: P.O. Box 26688, Los Angeles, CA 90026
Telephone: (323) 662-3750

Afro-Cuba Web
http://www.afrocubaweb.com
Description: This webpage is dedicated to promoting recognition and research of the African cultures in Cuba.

E-mail: acw@afrocubaweb.com
Address: P.O. Box 1054, Arlington, MA 02474

Timba.com
http://www.timba.com
Description: This multilingual website is put together and maintained by a global collection of aficionados of Cuba's contemporary dance music sensation, *Timba*. The site provides

detailed, accurate information on the origins and development of timba music, major groups and their albums, song lyrics, announcements of upcoming shows and tours, and music reviews.

Contact: Kevin Moore

E-mail: kevin@timba.com

Address: 6800 Bird Road, #267, Miami, FL 33155

CubaNOLA Collective

http://www.cubanola.org/

Description: CubaNOLA Collective brings together musicians, artists, scholars, and tradition bearers to explore and expand the ties between the musical, artistic, and cultural heritages of Cuba and New Orleans, Louisiana. The organization sees Cuba and New Orleans as cultural hubs for the Caribbean and Gulf South regions and builds relationships between artists and communities through performances, artist collaborations, educational programs, heritage tours, and documentaries.

Contact: Ariana Hall

E-mail: ariana@cubanola.org

DEMOCRACY AND HUMAN RIGHTS

Cuban Commission for Human Rights and National Reconciliation

Description: Elizardo Sánchez Santacruz is one of Cuba's leading human rights activists. He is distinguished from other dissidents as a social democrat who calls for fundamental changes in Cuba's political system, remaining in Cuba and publicly denouncing right-wing exile activities and the U.S. embargo.

Contact: Elizardo Sánchez Santacruz

Address: 3014 21st Street, between 30th and 34th Avenues, Playa, Havana, Cuba

Social Democratic Party
Description: Vladimiro Roca is a leading human rights activist and Cuban dissident. He was a member of the Cuban Dissidence Working Group that released the report "The Homeland Belongs to Us All," on June 27, 1997, denouncing the Cuban government. He served a long prison sentence (much of it spent in solitary confinement) following his arrest but has continued to work for human rights since his release.
Contact: Vladimiro Roca Antunez
Address: 105 36th Avenue, between 41st and 43rd Streets, Nuevo Vedado, Plaza, Havana, Cuba

Christian Liberation Movement (MLC)
www.mclpaya.org
Description: Founded in 1988 by a group of lay Catholics led by Osvaldo Payá Sardiñas, the Christian Liberation Movement is best-known for the Varela Project. The Varela Project seeks to start a civic dialogue, open up Cuba's political system, defend and promote respect for civil, economic, and human rights, and achieve national reconciliation through peaceful means. The MLC does not accept aid from the U.S. government and opposes the embargo.
Contact: Francisco De Armas, International Representative
E-mail: cromero@idcla.org; mclpaya2@compuserve.com
Telephone: (305) 285-7970

Freedom House, Cuba Country Report 2005
http://www.freedomhouse.org/template.cfm?page=22&country=6721&year=2005&view=mof
Description: The Cuba Programs of Freedom House seek to promote a peaceful transition to democracy in the island. Their strategy includes the distribution of publications and support for Cuban prodemocracy organizations and activists.
Contact: Lisa Davis, Xavier Utset
E-mail: fh@freedomhouse.org; utset@freedomhouse.org

Address: 1319 18th Street NW, Washington, DC 20036
Telephone: (202) 296-5101, Fax: (202) 296-5078

Human Rights Watch/Americas, Cuba Page

http://www.hrw.org/doc?t=americas&c=cuba

Description: The 2005 report begins with the following summary: "Cuba remains a Latin American anomaly: an undemocratic government that represses nearly all forms of political dissent. President Fidel Castro's government continues to enforce political conformity using criminal prosecutions, long- and short-term detentions, mob harassment, police warnings, surveillance, house arrests, travel restrictions, and politically-motivated dismissals from employment. The end result is that Cubans are systematically denied basic rights to free expression, association, assembly, privacy, movement, and due process of law."

E-mail: hrwdc@hrw.org

Address: 1630 Connecticut Avenue NW, Suite 500, Washington, DC 20009

Telephone: (202) 612-4321; Fax: (202) 612-4333

Amnesty International

http://web.amnesty.org/report2006/cub-summary-eng

Description: Amnesty International tracks and documents human and civil rights violations. The summary of the 2005 report concludes: "Restrictions on freedom of expression, association and movement continued to cause great concern. Nearly 70 prisoners of conscience remained in prison. The US embargo continued to have a negative effect on the enjoyment of the full range of human rights in Cuba. The economic situation deteriorated and the government attempted to suppress private entrepreneurship."

Human Rights Internet (HRI)

http://www.hri.ca

Description: Founded in 1976, HRI is a leader in the

exchange of information within the worldwide human rights community. Headquartered in Ottawa, Canada, HRI is linked to more than 5,000 organizations and individuals around the world seeking to advance human rights.

Contact: Juan Antonio Blanco

E-mail: hri@hri.ca; jab@hri.ca

Address: One Nicholas Street, Suite 301, Ottawa, Ontario, K1N 7B7, Canada

Telephone: (613) 789-7407; Fax: (613) 789-7414

Center for a Free Cuba

http://www.cubacenter.org/

Description: The Center for a Free Cuba (CFC) is an independent, nonpartisan institution dedicated to promoting human rights and a transition to democracy and the rule of law on the island. Established in November 1997, the center gathers and disseminates information about Cuba and Cubans to the news media, NGOs, and the international community. The center also assists the people of Cuba through its information outreach and humanitarian programs on the island.

Contact: Frank Calzón

E-mail: Freecuba@cubacenter.org

Address: Center for a Free Cuba, 1320 19th Street NW, Suite 600, Washington, DC 20036

Telephone: (202) 463-8430; Fax: (202) 463-8412

DIASPORA AND EXILE ORGANIZATIONS

Cuban American National Foundation (CANF)

http://www.canf.org/2004/principal-ingles.htm

Description: The Cuban American National Foundation (CANF) is a nonprofit organization dedicated to advancing freedom and democracy in Cuba. Established in Florida in 1981, CANF is the largest Cuban organization in exile, representing a cross-section of the Cuban exile community. CANF supports a nonviolent transition to a pluralistic, market-based democracy grounded in the rule of law and the protection of human, social, political, and economic rights.

Contact: Mariela Ferretti

E-mail: hq@canf.org; canfnet@icanect.net

Address: P.O. Box 440069, Miami, FL 33144-9926

Telephone: (305) 592-7768; Fax: (305) 592-7889

Cuban Liberty Council

http://www.cubanlibertycouncil.org/

Description: Formed in 2001 after a split with the Cuban American National Foundation (CANF), the Cuban Liberty Council (CLC) is a nonprofit organization committed to promote liberty and democracy in Cuba.

E-mail: info@cubanlibertycouncil.org

Address: 701 SW 27th Avenue, Suite 820, Miami, FL 33135

Telephone: (305) 642-0610; Fax: (305) 642-0410

Cuban Committee for Democracy

http://www.ccdusa.org/

Description: Working to support a peaceful transition to democracy in Cuba, the CCD is a moderate Cuban-American organization based in Washington, D.C.

Contact: Sean García

E-mail: ccd@us.net

Address: 1777 T Street NW, Washington, DC 20009

Telephone: (202) 319-0056; Fax: (202) 319-0058

Encasa/US-Cuba

http://encasa-us-cuba.org/

Description: As the name indicates, the Emergency Network of Cuban American Scholars and Artists for Change in US-Cuba Policy (ENCASA/US-CUBA) opposes current U.S. policy toward Cuba and seeks to eliminate the embargo and the restrictions on family contacts, while expanding the opportunities for academic exchange. Formed in 2006,

ENCASA seeks to break down the monolithic image of a uniformly hard-line Cuban-American community.

Contact: Rubén G. Rumbaut, Professor of Sociology and Codirector

E-mail: encasa-us-cuba@runbox.com; rrumbaut@uci.edu

Address: Center for Research on Immigration, Population, and Public Policy, 3151 Social Science Plaza, University of California, Irvine, Irvine, CA 92697

Telephone: (949) 824-2495; Fax: (949) 824-4717

Cuban American Commission for Family Rights

http://www.cubanfamilyrights.org/Contac/contact.html

Description: The Cuban American Commission for Family Rights is a broad coalition of Cuban Americans established to denounce the new government restrictions on travel and remittances to Cuba. Their mission is "to preserve the integrity of the Cuban Family and work to defeat those who want to divide it."

Contact: Silvia Wilhelm, Executive Director

E-mail: info@cubanfamilyrights.org

Address: P.O. Box 330017, Miami, Florida 33233

Phone: (786) 374-7220; Fax: (305) 858-9353

The Cuban American Alliance Education Fund (CAAEF)

http://www.cubamer.org/

Description: The Cuban American Alliance Education Fund (CAAEF) is a nonprofit national network of Cuban-Americans aimed at the development of mutually beneficial engagements between Cubans and Americans that promote understanding and human compassion.

Contact: Delvis Fernández Levy, President

E-mail: caaef@hughes.net

Address: 1010 Vermont Avenue NW, Suite 620, Washington, DC 20005

Telephone: (805) 627-1959; Fax: (805) 627-1959

TRAVEL AND TOURISM

Cuba Travel

http://www.cubatravel.cu/client/home/index.ph

Description: Official government site to promote tourism in Cuba.

HavanaTur

http://www.havanatur.cu/

Description: City of Havana official tourism site.

E-mail: eduardoj@cimex.com.cu

Address: Sierra Maestra Building, 1st Street, between 0 and 2, Miramar, Playa, Havana, Cuba

Telephone: (537) 203-9770; Fax: (537) 204-2877

Cuba Connection

http://www.cuba.tc/

Description: Having left the Turks and Caicos Islands to avoid the U.S. embargo, this organization has a solid group of associates on the ground in Cuba who can set up just about anything you need. The staff is multilingual, and its website features links to all major Cuban tourism companies. It also features a helpful list of hotels, car rental companies, good info on scuba in Cuba, tips for tourists, advice for U.S. travelers, and information on special marriage or honeymoon getaways to Cuba.

Contact: Carlos Ciaño or Katia Ramos

E-mail: cubanconnection@yahoo.com; cubacon@ip.etecsa.cu; or cubacon@enet.cu

Telephone: (941) 793-7157; Fax: (941) 793-5204

Marazul Tours

http://www.marazultours.com/

Description: The leading U.S.-based tourism agency catering to travel to Cuba. Its website has abundant information on U.S. travel restrictions and links to the U.S. Treasury Department's Office of Foreign Assets Control—the entity responsible for licensing travel to Cuba.

Contact: Mayra Alonso, Hilda Díaz
Address: 4100 Park Avenue, Weehawken, NJ 07087
Telephone: (201) 319-9670

Caribe Express
http://www.caribeexpress.com
Description: Caribe Express is located in the heart of the Cuban émigré community of West New York/Union City, New Jersey, and specializes in arranging family travel and sending care packages to Cuba. They are very friendly and efficient.

Contact: Linda
E-mail: caribexp@optonline.net; caribeexpress@optonline.net
Address: 6505 Hudson Avenue, West New York, NJ 07093
Telephone: (201) 869-7989

RELIGIOUS

Catholic Church in Cuba
http://www.nacub.org/
Description: The official website of the Cuban Catholic Church.

Vitral **Magazine—Center for Civic and Religious Formation**
http://www.vitral.org/ or http://www.diocesispinardelrio.org
Description: A publication Catholic Dioceses of Pinar del Río, this incisive and often critical bimonthly magazine is run by a group of dedicated and hopeful lay people. The Center and publication seek to provide an integrated framework with which to revitalize the values of human freedom and community solidarity with an eye toward rebuilding Cuban civil society.

Contact: Dagoberto Valdés Hernández, Director
E-mail: vitral@obipinar.co.cu
Address: C.F.C.R., Obispado de Pinar del Río, Calle Máximo Gómez No. 160 Between Avenue Rafael Ferro y Comandante Pinares, C.P. 20100, Pinar del Río, Cuba
Telephone: (53-82) 75-2359; Fax: (53-82) 77-8362

Caritas
Description: Cuba's principal Catholic Charity, in charge of distributing aid and donations to the Cuban population from abroad.
Contact: Dr. Rolando Suárez Cobián, Director
Address: 905 San Lazaro, Apartado 594, Centro Habana, Havana, Cuba
Telephone: (537) 870-4179

Christian Center for Reflection and Dialogue (CCRD)
http://ccrd.org/
Description: An active Protestant church located in the city of Cárdenas. The Centro publishes an on-line newsletter.
Contact: Rev. Raimundo García Franco, Executive Director
E-mail: ccrd@enet.cu; franco@enet.cu
Address: 1210 Céspedes, between 25th and 26th, A.P. 5363, Cárdenas, Matanzas, Cuba
Telephone: (53-45) 52-2923, (53-45) 52-1710; Fax: (53-45) 52-1000

Martin Luther King Memorial Center
Description: An important progressive social service and religious organization.
Contact: Daisy Rojas, Raúl Suárez
E-mail: rinternac@mlking.sld.cu
Address: 9609 53rd Avenue, between 96th and 98th Streets, C.P. 11400, Marianao 14, Havana, Cuba
Telephone: (537) 820-3940, 820-9741; Fax: (537) 827-2959, 833-2959

The Cuban Jewish Community
http://www.chcuba.org/english/index.htm
Description: This is the primary Jewish community center and charity of Cuba. It has extensive contacts in Israel and with Jewish communities in the United States.
Contact: Dr. José Miller
E-mail: patronato_ort@enet.cu; beth_shalom@enet.cu
Address: I Street at 13th Avenue, Vedado, Havana, Cuba
Telephone: (537) 832-8953; Fax (537) 833-3778
Related site and information: The Jews of Cuba—
http://jewishcuba.org/
Contact address in the United States: Jewish Cuba Connection, 4 Lighthouse Street, #12, Marina Del Rey, CA 90292

Yoruba Cultural Association of Cuba
Description: The Yoruba Cultural Association of Cuba has as its driving purpose the preservation, study, and promotion of the Yoruba cultural traditions in Cuba.
Contact: Antonio Castañeda Márquez, President
Address: 456 Gervasio, between Zanja and San José, Apartado 1, Centro Habana, Havana, Cuba
Telephone: (537) 879-6948

NEWS SOURCES

Granma International in English
http://www.granma.cu/ingles/index.html.
Description: International English version of Cuba's national newspaper.

Granma Daily National Newspaper
http://www.granma.cubaweb.cu/temas2/index.html
Description: Daily newspaper published by the Cuban Communist Party.

Cuba Encuentro
http://www.cubaencuentro.com/
Description: Site of the Cuban cultural journal *Encuentro de la Cultura Cubana* (Madrid), with the most balanced and up-to-date approach to news on culture, politics, and economics in Cuba. This site is also home to an extensive, easy-to-use, and penetrating collection of documents, links, human rights information, photographs, lists of Cuba-related publishers, a list of centers of Cuban, Caribbean, and Latin American Studies around the world, as well as PDFs of back issues.
Contact: Annabelle Rodríguez, President
E-mail: Association: asociacion@encuentro.net; Journal: revista@encuentro.net
Daily news on-line: enlared@encuentro.net; Portal: portal@encuentro.net
Address: Asociación Encuentro de la Cultura Cubana, Infanta Mercedes 43, 1° A, 28020 Madrid, España
Telephone: (34) 91-425-0404; Fax: (34) 91-571-7316

Miami Herald
http://www.miami.com/mld/miamiherald/
Description: Miami's major daily newspaper with extensive coverage of Cuba-related issues.

El Nuevo Herald
http://www.miami.com/mld/elnuevo/
Description: The Spanish-language publication of the *Miami Herald*. This version of the paper often has more sustained and in-depth coverage of Cuba.

CubaNet News
http://www.cubanet.org/
Description: CubaNet is committed to fostering a free press in Cuba. The website acts as a clearinghouse of news on Cuba,

with an emphasis on news directly from Cuba by independent journalists and a focus on human and economic rights.

Contact: Rosa Berre

E-mail: cubanetn@aol.com; cubanet@cubanet.org; laeditora@aol.com

Address: CubaNet News, 145 Madeira Avenue, Suite 207, Coral Gables, FL 33134

Telephone: (305) 774-1887; Fax: (305) 774-1807

Initiativo Cubaverdad

http://www.cubaverdad.net or http://www.cubaverdad.org

Description: This site is dedicated to human rights in Cuba and contains links to important news, reports, websites, and data. CubaVerdad also provides a free digest of a wide selection of articles from the international press about Cuba. The site also features an e-group with an archive of over 29,000 Cuba-related news articles: http://groups.yahoo.com/group.CubaVerdad/. The site also includes a link to a blog (http://cubadata.blogspot.com/) and a subdirectory dedicated exclusively to economic news (http://cubafacts.blogspot.com/).

E-mail: admin@cubaverdad.org; Cuba Verdad@yahoogroups.com

University of New Mexico—Cuba-L Direct Project

http://cuba-l.istec.org or http://www.unm.edu/~socdept/Faculty/valdes/valdes.htm

Description: Since 1986, Nelson Valdés has compiled one of the most extensive internet mailing digests on Cuba through his Cuba-L list. E-mail him for subscription information at: cuba-l@list.unm.edu.

Contact: Nelson P. Valdés, Director, Cuba-L Direct Project

E-mail: nvaldes@unm.edu; cuba-l@list.unm.edu

Address: Cuba Research and Analysis Group, Latin American and Iberian Institute

University of New Mexico, 801 Yale NE, Albuquerque, NM 87106

Telephone: (505) 277-3840, (505) 277-2501

MISCELLANEOUS

History of Cuba.com

http://historyofcuba.com/

Description: The mission of this site is to provide a clear and detailed journey through the themes, concepts, people, and ideas that make up Cuban history. The site features many useful features, including a general index of people and events, a detailed timetable of Cuban history, a comprehensive bibliography of works on Cuba, a list of links and resources, and an appropriately titled author's blog entitled simply "Cuba on My Mind."

Contact: Jerry A. Sierra

E-mail: ja378sierra@rcn.com

Domingo Soto—Homepage

http://www.domsoto.com/cuba/cuba2.htm

Description: A Puerto Rican Mobilian (that is, living in Mobile, Alabama), Dom Soto has set up this useful list of links for Cuba lovers. It includes links to everything from art and architecture, to human rights, to history and culture, to flora and fauna, to religion, to Spanish classes in Cuba.

Annotated Bibliography

BOOKS

Below I describe the books and other resources that were most useful to me in preparing this volume. In order to make this annotated bibliography more useful for future reading and research, I have divided it into thematic sections based on the chapters in the book's narrative section.

General and Miscellaneous

Understanding the life and thought of José Martí is essential as a basis for understanding Cuban history, politics, culture, and society. However, digesting the multivolume collected works in Spanish is a challenge for even the most ambitious and talented Cubanophile. Luckily, Esther Allen has done a stellar job of editing and translating some of the most relevant of his sometimes dense and always penetrating poetry, letters, journal entries, and essays, in *José Martí: Selected Writings* (Penguin, 2002). Also published in 2002 is the first ever two-volume English-language *Encyclopedia of Cuba: People, History, Culture* (Greenwood Press). Edited by Luis Martínez-Fernández, D. H. Figueredo, Louis A. Pérez, Jr., and Luis González, this essential collection of brief but informative entries on Cuba's history, politics, and culture is a gold mine of information on the island written by leading scholars both on the island and abroad.

Three major anthologies on Cuba have been published during the last twenty years. Most recently, Aviva Chomsky, Barry Car, and Pamela Maria Smorkaloff have edited *The Cuba Reader: History, Culture, Politics* (Duke University Press, 2003). This 700-page text contains an excellent and deftly edited collection of mostly primary materials arranged in eight chronological sections. Highlights of the reader include classic essays by Bartolomé de Las Casas, Fernando Ortiz, Manuel Moreno Fraginals, José Antonio Saco, José Martí, Miguel Barnet, Oscar Lewis, Che Guevara, Fidel Castro, Alejandro Portes, and Haroldo Dilla, as well as poetry and prose from leading Cuban authors including Juan Francisco Manzano, Gómez de Avellaneda, Nicolás Guillén, Alejo Carpentier, Reinaldo Arenas, Heberto Padilla, Nancy Morejón, and Roberto Fernández. Now in its eleventh edition, *Cuban Communism, 1959–2003* (Transaction Publishers, 2003) is focused on the economic, military, social, and political aspects of the revolution. Editors Irving Louis Horowitz and Jaime Suchlicki have recently added new readings under the heading "Transition to Civil Society," making the book especially useful to comparativists.

Philip Brenner, William M. LeoGrande, Donna Rich, and Daniel Seigel edited the excellent *Cuba Reader: The Making of a Revolutionary Society* (Grove Press, 1989) more than fifteen years ago. While some parts of it are dated, its more sympathetic approach to the socialist experiment is a nice complement to Horowitz and Suchlicki's more hard-edged collection. Especially enlightening are the essays by Cuban poet and social scientist Lourdes Casal. Brenner and LeoGrande, along with John M. Kirk and Marguerite Jiménez, are about to release an updated reader focused on the special period, entitled, *A Contemporary Cuba Reader: Reinventing the Revolution* (Rowman and Littlefield, 2007). Another useful anthology is *Toward a New Cuba? Legacies of a Revolution,* edited by Miguel Angel Centeno and Mauricio Font (Lynne Rienner, 1997). One final recent, well-written, and data-rich reference book on Cuba is *Cuba: A Country Study* (Federal Research Division, Library of Congress, 2002). Now in its fourth edition, edited and with an excellent introduction by Rex Hudson, this critical compendium of up-to-date information on the island includes sections on history, society, economics, political institutions, and the military, each penned by leaders in their fields.

Some of the most underestimated but most useful and informative resources on Cuba are the many guidebooks covering the island destination that have recently flooded the market. Few other resources combine readability with detailed facts and up-to-date information on seemingly everything under the sun. My most reliable companions on guiding me to, through, and out of the island now more than a dozen times are the handbooks on Cuba published by **Moon Handbooks** (Christopher P. Baker, Avalon Travel Publishing, 2000) and **Lonely Planet** (David Stanley, Lonely Planet Publications, 2000). (Both have been recently reissued in 2006 editions.) For comprehensive coverage, accurate, respectful reportage, and sheer readability, these two guides cannot be beat. Baker's 750-page guide manages to be truly encyclopedic without ever being boring and is the leader in the field. A bit more digestible is the 2006 Lonely Planet edition by Brendan Sainsbury, weighing in at just under 500 pages.

Geography, History, and Biography

General History and Geography. By far the clearest, most easily digestible, yet eminently serious and scholarly one-volume history of the island is *Cuba: A Short History.* Published by Cambridge University Press in 1993, this book is excerpted from Cambridge's multivolume *Cambridge History of Latin America.* Edited by Leslie Bethell, this slim book is under 200 pages and includes chronological chapters from the eminent scholars Hugh Thomas, Luis E. Aguilar, Louis A. Pérez, Jr., and Jorge I. Domínguez. For anyone wanting to dig deeper into Cuban history, the various books written by these same authors are an excellent guide and reference. First is Hugh Thomas's mammoth 1,700-page *Cuba or the Pursuit of Freedom* (rev. ed., DaCapo Press, 1998). Despite its enormous size, this book covers just 200 years of Cuban history (1762–1962) and as such does so in intricate and tantalizing detail. Thomas is a true master historian who can breathe life into the seemingly mundane just as well as he can tease apart the intricacies of the explosion of the USS *Maine* in 1898 or the events surrounding the failed Bay of Pigs invasion in 1961. Likewise, Cuban-American historian Luis E. Aguilar adeptly places the 1959 revolution in its proper historical context by walking us through the failed revolution of 1933 in his *Cuba, 1933: Prologue to Revolution* (Cornell University Press, 1972).

The most prolific historian writing today on Cuba is without a doubt Louis A. Pérez, Jr. Among his many very fine books on Cuba's history, his general overview *Cuba: Between Reform and Revolution* (now in its third edition, Oxford University Press, 2006) is perhaps the best to begin with. Besides being a fact-filled and entertaining general history, the book makes a clear, consistent, and convincing argument linking the Cuban Revolution of today to the country's history of frustrated attempts at independence and sovereignty. It also includes an incomparable annotated bibliography of an enormous amount of source material on Cuba that could be a book unto itself. Pérez has also published an excellent historical study of U.S.-Cuban relations, entitled *Cuba and the United States: Ties of Singular Intimacy* (University of Georgia Press, 1990). Finally, Jorge I. Domínguez has set the standard for institutional analysis of socialist Cuba in his detailed and critical-minded history of the island's twentieth-century politics, *Cuba: Order and Revolution* (Harvard University Press, 1978).

Also worth noting are journalist Richard Gott's *Cuba: A New History* (Yale University Press, 2004). A longtime itinerant journalist reporting from across Latin America since the 1960s, Gott has produced a quite comprehensive, readable, and fresh new history of Cuba. His book is especially good at recounting specific episodes from Afro-Cuban history, including the Aponte conspiracy, the Escalera massacre, and the 1912 "race war," as well as chronicling Cuba's hugely influential involvement in the African wars in Ethiopia and especially

Angola. Marifeli Pérez-Stable has written what is perhaps the clearest and most convincing historical sociology of the Cuban Revolution in her *Cuban Revolution: Origins, Course, and Legacy* (2nd ed., Oxford University Press, 1999). Finally, Cuban-American historian Jaime Suchlicki is the author of *Cuba: From Columbus to Castro and Beyond* (4th ed., Brassey's, 1997), which is especially useful on the colonial period and the student activism of the twentieth century. He is also responsible for the very useful reference work *Historical Dictionary of Cuba* (2nd ed., Scarecrow Press, 2001).

Apart from the above general histories of Cuba, the following classic works on sugar and slavery in the Caribbean with an emphasis on nineteenth-century Cuba are all highly recommended. The classic Cuban text on the island's allegorical battle between tobacco and sugar, *Cuban Counterpoint: Tobacco and Sugar* (Duke University Press, 1995), was written by Fernando Ortiz and originally published in Spanish in 1940. This new edition has been expertly translated by Harriet de Onís, with a fantastic new introduction by Fernando Coronil. After Ortiz, perhaps Cuban historian Manuel Moreno Fraginals' *Sugarmill: The Socioeconomic Complex of Sugar in Cuba, 1760–1860* (Monthly Review Press, 1976) is the next most important study of the socioeconomic impact that the sugar/slave nexus had on nineteenth-century Cuban society. This book was recently reissued by the Catalan publisher Crítica, under its original title in Spanish, *El ingenio: Complejo económico social cubano del azúcar* (2001). German explorer and intellectual Alexander von Humboldt first visited Cuba in 1800 and later penned one of the classic political studies of the Spanish colony, *Ensayo político sobre la isla de Cuba,* first published in 1826 as part of a larger work chronicling his travels throughout the Americas. His study has recently been reissued by Markus Wiener Publishers in a new critical edition, entitled, *Island of Cuba: A Political Essay* (2001), produced under the guidance of historians

Luis Fernández Martínez and Frank Argote-Freyre, and translated by Shelley Frisch.

Of equal importance is Herbert S. Klein's more general study, *African Slavery in Latin America and the Caribbean* (Oxford University Press, 1986). Similarly, Hugh Thomas has performed a masterful feat of historical research with his recently published study, *The Slave Trade: The Story of the Atlantic Slave Trade: 1440–1870* (Touchstone, 1997). Finally, there are two other books without which one cannot really begin to understand how slavery was lived on a day-to-day basis by the slaves themselves. The first is the life story of the *cimarrón* (escaped slave) Esteban Montejo, as he recounted it at 105 years of age to Cuban writer and anthropologist Miguel Barnet. The book was published in English as *Biography of a Runaway Slave* (Curbstone Press, 1994). The other Cuban slave narrative is perhaps the only document we have in all of Latin America actually written by a former slave himself. Juan Francisco Manzano's *Poems by a Slave in the Island of Cuba, Recently Liberated.* First translated and published in English by the Irish abolitionist Richard R. Madden in 1840, this book also contains the story of Manzano's early life, as well as a number of essays on slavery by Madden. Fortunately, the University of North Carolina at Chapel Hill has recently placed the entire text of this valuable document on-line at: http://docsouth.unc.edu/neh/manzano/manzano.html, where it can be viewed in open access, free of charge.

The War of 1898/The Spanish-American War. The Cuban War for Independence that began in 1895, leading to the so-called Spanish-American War of 1898, has produced a voluminous historical literature. Perhaps the most comprehensive and useful work that treats this period of Cuba's history is Benjamin R. Beede's *War of 1898 and U.S. Interventions 1898–1934: An Encyclopedia* (Garland Publishing, 1994). More than the War of 1898 itself, this high-quality reference work includes entries on the various U.S. military occupations of the island, all the major military and political personalities on the various sides, as well as entries on the many U.S. interventions both in the Caribbean and the Pacific that followed the invasion of Cuba in 1898. Louis A. Pérez, Jr., has set a new standard in critical historiography and national memory with his powerful and original *War of 1898: The United States and Cuba in History and Historiography* (University of North Carolina Press, 1998). This slim volume is anything but slight, as it takes on 100 years of scholarship on the war using a fresh, critical approach that questions many of the basic assumptions that led the United States to war and the basic lessons that we took from it as a nation.

The Origins and Impact of the Cuban Revolution. There are perhaps no more fertile years for Cuba in terms of personal memoir and scholarly analysis than those between Batista's coup in 1952 and the Cuban Missile Crisis just over ten years later in October 1962. Most recently, the Brooklyn-based, Cuban-Jewish political scientist Samuel Farber has written a detailed and original reappraisal of the events of those years in his *Origins of the Cuban Revolution Reconsidered* (University of North Carolina Press, 2006). Also groundbreaking in terms of its focus on the long neglected internal battle between the two wings of Castro's 26th of July Movement is Julia E. Sweig's *Inside the Cuban Revolution: Fidel Castro and the Urban Underground* (Harvard University Press, 2002). Two other important studies of that same period are Jules Benjamin's *United States and the Origins of the Cuban Revolution: An Empire of Liberty in an Age of National Liberation* (Princeton University Press, 1990) and Thomas G. Paterson's *Contesting Castro: The United States and the Triumph of the Cuban Revolution* (Oxford University Press, 1994). Finally, Thomas C. Wright's *Latin America in the Era of the Cuban Revolution* (Praeger, 1991) is a more broad-based study of the impact the Cuban Revolution had on the hemisphere as a whole. His book is especially useful in understanding how a successful revolution in Cuba provoked a violent backlash across the region that changed the nature of the U.S. relationship with the nations of Latin America. Wright's revised edition (Praeger, 2001) has new material on the impact of the fall of the Soviet Union on the image and influence of the Cuban model for the hemisphere.

Literally hundreds of personal and political memoirs have been written in Spanish by the Cuban participants on the various sides of the revolution. Although few of these have yet been translated into English, there are many fascinating first-hand accounts of the events of the revolution as witnessed by Americans. With different roles and often wildly differing political interpretations of the events, some of these observers include *New York Times* correspondents R. Hart Phillips and Herbert L. Matthews; U.S. diplomats Earl E. T. Smith, Philip Bonsal, and Wayne Smith; and U.S. Attorney General Robert F. Kennedy. The author who originally published under the byline R. Hart Phillips was actually *Ruby* Hart Phillips, who had originally accompanied her journalist husband to Cuba as *New York Times* photographer. After his untimely death, she became the *Times's* chief correspondent in the country, remaining at that post from 1933 until 1961, when she was jailed and then unceremoniously thrown out of the country. Among her various memoirs about her time in Cuba are the excellent **Cuban Sideshow** (Cuban Press, 1935) and the riveting **Cuba: Island of Paradox** (McDowell Obolensky, 1959). This last book was republished under the title **The Cuban Dilemma** in 1962, with a new section on what Phillips saw as the tragedy of the revolution.

Ironically, trying to avoid having her press credentials revoked by Batista, in early 1957 Phillips brought in the then famous editorial writer and foreign correspondent Herbert L. Matthews to make a rendezvous with Castro, and as it turned out with destiny, in the Sierra Maestra mountain range. Unlike Phillips, Matthews became quickly enamored with

Castro and his seemingly righteous revolutionary cause. After publishing a series of historic articles that proved Castro to be alive and introducing him to the world, Matthews had a falling-out with the newspaper over what it saw as his lack of objectivity. However, Matthews maintained to the end of his life, in his various books on Cuba, that Castro's intentions were genuine and the revolution was legitimate. These books include *The Cuban Story* (G. Braziller, 1961), *Fidel Castro* (Simon & Schuster, 1969), and *Revolution in Cuba: An Essay in Understanding* (Scribner, 1975). The entire fascinating tale has been retold recently by *Times* correspondent Anthony DePalma in his own book on the Matthews saga, *The Man Who Invented Fidel: Castro, Cuba, and Herbert L. Matthews of the New York Times* (Public Affairs, 2006).

Even more fascinating for aficionados of diplomatic intrigue are three memoirs written by three very different chief representatives of U.S. interests in Cuba. Like U.S. Ambassador Arthur Gardner before him, Ambassador Earl Smith went to Cuba in 1957 as a Republican political appointee with no foreign service experience and no knowledge of Spanish. As the title of his bitter memoir, *The Fourth Floor: An Account of the Castro Communist Revolution* (Random House, 1962), clearly indicates, Smith was convinced from early on that Castro had always been a communist and that his revolutionary group, the 26th of July Movement, was deeply infiltrated by communists. In the book, Smith maintains not only that Castro was a communist and that the "Fourth Floor" (lower-level State Department officials) knew it, but incredibly that they preferred him to Batista. From his primary briefing on Cuba by none other than *Times* correspondent Herbert Matthews, to his antagonistic relations with both the U.S. embassy staff and Washington's State Department officials, Smith seemed to be always on the defensive.

Although Wayne Smith was never an official ambassador to Cuba, his position as a State Department analyst in Washington and a political officer in the Havana embassy between 1957 and 1961 gave him an intimate perspective from which to view the breakdown of U.S.-Cuban relations during that period. Furthermore, Smith was the first chief of the U.S. Interest Section (the diplomatic equivalent of an ambassador) when the embassy was reopened, nominally as a section of the Swiss embassy, in 1978. While Earl Smith blames the breakdown in U.S.-Cuban relations on the "liberal" State Department's unwillingness to support a weakening president (Batista), Wayne Smith argues in his own account, *The Closest of Enemies: A Personal and Diplomatic Account of U.S.-Cuban Relations since 1957* (W. W. Norton, 1987), that the breakdown was due to the ineptness of an inexperienced ambassador and the ignorance, overconfidence, and neglect of President Dwight D. Eisenhower and Secretary Stephen Foster Dulles. A final valuable diplomatic memoir covering this period of U.S.-Cuban relations was published in 1971 by former ambassador Philip Bonsal. In his well-informed and evenhanded book, *Cuba, Castro and the United States* (University of Pittsburgh Press), Bonsal shows a clear understanding of Cuba's long history of frustrated attempts to gain true sovereignty and independence. He also is critical of U.S. government ignorance of this frustration, especially among people who should have known better, such as President Eisenhower. At the same time, in his detailed recounting of the crucial events between January 1959 and January 1961, the two years during which he served as U.S. ambassador, he argues that his many good-faith efforts to reach accommodation with Castro were repeatedly (and he thinks, purposefully) ignored.

When taking office in the early months of 1961, John F. Kennedy not only inherited a growing Cuba problem (diplomatic relations were broken in January 1961) but also found himself saddled with a plan for an exile invasion of Cuba that he reluctantly, and regretfully, allowed to go forward in April 1961. The best reflection on these events is *Politics of Illusion: The Bay of Pigs Invasion Reexamined,* edited by

James G. Blight and Peter Kornbluh (Lynne Rienner, 1998). The book is essentially an edited transcript of a revealing conference held in May 1996, which featured scholars, former members of the Kennedy White House, the State and Defense Departments, the CIA, and the Kremlin, along with former members of the Cuban opposition and invasion force, Brigade 2506. The book also includes an extensive appendix of maps, chronologies, and a number of key declassified documents.

President Kennedy's failed invasion and embarrassment at the Bay of Pigs led directly, if ironically, to his redemption as an authoritative and level-headed leader during the "thirteen days" of the Cuban Missile Crisis of October 1962. The essential events of those tension-filled two weeks are expertly recounted by Robert F. Kennedy, one of the principal actors in the episode, in his ***Thirteen Days: A Memoir of the Cuban Missile Crisis*** (Mentor, 1968). One of the sources for the 2000 Roger Donaldson/Kevin Costner film of the same name, Kennedy's book is a study in brinksmanship and of the difficulty of avoiding group-think in crisis situations. The Cuban side of the story is told by Cuba's former UN ambassador Carlos Lechuga in his memior, ***In the Eye of the Storm: Castro, Khrushchev, Kennedy and the Missile Crisis*** (Ocean Press, 1995). Aleksandr Fursenko and Timothy J. Naftali made expert use of exclusive access to the Soviet archives to tell the story from the perspective of the USSR in their book, ***One Hell of a Gamble: Khrushchev, Castro, and Kennedy, 1958-1964*** (W. W. Norton, 1997). A final useful resource on the events of those heady days in October 1962 is the compilation of declassified documents and participant interviews and memoirs published under the title ***The Cuban Missile Crisis, 1962: A National Security Archive Documents Reader,*** edited by Laurence Chang and Peter Kornbluh (W. W. Norton, 1999). The National Security Archive has made other declassified documents related to Cuba available on its website: http://www.gwu.edu/~nsarchiv/nsa/cuba_mis_cri/index.htm.

Castro and Guevara Biographies and Writings.
Although he finished it more than twenty years ago, the biography of Fidel Castro by *New York Times* reporter Tad Szulc remains the best. It was published in 1986 by Avon Books under the title *Fidel: A Critical Portrait* and is readily available in most bookstores. Also of note is the more recent biography by Robert E. Quirk, *Fidel Castro* (W. W. Norton, 1995). Though not exactly a biography, *Cuba Confidential: Love and Vengeance in Miami and Havana* (Random House, 2002) is a fascinating character study of the "family feud" that has raged for more than forty years between Fidel and his Miami enemies (and relatives). Written by investigative reporter Ann Louise Bardach, the book includes loads of original reporting and interviews by leaders on both sides of the conflict with information on the Elián González affair and an exclusive interview with Castro enemy and terror suspect Luis Posada Carriles. More recently, Bardach has resurrected an out-of-print and never before translated collection of twenty-one letters Castro wrote to his supporters while in prison on the Isle of Pines in the mid-1950s. Complete with a new introduction by Bardach, the full text of each letter (both in Spanish and English), and a new epilogue by the original publisher and recipient of the majority of the letters, Luis Conte Agüero, this valuable book is *The Prison Letters of Fidel Castro* (Nation Books, 2007).

Also valuable is the recent 800-page exended interview and conversational biography of Castro published by the European intellectual and Castro supporter, Ignacio Ramonet, *Cien horas con Fidel* (2nd ed., Havana: Consejo de Estado, 2006). The fruit of many more than the 100 hours of the title, this book provides intimate access to Castro in the twilight of his life. First published in the spring of 2006, the second edition is said to benefit from Castro's meticulous corrections and revisions done during the summer of 2006 in the lead-up to his provisional stepping down from power. For this reason, the book contains what are perhaps Castro's final sustained reflections, explanations, and justifications of a life of revolutionary power. The book is being published outside of Cuba under the title, *Fidel Castro: Biografía a dos voces* (Random House Mondadori, Debate) and will come out in an English translation by Penguin in the fall of 2007 under the title, *Castro: My Life.* A final recent study of the life of Fidel Castro, in tandem with a rare glimpse into the life and personality of his brother Raúl, is former CIA analyst Brian Latell's *After Fidel: The Inside Story of Castro's Regime and Cuba's Next Leader* (Palgrave Macmillan, 2005).

Since Ernesto "Che" Guevara's body was uncovered along with those of his comrades at arms, buried in a shallow grave on an abandoned airstrip in Valle Grande, Bolivia, in 1997, the world's bookstores have been flooded with biographies and assessments of the life and thought of the Argentine-Cuban revolutionary. The three most comprehensive biographies based on original research and new interviews with those who knew him best are John Lee Anderson's *Che Guevara: A Revolutionary Life* (Grove Press, 1997), Jorge G. Castañeda's *Compañero: The Life and Death of Che Guevara* (Vintage, 1997), and Paco Ignacio Taibo II's *Guevara, Also Known as Che* (St. Martin's Griffin, 1999). The first of these is more than 700 pages long but reads like a novel and is the most comprehensive and balanced of the three. Mexican diplomat intellectual Castañeda's well researched volume provoked howls of criticism from the Cuban government, which could be interpreted as a vote of confidence or a condemnation, depending on one's politics. Taibo's is by far the most sympathetic of the three. If you're looking for something a bit more abbreviated, try Eric Luther's *Che Guevara, Critical Lives* (Alpha Books, 2001), which condenses the findings and arguments of the three other biographies. (Full disclosure: I helped edit and wrote the preface to this last biography.)

Finally, if you're interested in reading some of Guevara's own prolific writings, many of his most important essays have been collected by Rolando E. Bonachea and Nelson P. Valdés in their edited volume *Ché: Selected Writings of Ernesto Guevara* (MIT Press, 1972). Similarly, Melbourne-based Ocean Press has recently issued the collection *Che Guevara Reader: Writings on Politics and Revolution* (2003). Ocean Press has also recently rereleased Guevara's *Motorcycle Diaries* (2004) to accompany the new Walter Salles film of the same name, as well as re-editing Guevara's other reflections on his guerrilla adventures, *The Bolivian Diary: The Authorized Edition* (2005) and *Reminiscences of the Cuban Revolutionary War: The Authorized and Revised Edition* (2005). Not to be missed, of course, is the book perhaps most associated with Guevara, his how-to manual on revolutionary struggle, *Guerrilla Warfare* (University of Nebraska Press, 1985), edited by Brian Loveman and Thomas M. Davies.

Cuba's Economy

Since Cuba entered an unprecedented economic crisis starting in 1988, which was immeasurably exacerbated by the fall of the Soviet Union and eventual cutoff of all preferential Soviet trade and aid, scholars from many different ideological (and geographical) positions have published books analyzing what went wrong and what could be done to remedy the situation. The first major book by a group of Cuban economists working within the system (then as members of a Cuban think tank, the Center for the Study of the Americas, CEA) to analyze the economic collapse and suggest ways to "restructure" the Cuban economy, while retaining its "socialist" character, was *Cuba: Restructuring the Economy—A Contribution to the Debate* by Julio Carranza Valdés, Luis Gutiérrez Urdaneta, and Pedro Monreal González. Originally published in 1995 in Cuba, the 1998 English edition was published by the Institute of Latin American Studies in London. A final helpful analysis of the economic and social changes that Cuba has undergone during Castro's tenure is available in *Back from the Future: Cuba under Castro* (Princeton University Press, 1994) by sociologist Susan Eva Eckstein.

In the United States, the Cuban economists Carmelo Mesa-Lago and Jorge Pérez-López (working both together and separately) have done more than any others to advance the study of the Cuban economy. While much of their excellent work on Cuba came out well before 1990, three important works published since then are their coauthored book *Cuba's Aborted Reform: Socioeconomic Effects, International Comparisons, and Transition Policies* (University Press of Florida, 2005); Mesa-Lago's systematic, historical comparison of Cuba's development strategy under socialism with that of two other very different regional economies, *Market, Socialist, and Mixed Economies: Comparative Policy and Performance—Chile, Cuba, and Costa Rica* (Johns Hopkins University Press, 2000); and Pérez-López's original study of Cuba's underground economy, *Cuba's Second Economy: From Behind the Scenes to Center Stage* (Transaction, 1995). Finally, Sergio Díaz-Briquets and Jorge Pérez-López have also recently published one of the only book-length studies of economic crime in Cuba, entitled *Corruption in Cuba: Castro and Beyond* (University of Texas Press, 2006).

Two recent collections of economic analysis on Cuba can be found in the edited volumes *The Cuban Economy at the Start of the Twenty-First Century* (Harvard University, 2004) and *The Cuban Economy* (University of Pittsburgh Press, 2004). The first of these was coedited by Harvard professor Jorge I. Domínguez, along with Cuban economist Omar Everleny Pérez Villanueva and Harvard scholar Lorena Barberia. It is unique among studies of the Cuban economy in that it successfully combines work done by leading economists and sociologists in Cuba with other essays written by North American scholars. The second collection, edited by Archibald R. M. Ritter, Canada's leading expert on the Cuban economy, has a clearly written overview of the macro and micro developments in the Cuban economy during the 1990s written by the editor, along with an eclectic and provocative selection of articles by leaders in the field. Also of note, though likely hard to find at this point, is Ritter's 1974 book on socialist Cuba's development trajectory up to that point, *The Economic Development of Revolutionary Cuba: Strategy and Performance* (Praeger).

Two final books that focus in detail on the crisis and survival of the Cuban economy after 1990 are Ana Julia Jatar-Hausmann's *The Cuban Way: Capitalism, Communism, and Confrontation* (Kumarian, 1999) and Oscar Espinosa Chepe's *Cuba: revolución o involución* (Aduana Vieja, 2007). The first of these is a concise but penetrating overview of the Cuban economy and U.S.-Cuban relations with a special focus on the split between the grassroots, and often illegal, form of capitalism *a la cubana* ubiquitous on the streets of Havana and the "bigger-is-better" capitalism practiced between the government and foreign investors. The second book is a comprehensive collection of articles by one of Cuba's leading independent journalists and economists who served nineteen months of a twenty-year sentence between 2003 and 2004 for his unauthorized activities. He was released in November 2004 due to his failing health and has been recognized by Amnesty International as a "prisoner of conscience."

Cuban Institutions

The institutionalization of the Cuban Revolution first during the 1970s under the new constitution, the newly reorganized Cuban Communist Party, and the Cuban military, and later during the late 1980s and early 1990s, is analyzed very well by Jorge I. Domínguez in his contributions to two works mentioned above, "Government and Politics" in *Cuba: A Country Study* (Library of Congress, 2002), and "Cuba since 1959" in *Cuba: A Short History* (Cambridge, 1993). More extended and detailed analysis is available in his *Cuba: Order and Revolution* (Harvard University Press, 1978).

Phyllis Walker also does an excellent job of picking apart the sometimes dense history of Cuba's military and state security apparatus in her own chapter on national security in *Cuba: A Country Study* (Library of Congress, 2002). Finally, Domínguez's Cuban colleague and sometimes collaborator, Rafael Hernández, has collected a number of his own penetrating essays on civil and cultural change in Cuba under the revolution in his recently translated book, *Looking at Cuba: Essays on Culture and Civil Society* (University Press of Florida, 2003).

Two outstanding recent collections of essays on the significant challenges facing Cuban society and state institutions are available in the edited volumes *Changes in Cuban Society since the Nineties* (Woodrow Wilson Center, 2005) and *Cuban Socialism in a New Century: Adversity, Survival, and Renewal* (University Press of Florida, 2004). The first of these volumes was edited by a diverse group of authors including Joseph S. Tulchin, Liliam Bobea, Mayra P. Espina Prieto, and Rafael Hernández, and includes contributions from leading Cuban scholars both on the island and in exile. Likewise, the other volume, edited by Max Azicri and Elise Deal, collects many penetrating essays by leading scholars both on and off the island on subjects as diverse as religion, the Cuban Communist Party, elections, presidential succession, the military, migration, and international relations. Also of note is Azicri's own book chronicling the survival of Cuban socialism during the crisis of the 1990s, *Cuba Today and Tomorrow: Reinventing Socialism* (University Press of Florida, 2000).

Finally, though they work from diverse ideological assumptions and come to sometimes wildly differing conclusions about the nature of Cuban society and polity, the following authors all clearly and critically explain the inner workings of Cuban socialism. They are Carollee Bengelsdorf, in her study of Cuba's experiment in democratic socialism, *The Problem of Democracy in Cuba: Between Vision and Reality*

(Oxford University Press, 1994); Peter Roman, in his detailed and updated analysis of the functioning of Cuba's National Assembly, ***People's Power: Cuba's Experience with Representative Government*** (Rowman and Littlefield, 2003); Javier Corrales, in his penetrating article "**The Gatekeeper State: Limited Economic Reforms and Regime Survival in Cuba, 1989–2002**," published in *Latin American Research Review* 39, no. 2 (June 2004): 35–65; Haroldo Dilla Alfonso and Philip Oxhorn, in their original and well-informed essay "**The Virtues and Misfortunes of Civil Society in Cuba**," published in *Latin American Perspectives* 29, no. 4 (July 2002): 11–30,); Mark Falcoff in his book, ***Cuba, The Morning After: Confronting Castro's Legacy*** (American Enterprise Institute, 2003); and Carlos Alberto Montaner in his many books on Castro and Cuban communism including, ***Cuba hoy: La lenta muerte del castrosmo*** (Ediciones Universal, 1996).

Cuban Identity, Culture, and Society

Recent investigations into Cuban identity, culture, and society have been as widespread as they have been penetrating. Here I will first present four more general surveys of Cuban national identity and culture, before going into a more detailed description of the most important works on religion, the Cuban diaspora, sexuality, race, and ethnicity, music and dance, art and architecture, and cinema and literature. The two leading analyses of Cuban national identity published in recent years are Louis A. Pérez's monumental ***On Becoming Cuban: Identity, Nationality, and Culture*** (University of North Carolina Press, 1999) and ***Cuba, The Elusive Nation: Interpretations of National Identity*** (University Press of Florida, 2000) edited by Damián Fernández and Madeline Cámara-Betancourt. While Pérez's work is an exhaustive analysis of the formation of Cuban national identity between 1850 and 1950 with special emphasis on the penetration and absorption of U.S. cultural influences in that process, the volume edited by Fernández and Cámara-Betancourt is a collection of essays on various themes including music, art, literature, and the Cuban diaspora. Damián Fernández has also published a slim but highly original monograph on the informal, personal nature of Cuban political culture, entitled *Cuba and the Politics of Passion* (Univeristy of Texas Press, 2000).

Two other important general surveys of Cuban culture are William Luis's *Culture and Customs of Cuba* (Greenwood Press, 2001) and the book of interviews by Canadian academic John M. Kirk and Cuban novelist and journalist Leonardo Padura Fuentes, *Culture and the Cuban Revolution: Conversations in Havana* (University Press of Florida, 2001). While Luis's volume is especially strong on the history and development of Cuban literature, cinema, and art, the Kirk and Padura Fuentes collection is more focused on the protagonists of Cuban culture working today in the areas of music, poetry, and cinema. Additionally, Mauricio A. Font and Alfonso W. Quiroz have recently edited two valuable collections of essays on Cuban history, politics, and culture. The first is entitled *Cuban Counterpoints: The Legacy of Fernando Ortiz* (Lexington Books, 2005) and the second is *The Cuban Republic and José Martí* (Lexington Books, 2006).

The two leading scholars of religion in Cuba and its diaspora are likely Margaret E. Crahan and Miguel A. de la Torre. While Crahan focuses more on the sociopolitical role of religion in Cuban society under the revolution in her edited volume *Religion, Culture, and Society: The Case of Cuba* (Woodrow Wilson Center, 2003), Miguel A. de la Torre has studied the role of religion as an inspirational force for counter-revolutionary activity in the Cuban-American community in the United States in his book *La Lucha for Cuba: Religion and Politics on the Streets of Miami* (University of California Press, 2003). De la Torre has also recently published a book, *Santería: The Beliefs and Rituals of a Growing Religion in America* (W. B. Eerdmans, 2004). In Cuba, the leading scholar of church-state relations is sociologist

Aurelio Alonso, author of *Iglesia y política en Cuba revolucionaria* (Havana, Editorial de Ciencias Sociales, 1997). A more openly critical voice coming from inside the Catholic church (but from within the laity) is that of Dagoberto Valdés, director of *Vitral* magazine and author of the collection, *Cuba: Libertad y responsibilidad (desafíos y proyectos)* (Ediciones Universal, 2005).

The four best historical, sociological studies of the "exceptionalism" of the Cuban community in the United States and its role in the formulation of a hard-line U.S. policy toward Castro are Guillermo J. Grenier's and Lisando Pérez's concise volume *The Legacy of Exile: Cubans in the United States* (Allyn and Bacon, 2003); Alejandro Portes's and Alex Stepick's historical and demographic analysis of the transformation of Miami into the "Capital of Latin America," *City on the Edge* (University of California Press, 1994); Silvia Pedraza's historical, demographic, and political comparison of the fates of Cubans and Mexicans in the United States, *Political and Economic Migrants in America* (University of Texas Press, 1985); and María Cristina García's *Havana USA* (University of California Press, 1996). Also of interest are *Latin Journey: Cuban and Mexican Immigrants in the United States* (University of California Press, 1985) by Alejandro Portes and Robert L. Bach, and *Political Disaffection in Cuba's Revolution and Exodus* (Cambridge University Press, 2007), recently published by Silvia Pedraza.

Other important, original, and incisive analyses of the Cuban diaspora in the United States include Gustavo Pérez Firmat's study of Cuban-American identity and popular culture, *Life on the Hyphen: The Cuban-American Way* (University of Texas Press, 1994); Joan Didion's excellent extended essay *Miami* (Simon & Schuster, 1987); and Jesús Arboleya's sociopolitical analysis of the history of the ongoing effort in South Florida to overthrow the Castro government, *The Cuban Counterrevolution* (Ohio University Press, 2000). Three other enlightening personal memoirs written by

Cuban-Americans are Gustavo Pérez Firmat's *Next Year in Cuba: A Cubano's Coming of Age in America* (Anchor Books, 1995); Román de la Campa's *Cuba on My Mind: Journeys to a Severed Nation* (Verso, 2000); and Mirta Ojito's riveting recent account of the Mariel boatlift twenty-five years later, *Finding Mañana: A Memoir of a Cuban Exodus* (Penguin Press, 2005).

Books on sexuality, race, and ethnicity under the revolution have been especially strong. The most important works on sexuality and sexual politics include Ian Lumsden's *Machos, Maricones, and Gays: Cuba and Homosexuality* (Temple University Press, 1996) and Lois M. Smith's and Alfred Padula's *Sex and Revolution: Women in Socialist Cuba* (Oxford University Press, 1996). For more on gender and sexuality, also see the work of Cuban historian Julio César González Pagés, including his *En busca de un espacio: Historia de mujeres en Cuba* (Havana, Editorial de Ciencias Sociales, 2003). By far the most comprehensive and authoritative study of racial politics in Cuba during the twentieth century is Alejandro de la Fuente's *A Nation for All: Race, Inequality, and Politics in Twentieth-Century Cuba* (University of North Carolina Press, 2001). Other useful and important books on racial identity in Cuba are the two volumes put together by Pedro Pérez Sarduy and Jean Stubs, *Afro-Cuban Voices: On Race and Identity in Contemporary Cuba* (University Press of Florida, 2000) and *AfroCuba: An Anthology of Cuban Writing on Race, Politics, and Culture* (Ocean Press, 1993). The most recent analysis of the revolutionary government's achievements in the area of racial equality is Mark Q. Sawyer's *Racial Politics in Post-Revolutionary Cuba* (Cambridge University Press, 2006).

Given Cuba's central role in the development and diffusion of popular dance music across the world during most of the twentieth century, there has been an outpouring of books in recent years attempting to chronicle and analyze this phenomenon. Perhaps the most comprehensive and accessible to nonspecialists is Ned Sublette's fantastic *Cuba and Its Music: From the First Drum to the Mambo* (Chicago Review Press, 2004). Sublette, musician, former coproducer of the public radio program *Afropop Worldwide,* and cofounder of the record label Qbadisc, which brought a cornucopia of contemporary Cuban music to the United States in the early 1990s, is a wizard with the details of Cuba's vast music history, which he manages to weave together in a spellbinding way. A bit more scholarly and focused on particular time periods are Robin D. Moore's two recent groundbreaking books on the history and development of Cuban music during the twentieth century, *Music and Revolution: Cultural Change in Socialist Cuba* (University of California Press, 2006) and *Nationalizing Blackness: Afrocubanismo and Artistic Revolution in Havana, 1920–1940* (University of Pittsburgh Press, 1997). Also very useful is the recently revised and updated edition of *Caribbean Currents: Caribbean Music from Rumba to Reggae* (Temple University Press, 2006) by Peter Manuel with Kenneth Bilby and Michael Largey.

For those who read Spanish any of the treasure trove of books on the history and development of Cuban music by Cristóbal Díaz Ayala is a good place to start, including *Cuando salí de la Habana (1898-1997): Cien años de música cubana por el mundo* (Ediciones Universal, 1998); his most recent, *Los contrapuntos de la música cubana* (Editorial Callejón, 2006); and his magnum opus, *Música cubana del areyto al rap cubano* (4th ed., Ediciones Universal, 2003). An earlier edition of this book has been translated into English as *The Roots of Salsa: A History of Cuban Music* (Excelsior Music Publishing, 2002). Useful and original books by other leading Cuban journalists and ethnomusicologists include Leonardo Acosta's *Cubano Be, Cubano Bop: One Hundred Years of Jazz in Cuba* (Smithsonian Books, 2003); Olavo Alén Rodríguez's *De lo Afrocubano a la Salsa: Géneros musicales de Cuba* (Editorial Cubanacán, 1992); Helio Orovio's dictionary, *Cuban*

Music from A to Z (Duke University Press, 2004); Leonardo Padura's book of interviews with Cuban and Caribbean music greats, *Faces of Salsa: A Spoken History of the Music* (Smithsonian Books, 2003); and the anthology, *Panorama de la música popular cubana* (Editorial Letras Cubanas, 1995), edited by Radamés Giro, which includes articles by Cuban musicologists Argeliers León and Leonardo Acosta and musicians Emilio Grenet, Rosendo Ruiz, Jr., and Noel Nicola.

The recent cache of all things Cuban has led to a glut in the market of beautifully photographed but none too deep coffee table books highlighting Havana's many architectural and natural wonders. Luckily there are also a number of more serious studies of the history, photography, and architecture of the country's capital city. The leader in this field is surely the coauthored book on Havana by Joseph L. Scarpaci, Roberto Serge, and Mario Coyula, *Havana: Two Faces of the Antillean Metropolis* (University of North Carolina Press, 2003). Now in its second edition, the book is the only English-language history of the city that also has chapters describing urban planning, architecture, public policy, and the many current social and economic challenges facing this most beautiful of cities. A more recent chronicle of the storied history of Cuba's capital is the engrossing *History of Havana* (Palgrave Macmillan, 2006), coauthored by the North American novelist and translator Dick Cluster and the Cuban editor and political scientist Rafael Hernández. A good visual guide to accompany these books, as well as any architecture lover's handbook on the buildings of modern Havana, is Eduardo Luis Rodríguez's *Havana Guide: Modern Architecture, 1925–1965* (Princeton Architectural Press, 2000). Another fantastically photographed architectural history of the city is the elegant *Havana: History and Architecture of a Romantic City* (Monacelli Press, 2000) by María Luisa Lobo Montalvo.

Two other excellent books of photography and essays are *Cuba: Going Back* (University of Texas at Austin, 1997) by Tony Mendoza and *Cuba on the Verge: An Island in*

Transition (Bulfinch Press, 2003), edited by Terry McCoy, with an introduction by William Kennedy and an epilogue by Arthur Miller. This second book showcases the work of leading Cuban and American writers, journalists, and photographers including writers Antonio José Ponte, Abilio Estévez, Reina María Rodríguez, Nancy Morejón, Mayra Montero, Susan Orlean, Abelardo Estorino, Ana Menéndez, Jon Lee Anderson, Achy Obejas, Cristina García, and Pablo Medina, and photographers Manuel Piña, Abigail González, Abelardo Morell, and Carlos Caraicoa. Another important contribution to the history of Cuban architecture and photography is John Loomis's judiciously written and breathtakingly photographed book on the birth, short life, abandonment, and slow death of Cuba's architecturally revolutionary National Art Schools, *Revolution of Forms: Cuba's Forgotten Art Schools* (Princeton Architectural Press, 1999).

The best two books on twentieth-century Cuban art are Juan A. Martínez's *Cuban Art and National Identity: The Vanguardia Painters, 1927–1950* (University Press of Florida, 1994), which covers Cuban modernism, and Luis Camnitzer's *New Art of Cuba* (University of Texas Press, 1994), which chronicles art during the revolutionary period with an emphasis on the 1980s. Although Cuban film has distinguished itself as one of the leading forms of art under the revolution, there are few serious English-language studies of the form. The only book-length study currently available is Michael Chanan's *Cuban Cinema* (University of Minnesota Press, 2004). Luckily, this much revised and augmented edition of Chanan's 1985 *Cuban Image: Cinema and Cultural Politics in Cuba* (BFI Publishing) is a tour de force that chronicles many of the achievements of ICAIC (the Cuban Film Institute), while providing rich, nuanced descriptions of the periodic controversies to beset Cuba's revolutionary film industry. If you read Spanish, Juan Antonio García Borrero's *Guía crítica del cine cubano de ficción* (Editorial Arte y Literatura, 2001) will be an indispensible guide.

Cuban literature (both on the island and in exile) has attracted many critical assessments and scholarly analyses, among which two books can serve as a solid introduction. The first is the groundbreaking study of Cuban and Caribbean literature by Antonio Benítez-Rojo, *The Repeating Island: The Caribbean and the Postmodern Perspective* (Duke University Press, 1992). The second is Isabel Álvarez Borland's accessible introduction to the literature of the Cuban diaspora, *Cuban-American Literature of Exile: From Person to Persona* (University Press of Virginia, 1998). Another recent book that focuses on the development of the Cuban crime novel with a special emphasis on the work of contemporary Cuban novelist Leonardo Padura Fuentes is *Detective Fiction in Cuban Society and Culture* (Peter Lang Publishers, 2006) by Stephen Wilkinson. There are also a number of collections of Cuban literature (novels, poetry, essays, and short stories) translated into English. Two good introductions are Cuban-American novelist Cristina García's recent inclusive collection *¡Cubanísimo! The Vintage Book of Contemporary Cuban Literature* (Vintage Books, 2002), and Ruth Behar's collection, *Bridges to Cuba / Puentes a Cuba* (University of Michigan Press, 1995).

Finally, though it has yet to find itself translated into English, the single best book I have ever read about Cuban culture under the revolution, indeed about the Cuban revolutionary period in general, is Eliseo Alberto's *Informe contra mí mismo* (Alfaguara, 1996). A highly personal, provocative exposé of the manipulative strategy of turning the entire country into government informants, the book's title roughly translates as "secret report against myself." The book also serves as a kind of midlife memoir and critical reflection on Cuban culture and governmental repression. The author, who lives in exile in Mexico City and is known to his friends as *Lichi,* also wrote the screenplay for the movie *Guantanamera* and is a member of one of the leading families of Cuban culture (son of poet Eliseo Diego).

Cuban Language, Food, Etiquette, and Holidays

The best place in the United States to find books on Cuban Spanish (and on many other Cuban-related topics) is the Miami-based bookstore and publishing house Ediciones Universal. Their collection of books about Cuba in Spanish is unsurpassed; their catalogue is on-line at: http://www.ediciones.com. There you can find two of the books most helpful to me in writing the section on language: Carlos Paz Pérez's *Diccionario cubano de habla popular y vulgar* (Agualarga, 1998) and José Sánchez-Boudy's *Diccionario mayor de cubanismos* (Ediciones Universal, 1999). Also helpful in understanding the nuances of Cuban syntax and phonology is Pablo Julián Davis's entry "Cuban Spanish (Language)" in the aforementioned *Encyclopedia of Cuba: People, History, Culture* (Greenwood Press, 2002). Finally, Cuba's Fernando Ortiz Foundation publishes *La Fuente Viva*, a new series of monographs focusing on specific areas of Cuban culture. Included among them is Gema Valdés Acosta's *Los remanentes de las lenguas bantúes en Cuba* (2002). Helpful in preparing the section on Cuban cuisine were Alex García's *In a Cuban Kitchen* (Running Press, 2004) and the incomparable Nitza Villapol's *Cocina cubana* (Editorial Científico-Técnica, 2002).

Videos, Documentaries, and Feature Films

The following is only a partial listing of Cuban-made or Cuban-themed movies and documentaries. For a more detailed and comprehensive listing of such films, readers should consult Michael Chanan's *Cuban Cinema* (University of Minnesota Press, 2004). Also, though most of its films lack English subtitles, the Miami-based distributor, Marakka2000 (http://www.marakka2000.com), has the most extensive on-line catalogue of Cuban films and documentaries.

Cuban Music. "¿De dónde son los cantantes?" (1976): Luis Felipe Bernaza (32 min.)—Made in Cuba, this is a documentary about the famous Santiago "son" group Trio Matamoros.

"The Routes/Roots of Rhythm" (1984): Howard Dratch (55 min.)—Narrated and hosted by Harry Belafonte, this is a chronological documentary history of the African roots of Cuban popular music, including son, rumba, Latin Jazz, and salsa.

"Machito: A Latin Jazz Legacy" (1987): Carlos Ortiz (58 min.)—Bio pic of Latin Jazz great Frank "Machito" Grillo, lead man and cofounder of Machito's Afro Cubans.

"Ache Moyuba Orisha" (1990): Cristina González (42 min.)—An excellent documentary film about Cuban santería, made in Cuba.

"La última rumba de Papá Montero" (1992): Octavio Cortázar (57 min.)—This cross between a documentary and filmic re-creation of the investigation of the mysterious death of the famous rumbero Papá Montero features examples of the various rumba styles as well as interviews with some of Cuba's leading ethnomusicologists.

"Voices of the Orishas" (1994): Alvaro Pérez Betancourt (37 min.)—A documentary that chronicles Cuba's Yoruba heritage and traditions.

"Yo Soy, Del Son a La Salsa" ("I Am, From Son to Salsa," 1997): Rigoberto Mercado (100 min.)—With a screenplay written by leading Cuban novelist Leonardo Padura Fuentes and narration provided by Cuban salsa sensation Issac Delgado, this film provides a documentary overview of 100 years of Cuban popular music at home and abroad.

"Zafiros: Locura Azul" ("The Zafiros: Blue Madness," 1997): Manuel Herrera (115 min.)—A rare Cuba-U.S. coproduction, this film is a musical homage and biography of the early-1960s Cuban vocal group Los Zafiros (The Saphires), a Cuban version of the Platters.

"Cinco joyas de la música cubana" ("Five Jewels of Cuban Music," 1998): Luis Felipe Bernaza, Oscar Valdés, and

Constante Diego (95 min.)—Five short documentaries on Ignacio Piñeiro, María Teresa Vera, Ernesto Lecuona, Benny Moré, and Bola de Nieve.

"Buena Vista Social Club" (1999): Wim Wenders (105 min.)—A documentary on Cuban "son" music featuring the stars of the original Buena Vista Social Club album.

"Calle 54" (2000): Fernando Trueba (105 min.)—A film featuring performances of some of the living legends of Latin Jazz, including Cachao, Paquito D'Rivera, and Chucho Valdés.

"For Love or Country" (2000): Joseph Sargent (120 min.)—Bio pic of Latin Jazz trumpeter Arturo Sandoval, featuring Andy García in the lead role.

"La Tropical" (2002): David Turnley (90 min.)—Set at the (in)famous open-air Havana club of the title, this sophisticated documentary is a vibrant tribute to the central but complex place music and dancing play in the lives of everyday Cubans.

"Cuban Hip Hop All Stars" (2004): Joshua Bee Alafia (60 min.)—A film that collects videos of some of Cuba's leading hip hop groups.

"La Fabri-K: The Cuban Hip-Hop Factory" (2005): Lisandro Pérez-Rey (64 min.)—A documentary film about two of the leading Cuban Hip-Hop groups.

"Rumba en La Habana con Yoruba Andabo" (2005): José Luis Lobato (103 min.)—A DVD that is perfect for classroom use as it includes performances of the many different kinds of sacred and profane Afro-Cuban music and dance.

"Habana Blues" (2005): Benito Zambrano (110 min.)—The classic tale of two kids from the barrio with big dreams of musical stardom who face the dilemma of getting exactly what they have long been wishing for—a recording contract—that will take them to Spain and away from everything and everyone they know and love.

"East of Havana" (2006): Jauretsi Saizarbitoria and Emilia Menocal (82 min.)—A taut tale of the underworld of Cuban hip-hop and the difficulties of navigating between artistic integrity and government bureaucracy.

"El Benny" (2006): Jorge Luis Sánchez (132 min.)—A bio pic of the great Cuban crooner, Benny Moré.

Emigration and Exile. "El Super" (1979): Leon Ichaso and Orlando Jiménez Leal (90 min.)—A Cuban exile in New York City works as a building superintendent but yearns for his lost homeland.

"90 Miles" (2001): Juan Carlos Zaldívar (75 min.)—A filmmaker's return trip to his homeland.

"Balseros" ("Rafters," 2002): Carlos Bosch and Josep Maria Domènech (120 min.)—This documentary film follows seven Cubans who risk it all to start over in the United States.

"Adio Kerida" ("Good-bye Dear Love," 2002): Ruth Behar (82 min.)—U.S. anthropologist Ruth Behar returns to her native Cuba to profile the remnant of the Sephardic Jewish community there and trace her own family's journey to the United States as Cuban-Jewish exiles.

"Beyond the Sea" (2003): Lisandro Pérez-Rey (80 min.)—A history of the Mariel boatlift.

"Viva Cuba" (2005): Juan Carlos Cremata (80 min.)—A poignant film that follows the wanderings of two Cuban run-away children as they make their way across the island in search of one's long lost father.

"The Lost City" (2006): Andy García (143 min.)—A music-filled film about the end of an era in Cuba and the start of the revolution as experienced by one family torn apart by politics.

Homosexuality. "Improper Conduct" (1984): Néstor Almendros and Orlando Jiménez Leal (112 min.)—A documentary chronicling the treatment of homosexuals under the Cuban Revolution.

"Fresa y chocolate" ("Strawberry and Chocolate," 1994): Tomás Gutiérrez Alea and Juan Carlos Tabío (108 min.)—The poignant story of a friendship between a cultured homosexual and a square party militant, and the lessons that they teach each other.

"Before Night Falls" (2000): Julian Schnabel (133 min.)—The film version of the fantastical autobiography of Cuban writer, dissident, and exile Reinaldo Arenas.

Cuban Women. "Lucía" (1968): Humberto Solás (160 min.)—This important, but overly long and melodramatic film chronicles the tumultuous lives of three Cuban women during three different periods in the country's history (1895, 1932, and the 1960s).

"De cierta manera" ("One Way or Another," 1974): Sara Gómez (79 min.)—The only feature-length film by this acclaimed Cuban documentary filmmaker, this film blurs the lines between the two forms as it describes the construction of a new neighborhood.

"Retrato de Teresa" ("Portrait of Teresa," 1979): Pastor Vega (103 min.)—Cuban cinema's most unflinching look at machismo, this film presents Teresa, a "new woman" who struggles to simultaneously fulfill her duties as mother, wife, worker, and revolutionary.

"María Antonia" (1990): Sergio Giral (111 min.)—The story of María Antonia, a mulata who lives in a Havana slum of the 1950s, and struggles with life, love, and santería.

"Mujer transparente" ("Transparent Woman," 1993): Mario Crespo, Ana Rodríguez, Mayra Segura, Mayra Vilasis, Héctor Veitia (82 min.)—This five-part film, each part directed by a different filmmaker, explores different facets of contemporary Cuban womanhood.

"¿Quién diablos es Yuliet?" ("Who the Hell Is Juliette?," 1997): Carlos Marcovich (90 min.)—This film (or is it a documentary?) is about a streetwise Cuban teenager and sometime prostitute who is orphaned by her father's immigration and her mother's suicide.

"Cuban Women: Branded by Paradise" (1999): Mari Rodríguez Ichaso (113 min.)—This documentary chronicles the impact of the revolution on a number of exiled women, including singer Celia Cruz, novelist Zoé Valdés, and poet María Elena Cruz Varela.

Politics, Polemics, and Personalities. "Soy Cuba" ("I Am Cuba," 1964): Mikhail Kalatosov (141 min.)—A clearly propagandistic condemnation/celebration of the "before" and "after" of the revolution, this Soviet-made film also paints a cinematographically brilliant picture of Cuba.

"Alicia en el pueblo de las maravillas" ("Alice in Wonderland," 1990): Daniel Díaz Torres (94 min.)—Banned in Cuba after the briefest of openings, this film parodies the absurdities of life in a town named Maravillas (Wonders), where people are sent to be redeemed.

"Azúcar amarga" ("Bitter Sugar," 1996): Leon Ichaso (102 min.)—A portrait of the daily struggles and bitter contradictions of life in Cuba in the early 1990s as lived by one family.

"El Che: Investigating a Legend" (1997): Maurice Dugowson (83 min.)—A riveting, revealing documentary portrait of Ernesto "Che" Guevara and his role in the Cuban Revolution.

"Thirteen Days" (2000): Roger Donaldson (145 min.)— Based in part on the book of the same name by Robert F. Kennedy, this film focuses on the tense decision-making process in the White House during the Cuban Missile Crisis of October 1962.

"Fidel" (2001): Estela Bravo (91 min.)—A revealing, if sympathetic, bio pic of the Cuban leader.

"Comandante" (2003, 99 min.) and "Looking for Fidel" (2004, 57 min.): Oliver Stone—The controversial pair of made-for-TV HBO films focusing on the personality of Fidel Castro. The first, more sympathetic, "Comandante," was pulled from circulation in the United States after Castro cracked down on hijackers and dissidents in the spring of 2003. The second, "Looking for Fidel," is a more tough-minded interview with Castro about Cuba's human rights record. Incidentally, Stone was fined by the U.S. government for illegally traveling to Cuba to make these films.

"The Motorcycle Diaries" (2004): Walter Salles (128 min.)—Based on Ernesto "Che" Guevara's early diaries and staring Gael García Bernal, this beautifully filmed movie covers the future revolutionary's coming of age on a journey across the South American continent.

"Monte Rouge" (2004): Eduardo del Llano (15 min.)—This independent film short pokes fun at the often dreary realities of Cuban life, starting with government spying and hypocrisy. It was filmed with a borrowed camera on a $500 budget and distributed underground in Cuba and abroad via the internet at: http://www.cubaverdad.net/monte_rouge.htm.

"He Who Hits First, Hits Twice: The Urgent Film of Santiago Álvarez" (2005): Santiago Álvarez and Travis Wilkerson (147 min.)—This compilation of some of the best "propaganda art films" from reknowned Cuban director Santiago Álvarez, selected by U.S. filmmaker Travis Wilkerson, includes seven films originally released between 1965 and 1973: *Now* (1965, 5 mins.), *Cerro Pelado* (1966, 34 mins.), *Hanoi Martes 13* (1967, 38 mins.), *Hasta La Victoria Siempre (LBJ)* (1968, 18 mins.), *79 Primaveras* (1969, 25 min.), *El Sueno del Pongo* (1970, 11 mins.), and *El Tigre Saltó y Mató, Pero Morirá... Morirá...* (1973, 16 min.). The two-DVD set also includes a film portrait of Álvarez by Wilkerson, entitled *Accelerated Underdevelopment*.

"Habana: Arte nuevo de hacer ruinas" (2005/2006): Florian Borchmeyer and Matthias Hentschler (86 min.)—This film is a German-made portrait of the inhabited ruins of Havana and their strange blend of magic and demolition. It follows five real-life Havana residents, capturing the final moments of their lives in the buildings they inhabit before they're renovated—or simply collapse altogether.

"Páginas del diario de Mauricio" (2006): Manuel Pérez (135 min.)—On a September day in 2000 as the Sydney Olympics begin a solitary Cuban man comemorates his sixtieth birthday by remembering key moments from the last twelve years of his life, a time of deep personal, political, economic, social upheaval both for him and for his island nation.

"Revolución: Five Visions" (2006): Nicole Cattell (57 min.)—A breathtakingly photographed documentary film about five very different, but each very genuine, Cuban photographers as they struggle to chronicle the epic of revolutionary Cuba.

"Cuban Mysteries: An Interview with Leonardo Padura" (2006): Claudia Ferman (30 min.)—An extended interview with Cuba's leading novelist, Leonardo Padura Fuentes, interspersed with scenes from some of his recent crime novels set in Havana.

"Sicko" (2007): Michael Moore (113 min.)—Aw shucks guerrilla documentary filmmaker Michael Moore's newest documentary criticizing the U.S. health care system. The second half of the film takes viewers to Canada, Great Britain, France, and finally Cuba, in order to contrast those countries' universal state-run systems with the U.S. private system. The movie ends with an emotional bang as Moore takes a group of 9/11 rescuers to Cuba to get care they could not get at home.

By Tomás Gutiérrez Alea. "La muerte de un burócrata" ("The Death of a Bureaucrat," 1966, 85 min.): When an honored worker is buried with his ID card, his wife discovers that she cannot get her pension unless she figures out a way to get it back.

"Memorias del subdesarrollo" ("Memories of Underdevelopment," 1968, 97 min.): When his wife and family leave for Miami, Sergio, a formerly wealthy aspiring writer, decides to stay behind in the new Cuba but cannot quite come to embrace the revolution.

"La última cena" ("The Last Supper," 1976, 120 min.): Set in the 1790s, just after the Haitian revolution, a naive plantation owner decides to re-enact Christ's last supper by serving his slaves a meal, but they take their newfound Christian brotherhood seriously and revolt.

"Fresa y chocolate" ("Strawberry and Chocolate," 1994)— See description on page 545.

"Guantanamera" (1995, 105 min.): Codirected with Juan Carlos Tabío, this is the story of what happens when an aging diva from Guantánamo dies unexpectedly while visiting her hometown. The rest of the movie is a hilarious farce chronicling the endless bureaucratic maneuvering needed to transport her body back to Havana for burial.

By Fernando Pérez. "Madagascar" (1994, 50 min.): A teenage girl looks for meaning in a world gone mad and a city in ruins.

"La vida es silbar" ("Life Is to Whistle," 1998, 106 min.): Three characters in present-day Havana must overcome their fears in order to live a fuller, freer life.

"Suite Habana" (2003, 84 min.): Shot almost entirely without dialogue, this film is a sad but proud tribute to the city of Havana and its resourceful, tenacious inhabitants. It provoked both controversy and tearful standing ovations when it was debuted in Cuba.

"El madrigal" (2007, 112 min.): In the style of American filmmaker David Lynch, this film plays with the conventions of cinema by presenting a story within a story, while refusing to clarify which of the two is fact and which is fiction.

Discography of Cuban Music

As with the previous listing of films, this hit parade of Cuban music is a bit of a grab bag of personal favorites organized by musical genre. Literally thousands of albums could be added to this list, with truly great ones numbering in the hundreds. I refer readers to Ned Sublette's **Cuba and Its Music: From the First Drum to the Mambo** (Chicago Review Press, 2004) for a clear, entertaining social history of Cuban music up to the early 1950s. The best beginner's guides to the many groups, albums, and genres of Cuban music that I know of are Philip Sweeney's **Rough Guide to Cuban Music** (Rough Guides, 2001), and the more scholarly Cuban musical dictionary by Helio Orovio recently translated into English, **Cuban Music from A to Z** (Duke University Press, 2004). If you make it to New York City, you can make a pilgrimage to the recently reopened Record Mart, located inside the 42nd Street/Times Square subway station. If you are lucky the store's once and future owner, seventy-three-year-old Jesse Moskowitz or the store's legendary buyer and floor manager Harry Sepulveda might be kind enough to guide your purchases and give you a musical education.

Compilations: Various Artists and Various Genres. "Yo Soy, Del Son a la Salsa" (two CDs), RMM Filmworks Soundtrack, 1997.

"Cuba, I Am Time" (four CDs), Blue Jakel Entertainment, 1997.

"Official Retrospective of Cuban Music" (four CDs), Center for the Investigation and Development of Cuban Music, Tonga Productions/Salsa Blanca, 1999.

"100 Canciones Cubanas del Milenio" (four CDs), Alma Latina, 2000.

"Rarezas del siglo," Vols. I and II, produced by Helio Orovio, EGREM and UNEAC, 2001.

Cuban Instrumental and Classical Music: Contradanza, Danzón, etc. Rotterdam Conservatory Orquesta Típica, "Cuba: Contradanzas and Danzones," Nimbus, 1996.

Ernesto Lecuona, "The Ultimate Collection: Lecuona Plays Lecuona," BMG Music, 1997.

Various Artists, "The Cuban Danzón: Before There Was Jazz, 1906–1929," Arhollie, 1999.

Bola de Nieve, "Bola de Nieve," Egrem/Nuevos Medios, 2003.

Son. Trio Matamoros, "The Legendary Trio Matamoros," Tumbao, Cuban Classics, 1992.

Arsenio Rodríguez y su Conjunto, "Dundunbanza, 1946–1951," Tumbao Cuban Classics, 1994.

Buena Vista Social Club, "Buena Vista Social Club," World Circut/Nonesuch, 1997.

Afro-Cuban All-Stars, "A Toda Cuba le Gusta," World Circut/Nonesuch, 1997.

Polo Montañez, "Guajiro Natural," Lusafrica, 2000.

Vieja Trova Santiaguera, "Dominó," Virgin Records, 2000.

Benny Moré, "Canto a mi Cuba," EGREM, 2004.

Rumba. Lydia Cabrera and Josefina Tarafa, "Havana, Cuba, ca. 1957: Rhythms and Songs for the Orishas," Smithsonian Folkways Recordings, 2001.

Lydia Cabrera and Josefina Tarafa, "Matanzas, Cuba, ca. 1957: Afro-Cuban Sacred Music from the Countryside," Smithsonian Folkways Recordings, 2001.

Los Muñequitos de Matanzas, "Rumba de Corazón—50 Aniversario," Bis Music, 2002.

Mambo. ¡Cubanismo!, "Mardi Gras Mambo," Hannibal Records/Rycodisk, 2000.

Benny Moré y Dámaso Pérez Prado, "30 exitos (30 Hits)," Orfeon, 2001.

Cha-cha-chá. Orquesta América with Félix Reina and Richard Egües, "Cha-cha-chá-son," Tumi Cuban, 2004.

Latin Jazz (Afro-Cuban Jazz). Gonzalo Rubalcaba, "Gonzalo Rubalcaba," EGREM, 1995.

Maraca y Otra Visión, "Habana mía," OK records/Caribe Productions, 1998.

"Calle 54—Music from the Miramax Motion Picture," Blue Note Records, 2001.

Chano Pozo with Dizzy Gillespie, "The Real Birth of CuBop: Manteca," Tumbao, 2001.

Machito and His Afro-Cubans, "Ritmo Caliente," Proper Records, 2002.

Salsa. Willie Colón and Rubén Blades, "Metiendo Mano," Fania Records, 1977.

Willie Colón and Rubén Blades, "Siembra," Fania Records, 1978.

Rubén Blades y Seis del Solar, "Buscando América," Electra, 1984.

Fania All-Stars, "Hot Sweat: The Best of Fania All-Stars Live," Vampisoul, 2005.

Celia Cruz and Johnny Pacheco, "Celia and Johnny," Fania Records, 2006.

Gloria Estefan, "Mi Tierra," Epic, 1993.

Timba—Modern Cuban Dance Music. Manolín, El Medico de la Salsa, "Para mi gente," Milan, 1996.

Los Van Van, "Llegó ... Van Van (Van Van Is Here)," Havana Caliente/Atlantic, 1999.

Issac Delgado, "Malecón," Bis Music, 2000.

David Calzado y su Charanga Habanera, "Soy Cubano, Soy Popular," EGREM, 2004.

Bolero/Fílin (Feeling). Olga Guillot, "La Reina de Boleros: Sus 22 Mejores Boleros," Gema Records, 1995.

Armando Garzón with the Quinteto Oriente, "Boleros," CoraSon Records, 1996.

Bebo Valdés and Diego Cigala, "Lágrimas Negras," RCA, 2003.

La Lupe, "La Lupe es la reina," Fania Records, 2006.

Vieja Trova. Los Compadres Original, "Epoca de oro del duo," EGREM, 1996, Sonodisc, 2000.

María Teresa Vera, "La embajadora de la canción de ataño," EGREM, 2002.

Nueva Trova. Silvio Rodríguez, "Canciones Urgentes, Los Grandes Éxitos," Luaka Bop, 2000.

Pablo Milanés, "Como un campo de maíz," Epic Records, 2005.

Pedro Luis Ferrer, "Rústico," La Escondida Records, 2005.

Cuban Rock (Novísima Trova). Carlos Varela, "Carlos Varela en vivo," Bis Music, 1993.

Habana Abierta, "24 Horas," Ariol, 1999.

Buena Fe, "Dejame Entrar," EGREM, 2002.

Cuban Hip-Hop. Orishas, "A lo cubano," Universal Latino, 2000.

Punto Cero, "Punto Cero," Bis Music, 2001.

Various Artists, "Cuban Hip Hop All Stars," Papaya Records, 2001.

Index

555

About the Author

Ted Henken holds a doctorate degree in Latin American studies from Tulane University and is a professor of sociology and Black and Hispanic studies at Baruch College, City University of New York. He has taught courses on contemporary Cuban culture and society, the origins and development of Cuban music and cinema, and Cuban history and politics. He is currently co-authoring a book about the development of microenterprise and the underground economy in socialist Cuba. He has published articles about Cuba in the journals *Cuban Studies*, *Latin American Research Review*, *Latino Studies*, *Encuentro de la Cultura Cubana*, and *Cuba in Transition*. He is frequently interviewed by leading newspapers and news media outlets on Cuba, having been a consultant for CNN and the U.S. Department of State.

Henken is a fellow at the Bildner Center for Western Hemisphere Studies (CUNY, Graduate Center), where he helps organize events about Cuba. He is also on the board of directors of the Association for the Study of the Cuban Economy. He has promoted scholarly and cultural exchanges with Cuba through Tulane University's Cuban and Caribbean Studies Institute and the nonprofit cultural exchange group CubaNola Collective. In the mid-1990s, he worked for Catholic Social Services in Mobile, Alabama, helping to resettle Cuban refugees from the U.S. Naval Station at Guantánamo Bay. He has visited Cuba more than a dozen times since 1997.